THE SUPREME COURT JESTER

THE SUPREME COURT JESTER

JAMES M. ROSE

Copyright © 2004 by James M. Rose.

Library of Congress Number: 2004097672
ISBN : Hardcover 1-4134-6793-8
Softcover 1-4134-6792-X

All rights reserved. No part of this book may be reproduced or transmitted in any form or by any means, electronic or mechanical, including photocopying, recording, or by any information storage and retrieval system, without permission in writing from the copyright owner.

This is a work of fiction. Names, characters, places and incidents either are the product of the author's imagination or are used fictitiously, and any resemblance to any actual persons, living or dead, events, or locales is entirely coincidental.

This book was printed in the United States of America.

To order additional copies of this book, contact:
Xlibris Corporation
1-888-795-4274
www.Xlibris.com
Orders@Xlibris.com

22693

CONTENTS

Introduction 11

Chapter One
Time And Its Discontents

The Judge Who Didn't Know What Time It Was 17
The Night They Raided The Annual Dinner 26
The Course Of True Time In Albany Never Did Run Smooth 31
Frozen Assets: The Law Of Life After Death 35
Obituary: John Doe, Famous Litigant, Dies In Accident, Many
    Wrongful Death Suits Expected To Follow 42
United States Ex. Rel. Row V. Waite; When Is A Flag A Flag? 47
Whose Quality Of Life Is It Anyway? 51
Will New York Nikes Become Pyrrhic Victories? 58
The Wisdom Of Solomon On Appeal: Splitting Heirs? 64
Application Of The Scaffold Law To Injury On Gallows 68

Chapter Two
Is "Hostile Work Environment" A Redundancy?

"What's Round On The Ends, High In The Middle, And Late
    In The Union?" Will Become A Legal Question 75
Current Positions Of The Parties In Collective Bargaining 81
Evidentiary Rules At Administrative Hearings: Are There Any? 82
An Employee's Right To Drink Alcoholic Beverages 86
Law Firm Of Tummler, Schnorrer, Pischer, & Verblungent, P.C. 90
The HMO Was A Success But The Patient Died 93
An Employee's Right To Hibernate In
    The Winter Without Being Fired 98

Chapter Three
*This Legal Advice Is Only Good On
A Day That Ends In "Why?"*

What Is The Appearance Of Justice? 103
Suicide And Homicide—Another Side? 112
Does A Voter Have A Right To Know For
  Whom He Is Voting? 116
Sgt. Preston, You Con: Do You Always Get Your Land? 122
Much Swearing Necessary At Closings 128
The Law Of Unintended Consequences And Nicotine As An
  Addictive Drug: Are Non Smoking Statutes In Schools
  Now In Violation Of Federal Law? 131
The Answers To Life's Persistent Questions 136
Bigfoot Loses Ten Pounds A Day Eating Elvis On Diet Space
  Aliens Gave Princess Di or Ias, Iola, Aye Yi Yi 139
The Law And The Hendiadys 143
Further Asides 147
The Law Of Monkey Business 149
What Is The Meaning Of This? Or When Is It Night In The
  Penal Law But Not In The Criminal Procedure Law? 156
Is It Time For A New State Motto For New York? 161
Religious Freedom Restored In 1993 166

Chapter Four
*Supremely Courting Disaster
(By An English To Law And Law To English Interpreter)*

Does The FDA Have Jurisdiction Over Miracles? 175
Parsing The Federal Uniform Restroom Labeling Act Of 1986:
  The Lady Or The Tiger? 179
The Rights Stuff 182
Must Dogs Wear Seat Belts? 183
Sex And The Single Family Residential Zone 188
Toward A Reconciliation Of Seemingly Unrelated Supreme Court
  Cases—Warping And Woofing In The Seamless Web 194
Evolution Still Makes A Teacher Into A Monkey's Uncle 197
The Electoral College: One Person,596 No Vote? 201

Chapter Five
Forms For The Uninformed

The Very Model Of A Modern Major General Release 207
The Revised Request For Judicial Interference Form:
    Back Despite Popular Demand 214
Agreement For The Sale Of Body To Science And
    Lease Back For Tax Purposes 217
Standard Form Side Letters For Outside Counsel 222

Chapter Six
"How Long Is A Trial?"
"How Long Is A Piece Of String?"

Can Courts Legislate Politeness For Lawyers? 227
Why Lawyers Are Advising "Trespassers Must Shoot Rats"
    Signs For Crack Houses 232
A "Simple" Case Of Driving
    With An Expired Registration 236
Rules Of Evidence And Procedure For TV Cops And Lawyers:
    A/K/A The Rules In Telly's Cases 240
Book Review—The Law Of Vegetable Rights 244
In Praise Of Appraisal 248
How Arbitrary Is The Definition Of Arbitrary? Or Reading This
    Article To The End May Not Get You Any CLE Credits,
    But It Could Be Worth A Free Beer 252
Stambovsky V. Ackley: Will It Haunt Ghost Writers
    In The First Department? 256
Legal Fictions And Illegal Ones Or Liable For Libel? 262
Recent Developments In The Law Of Ethnic Slurs 267
The Nuts And Bolts Of Mental Hygiene Practice:
    Part I—The Nuts 271
CLE-ver Ways To Get CLE Credits 274
Suing The Devil In New York 278
Disorders In The Court—All Rise 283
Dr. Ipsie Dixit's Advice To The Law Lorn:
    "Be Upstanding In Court" 288

Chapter Seven
*On A Scale From Excellent To Poor,
All's Fair In Love, War And Taxes*

"Don't Look For Truth In My Courtroom,
    It's Not A Lost And Found" 293
Deep In The Heart Of Taxes; Or Few Happy Returns 300
A Fine Legal Mess You've Gotten Us Into Now, Ovie!" 305
Agreements Between A Husband And Wife To Engage In
    Sexual Intercourse Must Be In Writing To Be Binding 308
Tax Consequences Of Acquiring A Trophy Spouse 311

Chapter Eight
Criminal Practice Never Made Perfect

Legal Status Of Combatants In The War On Drugs 317
Ogling Recent Bare Breast Cases: Prohibitions In
    Search Of A Rationale? 322
The Constitutional Right Of Minors To Keep And Bear Squirt
    Guns, Or Arms And The Child 330
The Effects Of Gravity On The Law And Vice Versa 335
"When The Bill Of Rights Comes—Don't Pay It!" 340
New Defenses For New Causes Of Action 344
Can The Courts Fashion A Remedy For Dodge Ball? 350
Are Street Gangs Indian Tribes? 358
Inevitable Issues At Inevitability Discovery Hearings 363
Gullibul's Travails 366
Petty Thoughts And Grand Illusions; The Value Of Money 372
Money Speaks, But Is It Worth Listening To? 375

Chapter Nine
*Grimm & Barrett, Esqs.
A Fantasy Dream Team*

The Story Of The Three Little Piggs, Ltd. 381
The Defense Of Hansel And Gretel 385

The Legal Consequences Of Building A Better Mousetrap 390
Can The Courts Prosecute The Tooth Fairy? 396

Chapter Ten
From The Desk Of The Chief Shop Steward, Union Of Unconcerned Nuclear Scientists

A Proposal For An Investigation Of The Mating Habits And
   Morals Of Hosaria Midcalfus 403
Results Of An Interdisciplinary Survey At A Large University
   Reveal Thirteen Of The Top Ten Reasons Why 406
Confirmation Of The Existence Of The Sub Atomic Particle
   The Wishon By Experimental Data 409
An Inquiry Into The Proximity Of Mobile Homes And
   Tornadoes: A Study To Determine If Mobile Homes
   Attract Or Create Tornadoes 413
Where Paper Profits Go When You Lose Them In
   The Stock Market 416
The Effects Of Gravity Upon The Law And Vice Versa 419
A Proposal To Investigate What An Infinite Number Of
   Monkeys Would Write 424
Interdisciplinary Ruminations On The Origins Of
   Law And Justice 429
Sacharomyces Carlsbergenis: The Beer Making Microbe That
   Put The Fun In Fungus 433

Chapter Eleven
Short Ribs Or When You Finish Chapter Eleven, You're Discharged

When Life Hangs A U Turn 439
St. Patrick And The Snakes 441
NAFTA's Why Santa Claus Is Not Comin' To Town 443
If You Can't Sue Yourself, Who Can You Sue? 449
Errata, Corrections, Apologies And Mea Culpas 451

Introduction

The articles contained in this book were written by me over the past twenty-five years. Most have appeared in the Westchester *Bar Journal* and The Westchester Bar Journal *Newsletter,* although some were also printed in the New York *Bar Journal*, The *Journal of Irreproducible Results,* and *Law Office Economics & Management.* Some are seeing the light of day for the first time here. Over the years my peers have urged me to do a comprehensive collection of them, although that may just be so that they can find them when it comes time to institute litigation against me, or cite to them against me in court.

All of them are intended to amuse, and some are just intended to be silly. However, others have a purpose and a point of view, and are intended to get the reader to think about the topic. For example, "Don't Search for Truth in My Courtroom" raises the issue of whether a trial is a search for the truth, dismisses it, and concludes that a trial is intended to be a way of resolving conflicts between people under a set of applicable rules that sometimes work to exclude the truth from a trial. If the reader wants to think about whether this is what a trial should be, or concluded that a trial is something else, or even look at the application of certain exclusionary rules in a new light, then the piece has accomplished something more than mere amusement. Often a piece will attempt to fathom the reason for a rule, by raising the rule in a humorous context.

Lawyers say that bad cases make bad law, so absurd cases should make absurd law. Placing familiar rules of law on bizarre landscapes is one of the *modus operandi* of these pieces. Other articles are just satire, and were written to get serious people to lighten up a bit.

Most of the citations to cases or articles in these pieces are real, although some are obviously not meant to be, and I hope the reader is able to distinguish which are which. Most of the scientific articles are based upon bogus intellectual journal citations. Some of the articles dealing with the future allow me to make up my precedents and give them futuristic citations.

I have arranged the articles into somewhat arbitrary chapters. The chapter "Time and its Discontents" deals with issues relating in some way to time, how it is measured, what it is, and what its passage does. These articles frequently start with a fax or an e-mail from the future via some time travel mechanism, and allow me to explore the law of the future. This is a new genre, "legal science fiction" which allows me the freedom to make up worlds, just like the science fiction novelist does.

The chapter "Is 'Hostile Work Environment' Redundant?" deals with labor and administrative law, a field with which I am familiar because of my practice. Some of the articles were inspired by things I learned or situations I actually encountered in practice. No actual clients were harmed in the writing of these pieces, which were first tested on members of my family. The chapter "On a Scale from Excellent to Poor, All's Fair in Love, War and Taxes" lops together matrimonial and family law issues, as well as taxes. Sometimes the two issues overlap—and then they seem to mix like oil and tax loopholes.

The scientific articles, many of which have not appeared anywhere before, are in the chapter "From the Desk of the Chief Shop Steward, Union of Unconcerned Nuclear Scientists." The issue of how "nuclear" is to be properly pronounced is beyond the scope of this book.

The chapter "Supremely Courting Disaster, By an English to Law, Law to English Interpreter" deals roughly with interpretation of statutes, rules, case law and the like, although what there is to like about them is not only beyond the scope of this book, it is beyond me. These interpretations must be good for something, and perhaps what they are good for is a good laugh.

"How Long is a Trial? As Long as a Piece of String" is a chapter that deals with trial practice, roughly. That is, it not only is trial practice "roughly" the *category*, it is treated fairly roughly as well.

More frequently than you would imagine, a client will ask how long a trial or hearing will be. I respond with the question, "How long is a piece of string?" although I should, no doubt, give a more respectful and precise answer, like "Well beyond the endurance of your kidneys."

The chapter "Criminal Practice Never Made Perfect" deals with the criminal law, a statement so obvious that even defendants who confess after full *Miranda* warnings could no doubt figure that out. If you don't like this chapter, I have several alibis, many left over from clients who need not worry about being homeless, as they are currently guests of the state of New York.

"This Legal Advice Only Good on Days that End in "Why?" is from the title of a Country and Western song that I am writing. Lawyers are much better on the "who, what, where, and when" than they are on the "why" I surmise. They tend to deal more with fact than motive, even when they have the opportunity. The layman often wants to know why certain things are happening to him, and by "why" I mean in the cosmic sense. It is amazing how often a client asks why the other side has taken the position that they have, when it is frequently difficult enough for the lawyer to figure out why his own client has taken the position he has. Sometimes it is even difficult for a lawyer to understand why *he* is doing what he is doing. This chapter is a kind of miscellaneous catchall for the things that didn't fit neatly into some other category.

"Short Ribs" is the final chapter, and fittingly is Chapter Eleven. When you're finished with a Chapter Eleven you're discharged, and so it is with this book. When you finish it, you, like this book, will be released in your own recognizance. This chapter is a collection of some of the shorter pieces, often newsletter columns, and little pieces that never seemed to fit anywhere else, but need somewhere to go.

I would like to thank all my colleagues who were so generous with their gratuitous advice, censorious comments, and annoying suggestions that indicated they didn't get my point. If there are any errors of fact or judgment in these chapters, they are the fault of all that officious interloping.

13

And finally, I would like to than my family for putting up with me while I was writing this book and the pieces in it. Not only did they deserve better then, they will deserve better in the future, when I pester them to sell copies of this book to their friends and acquaintances. I especially thank my wife, Natasha, for her suggestion (insistence) that I undertake this project, for financing it, and for the extravagant and laudatory blurb I intend to write under her signature for the advertizing campaign.

Jim Rose
White Plains, New York
July, 2004

CHAPTER ONE

TIME AND ITS DISCONTENTS

THE JUDGE WHO DIDN'T KNOW WHAT TIME IT WAS

by James M. Rose[1]

A recent New York court decision concerned the property of the missing international entrepreneur, Maxwell Robert. Mr. Robert was in Fiji vacationing. At a protracted Sunday night party he and a charming female companion named Marie had a bit too much to drink, and around 1 AM, Monday, April 1, they had a clergyman at the party marry them. They had a delightful honeymoon all that day. But when they sobered up on Tuesday, April 2, his tax advisers explained that the marriage would be a financial nightmare. An obliging local judge annulled the marriage for him shortly after 9 AM.

Maxwell Robert then met several sellers of the tabloid New York *Daily Voyeur*, which he purchased. At the same time he executed a will leaving the *Voyeur* to certain lenders in the event of his death prior to repaying several huge obligations to them, including a million dollars in cash advanced at the closing for operating expenses. His private plane took off for New York. It disappeared just after reporting that it was traveling through rough weather in the area of the International Date Line, and was heading for American Samoa. No trace of it or the restless Mr. Maxwell Robert has ever been found despite an extensive search. The aircraft disappeared approximately 5:15 PM Fiji time on Tuesday April 2.

---

[1] White Plains, New York. Mr. Rose doesn't have the time to write this sort of thing.

Several claimants began litigation a few months later in New York concerning the ownership of the newspaper. One claimant was Marie. To dispose of her claims on the *Voyeur* appeared to be deceptively simple. She was not the decedent's wife when he acquired the paper, and in any event an annulment made the marriage void *nunc pro tunc*.

Deceptively, however turned out to be the key word. Fiji is on the other side of the International Date line from American Samoa, and although they are less than a thousand miles apart, American Samoa is twenty three hours earlier in time.[2] The annulment was procured on Tuesday in Fiji, she argued, but the plane crossed the International Date Line. At the time the plane was last heard from it was 6:15 PM, Monday, April 1 American Samoan time, a date and time on which she was still married to Robert.

In other words, she argued, although an annulment had been procured earlier in the day in Fiji, there were parts of the world in which she was still married, and Mr. Robert died in one of them.

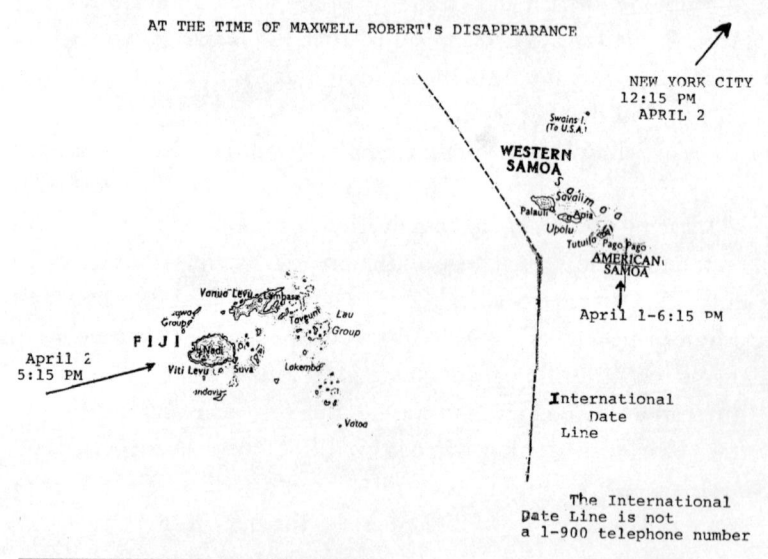

AT THE TIME OF MAXWELL ROBERT's DISAPPEARANCE

NEW YORK CITY
12:15 PM
APRIL 2

WESTERN SAMOA

AMERICAN SAMOA

April 1-6:15 PM

April 2
5:15 PM

FIJI

International
Date
Line

The International Date Line is not a 1-900 telephone number

---

[2] See, 15 U.S.C. 263 establishing Samoan Standard Time and 49 C.F.R. §71.13. Time zones are explained in *State v. Johnson*, 77 NW 293, 294, 74 Minn. 331.

Marie claimed that the transfer of the newspaper occurred 9 PM New York time, also a time at which she was still married to Maxwell Robert, and entitled to the paper as a joint marital asset.

The contract of sale for the newspaper indicated it was to be interpreted by the laws of New York. New York law means New York time because of General Construction Law § 53, it was argued.[3] Thus New York time would govern the contract in this saga, whether or not it was tomorrow in Fiji.[4]

While Marie could not contest that an annulment has the effect of voiding a marriage *nunc pro tunc*, this one was issued April 2 and had not taken effect yet in Samoa or New York, where it was still April 1 when the property was acquired. The marriage could not be void *nunc pro tunc* until April 2 dawned in Samoa.[5] By then Robert was dead, since he disappeared 6:15 PM April 1. One

---

[3] General Construction Law § 52 provides that Eastern Standard Time (or Eastern Daylight Time) shall be observed by the courts of New York, and § 53 applies that time when determining if an act required to be performed "at or within a prescribed time" was performed. It mentions nothing about applying that time to determining the happening of events. Compare 15 U.S.C. §262, which provides in part that the duty to observe the standard time zones of the United States is imposed upon the judicial branches, and that ". . . it shall be understood and intended that the time insofar as practicable be the United States standard time of the zone within which the act is to be performed."

[4] For example, a law that takes effect at midnight January 1 in England would govern events that happened in Hong Kong on Dec. 31 if the law was already in effect in England, *Regina v. Logan*, 2 QB 589 (1957); and an amendment to the Code of Military Justice in effect in Washington D.C. governs servicemen in Korea despite the local time there, *Sunday v. Madigan* 301 F. 2d 871 (9th Cir., 1962).

[5] A marriage that is voidable rather than void is not dissolved until the order of the court annulling it is entered, see 45 *NY Jur* 2d § 46 (Domestic Relations).

cannot obtain an annulment after death.[6] The court was left to determine if, under Marie's theory, there were parts of the world where Maxwell Robert was alive and others where he was dead according to local time.

Marie's opponents argued that General Construction Law §§ 52 and 53 did not apply. They first went into effect in 1884 at the request of the railroads who needed uniform time. Local time differed from city to city prior to that date, depending on longitude.[7] However, the presumption that someone is dead who is missing after exposure to a particular peril was first enacted as a law in 1966, and could not incorporate the General Construction Law by reference because such incorporation is forbidden by New York Constitution Art. 3 §16.[8] Thus, they argued, the Fiji date and time govern the annulment obtained there.

The court was left to determine not only what law to apply to the marriage, the annulment,[9] and the will, but also what time.[10]

The prior owners of the *Voyeur* had an unusual claim as well. Since

---

[6] At least there are no reported cases of dead persons obtaining annulments. In *Byron v. Byron,* 134 App. Div. 320 it was held an action for divorce abates upon the death of the plaintiff when an interlocutory decree has been entered but has not yet become final, and the divorced spouse would inherit despite the decree.

[7] In the Eastern Standard Time Zone when it is noon standard time in both New York and Cleveland, the solar time is 12:04 PM and 11:38 AM in each location respectively.

[8] The statutory rule restated case law, which derived from a common law presumption. The court fretted that following the English Common Law may require it to follow Greenwich Mean Time.

[9] No one indicated if the Fijian decree was final or a *decree nisi*. New York has held that a person who is subject to a *decree nisi* can get married in New York despite the other state's prohibition (*Cityrnell v. Cityrnell,* 86 Misc 2d 60), but no New York court has ever permitted one to die while the decree is pending.

[10] While the General Construction Law defines "day" and other terms one associates with chronology, it does not indicate *whose* time. The judge opined that he would benefit more in this case from a General Deconstruction Law.

Robert was missing after exposure to a particular peril the courts can declare that he died. Because he had crossed the International Date Line he was missing and presumed dead April 1, and because all the sale papers were dated April 2, Robert died before the sale took place! An estate can acquire property after the death of its creator, but the signature of a dead man has no legal effect if he died before he signed.

They even cited precedent for such a novel proposition. Civil Rights Law § 79 (a) (1) considered felons under a sentence of life imprisonment legally dead. As a matter of law, they could make no legal contracts, the courts held.[11] Therefore, although they were living flesh and blood, they were dead as a matter of law, and could not marry or engage in activities with legal consequences. This law stated the public policy of New York that men who are legally dead should not be permitted to enter into binding contracts during the period when they are still dead,[12] they concluded.[13]

Their opponents argued that cases interpreting E.P.T.L. § 2-1.7 (which creates the presumption of death after someone is missing for five years) hold a person will be presumed to have died at the *end* of the five year period.[14]

However, that language only applies to a person missing for five years, and is not contained in subdivision (a)(1) concerning persons missing after exposure to a particular peril.[15] Maxwell

---

[11] see, *Fitzpatrick v. Smith*, 90 App.Div. 2d 974 (1982), aff'd 59 NY2d 916, cert. den. 78 L. Ed. 2d 340.

[12] but can enter contracts afterwards when they are no longer legally dead, *In re Petras*, 123 Misc. 2d 665 (1984).

[13] After *Stambovsky v. Ackley*, 169 App. Div. 2d 264 (1st Dept, 1991) in which a house was held to be haunted as a matter of law, what rights ghosts can claim is a question the court held was "up in the air."

[14] *Caporino v. General Foods Corp.*, 122 App.Div. 2d 470.

[15] If he disappeared after facing a particular peril such as a storm, there is no presumption that he died at the beginning of the period as opposed to some time during or thereafter, (*Cohen v. U.S. Life Ins. Co.*, 143 App. Div. 2d 6.) and could be deemed to have died on the actual date of his disappearance. *In Estate of Rose*, New York *Law Journal*, Nov. 2, 1977, p. 15, col. 1; *Matter of Zucker*, 31 Misc 2d 177 (1961).

Robert could only be presumed to be dead at the time he actually died, but what day he died depends on whose time is applied.

The opponents of the will were Robert's children, who would be his beneficiaries if Robert died intestate. They argued that a will dated April 2 cannot take effect on April 1, and the decedent died without a will.[16] A will dated April 2 cannot go into effect April 1, no matter what the testator's intentions were, they said.[17] The court noted that a will is an ambulatory document that speaks at time of death,[18] although perhaps not as ambulatory as Maxwell Robert. The court found several treatises on conflict of law, but none on conflict of time.

While such an argument is ingenious, one would think that it would eliminate any claims on the *Voyeur* which was property acquired on April 2, a day after death. They argued that the *Voyeur* was part of the estate however, because Robert had clearly executed all the papers prior to his death. The day April 2 eventually broke on this side of the International Date Line, so the contract sprung into effect on that date on this side of the line like a post dated check.[19]

The case was complicated by the situs of death as well. Maxwell Robert's private plane reported that it was unsure of its location. If he died the day before his will was to go into effect, the property would pass by intestacy. If Maxwell died on the Fijian side of the line, his death would be presumed to have occurred on Tuesday, and his will would therefore be valid. If New York time were applied to the death the problem was more complicated, but it appeared

---

[16] A will does not have to be dated at all (*Re Sniffen's Will*, 113 Misc. 307 (1920)).

[17] "Our courts have repeatedly held that the validity of a will or any portion thereof must be determined by the date of death of the testator and not in light of what has actually occurred," *Matter of Doughty*, 24 Misc 2d 625, 630. (1959).

[18] *In Re Tucker's Trust*, 41 Misc 2d 405.

[19] A post dated check will take effect after death and is not invalid, *Matter of Samuels v. Marella*, 15 App. Div. 2d 618 (3rd Dept., 1961).

his will would be valid. It was dated April 2 and he died fifteen minutes into April 2 New York time, even though the will was not signed until midmorning April 2 (Fiji time). Courts will not take into consideration a fraction of a day, following the maxim "A day begun is a day done."[20] Applying this rule a man who is already dead man can make a will as long as he dates it the same day he dies.

The report of this case concerns the motion to reargue and renew. The court awarded the *Voyeur* to Marie and the sons in a judgment dated July 3, but the lenders had commenced a similar action in Fiji. The Fijian court had rendered a determination that the lenders were to take the estate in a judgment dated July 4. The New York judgment dated July 3 should take precedence over the Fijian one, Marie argued. However, the lenders replied that the July 4 decision prevails.

Although it was dated July 4, chronologically it was effective before the New York court's decision. The judgment was entered on the other side of the International Date Line at 9:15 AM on July 4 Fijian time. The New York judgment was dated July 3, but was entered at 4:30 PM, so the Fiji order was actually signed before the New York one was. Courts consider fractions of a day if it is important to the ends of justice[21] and if rights are in conflict they may determine "an instant of time."[22]

Next the court was faced with the issue of what kind of time to apply as well. Three choices presented themselves—standard time, solar time, and sidereal time. General Construction Law § 53 provides that eastern standard time is to be used in regard to acts required by or to be performed at or within a prescribed time, and the failure to include any reference to determining when things actually did occur could be taken as an expression by the Legislature that some other time should be used for that purpose.

---

[20] *Mandell v. Passaic National Bank & Trust Co.*, 18 NJ Misc. 455, 14 A.2d 523.
[21] *Louisville Turnpike v., Portsmouth Savings Bank*, 104 U.S. 469.
[22] *Matter of Lanni v. Grimes*, 173 Misc. 614 (1940), involving two conflicting bills signed by the Governor at approximately the same time.

Solar time is the actual time at a location on earth determined by the position of the sun. It differs according to the longitude of the location.[23] Since time zones are approximately 15 degrees wide, the solar time at the eastern end of the time zone differs from the solar time at the western end.[24] Thus, in *Morse v. State*[25] solar time differed from central standard time by twenty minutes, and from Central War Time by an hour and twenty minutes. That case noted that navigators use sidereal time, which is fixed by reference to the stars, and not solar time which also varies by time of year.[26]

While the Fijian order was signed earlier if one uses standard time zones to determine the time it was signed, because New York is at the eastern end of its time zone using solar time to determine when the New York judgment was signed would reverse the result.[27]

No wonder, the court concluded, the Court of Appeals found, "All rules for computing time are purely arbitrary."[28]

The opponents of reargument argued that July 4 was a holiday in New York[29] on which courts are closed by law,[30] and the transaction of public business is enjoined.[31] When court process is

---

[23] *Globe & Rutgers Fire Ins. Co. v. David Moffat Co.*, 154 Fed. 13 at 20.

[24] Four minutes for each degree of longitude, *Parker v. State* 295 SW 480, 481; 35 Tex. Cr. 12.

[25] 147 Tex. Cr. 272, 180 SW 2d 347.

[26] Because the Earth tilts on its axis, causing the distance from the sun to vary.

[27] *If* one can use solar time to determine when a New York court did something in the face of the command of General Construction Law § 52. There about 24 minutes difference between Fiji and New York using solar time for both locations, but neither location does. The result would only be reversed by comparing New York solar time to Fiji Standard time, which is like comparing apples to pineapples.

[28] *Aultman & Taylor v. Syme*, 163 NY 54 at 58 (1900).

[29] In ancient law a *dies non juridicus*.

[30] But see *Flynn v. Union Security Co.*, 170 NY 145 (1902) for a case holding courts can transact business on holidays.

[31] *County of Westchester v. Morella*, 85 Misc. 2d 251 (1976) at 258.

mistakenly made returnable on a day when the courts are not open, it will be heard the next day. They argued that any judgment dated July 4 should be treated as if it were dated July 5, the next day the courts were open.[32]

The reply was that the order was actually made on July 3 New York time, and that the court should calculate interest on the judgment dated July 4 from July 3, the equivalent New York time![33]

When one of the attorneys began discussing Einstein's Theory of Relativity and the relativity of time,[34] the court found a way to cut this Gordian knot. EPTL § 2-1.7(a)(1) allows a court to declare a person to be dead if he is missing after exposure to a specific peril, such as a journey in a storm from which he does not return.[35] The court noted that Robert had a million dollars in cash, and that "rough weather" was not a peril. It concluded that no one had established that Maxwell Robert had died. The case was dismissed.

---

[32] *In re Kennedy's Estate*, 151 Misc. 292.

[33] Since by analogy interest on money accrues on holidays, General Construction Law § 25 (3).

[34] A discussion of Einstein's Theory of Relativity in excruciating detail is beyond the scope of this article. It has something to do with time being relative to the speed of an object as it approaches the speed of light. Since Maxwell's plane was not going near the speed of light, it was argued, under the doctrine of *expressio unis est exclusio alterius*, Marie was not his relative at the time.

[35] *In re Estate of Cowan*, New York *Law Journal*, March 31, 1980, p. 15. He will be held to have died some time within the voyage, *Gerry v. Post*, 13 How. Prac. 118 (1855).

James M. Rose

THE NIGHT THEY RAIDED THE ANNUAL DINNER

UNIFIED COURT OF THE STATE OF NEW YORK
COUNTY OF WESTCHESTER
_____X

PETER SOW,
               Plaintiff,

-against-

THE WESTCHESTER COUNTY BAR ASSOCIATION,

               Defendant.

_____x

Apochrypha, J.

The case comes to the court upon cross motions for summary judgment in to a RICO (Racketeer Influenced Corrupt Organization) prosecution of the Westchester County Bar Association (hereinafter "the County Bar"). The motions present issues which arose when the defendant's members sang the National Anthem at their annual dinner at the Rye Town Hilton Hotel. This has been their practice for more than a century. Unfortunately, the Rye Town Hilton had not applied for a cabaret license for the occasion, and it is now alleged by plaintiff that the live performance of musical entertainment requires a cabaret license and an environmental impact statement.

A. Is the Annual Dinner a Cabaret?

The County Bar first alleges that the patriotic gesture of singing the Star Spangled Banner is not the running of a cabaret.

The proposition has some surface appeal. A cabaret, it claims, is understood to be a barroom with singing, dancing, and frivolity; whereas the singing of a patriotic song has a serious purpose.

The statute in question defines a cabaret as "a room where musical entertainment, singing, dancing or similar amusement is permitted in conjunction with the selling of food and drink to the public."

Here food and drink were sold to the defendant's members, and singing accompanied by a piano occurred. This conduct appears to fit the definition of a cabaret found in *People v. Ginsberg*, 12 Misc 2d 396.

In so determining the court is not concerned with the dictionary definition of "cabaret," but rather the statutory one. If this is not a cabaret in the dictionary sense, it may be a cabaret in the statutory one. If this was not a cabaret in fact, it may be one in law.[36] A man considers his wife to be a female, but Penal Law § 130.00 (4) defined "female" as "a female person other than the actor's spouse."[37] To put it another way, something may be one thing *de facto*, and quite another when the judge charges *de jure*. As the great legal scholar Liza Minelli all too often reminds us "*Life* is a cabaret."[Emphasis added]

The County Bar next argues that there was no cabaret in fact, because it did not *mean* to entertain. However the County Bar's intentions are irrelevant, as motive is not a concern of the statute. Perhaps the County Bar's intentions were not to entertain (But See Part B, *infra.*) And perhaps its singing was not sufficient to entertain or amuse. Whether the County Bar's singing was *malum in se* or *malum prohibitum*, once it is attempted, it is amusing and bad as a matter of law.

---

[36] See, for instance *Sterling v. Lapidus*, 17 Misc. 2d 587 in which a doctor's office was held to be a store (reversed at 10 App. Div. 2d 180).

[37] This definition, used to define "female" for the purposes of the rape statute, has since been amended, but did read this way when this article first was published.

B. Is the County Bar's Singing Entertainment or Amusing?

Next, the County Bar alleges that singing the National Anthem is not "entertainment" or "amusing" as those terms are contemplated by the statute. No suggestion has been made that the County Bar's attempt at vocalization was not "singing." The statute conclusively presumes that singing is entertainment or amusement, even if the singing is not successful. Whether the County Bar's singing was or was not melodious is beside the point, as is the issue of whether it was done for a higher purpose. The statute designates singing as entertainment, and this conclusion is not a presumption that can be overcome. The complainant need not produce a witness to testify he would rather hear several hundred attorneys struggling to sing an old English Drinking song in the key of B flat than watch the Weather Channel or Australian Rules Football on cable television. Bad as well as good singing may entertain certain segments of the public, as the television show "American Idol" has demonstrated. The tune for the Star Spangled Banner was appropriated from an old drinking song that was once sung in taverns to entertain. Entertainment and patriotism are not exclusive concepts, as the Statue of Liberty rededication extravaganza and any number of Macy's Fourth of July fireworks displays attest.

The cabaret statute does not require the court to determine what entertains or amuses. The law wisely declines to cast the court in the role of a music critic, a function for which it is ill-suited. That power resides in the Court of Public Opinion, and is one of the powers reserved to the people by the Tenth Amendment. Unlike pornography, entertainment may be something that the courts do not even recognize when they see (or hear) it.

The County Bar next argues that the singing was only incidental, and played such a minor part in the evening's activities that it should be considered *de minimus*. The County Bar argues that long speeches followed the singing. Their function was to educate, and they were not at entertaining at all in the manner that televised gossip, sex and mayhem is. However, the law forbids entertainment accompanied by alcohol regardless of the length of the entertainment, expressing the wise sentiment that alcohol and singing require stringent vetting and regulation.

C. The First Amendment Right to Freedom of Song.

As part of its First Amendment defense, the County Bar next argues that singing the National Anthem may be every bit as constitutionally protected as live nude dancing, see, *Shad v. Borough of Mount Ephriam*, 452 U.S. 61; *Bellanca v. New York State Liquor Authority*, 50 NY2d 524. It is true that the First Amendment grants us the right to do in public things we would never consider doing in the privacy of our own homes. However, the licensing of cabarets has withstood challenges that it is not an appropriate use of police power, c.f., *Club Winks v. City of New York*, 99 Misc. 2d 787. To paraphrase a famous Supreme court decision, alone with shouting "Fire!" in a crowded building, there are apparently other things that you cannot say, and singing the National Anthem without a license is one of them. By way of analogy, reciting the Pledge of Allegiance while driving does not mean that the driver does not need to be licensed.

The County Bar's freedom of expression was not chilled, its freedom to eat and drink was. The Bar could have chosen to *recite* the Star Spangled Banner, or to sing it without spirits and nourishment present. There is no constitutional right to eat and drink while singing.[38]

The plaintiff, Mr. Sow, was passing the banquet hall, and claims to have been annoyed by the sounds emanating therefrom. He

---

[38] Compare with the following passage from *Bellanca v. New York State Liquor Authority*, op. cit. at 531 ftn 7 : "Of course, when the State seeks to prohibit more traditional forms of expression it must show a compelling need for the restriction. For instance, it would be difficult to sustain a law prohibiting political discussions in places where alcohol is sold by the drink, even though the record may show, conclusively, that political discussions in bars often lead to disorderly behavior, assaults, and even homicide."

asks for treble damages, that is three fold damages, and not damages done to the treble clef.

It is difficult to contemplate that the County Bar could be a Racketeer Influenced Corrupt Organization. The charter of the Westchester County Bar Association says that its purpose is to "foster the spirit of brotherhood among its members." Although some rather sinister organizations have been described as "brotherhoods," it does not mean that this organization has as its purpose conspiracies. Mr. Sow argue that there is a pattern of conduct, as required by the statute, to sing the National Anthem on many occasions since the first annual dinner of the County Bar in 1897. He says, "[t]hree generations of impresarios are enough."

However, before damages can be awarded the plaintiff must show that he was injured in his business or property. An offense to the aesthetic sensibilities of a passer-by will not qualify. It is the purse and not the ear of the plaintiff that must suffer. Plaintiff cannot make a silk purse out of a Sow's ear. Motion for summary judgment denied to plaintiff and granted to defendants.

THE COURSE OF TRUE TIME IN ALBANY NEVER DID RUN SMOOTH

by James M. Rose[39]

You probably believe that you know how fast time passes in Albany because you spent a week there one afternoon. It was once suggested in this publication that a sentence to spend a weekend in Albany was cruel and unusual Capitol punishment.[40] However a decision of the Appellate Division, Third Department has recently shed some darkness over the subject of how fast time passes in Albany County.

The case, *Labello v. Albany Medical Center Hospital et. al.* as reported in the New York *Law Journal* [41] involved a medical malpractice lawsuit which could only be commenced within a period of ten years. The Court then noted that the malpractice complained of occurred November 9, 1982 and the action was commenced by November 2, 1992. The court concluded that the ten year period[42] had been exceeded![43]

Albert Einstein's theory of Relativity tells us that the passage of time is relative to the speed at which one travels. Until now, we believed that time in Albany traveled slowly because there are so many bureaucrats and legislators there.[44]

---

[39] White Plains, New York, Occupant of the Bob Dylan Chair of Wind Direction at the Federal State School of Law and Comity Club.

[40] Rose, "Out of the Hopper", 3 *Westchester Bar Topics* 50 at 51. OK, it's a bad pun, but I was young.

[41] New York *Law Journal*, July 15, 1994 p. 25 col 3.

[42] CPLR § 208 and 214-a.

[43] As the eminent professor of Linguistics Casey Stengel used to say "You could look it up!"

[44] "*Nullum tempus occurrit regi*." ("Time is no object to a government department.") A.P. Herbert, *Uncommon Law*, p. 200 (1969).

Legislators possess not only the ability to make time seem like it is standing still when they give a speech, they have the ability to actually suspend time by "stopping the clock." This they do[45] by directing that the clocks in the Senate and Assembly chambers be physically halted short of midnight so that midnight does not occur—at least inside the halls of the state capitol.[46] Since digital clocks are not used, the blinking twelve o'clock that occurs whenever a VCR is first plugged in never is reached. Time stands still. They can do it when the budget is due by April 1[47] or at the end of the Legislative session.

It is possible that holding back time in Albany affects the physical consistency of it. If it is too lumpy in the Senate and Assembly Chambers, time can become too thin and fast outside.[48]

However, we did not know until now that time could also speed up in Albany as well. Perhaps because it is held back so long it must gush forward like water bursting from confinement behind a dam. Perhaps holding back time causes friction which heats up time and makes it go faster when released like the molecules in a chemical reaction.[49]

Time and space can be warped by strong gravity such as that which exists around black holes. The gravity of the subjects

---

[45] Perhaps while singing "hold back the hands of time."

[46] This is the converse of the problem of people on budgets who have too much month left over at the end of the money.

[47] State Finance Law § 3 (1) provides that (after 1943) the first day of the fiscal year is (appropriately) April Fool's Day. In 1942 the fiscal year ran from July 1, 1942 to March 31, 1943—apparently due to war shortages.

[48] Or perhaps this is just a corollary to the Einsteinian theory of relativity that the faster you travel the slower time passes. The slower you travel the faster time passes, and things in general move so slowly in the bureaucracy in Albany that time actually passes quicker. The state has so much time left over that it can give a lot of time to its convicts.

[49] Somewhat akin to "Brownian movement"—named after *Brown v. Board of Education of Topeka, Kansas*, 347 U.S. 483, because the molecules in question move with all deliberate speed.

considered by the state Legislature[50] or the black hole into which your tax dollars disappear may affect the speed of time there as well.

On what legal authority does the Legislature rely to stop time? It may be the "new style" of time computation. General Construction Law § 50 provides "Time shall continue to be computed in this state according to the Gregorian or new style. The first day of each year after seventeen hundred and fifty-two is the first day of January according to such style.["51] We know what the Gregorian calendar is, but what was the purpose of adding "or" before the words "new style" in the statute? The Gregorian calendar had already been mentioned so "new style" must mean something else if it is connected by the use of the preposition "or." Otherwise the presence of "new style" in the statute would be superfluous. Where is the definition of "new style?"[52] There are no less than four definitions of "time" in the General Construction Law,[53] but none of them provide for suspending it.[54]

---

[50] Such as the selection of the official state muffin (State Law § 84—it's the apple muffin), or repealing laws not yet in effect. L. 1990 c. 747 § 2 effective (October 20, 1990) repealed subdivision (d) of Insurance Law § 2335 which had yet to be enacted. Chapter 747 thus had the effect of repealing Chapter 932 prior to its enactment! (See Codification note to Insurance Law § 2335.)

[51] "What the first day of each year was before that is beyond the scope of this article.

[52] The statute tells us when new style begins (i.e., January 1). We know when it begins, but what is it?

[53] Sections 50 ("Time, computation"), 51 ("Time, night"), 52 ("Time, standard"), and 53 ("Time, use of standard.")

This list does not include § 48 of that law ("Tense, present") which provides that the present tense includes the future. This is something we have discovered when we noted that the tense present is always followed by a tense future.

[54] Of course it could be argued that General Construction Law § 52 requires the use of Eastern Standard or Daylight time. However, it could also be argued that Eastern Standard is only the time that must be used when the state uses time at all. By analogy, although the courts use the Gregorian calendar that does not require them to transact business on Sunday.

Perhaps the authority to halt time falls within the general duties of the secretary of each Legislative Committee who has the job of keeping the minutes. If they keep enough of them they add up to hours![55]

Or it could be that the state constitution's provision which grants each house the power to determine the rules of its own proceedings (Article III § 9) give it the power to determine the time as well.[56]

But then who are *we* to question what the Legislators do?[57] The State Constitution Art. III § 11 provides that for any speech or debate in either house of the legislature the members shall not be questioned in any other place. That would include this journal— so case closed![58]

---

[55] If the clock in the state capital is stopped for more than two weeks do the Legislature's employees get paid? (This is the opposite of "no show" jobs in which people get paid by the Legislature although they do not perform some service "at some time." *People v. Ohrenstein,* 77 NY2d 38 at 53. Here employees work "around the clock"—but *it* doesn't.)

However, if this piece of Legislative legerdemain continues past April 15, do not elect not to file your New York State income tax on the theory that it is still March 31 in Albany. It may be *inside* the capitol building, but at the State Department of Taxation time marches on. If you have a statute of limitations in a lawsuit against the state of New York that expires April 2 and the clock is stopped inside the capitol, can you sue the state on what is April 5 in the rest of the state, but not yet April 1 for purposes of state government?

[56] See, *New York Public Interest Research Group v. Steingut* 40 NY2d 250, 257 "It is not the province of the courts to direct the legislature how to do its work."

[57] We just pay their salaries!

[58] **EDITOR'S NOTE:** Or perhaps the *Law Journal* report of the case contained a typographical error. The official report at 202 App. Div. 2d 299 at 300, 614 NYS2d 459 recites the action was commenced on November 23, and not on November 2 as the *Law Journal* had reported. It only goes to prove the old adage "Times change!"

FROZEN ASSETS:
THE LAW OF LIFE AFTER DEATH

From time to time, cases and briefs from the future appear on the author's fax machine from his great, great, granddaughter who is (will be?) a famous time traveler in the twenty second century.

A report of an oral argument in such a case by famous trial lawyer (and former Chief Judge of the Court of Appeals) Moon Unit Zappa III dealt[59] with the estate of the late Walter "Pop" Sickle, a famous felon. Sickle, a fairly successful Northern Westchester County apple farmer, was convicted of a murder and sentenced to "from twenty years to a maximum of his natural life in prison." Just prior to the trial he learned that he suffered from an inoperable brain disease, and he agreed to participate in an experiment in which he would be cryogenically frozen while in an "irreversible" coma and "preserved" to see if he could be revived when a cure was found.

"Pop" Sickle wrote a holographic will before he was convicted. In it he placed his apple farm in trust for "my son, then my grandson, and his heirs and their heirs for as long as I remain dead, but in the event that I am resuscitated the trust shall cease and the property shall be returned to me."

His body was deposited in the First National Sperm Bank[60] and Perpetual Cryogenic Repository (FDIC).[61] His descendants had less faith in science than he did, and had the medical examiner issue a death certificate because after he was frozen his brain had

---

[59] will deal?

[60] The First National Sperm Bank had previously been prosecuted for violating Banking Law § 132 which prohibits any institution from using the work "bank" in its title unless it is approved to conduct banking by the Superintendent of Banking. In a consent order it agreed not to advertise certificates of deposit, Tots 'N Trusts, or publicize the fact that its employees encouraged depositors to make premature withdrawals.

[61] Frequent Deposits Iced Continuously.

ceased to function.[62] His estate was probated in the 1970's. When the suburbs encroached on the less than prosperous farm, his descendants switched crops from apples to IBM—leasing the land to IBM for nine hundred and ninety-nine years.

In 2150 "Pop" Sickle was one of the first persons to be defrosted successfully. His son, grandson, and great grandson had predeceased him, and his great grandson's sole heir was his distant cousin Kareem Sickle[63]—who refused to either terminate the supposed trust or give "Pop" Sickle the rent from the property. A lawsuit followed. Kareem was represented by the prestigious Westchester firm of Doty, LaSeaux, Fahmi, Re and Doe. "Pop" Sickle retained the firm of Dox & Dox.[64]

Zappa said the first hurdle "Pops" Sickle faced was his attempt to prove that he was now alive not dead.[65] He needed to do this is in order to show he was the same person who was named in the will to take the corpus of the trust when it terminated. Sickle had been declared dead, and a death certificate had been filed. The information in it is *prima facie* proof of its contents,[66] but that can be rebutted by proof to the contrary.[67] "Pops" Sickle was prepared to do that.

Anyone who knew or could recognize him was long dead. There were scant records from the bank concerning which frozen body was which, and no one to testify about them. Sickle had his fingerprints taken and had a technician compare them to those on file in Sing Sing, where he had been imprisoned. The technician was prepared to testify that the fingerprints matched, but the

---

[62] The Court of Appeals has accepted that the definition of life or death is affected by advanced medical technology, since it has held that a person may be declared dead when there has been an irreversible cessation of brain function, notwithstanding that other organs have been technically kept alive through the use of machines (see, *People v. Eulo*, 63 NY2d 341).

[63] The descendant of one of Pop's distant cousins.

[64] Known locally as "a pair o' Dox."

[65] "Pop" Sickle was willing to tell some tales and wear plaid as proof.

[66] When properly certified by a registrar, a death certificate is *prima facie* proof of the facts contained therein, Public Health Law § 4103 (2).

[67] *Lewis v. Lewis*, 85 Misc 2d 610, 381 NYS2d 631.

testimony about taking the fingerprints in 2150, Zappa argued, is a transaction between a witness and a "decedent," and was therefore barred by the Dead Man's Statute![68]

Sickle could not testify himself, Zappa argued, as that would be a self-serving declaration,[69] and a violation of the Dead Man's Statute. Sickle responded that he was not trying to claim as an *heir* of the dead man, but as the dead man himself. But the statue prohibits parties who would claim a portion of the deceased person's estate from testifying to transactions with the dead man, and that must include the dead man himself if he is claiming his estate back.

However Sickle's attorney, Ortho Dox, pointed out that there is an exception in the Dead Man's statute that permits a man who is already dead to testify himself since CPLR § 4519 provides "... except ... where ... the testimony of the ... deceased person is given in evidence concerning the same transaction." This language, Dox said, showed that the Legislature anticipated this problem long ago, and § 4519 evinced the Legislature's intent to allow men who are dead (as well as those with whom they transact business) to testify in court.

---

[68] CPLR § 4519 reads as follows: Personal transaction or communication between witness and decedent or mentally ill person.

Upon the trial of an action or the hearing upon the merits of a special proceeding, a party or a person interested in the event, or a person from, through or under whom such a party or interested person derives his interest or title by assignment or otherwise, shall not be examined as a witness in his own behalf or interest, or in behalf of the party succeeding to his title or interest against the executor, administrator or survivor of a deceased person or the committee of a mentally ill person, or a person deriving his title or interest from, through or under a deceased person or mentally ill person, by assignment or otherwise, concerning a personal transaction or communication between the witness and the deceased person or mentally ill person, except where the executor, administrator, survivor, committee or person so deriving title or interest is examined in his own behalf, or the testimony of the mentally ill person or deceased person is given in evidence, concerning the same transaction or communication.

[69] *In Re Estate of Gilchrist*, 95 Misc 2d 873, 408 NYS2d 684 (1978).

Sickle testified that he was the same old Walter "Pop" Sickle that died in 1972. However, Zappa adduced proof that the primitive cryogenic equipment did extensive damage to Sickle's body, and over 61.5% of the organs, tissue, and fluid had to be replaced with artificial parts when he was defrosted. "He is *not* the same old "Pop" Sickle, Zappa opined, he is a *brand new* old "Pop" Sickle, since more than half of him is replacement parts. He cannot be the same "Pop" Sickle if the majority of him is new.

Moreover, "Pops" was dead in the eyes of the law for several reasons. In addition to the death certificate, Zappa reminded the court, the law presumed "Pops" to be dead because he had not been heard from well past the span of life for any human being.[70]

Another reason that "Pops" was dead in the eyes of the law was that "Pops" was serving a life sentence at the time of his demise and, under section 79-a of the Civil Rights Law,[71] when a convict

---

[70] "The law is clear to the effect that the demonstration that a person was once alive gives rise to an inference that he was still alive on a subsequent date, unless such later date would extend his life beyond the usual span of human existence." [Emphasis added]. *Matter of Harris*, 23 Misc. 2d 595, 201 NYS2d 28; *Re Powers Estate*, 96 NYS2d 25 (1950).

[71] § 79-a. Consequence of sentence to imprisonment for life

1. Except as provided in subdivisions two and three, a person sentenced to imprisonment for life is thereafter deemed civilly dead; provided, that such a person may marry while on parole, or after he has been discharged from parole, if otherwise capable of contracting a valid marriage . . .
2. A sentence to imprisonment for life shall not be deemed to suspend the right or capacity of any person so sentenced to commence, prosecute or defend an action or proceeding in any court within this state or before a body or officer exercising judicial, quasi-judicial or administrative functions within this state . . .
3. This section shall not apply to a person sentenced to imprisonment for an indeterminate term, having a minimum of one day and a maximum of his natural life.

is imprisoned for life he is deemed to be "civilly dead." This does not mean that he lacks the capacity to inherit, Dox pointed out, referring to case law.[72] But Zappa replied that "Pop" Sickle could not reclaim the land because of the wording of the trust instrument Sickle had penned. Others were to hold the property "as long as I remain dead," and Pops remained "civilly dead" in the eyes of the law.[73] Whether or not Sickle is dead is a *legal* question and not a factual one, he argued. After his resurrection he is still required to serve the remainder of his life sentence, Zappa argued.

Ironically, Dox pointed to the death certificate as proof that the life sentence was over. He argued "Pop's" "natural life" sentence was *over* when he first died, and when his sentence was over his legal disability ceased. Since the sentence was for his "*natural*" life, he argued, the Legislature carefully differentiated when it authorized such a sentence (and when it wrote Civil Rights Law §79-a) between a "natural" and an "unnatural" life—and nothing could be more unnatural than to be composed of more than 61.5% foreign material and to be alive almost two hundred years after your death was declared.

Zappa then alleged that the trust violated the Rule against Perpetuities. (as did Sickle himself!) The trust did not terminate within twenty-one years plus a life in being,[74] but some one hundred seventy-eight years later. Since the initial trust instrument was in violation of the rule, it was void. However, Kareem was still entitled to the property since he was the only person who could take by intestacy.

---

[72] *Matter of Hartman*, 76 Misc. 2d 339, at 340-1, 351 NYS2d 43 held "The law is that even where a person is deemed civilly dead, following a criminal conviction, such person does not lose his property rights and is qualified to take testamentary gifts or inherit property as a distributee (7 *Warren's Heaton*, Surrogates' Courts, § 11, par. 3; *Matter of Cirello*, 50 Misc. 2d 1007).

[73] The concept of "civil death" has been referred to as a "relic of medieval fiction" (*Shapiro v. Equitable Life Assur. Soc. of U. S.*, 182 Misc. 678, 680, supra), and as an "outdated and inscrutable common law concept". (*Urbano v. News Syndicate Co.*, 358 F. 2d 145, 148, n. 3.)

[74] His own life ceased to be "in being" when he was frozen.

"Pop" Sickle argued that *he* was the closest relative to the "deceased" intestate "Pop" Sickle, because he has 39.5% of the body parts, and one hundred percent of the same chromosomes as the decedent "Pop" Sickle, whereas his distant descendent Kareem had practically none.

Zappa argued "Pop" could not claim from his own estate by intestacy because a person is not related to himself.[75] Dox replied that intestacy is governed purely by statute. EPTL § 204-1.1 provides:

§ 4-1.1. Descent and distribution of a decedent's estate

The property of a decedent not disposed of by will shall be distributed as provided in this section . . . Distribution shall then be as follows: (a) If a decedent is survived by:

. . . (5) Issue of parents, and no spouse, issue or parent, the whole to the issue of the parents, by representation."

Kareem was not issue of "Pops" or "Pop's" parents, Dox argued, but "Pops" was clearly issue of his *own* parents. He could therefore claim his own estate by intestacy.

Zappa countered that § 4-1.1 deals with who survived at the time the decedent first died, and since "Pops" did not survive his own death (but was dead for over one hundred seventy eight years), he did not come within the statute's language.

But Sickle had another ingenious rejoinder. *He* had never consented to the issuance of a death certificate, (which he could now rebut and which consequently must be revoked).[76] His estate never should have been probated because he was never truly dead, but only in a state of suspended animation. Therefore he *never* died.

Zappa countered by arguing that it did not matter whether "Pop" *died*, as long as he was not *alive*, and was not a life "in being" during the one hundred and seventy eight years the state put him both literally and figuratively "on ice."

---

[75] Unless he is born as a consequence of an incestuous union.
[76] Since under the *Eulo* test (see footnote 5 supra.) it was *now* clear that his brain did not cease to function "irreversibly."

Zappa argued to Justice Victor G. T. Spoilz[77] that the policy underlying the Rule Against Perpetuities should prevail. That policy can be stated as follows: The law does not permit long restraints on the alienation of property that tie up titles to property. He quoted *Matter of Wagener*[78] at page 288 as follows: "Rights are not to be held in abeyance indefinitely on account of the absence of a person of whom no trace can be found. He may not be dead, but he *will be presumed to be dead* for the purpose of fixing the rights of those known to be living." [Emphasis added].

Therefore, Sickle was shown to be dead by death certificate, by the fact he had not been heard from, by the passage of close to two hundred years, by the fact that he was "civilly dead" even if he was uncivilly alive, and by the fact that he was composed of more than 50% non-"Pops" Sickle parts. As a matter of law and policy, and in the interests of the stability of society, he should be irrebuttably presumed to be dead. The law allows but one life and one death per customer, and the "New "Pop" Sickle had exceeded the legal limits.

The author hopes that the decision of this case will be faxed to him as well.[79]

---

[77] Who remarked that after *this* case nothing was sure but taxes.
[78] 143 App. Div. 286.
[79] And, if she would like to financially secure her future, he hopes that his great, great granddaughter will also fax next week's winning Lotto numbers along with some hot stock tips for the next twenty years.

OBITUARY:
JOHN DOE, FAMOUS LITIGANT, DIES IN ACCIDENT, MANY WRONGFUL DEATH SUITS EXPECTED TO FOLLOW

by James M. Rose[80]

It was reported earlier this week that the world's most famous litigant, John Doe, age unknown,[81] died in an accident.[82] Although the circumstances of the accident are not clear, it appears it involved several common carriers and many unknown drivers, and occurred under circumstances that may involve a myriad of defenses from sovereign immunity to last clear chance. "The only thing I can say now," said his lawyer and cousin Rollyn N. Doe, "is that there are a lot of unique issues presented, and there will likely be many reported decisions concerning them." There was some initial confusion concerning whether John Doe had died, but a telephone call to the morgue confirmed that there was indeed a John Doe there.[83] Mr. Doe,[84] who resided on his family estate Black Acre,

---

[80] White Plains, New York. This piece did not appear previously in *Rodent Track—The Magazine of the Rat Race*.

[81] His exact age is unknown, although it is reported he was an infant in 1969 when he was surrendered for adoption, *People ex. rel. Jane Doe, Mother on behalf of John Doe, an Infant v. Edwards* 23 NY2d 925. He was of draft age in 1974 when he attempted to get into the Army in a case in which the author appeared, *Doe v. County of Westchester*, 45 App. Div. 2d 308, although the author never saw him. However, he was supposedly a hit and run driver in 1965 (*Creswell v. Doe* 22 App. Div. 2d 942) and a union president in 1968 (*Oakland Coat Company v. John Doe* 29 App. Div. 2d 888)! He was young enough to be a parent in 2001 *Guardianship of Doe*, 189 Misc 2d 512.

[82] Although there are many cases involving Mr. Doe, no photograph of him is known to exist.

[83] Surprisingly there were several.

[84] Sometimes he spelled it with an asterisk, sometime with quotation marks, without either the asterisk or quotation marks, or with both.

was famous for his litigiousness, and was often suing his neighbor and rival, Richard Roe of White Acre.[85] Together they were thought of as the Hatfields and the Mc Coys of litigation. He is one of a long line of John Does[86] and a direct descendent of the famous John Doe often named in actions of ejectment.[87] Mr. Doe is survived by numerous offspring who are likely to carry on the family tradition.[88] They included Juan Doe, III, who bears such a resemblance to the rest of the family that it was often said, "If you've see Juan Doe you've seen them all." The Japanese branch of the family is headed by Nint N. Doe. The Spanish branch is headed by a Chinese—Spanish descendant Kwan Doe, and the French by Jean Deau. Mr. Doe's litigious wife, Jane "Cookie" Doe,[89] was said to be staying with her daughters Twae Kwon Doe and Bambi Doe. The couple was divorced in 1987,[90] although she had been declared incurably insane in 1972.[91] John Doe was an adoptive parent in 1993,[92] but he had his parental rights to his daughter Olivia Doe born in 2001 terminated shortly thereafter.[93] His children include his son Richard[94] and John Doe, Jr.[95] Their son, the famous

---

[85] He sued Jane Doe, a doctor for disclosing his HIV status in 1993 in *John Doe v. Jane Roe, M.D.* 190 App. Div. 2d 463 (4th Dept., 1993), 61 USLW 2796.

[86] and Don'ts. He used several aliases such as "Nathaniel Jackson" (See, *People v. Jackson,* 213 A. D. 2d 257 (1st Dept., 1995)); "Richard Brownstein" in (See, *People v. Brownstein,* 211 A.D. 2d 538 (1st Dept., 1995)); "Richard Devone" in *People v. Devone,* 163 Misc. 2d 581; and "Ronald T. Freeman" (See, *People v Freeman,* 198 A.D. 2d 725 (11st Dept., 1993)).

[87] See, *Black's Law Dictionary* (3rd Ed.) 569.

[88] see *Diane Doe, Deborah Doe et. al. v. City of Mount Vernon* 156 AD2d 329.

[89] See *Doe v. Roe,* 33 NY2d 902.

[90] *Jane Doe v. John Doe,* 136 Misc 2d 1015.

[91] *Roe v. Doe,* 68 Misc 2d 833.

[92] *Raymond AA v. Doe* 217 App. Div. 2d 757 (3rd Dept., 1995).

[93] *Guardianship of Doe,* 189 Misc. 2d 512.

[94] *In re Doe,* 181 Misc 2d 787 (Richard was still a minor in 1999).

[95] *People v. Cuevas,* 167 Misc. 2d 738. John Doe, Jr. was accused of a crime in that case.

square dance caller, Doe C. Doe, could not be reached for comment. John Doe had many children born out of wedlock, often from his tempestuous love hate relationship with the Roe family.[96]

"We never talk to the press about Uncle John and his, shall we say 'behavior'," said his cousin, Ian. U. N. Doe. Many people thought that John Doe was retired, specially after the famous case *Roe v. Wade* carried the name of his traditional rival. Mr. Doe scoffed at the reports, and retorted "*Roe vs. Wade*, indeed. It sounds like two ways of crossing the Potomac." At the time of his death, John Doe was on his way to Federal Court to file a trademark infringement and right of privacy suit against the inventors of Tic Tac Doe. John Doe was often seen filing lawsuits against Richard "Front" Roe and his daughter Eve N. Roe, and son Mort "Death" Roe. Many involved the complicated land title problems at Black Acre that resulted from the application of the Rule in Shelley's Case, the Rule Against Perpetuities, and "race-notice" statutes; and are familiar to the takers of bar examinations. Much of Doe's legendary wealth, acquired by the right of estover, was dissipated in legal fees. "The legal profession will miss him, especially the students. As a plaintiff he was matchless," said his distant cousin Law School Dean R. Guen Doe, of the Close Cover Before Striking School of Law and Computer Repairs. "He'd sue you at the drop of a hat. We miss his kind now that there are fines for frivolous law suits."

No one knows exactly what his profession was. He was reported

---

[96] E.g., *Mary Roe v. John Doe* 51 Misc 2d 875 (1966); *Mildred Roe v. John Doe* 56 Misc 2d 59 (1968), *Jane Roe v. John Doe* 58 Misc 2d 757 (a child born in 1964); *Matter of Roe v. Doe* 26 NY2d 672, *Doe v. Dept. of Social Services of City of Poughkeepsie* 71 Misc.2d 666 (1973). In the tradition of suing people whose names rhymed with his he also sues his attorney Peter Poe in *Doe v. Poe* 191 App.Div. 2d 606 and 189 App. Div.2d 132.

to be a doctor[97]; or a judge[98]; or an election commissioner.[99] At one time he was involved with a shady business converting cruzeros to traveler's checks.[100] The report of his death has caused District Attorneys to throw out drawers full of arrest warrants, and lay off grand juries. He was supposedly the target of numerous grand jury investigations and reports. John Doe was a hit and run driver in 1965,[101] 1969[102] and 1996.[103] In 1968 he was a union president.[104] He was identified as a squatter in rent controlled premises in 1975,[105] as well as a recipient of public assistance in Ulster County in 1978.[106] In 1979 he was "a person entitled to legal immunity from suit and legal process under Section 7B of Public Law 291, 79th Congress" (i.e., diplomatic immunity).[107] Although he was employed as a law clerk[108] in 1981, and a former

---

[97] in *Doe v. State of New York* 59 NY2d 655, in *In the Matter of John Doe doing business as Anonymous Hospital v. Kuriansky* 58 NY2d 1110, and in a suit against a psychotherapist, *Doe v. Young* 95 App. Div. 2d 673. He was a doctor at the Westchester Medical Center in *Reed v. County of Westchester* 222 App. Div. 2d 757 (3rd Dept., 1995), and at Kingsboro Medical Center in 1992 in *Doe v. Roe* 210 App.Div. 2d 932 (1st Dept 1994). He was a doctor who was involved with discipline in *John Doe v. Novello*, 193 Misc. 2d 457. He was suspended as a doctor for six months in 1994 in *Maryanne Roe v. John Doe*, 160 Misc. 2d 1074.

[98] *Matter of New York State Commission on Judicial Conduct v. Doe*, 61 NY 2d 56.

[99] *Matter of Camacho v. Doe*, 7 NY 2d 762.

[100] *Banco Brasilero v. John Doe*, 36 NY 2d 592.

[101] *Creswell v. Doe*, 22 App. Div. 2d 942.

[102] *Galente v. Doe* 68 Misc 2d 295.

[103] *Gomez v. Doe*, 230 App.Div. 2d 892 (2nd Dept, 1996).

[104] *Oakland Coat Co. v. Doe* 29 App. Div. 2d 888.

[105] *Dunbar Paint Supply v. Doe*, 50 App. Div. 2d 533.

[106] *Doe v. Greco*, 62 App. Div. 2d 498.

[107] *People v. "John Doe,"* 101 Misc 2d 789 at 790.

[108] *Matter of Alim v. Doe* 74 App. Div. 2d 732.

Assistant District Attorney in Nassau County in 1995,[109] he was married in 1985 while serving a term of imprisonment in the Auburn Correctional Facility.[110] Based upon his criminal record he was denied an appointment as a special patrolman[111] perhaps because of his convictionfor sexual abuse in the first degree.[112] Sometime in the 1980's he was a pharmacist.[113] In 1995 he was a teacher (but got fired),[114] and he was also a Deputy Sheriff that year.[115]

The American Civil Liberties Union praised him as a staunch defender of the rights of privacy who was often willing to lend his name to a publicity shy plaintiff. This practice was waning in his later years, and he bitterly attributed it to the "lust for headlines and the big bucks from mini-series the networks are willing to pay big name plaintiffs."

---

[109] *Doe v. District Attorney of the County of Nassau,* 166 Misc 2d 188.

[110] *Matter of Doe v. Coughlin,* 71 NY2d 48.

[111] *Doe v. Safir,* 184 Misc 2d 198.

[112] *Doe v. Division of Parole and Correction Alternatives,* 171 Misc 2d 210.

[113] *County of Westchester v. New York State Div. Of Human Rights,* 199 App. Div. 2d 390 (2nd Dept, 1993).

[114] *Doe v. Madrid-Waddington Cent. S. Dist.* 232 App. Div. 2d 992, 114 Ed. Law Rept. 257.

[115] *Santiamagro v. County of Orange* 226 App. Div. 2d 359 (2nd Dept., 1996).

UNITED STATES EX. REL. ROW V. WAITE;
WHEN IS A FLAG A FLAG?

This opinion fell out of an incomplete volume of future court opinions, which itself fell out of a time warp a few years ago.

The case deals with when a flag becomes a flag. It involves the application by a petitioner to enjoin a prosecution by Judge Waite for desecration of the flag on the grounds that it chilled his First Amendment rilghts. The proceeding is (will be?) Captioned *United States of America ex. rel. Row v. Waite.*

After the Constitution was amended in 2010 to allow the states to prosecute flag burning despite the First Amendment, New York passed a statute making it a crime to destroy, mutilate, deface, or trample the flag of the United States in a manner which desecrates the flag.[116] Obviously, tattered and torn flags could be burned, as was the previously approved custom.

The petitioner, a member of the True American Patriots, Inc., a fraternal organization dedicated to protect the purity of American institutions, took a dislike to the flags being produced by the Grand Ole Gonfalon Co.,. He believed that the owner of The Grand Ole Gonfalon Co., a "hippie looking" man named Bryan, produced flags that were not true and correct, but were subtle parodies of the proper American flags. Specifically, he believed that the stripes produced by the company were "fat, bloated looking, lazy, and complacent" and not in true fighting trim. He said they were too big in relation to the union, or blue part of the flag. He believed that the stars in the union of the flag were "lopsided looking and grayish—not pure white but puny and misplaced."

---

[116] New York's previous flag desecration state, General Business Law § 136, had been declared unconstitutional as over broad, *Long Island Vietnam Memoriam Committee v. Cahn*, 437 F. 2d 344, aff'd 418 U.S. 906 (1970); *Street v. New York*, 394 U.S. 576 (concerning a prohibition on casting contempt on the flag or harming it); *U.S. ex. rel. Radich v. Criminal Court of the City of New York*, 385 F. Supp. 165 (1974). It was held that the prior statute was designed to the outbreak of violence and a breach of the peace when the flag was treated contemptuously in public, *People v. Street*, 20 NY2d 231 (1967).

Finally, he alleged that Grand Ole's flags began and ended with a white stripe, whereas true flags begin with a red stripe.

Row stewed over this alleged disrespect to the flag,[117] and one hot July afternoon he ran into the Grand Ole Gonfalon factory yelling, "You're making fun of the flag. This is a satire of the flag, and not a true flag!" With that, he splashed acid all over a workbench containing some work that Grand Ole Gonfalon has in progress and destroyed it.[118] Gonfalon now concedes that there was no finished flag on the table, and how fully formed the flag was at the time remains in question.

Row said that he was a true patriot doing a true patriot's duty, and that Bryan was desecrating the flag. His attorney noted that "A person gets from a symbol the meaning that he puts into it," quoting *Board of Education v. Barnette*.[119] The flag occasions deep emotional feelings[120] in many people.[121] Row felt the charges against him were like a bayonet pointed at my heart—sharp and ironic."

The court was required to wrestle with the difficult question of what *is* the flag of the United States, and when does a flag become

---

[117] 36 U.S.C. § 176 provides in part, "no disrespect should be shown to the flag of the United States . . ." It has been held to be a code of conduct that does not have the force of law.

[118] Gonfalon's workers were outraged.

[119] 319 U.S. 624, 632-3.

[120] One expects that it instills more patriotic feeling than other symbols. Indeed, that is the very reason for a flag. General Business Law § 136 makes it a misdemeanor to desecrate the flag of the State of New York. One can imagine how much less furor would be occasioned by the desecration of other state symbols, such as the official state seal (State Law § 730), State Flower (the rose, of course—State Law § 75), state tree (the sugar maple—State Law § 75, state gem, the garnet, state bird (the bluebird), state animal (the American beaver), state fish (the brook or speckled trout), state fruit (the apple), state beverage (milk), state fossil (*Eurypterus remipes*), state muffin (apple muffin), state shell fish (bay scallop), and state insect (ladybug (State Law Sections 74 through 86).

[121] *Haller v. Nebraska*, 205 U.S. 34; *People v. Radich*, 26 NY2d 114, *Lapollla v. Dullagham*, 63 Misc. 2d 157, 161.

a flag. The flag of the United States is described in 4 United States Code § 1as follows: The flag of the United States shall be thirteen horizontal stripes, alternate red and white, and the union of the flag shall be forty-eight stars, white on a blue field." Section 2 then allows a new star to be added to the union of the flag on the admission of a new state. The definition is silent as to how may of the stripes should be red and how many white. Grand Ole argues that it has both red and white alternating stripes on its flags, but Row argues that the definition means commencing with a red stripe, and then alternating.

Also presented to the court is the perplexing issue: Is a flag a flag from the moment of its conception (as a flag)? Even if the seamstress had created but a single star, can that be conceived of as a flag (or embryonic flag) because it would have eventually become a flag able to fly on its own (except for the intervening efforts of Row to abort the process)? Is the flag only a flag when an observer is able to identify it as a flag—that is, when its features are so complete as to resemble an immature flag?[122]

---

[122] 18 U.S.C. § 700, the Federal statute that prohibits desecration of the flag notes that:

> (B) the term "the flag of the United States" *as used in this section*, shall include any flag, standard, colors, ensign, or any picture or representation of either, or of any part or parts or either, made of any substance or represented in any substance, of any size evidently purporting to be the flag of the United States of America, or a picture or representation of either, upon which shall be shown the colors, the stars and stripes, in any number of either thereof, of any part or parts of either, by which the average person seeing the same without deliberation may believe the same to represent the flag, standards, colors, or ensign of the United States of America. [Emphasis added].

However, that definition is for use in that section only, as it defines objects that clearly are not flags, which are defined in U.S.C. § 1.

The former New York law, General Business Law § 136 did not define "flag of the United States" and omitted the "average person" test in favor of the words "the person seeing the same."[123] Thus, under the former law, a person could theoretically be prosecuted for desecrating an object that the complainant *thought* was a flag but was not.[124] Happily, the court noted, this law does not go that far.

However, if the test is when the object is capable of being interpreted as a flag, is there a moment in time (which the courts are left to define by Congress) when a flag become a flag and more than just a potential or possible flag? When is that moment of viability for a flag? In the first, second or third trimester of its gestation?

Or, if a flag is only a flag when it is complete and can be delivered into the world by those that conceived it?

Does a person have a right to abort a flag that he thinks will be irregular, misshapen, and defective?

Whose version of the flag is correct?[125] Row argued that it was Bryan who should be prosecuted for his "parodies" of the flag. But under the law, Bryan was not desecrating the flag by creating it, he argued. In fact, if Bryan were making a parody and not a real flag, could anyone be prosecuted? And who is to say that a less than perfect attempt to make a flag is any less patriotic than a perfect version? Doesn't something that is less than perfect still have a right to exist?

Unfortunately, the volume of the reports we have ended at that point.

---

[123] See, Uniform Flag Law, 9B Uniform Laws Annotated [1966], pp. 51-54.

[124] Thus enshrining in law "It's the thought that counts."

[125] Executive Order Number 10834 (24 Code of Federal Regulations § 6865) establishes the proportions of the flag manufactured or purchased exclusively for the use of executive agencies of the federal government. It establishes the dimensions by hoist (width) and by fly (length), as well as the size of the union and the size (.0616 of the fly of the flag) of the stars and their location.

The flag is traditionally referred to in the feminine, "She's a grand old flag!" even though it has a fly.

No rule establishes the dimensions of flags manufactured for private ownership.

WHOSE QUALITY OF LIFE IS IT ANYWAY?[126]

by James M. Rose[127]

One evening State Sen. Alfonzo Pothola (R-L.I.) was watching the evening news. After a long piece on the Tawana Brawley defamation case that made it appear the trial might itself violate the Rule Against Perpetuities, he saw a heart rending scene. A murder defendant had been convicted, but on appeal the conviction was reversed because of due process and discovery violations of the defendant's rights. A relative of the deceased was being interviewed, and angrily complained that no one had given the victim of the crime due process. The killer had violated the constitutional rights of the victim, she noted.

Sen. Pothola was moved by the remark, and set out to remedy the situation. When he believed that defendants had been abusing the insanity plea,[128] he co-sponsored a bill to shift the burden of proof from the prosecution to the defendant.[129] He decided to combine two concepts familiar to lawyers—the prior notice provisions of Tort law[130] (which require the potential victim of a defect in a road to send the city advanced

---

[126] For more information visit us at our Web site—www.hisownrecognizance.com.

[127] White Plains, New York. When it comes to cross discovery, no one is crosser than Mr. Rose.

[128] It took attorneys a long time to get the insanity plea right. In the Salem witch trials they alleged that *the judges* were insane. In the trial of John Peter Zenger in colonial times in New York (17 Howell's State Trials, 675), they alleged that *the law* was insane. It took a while until they settled on arguing that *the defendant* was insane.

[129] See Penal Law § 40.15 and *People v. Kohl*, 72 NY2d 191, 532 NYS2d 45 (1988).

[130] Sometimes known as pothole laws. See for example, Village Law § 6-628 and Admin. Code of the City of New York § 7-201 (c), as well as *Poirier v. City of Schenectady*, 85 NY 2d 310 at 314.

notice that he intends to injure himself at a specific location in a particular defect),[131] and Megan's Law[132] that requires a felon

---

[131] The Pothole Law provides that "[n]o civil action shall be maintained against the City for damage to property or injury to person or death sustained in consequence of any street, highway, bridge, wharf, culvert, sidewalk or crosswalk * * * being out of repair, unsafe, dangerous or obstructed," unless prior notice is established in one of three ways: by "written notice of the * * * condition * * * actually given to the commissioner of transportation"; by "previous injury to person or property as a result of the * * * condition, and written notice thereof * * * given to a city agency;" or by "written acknowledgment from the city of the * * * condition".

[132] Megan's Law became effective in New York on January 21, 1996 (see, L 1995, ch 192, §3). The stated purpose of New York's "Sex Offender Registration Act" (Correction Law, art 6-c, §168) is "predominantly regulatory" (Bill Jacket, Senate Memo in Support, L 1995, ch 192, at 6; see, *Doe v Pataki,* 120 F3d 1263, 1276-1277; Greenberg, et al., New York Criminal Law §10.1, at 221). The Legislature's goals are to protect the public from "'the danger of recidivism posed by sex offenders,'" to assist the "'criminal justice system to identify, investigate, apprehend and prosecute sex offenders,'" and to comply with the federal crime control bill (Correction Law § 168, Legislative Findings and Intent of L 1995, ch 192, §1).

The requirement for sex offenders to register under the Act has been upheld by the Federal Court in *Doe v Pataki* (940 F Supp 603, affd in part, revd in part 120 F3d 1263).

The Second Circuit Court of Appeals recognized that the statute was civil and remedial and not criminal and punitive in purpose (see, *United States v One Assortment of 89 Firearms,* 465 U.S. 354, 362) and upheld it against challenge on the basis that the requirements for notification and registration did not constitute punishment (*Doe v Pataki,* supra).

The provisions also require the offender to give notice he is moving into the neighborhood to a group of neighbors designated as the Unwelcome Wagon.

convicted of a sexual offense to advise the neighbors he was moving into the neighborhood.[133]

He proposed an amendment to the discovery provisions (Article 240) of the Criminal Procedure Law. The new provisions required a felon intent upon causing death or serious physical injury[134] to send prior notice to the police of the location of the crime. The stated purpose of the law was to insure that full discovery be afforded to criminal defendants by making sure that a full forensics unit was available at the location where the crime was to be committed to collect evidence of the crime. The failure to send the notice prior to the crime meant that the defendant would be denied all "reciprocal" discovery.

Defense attorneys reacted quickly. Their alter ego organization, Big Applesauce Notification Corporation, filed maps of the state of New York with all police departments, claiming that the locations of all future crimes could be found somewhere on the maps. This strategy was successful for tort lawyers who needed to comply with the pothole law.[135] For a small fee, the corporation would provide proof to a defense

---

[133] Apparently in the belief that he intended to commit violations in the future, and the lynch mob would need to find his correct address quickly and accurately.

[134] That term is defined in Penal Law § 10.00 (10). The opposite of "serious physical injury" is "humorous physical injury," which is the kind often seen on "America's Funniest Home Videos" (such as small children smashing a parent between the legs with wiffle ball bats, soccer balls, etc).

[135] Maps prepared by Big Apple Pothole and Sidewalk Protection Committee, Inc. and filed with the Department of Transportation serve as prior written notice of defective conditions depicted thereon (see, *Weinreb v City of New York*, 193 App. Div 2d 596, 598; *Acevedo v City of New York*, 128 App.Div. 2d 488, 489; *Matter of Big Apple Pothole & Sidewalk Protection Comm. v Ameruso*, 110 Misc 2d 688, 691, affd no opn 86 App. Div. 2d 986, lv. denied 56 NY2d 507).

attorney that it had sent such a notice, so his client would be entitled to discovery.

Pothola realized that the law required more detail, so he then had it amended to require the "intention notice" to be sent to the potential victim of the crime. It was required to state the exact nature of the crime, and the name of the defendant who intended to commit it. He called it the "Guarantee of Due Process for Crime Victims Act." He argued to the Legislature that innocent people had due process constitutional rights just as well as criminals. As between criminals and innocent victims, the state ought to prefer the victims when rights come into conflict.[136]

Critics saw some Fifth Amendment problems with the law immediately. However, Pothola pointed out, the concept of cross discovery does not offend the Fifth amendment the Court of Appeals has held in *People v. Copicotto*.[137] His notice to the victim required that the victim be given due process he claimed, and was no more than a balancing of the rights of a criminal against those of a law abiding citizen and the government in general.[138]

---

[136] In *Snyder v. Massachusetts* (291 U.S. 97, 116), Mr. Justice Cardozo, writing for the majority, stated: "But justice, though due to the accused, is due to the accuser also. The concept of fairness must not be strained till it is narrowed to a filament. We are to keep the balance true" (p. 122). He further added: "There is danger that the criminal law will be brought into contempt—that discredit will even touch the great immunities assured by the Fourteenth Amendment—if gossamer possibilities of prejudice to a defendant are to nullify a sentence pronounced by a court of competent jurisdiction in obedience to local law, and set the guilty free" (p. 122 [emphasis supplied]).

[137] 50 NY2d 222, 428 NYS2d 649 (1980) See also *Wardius v Oregon*, 412 U.S. 470 and (L 1974, ch 420, § 1).

[138] See, *Globe Newspaper Co. v Superior Ct.*, 457 U.S. 596, 607; *Milkovich v Lorain Journal Co.*, 497 U.S. 1, 14; a defendant's rights of confrontation "must occasionally give way to considerations of public policy and the

In *People v. Donovan*[139] Judge Burke noted in his dissent:

> It is only when we consider counterbalancing interests (such as those of the next person who may be molested by the freed criminal) that we must pause before devising all possible rules, far beyond the requirements of due process, to reinforce the criminal defendant's rights to the limit. In striking the proper balance, it is not amiss to note that this court is not confronted with the police persecutions of a despotic state. It is confronted with the too often impeded efforts of a civil service police force and of a District Attorney elected by the citizens of the community to control the increasing rate of crime.

Moreover, the so called "intention notice" could not be used as evidence in chief in the people's prosecution of the defendant, but only on rebuttal if the defendant took the stand.[140]

It did not violate Fifth Amendment rights of the accused because the defendant was not being forced to testify. He was only being required to help the police and notify a citizen[141] by producing a

---

necessities of the case" (*Mattox v United States*, 156 U.S., at 243, supra), "We believe, results in a rule that strikes a proper balance between the State's manifest interest in protecting the child witness in child sexual abuse prosecutions (see, *People v Groff*, 71 NY2d 101, 108-109."

[139] 13 N Y2d 148, 243 NYS2d 841 (1963).

[140] The prosecution may not, therefore, use at trial the fact that a defendant stood mute or claimed his privilege to remain silent in the face of accusation according to *Miranda v. Arizona*, 384 U. S., at p. 468, n. 37.) But, the scope of *Miranda* was modified by *Harris v. New York* (401 U. S. 222) where Chief Justice Burger, writing for the majority, stated that "[t]he shield provided by *Miranda* cannot be perverted into a license to use perjury by way of a defense, free from the risk of confrontation with prior inconsistent utterances." In that case a confession suppressed because of a *Miranda* violation was used to cross examine the defendant when he took the stand.

[141] as in the Megan's Law cases.

document,[142] Pothola argued. Producing a document is like giving a blood sample,[143] requiring a defendant's accountant to produce a paper in his posession,[144] and is not compelled testimony.

It is true that the notice would make it easier for the police to identify a criminal and catch him before the crime happened, but there is nothing unconstitutional about helping the police catch criminals.[145] No one has a right to commit a crime, he noted.

The opponents of the bill pointed out that it was a cynical attempt to curry favorable publicity. No one would actually send a notice of his intention commit a crime in the future,[146] and so this was a way of denying defendants who would not comply with the law discovery and other due process.

At the urging of Pothola the bill was passed, and the notice

---

[142] *In Garner v. Los Angeles Bd.* (341 U. S. 716), the Supreme Court of the United States upheld an ordinance of the City of Los Angeles which required every employee to execute an affidavit, stating whether or not he was or ever had been a member of the Communist party or the Communist Political Association. Mr. Justice Clark, writing for the court, said (p. 720):

"The affidavit raises the issue whether the City of Los Angeles is constitutionally forbidden to require that its employees disclose their past or present membership in the Communist Party or the Communist Political Association."

An apocryphal story is told about a criminal court judge who was believed to be a leading Liberal opposed to anti-Communist oaths. He was asked if he would take an oath that he would support the Constitution. He replied, "Why not? Its been supporting me for years."

[143] *Schmerber v. California*, 384 U.S. 757.

[144] *Fisher v. United States,* 425 US 391 at 411.

[145] He claimed his notice provision was no more unconstitutional than fingerprints, voice prints, DNA testing or other modern forensic devices that help catch wrongdoers.

[146] Except perhaps a slightly off kilter person under the influence of a drug interaction, the former Chief Judge of the Court of Appeals who had sent one pointed out.

was duely accored the nickname "Pothola Notice" by the criminal defense bar.

Senator Pothola felt quite proud that he had contributed to a leveling of the field of criminal justice, until one day he received an "Pothola Notice" in the mail.

RES IPSA LOQUITUR (Humor)[147]

WILL NEW YORK STATE NIKES BECOME PYRRHIC VICTORIES?[148]

Law of the twenty-first century appears on the author's fax machine from time to time. It is supplied by his great great granddaughter, who will figure out how to manipulate time in the future. Her company, Nunc Pro Tunc Filings Inc., was an immediate success with harried attorneys who had to be in two courts at once, and who needed to file a brief for which they were already in default and pleadings after the statue of limitations had run.

She has recently advised me what will happen in the next few years in the wake of the United States Supreme Court's decision in *College Savings Bank v. Florida Prepaid Postsecondary Educ. Expense Bd.*[149] The case stands for the proposition that states cannot be sued for violating patents. The New Jersey plaintiff had developed a patented method of marketing certificates of deposit to save for college education expenses. It alleged under the Trademark Remedy Clarification Act § 43 (a)[150] that its patent was being infringed by the State of Florida. The court, in a decision by Judge Scalia, ruled that the federal courts had no jurisdiction over the matter, as the Eleventh Amendment to the Constitution forbids out of state residents from suing a state in Federal Courts where Congress did not specifically authorize it and the state did not waive sovereign immunity.

---

[147] by James M. Rose, White Plains New York. Research for this column was funded by the Irving Knotzo Charitable Foundation.

[148] Bad pun based upon the fact that "nike" is Greek for "victory." This footnote is required by the Federal Witless Assistance Program for the humor impaired, which is obviously not someone like *you*.

[149] 527 U.S. 666 (1999).

[150] 15 U.S.C. § 1125(a).

In the future, another resident of New Jersey, P. S. De Raysistans Esq., wrote to the governor of the State of New York. He suggested (as a public service for which he claimed pro bono time credit) that New York could market its own version of expensive patented or trademarked items of apparel at lower costs.[151]

The governor saw a chance for increasing his state's revenue and quickly began to put out New York made Nike Air shoes. They were manufactured (with the distinctive Nike swoosh on them) in New York state prisons, which still paid its workers more than Nike employee in Third World counties. He wasn't worried that Nike would sue or threaten to move its plants out of the state, since all of its plants were in Third World countries where the hourly wage won't buy a lotto scratch off ticket.

The shoes were indistinguishable from authentic Nikes except that they cost $29.95.[152] Nike was without a remedy since it could not sue a state for trademark infringement.

However, Mr. De Raysistans wanted something for his brilliant idea. He wrote to the governor and demanded that he acknowledge the source of this great idea. The governor demurred.

Mr. De Raysistans then hired a New Jersey attorney, Jack L. N. Hyde of Hyde & Seik, P.C. to write to the governor demanding the governor acknowledge his debt of gratitude and give his client "the credit he deserves for his services to New York."

Much to Mr. Hyde's shock, the Attorney General of New York responded by suing Hyde & Seik under the FDCPA.[153] That statute[154] prohibits persons (including attorneys) from taking certain actions to collect the debts of their clients. Hyde

---

[151] New York did not have enormous advertising costs or endorsement contracts with famous athletes.

[152] Thus disproving Gerald Ford's comment at a dinner on February 7, 1976 that if the government made beer it would cost $50.00 a six pack.

[153] Which stands for Fair Debt Collection Practices Act, and not Federal Dumb Court Pronouncements Act as some attorneys have been asserting.

[154] 15 U.S.C. § 1692 *et. seq.*

asserted that he did not come within the act, but Assistant Attorney General Mort Mane replied that he did. Section 1692 (a) (4) defines a creditor as a person to whom a debt is owed. In this case it is a debt of gratitude. Hyde asserted that the debt was not one that came under the statue.[155] The definition includes "an obligation owed for credit or services." Here De Resistans himself alleged that he had performed a public service and deserved credit for it. Judge Hugh De Mann ruled that the statute did cover the governor, who was a consumer of advice. The advice benefitted not only the state of New York, but the governor personally. His popularity in the polls went up 10 points when he brought out the cheap Nikes.

The governor denied in court that Mr. De Raysistans was the sole source of his inspiration. He insisted that he had always planned to charge residents of the state for Air of some kind, since it was one of the few items the state had not figured out how to tax. To charge them for New York Nike Airs was just a part of his plan.

De Raysistans was not through, however. He went to the District Attorney of Albany County, Max Termm, Esq.—a political rival of the governor. The District Attorney then brought criminal charges against the state under Penal Law § 170.45 for Criminal Simulation. That section of the Penal Law makes it a crime for a person to pass off as authentic some item that appears to have a source it does not in fact possess.[156] The section

---

[155] cases have held that debts include a dishonored check, *Snow v. Jesse L. Riddle, P.C.*, 143 F 3d 1350 (10th Cir., Utah 1998); or rent, *Romea v. Heilberger & Assoc.* 988 F. Supp. 712 (SDNY 1997); or insurance premiums, *Kahn v. Rowley* 968 F.Supp. 1095 (MD La. 1997); and dues to homeowners associations *Thies v. Law Offices of William A. Wyman* 969 F. Supp. 604 (SD Cal. 1997).

[156] When the Legislature decided (will decide?) to go into the Nike business, it will amend Penal Law § 165.70 so that the state's own use of a trademark will not constitute Trademark Counterfeiting.

has been held to apply to sweatshirts from Hardrock Cafe[157] even when the seller does not say that they are genuine. "These shoes are not *Air* Jordans," Termm told the press, "They're *er*satz."[158]

But Assistant Attorney General Mane argued that the District Attorney of a single county (which is itself but a subdivision of the state of New York) could not charge the state itself with a crime. Max Termm replied that the definition of "person"[159] in Penal Law § 10.00 (7) includes where appropriate a government.[160] "Besides," he said, it is not the County that is prosecuting the State of New York, it is "The People of the State of New York."[161] The People themselves are often unhappy with their government.[162]

He cited a variety of cases in which the state, or one of its

---

[157] *People v. Tanner*, 153 Misc 2d 742, 582 NYS2d 641 (Crim. Ct., 1992).

[158] In the future, the author's great great granddaughter advises me, atheists will attempt to get sellers of the Bible prosecuted for Criminal Simulation under the theory that it is passing itself off as having a divine origin, but the district attorney will decline to bring charges.

[159] Definitions are important in criminal law. The Court of Appeals determined in *People v. Owusu*, 93 NY2d 398, 1999 WL 319089 (May 13, 1999) that teeth used to bite a victim are not "dangerous instruments" because body parts are not instruments. The court literally followed the advice of the crime dog Mc Gruff, and took a bite out of crime.

[160] Thus waiving any argument concerning sovereign immunity.

[161] Criminal Procedure Law § 1.20 (1) provides, inter alia, that "Every accusatory instrument, regardless of the person designated therein as accuser, constitutes an accusation on behalf of the state as plaintiff and must be entitled "the people of the state of New York" against a designated person, known as the defendant."

[162] And hence the hoary saying "When the Legislature is in session no one's property is safe."

departments had sued itself or another one of its departments.[163] He argued that it was specifically acknowledged that the state could sue itself in the Civil Practice Law and Rules.[164] Unlike the prohibition on trademark counterfeiting, which was intended to protect the trademark owner, this section is intended to assure the buyer that he gets what he thinks he's buying, Termm argued.

---

[163] *New York State Department of Mental Hygene v. New York State Division of Human Rights,* 66 NY2d 752, 497 NYS2d 361, 488 NE2d 107 (1985); *New York State Dept. of Audit and Control v. Crime Victims Compensation Bd,*. 76 App. Div. 2d 405, 431 NYS 2d 602 (3rd Dept. 1980); *Matter of New York State Dept. of Civil Service v. New York State Division of Human Rights,* 66 App. Div. 2d 309, 414 NYS2d 46 (3rd Dept. 1979); *Matter of New York State Div. of State Police v. Mc Call as Commissioner of the State Div. of Human Rights,* 98 App.Div. 2d 921, 470 NYS2d 916 (3rd Dept., 1983); *New York State Education Dept. v. New York State Div. of Human Rights,* 92 App. Div. 2d 648, 460 NYS2d 176 (3rd Dept. 1983); *People of the State of New York ex. rel. Dew v. Ogden Reid as Commissioner of the State Dept. of Environmental Conservation,* 82 Misc 2d 583, 372 NYS2d 462 (S.Ct. Oneida Co., 1975); *People v. New York State Division of Parole* ___NY2d___ (mot.537) New York *Law Journal,* July 2, 1999, p. 30 col 6 B; *People of the State of New York ex. rel. Nunez v. New York State Division of Parole* 255 App.Div. 2d 159, 679 NYS2d 582 (1st Dept., 1998) to name more than a few.

[164] CPLR § 8601 is captioned "Fees and other expenses in certain actions against the state." It provides that ". . . a court shall award to a prevailing party, other than the state, fees and expenses incurred by such party on any civil action brought against the state." He argued that the language of the statute which literally referred to a party other than the state prevailing in an action against the state recognized that the state could sue the state and prevail in such an action.

When two state entities sue and one prevails as in footnote 15 supra., does the losing party that appeals get the automatic stay in CPLR § 5519(a)(1) available to the appellant when it is the state?

Besides, Max Termm argued, if the state can produce Nikes without paying exorbitant sums to self absorbed athletes, our way of life (and sport) as we know it will come to an end. Our athletes *must* receive astronomical sums of money that look like telephone numbers with area codes, he argued, or they might actually be the target of bribe attempts—like the famous Chicago Black Sox "Shoe Contract-less" Joe Jackson.

As usual, the author's great great granddaughter refused to let us know the result of the case, so as not to alter history or subject the author to inside trading temptations.

JAMES M. ROSE

THE WISDOM OF SOLOMON ON APPEAL: SPLITTING HEIRS?

A tattered old Hebrew manuscript recently changed hands on e-Bay, and, when it was translated, it turned out to be an ancient report of an appeal of a famous case often cited to exemplify the wisdom of King Solomon.

The decision of the Sanhedrin of Israel dealt with an appeal from the Jerusalem Family Court. Judge Solomon Ben David had ruled in a custody dispute between two women, each claiming that a child was hers (and that a dead child was the issue of the other woman).[165] Solomon had ordered that the child be split in half, and divided between the two women.[166] In order to protect the anonymity of the two women, the putative mothers were referred to in the decision only as Ms. Aleph and Ms. Bet.

When Ms. Aleph withdrew her petition for custody rather than see the child split, but Ms. Bet did not, Judge Solomon awarded custody of the child to Ms. Aleph. Ms. Bet then appealed on the ground that there was no jurisdiction to award a child to someone who had withdrawn her petition, and was therefor no longer a party in the case before the court.

In the appeal to the Great Sanhedrin, Ms. Aleph was represented by Irving Nottzoh of Nottzoh, Fast & Loos.[167] Ms. Bet was represented by Morris Tummler of the firm of Schnorrer, Gonniff,

---

[165] One woman was reported to have inadvertently crushed her own child in her sleep. It was then alleged that the dead child's mother switched her dead child for a living one sleeping near the other litigant.

[166] Solomon referred to it as his "Disputed Nativity Assessment" (or "DNA") test. It is ironic that the first ever recorded DNA test was used to determine the *mother* of a child and not the father!

[167] That firm became famous when it brought a lawsuit (*Application of Shellach*) for a young scholar who had flunked her Hebrew grammar test because she could not remember the gender of her nouns. She alleged that languages that assigned genders to nouns were guilty of sexual discrimination.

& Kvetch. To represent the interests of the child the court had appointed as Law Guardian Emmanuel Ricompte of Phlordah.

In the Great Sanhedrin the youngest judge of the seventy[168] always delivered his opinion first, so as not to be influenced by the opinions of the famous elder justices. Therefore, the opinion of Justice Pischer was reported first. He attacked the actions of the judge below—and scoffed at any order to split a baby in half as uncivilized "in this modern day when the humane practice of stoning had replaced such barbaric procedures." He noted that the Judge below should not have ordered the child "cleaved in twain"—which would kill it. Did not Solomon Ben David himself once say "A live dog is better than a dead lion?" He suggested that the judge below was suffering from "mental incontinence."

He said that the decision was a disgrace to Solomon's "brethren and sisterns" on the bench. Finally, he noted that Solomon confused the policy of the country to encourage having children with halving children—a remedy not contained in the statutes.[169]

Justice L. X. Talionis suggested that the court reporter had gotten a bit confused in transcribing the record. He indicated that Solomon, acting on a motion to bifurcate the claims, may have said to sever the trial and not the child.

He noted that the two women were screaming at one another and cursing.[170] The record indicated that Ms. Aleph had said to Ms. Bet "May all your children be as stubborn as you are."[171] Perhaps it was Solomon's decision that *the custody* of the child be split. He believed that Solomon referred to joint *custody* and not custody of the child's *joints*, and he suggested the case be remitted to clarify the record.

---

[168] With seventy judges the decision was never unanimous. Hence the saying where there are seventy lawyers you have one hundred forty opinions. In this case, a divided court was no doubt appropriate.

[169] Despite the physical location of Israel, he felt the court should not have referred to the child as "a youth in Asia."

[170] Not unlike a modern Jerry Springer or Judge Judy confrontation.

[171] He reminded us that more teenagers are being born every day!

The manuscript reports a dispute in the Sanhedrin between the Pharisees and Sadducees over language in Solomon's decision. They could never agree in any case, and this was no exception. In his opinion Solomon had referred to the two women, each with newborn babies sharing a dwelling together, as practitioners of "the world's oldest profession." The Sadducees approved of the language, but the Pharisees pointed out that growing the fig trees for fig leaves was Adam and Eve's first job,[172] and hence the world's oldest profession was horticulture, and that their brothers on the bench had perhaps forgotten to include the last three syllables in this description of the oldest profession.

The decision of the majority of the court was delivered by Justice Mensch, with Justices Iddo the Seer and Deborah the Prophetess and approximately fifty others concurring. They noted that the best interests of the child was the standard to be applied. Solomon had listened to the law guardians suggestion that neither prostitute should be permitted to keep the child, but determined that the Respondent should be awarded custody and not Ms. Bet, or some stranger or institution. As long as the law guardian was before the court, there was jurisdiction to entertain the custody dispute.

The Sanhedrin had only the written record before it, and could not evaluate what Solomon had seen. "The wisdom of Solomon was not displayed by the clever trick he devised," they wrote. "Clever street vendors peddle red strings for good luck (in imitation of the one used by Rahab in the time of Joshua to ward off the evil eye), but they are in no way wise. Concocters of clever schemes fill our jails."

"In Ninety-nine percent of Family Court custody cases, both litigants would ask Solomon not to harm the baby. But Solomon could see that one mother truly wanted the baby, and the other merely had a child because she was infatuated with its father."[173]

---

[172] Exodus 3:7.

[173] Or, as Solomon wrote, "heels over head in love, to quote the *Kaballah Sutra*."

"In this case, Solomon displayed the wisdom and understanding heart attributed to him by many. He did so not by devising this trick (that seems at first blush to be too clever by half), but by his insight into the litigants. He could see past their carefully prepared stories for court, and the fact that they were prostitutes brawling for custody,[174] and understand the motivations of each woman. His wisdom and understanding told him that this case was that one case in a hundred where this ruse would actually work."

The decision of Solomon was affirmed.

---

[174] "Brawling For Custody" is *not* the name of a new fall offering from the Fox Network.

APPLICATION OF THE SCAFFOLD LAW TO INJURY ON GALLOWS

by James M. Rose[175]

We previously reported to you that we had come into possession of some decisions from the future, thanks to a time warp. Here is another one.

The case we came across is in 250 Appellate Division Reports, 3d; and deals with capital punishment. After the Legislature re-instituted capital punishment[176] the new oil embargo made its cost prohibitive at any time other than off peak hours. The brown outs from reduced electrical service in the summer made it impossible to get up enough volts to do anything other than warm up a felon's hindquarters like a good switching in school. The Legislature then re-introduced hanging. After two years of litigation concerning whether Article V section 6 of the New York Statute Constitution required a civil service examination for the position of hangman[177] and five years of litigation about the appropriateness of the questions on the examination (*Gibbet v. N.Y.S. Civil Service Commission*),[178] two years of litigation concerning the correctness of the list and whether it had expired, an official position of Executioner was established. After two years of litigation whether the position should be in the Executive Department, the Department of Corrections, or the Department of Criminal Justice

---

[175] White Plains, New York. Mr. Rose is not the Official Court Jester for the 9th Judicial District.

[176] At the insistence of the Pro-Life Lobby.

[177] The issue was whether this was a position where book learning was important, or whether the position required an incumbent to possess certain intangibles that could not be tested for such (as the ability to get along well with the public).

[178] For example, there were objections to questions showing a hood with eye holes and one without which asked the candidate which one the condemned and which one the executioner wore.

Services[179], and two years of hearings whether a high school degree requirement was discriminatory,[180] a gallows was finally built on state property. Then the litigation *really* began.

While preparing for a hanging one day, the executioner slipped and fell through the hole reserved for the plummeting condemned. He brought suit[181] alleging that Labor Law § 240 (1), the so-called Scaffold Law, established absolute liability for injuries to workers who must travail on such platforms. He further alleged that he suffered psychological traumas as a result of his fall that caused him to dislike him job, and that he was no longer able to cheerfully execute people.

There was a flurry of motions, and several interesting defenses were asserted.

The first involved prior notice, or the so-called pot hole law. To simplify to the point of distortion, such laws require that, prior to having an accident, someone send a municipality a notice indicating that he or she intends to trip or fall in a presently existing hole in the sidewalk, roadway, pier, or other municipal facility in the near future, and the exact location where the accident will occur.

Only if the municipality has received such a notice will it be held liable. Without such a notice (the legal fiction goes) cars, people, small animals and even municipal busses and garbage trucks that theoretically ply the streets on a daily basis may disappear without the appropriate municipal government having an inkling of such occurrences.

That defense was rejected by the Court of Claims because the condition of the scaffold was created by the State itself, so it was held to have notice of it. Indeed, had there been no trap door in

---

[179] Or whether it should be contracted out to the private sector where several pest control services were vying for the contract.

[180] It was, and the courts ruled that the state would have to accept as suitable equivalent experience 3 years as a gang member or hit man.

[181] *Jack Ketch v. New York State Department of Executional Services* 250 A.D. 2d 175 (5th Dept., 2009).

the gallows through which the candidate for eternity is intended to plummet, he would simply have to stand there with a rope around his neck. The court referred to several products liability cases in which governments sued manufacturers on account of ineffective or defective gallowses.[182]

The next defense asserted by the State was sovereign immunity. The basis for such a doctrine is the theory that the state can only be sued to the extent it permits itself to be sued, because all laws flow from the sovereign state. The basis for *that* assertion in turn is that the sovereign *is* the law, and the historical basis for *that* assertion was that the sovereign was believed to be divine, and you couldn't very well sue a divinity could you? The court laughed.[183] It could find nothing in the government of the State of New York that was divine, and certainly nothing that a Supreme Court could not assert jurisdiction over.

The defense of contributory negligence was asserted next. A hangman working around a trap door could well have kept the door closed, and not clowned around on the scaffold with a black hood over his eyes, the State argued.

In considering that assertion the court first examined the seminal case of *Dole v. Dow*. Although it concluded the case was irrelevant to this particular issue, it nevertheless felt it imperative to begin a consideration of the issue with the examination of the seminal case of *Dole v. Dow* in hopes that the court might finally understanding it. The court rejected contributory negligence as a defense because the statute was intended to impose absolute liability.[184]

The argument that a hangman assumes the risk of falling through his own trap door was likewise politely hooted out of court with appropriate references to OSHA and similar state guarantees of a safe workplace. The defense was rejected despite

---

[182] *Federal Trade Commission v. Merchants of Death Inc.*, 34 F4d 395; *Florida v. Gator Gallows Group*, 385 Fla. 459; *Texas v. Corvair Gallows Fabricators*, 256 S. 3d 341; *Alabama v. ABC Noose* and *Arkansas v. Guys n' Gallows* 34 F4d 35.

[183] "Ha, Ha., *Id.*"

[184] *Wright v. State* 110 App.Div. 2d 1060, aff'd 66 NY2d 452.

the fact that the hangman was not wearing the safety harness required by OSHA regulations for hangmen and hangwomen, nor a parachute (arguably called for by the same obscure provisions of the Code of Federal Regulations)! The Court made passing reference to the fact that the state had not filed an Environmental Impact statement with the Federal Government before constructing the structure, and had not obtained a Certificate of Occupancy for it. (The gallows was a non-conforming use as the area in which it was constructed was not zoned for "business," it exceeded local height limits on structures, and the gallows could not be considered a home as it had no mandatory smoke detector. In addition, OSHA found, the stairs to be used by the condemned did not have a proper surface preparation on the treads and could cause a nasty fall, thus ruining the condemned prisoner's whole day.

The State argued that the gallows was necessary after litigation from several groups led to the abandonment of the plan to throw a rope over a tree branch, and swat the back of a horse on which the condemned rode. First the Sierra Club sued because of potential damage to the tree, and then the ASPCA chimed in about abuse of the horse.

The defense that the state did not breach a warranty of fitness for a particular purpose (UCC § 2-315) split the court. The strict constructionists felt there had been a breach, but the deconstructionists did not. The latter decide cases based upon what the result *should be,* and only then look for support for their position. They believe courts should not be bound by precedents, with the possible exception of the precedents that the deconstructionists themselves write.[185]

They argued that a gallows is constructed to maim or kill someone. If it **does** maim or kill, it cannot be said to breach a warranty of fitness for that particular purpose, even if the person it maims or kills is an innocent bystander.[186]

---

[185] *All Fours v. Brown Cow*, 200 App.Div. 3d 197.

[186] The court noted that under our law all bystanders are presumed innocent until proven guilty.

However, the dissenters noted that if a gun fails to fire when the trigger is pulled, and will not fire until its user looks down the barrel[187] the warranty may be breached.

As part of the damages, the claimant presented the testimony of a psychiatrist who noted that the claimant had been a cheerful person who looked forward to his work. After the accident the claimant became morose, and looking at the gallows depressed him. He opined that the claimant could no longer perform his work as a hangman. In addition he was no longer able to enjoy horror movies, sick jokes or most of the New York *Post*. In addition the claimant contended he was not capable of performing his job duties due to an injury to his back.

The State's doctor interviewed the claimant and found him to be fit for the position of executioner, if he returned on a "light duty" basis and did not execute anyone weighing more than 125 pounds.

The Court remanded for further testimony on the issue of whether the trap door in the gallows was required by safety regulations to be surrounded by guard rails.

---

[187] *Wiley Coyote v. Acme Novelty Co. Inc.*, 239 Ariz. 3d 197.

CHAPTER TWO

IS "HOSTILE WORK ENVIRONMENT" A REDUNDANCY?

"WHAT'S ROUND ON THE ENDS, HIGH IN THE MIDDLE, AND LATE IN THE UNION?"[188] WILL BECOME A LEGAL QUESTION

by James M. Rose[189]

Because of a legal loophole in the laws of physics, from time to time the author's great great granddaughter who is (will be?) a Forensic Chronoloquitur[190] in the twenty second century sends him decisions of note on his fax machine. She can do that because of a rent (actually a triple net lease) in the fabric of space time caused by the manipulation of lawyer's time sheets.

One case of interest to labor practitioners involves a suit brought by the conglomerate HMBC—Humongous Multinational Behemoth Corp (Huge.com) involving a secondary boycott of its subsidiary Granny's Homemade Movies. The company was making the seventeenth Star Wars movie—"The Big Bang—Really Really Long Ago and Very Very Far Away" (The prequel to the prequel's

---

[188] The riddle "What's round on the ends and high in the middle" refers to the name of the state of Ohio.

[189] White Plains, New York. Mr. Rose is a member of the New York State Bar, which reports he is a potential Supreme Court Justice, and always will be. The references to past events in this piece are true.

[190] In the future, chronoloquiturs will be scientists who have solved the riddle of time, and are able to send messages backward in time through a process that allows them to access and manipulate time sheets attorneys submitted in the past, and modify them retroactively. (Editor's Note: The author, James M. Rose, Esq. is not associated with the Rose Law Firm of Little Rock, Arkansas.)

prequel) when it was struck by a labor union. The IUGGBBFA & YM (International Union of Gaffers, Gofers, Best Boys, Foley Artists and Yes Men, AFL-CIO) threw a picket line around the set. Another union's members refused to cross the line and perform in the movie.

That union, BRAIN (Brotherhood of Robots and Androids International Network AFL-CIO-PPPLO (Parliament of Pan-Planetary Labor Organizations), was then sued. The pleadings alleged that the union was conducting a secondary boycott in violation of the Labor Management Relations Act of 1947—also known as the Taft-Hartley Act.[191]

BRAIN did not deny the allegation but its attorney, Joy Finn Nagel of the law firm of Thrust, Perry & Lunnj, offered a unique defense. She requested Federal District Court Judge Solomon Maven to declare an obscure act of Congress passed on August 1, 1953 by the Senate to be partially unconstitutional. The law was the one which admitted the State of Ohio to the union on August 8, 1953.

While many believe that Ohio was admitted to the Union on March 1, 1803,[192] that is a mistaken belief. In 1953, when the state was preparing to celebrate the 150th anniversary of its admission to the union, it was discovered that the last act in the statehood process, an acceptance vote by Congress, had never occurred.[193] As a formality that vote occurred on August 1, 1953.[194] The act made the admission of Ohio retroactive to March 1,1803.[195]

It is that portion of the act that BRAIN challenges. The reason

---

[191] 61 Stat. 136-52 (1947) 29 U.S.C. §§ 141-97.

[192] Just about the time that *Marbury v. Madison* was being argued before Justice Marshall in the Supreme Court.

[193] Cong. Rec August 1, 1953 at 10799 col. 2. Really! Look it up yourself!

[194] See Cong. Rec. August 1, 1953 at 10800 col 1. passing H.J. Res. 121 and New York *Times* August 2, 1953 p. 29 col. 2, "Ohio Definitely a State, Congress Says So."

[195] See, New York *Times* August 8, 1953 p. 18 col. 2, "Eisenhower Makes Ohio a Member of the Union."

why it is part of BRAIN's defense is less than obvious, but BRAIN's argument is that the Taft-Hartley Act was made law on June 24, 1947 and was introduced by Sen. Robert A. Taft (R-Ohio). Taft could not have been the Senator from Ohio if it had not been a state, the argument goes, he could not have introduced the bill. It could not be a law if it had not been legally introduced.[196]

Judge Maven had to consider the constitutionality of admitting a state to the Union retroactively. How could Ohio's representatives[197] introduce such a bill if they were not, in fact, representatives of a state in the Union?[198] How could representatives of states such as Arizona have a vote on the issue if their states were not in the Union in March of 1803? The Louisiana purchase was still a month away.[199] None of the territory west of the Mississippi River belonged to the United States, and most certainly could not send voting representatives to the Senate or the House of Representatives.

California, for example, was not even United States territory at the time. Rather it was a possession of Spain, and certainly our Constitution does not permit residents of foreign countries to decide whether states can be admitted to our federal union.[200]

---

[196] The bill was passed over the veto of President Truman by a vote of 68 to 25. Even if Taft and fellow Republican Bricker of Ohio had not voted, two thirds of the eligible Senators (64) voted to override the veto. It passed in the House by a vote of 331 to 83—a 4 to 1 margin.

[197] The bill was sponsored by Senator Bricker of Ohio, who was the presiding officer in the Senate when it was passed (See Cong. Rec. for August 1, 1953 at 10799 col. 3), and by Representative Bender from Ohio in the House.

[198] HMBC's attorney, Ike A. Rumba of the law firm of Sturm & Drung, argued that once the retroactivity took effect they would be representatives *nunc pro tunc*. When Judge Maven asked if that was not circular reasoning, Rumba replied it more closely resembled a Mobius strip.

[199] And the actual ratification of the treaty did not occur until the end of 1803.

[200] But vote they did. Senator Hayden of Arizona was concerned that his state would no longer be the youngest in the Union, but was assured that the act would be retroactive. (Cong. Rec. August 1, 1953 at 10799.) Sen. Barrett of Wyoming spoke in favor of the bill.

Even if only the representatives of the sixteen states that had been admitted to the union before Ohio were permitted to vote the act could still not have been legal.[201] There would have been a total of thirty-two senators in March of 1803. In 1953 there were forty-seven states (excluding Ohio) each with two Senators, and thus a bill was required to pass by more than 47 votes if all were present.[202] A unanimous vote of the thirty two Senators from the states that preceded Ohio into the union would not a pass a bill in what was obviously a session of the Eighty—third Congress.

The Senate and House of Representatives had a much different political composition in 1803. The Federalists and Democratic Republicans were in power, and it would be almost four score years until the Republicans would elect a President. It cannot be said that the twentieth century representatives of the founding states could be representative of the voters in their constituencies in 1803, or knew their hearts and minds. None of the senators who voted in 1953 had represented their states in 1803—not even Strom Thurmond. To pass a bill which was retroactive to 1803 would be to make laws for the voters of that time, and not of 1953. The Seventh Congress, which had been elected and selected in 1803 from Federalists and Democratic Republicans was selected by a polity that did not include women, blacks and non-land owners. The Eighty-third Congress that was elected in 1953 was chosen by a much different pool of eligible voters of that time, from Republican and Democratic candidates. It had no mandate from the voters of 1803.

Moreover, for a bill to be effective in 1803, the president would have to sign it. Judge Maven took judicial notice that the President

---

[201] The Congressional Record does not indicate the vote count or who voted, but reads tersely "The joint resolution (H. J. Res 121) was ordered to a third reading, read the third time, and passed . . . The preamble was agreed to." Perhaps it was a voice vote.

[202] What would constitute a quorum in this unique circumstance? A quorum of the Eighty-Third Congress or of the Seventh one?

of the United States in 1803 was Thomas Jefferson and not Dwight Eisenhower. Jefferson was a Democratic Republican, a party that had ceased to exist prior to 1953. Eisenhower was a Republican, a party that did not yet exist in 1803. They were not selected by the same Electoral College.[203]

BRAIN also pointed out that Article I Section 9 of the Constitution explicitly prohibits ex post facto laws.[204] "If this is not an ex post facto law attempting to legitimize something after the fact,[205] then what is?" Judge Maven pondered.[206]

If Ohio was not a state in 1947, then Senator Taft was not a Senator, and could not have introduced any bills in the Senate. Both his vote and the vote of Senator Bricker to override the veto of the Taft-Hartley Act would have been illegal.

Finally, Article I § 3 of the Constitution requires that a senator be an inhabitant of the *state* for which he is chosen, but if the territory from which he is chosen is not a state, then he cannot be a Senator.

In a final irony, Robert A. Taft did not live to see his native

---

[203] Although an electoral college *sits*, its members take no SAT's to get into the college. Eisenhower was a graduate of West Point, but may have gotten through the electoral college on the G.I. Bill.

[204] "Ex post facto" is a legal term composed of "ex" (meaning "out of") "facto" (meaning "by reason of a fact") and "post" (meaning "having to do with the mails"). "Ex post facto" is roughly translated as "because it got lost in the mail."

[205] The result would mean that Warren G. Harding, a resident of Marion, Ohio, would not have been a legitimate President of the United States—something scholars have long suspected. Art II § 1 of the Constitution establishes the eligibility requirements to be president. They include being a resident of the United States for fourteen years. They also require a candidate to be "a natural born citizen," which eliminates all those people born by caesarean section.

[206] Judge Maven had recently received a speeding ticket, a few days before all speed limits on interstate highways were repealed in 2163. He wondered if Congress could repeal the speed limit retroactively, too.

Ohio become a state in 1953. He died the day before the Senate vote.[207]

The Taft-Hartley Act was therefore the work of a citizen who had no power, jurisdiction or authority to introduce it as a bill, and it could not become a law.

What happened next in the case is unclear, as the author's fax ran out of paper and his great great granddaughter[208] did not load the paper retroactively to compensate for the problem.

---

[207] See Cong. Rec., July 31, 1953 at 10038 and August 1, 1953 at 10868.

[208] The author has not named his great great granddaughter, as he believes it would be presumptuous of him to do so when that will be function of his descendants.

CURRENT POSITIONS OF THE PARTIES
IN COLLECTIVE BARGAINING

MANAGEMENT'S DEMANDS *UNION RESPONSE*

1. No salary increase
2. Random Drug testing
3. Longer work day
4. Switch to provide HMO
5. Charge fee for parking
6. No coffee on premises
7. Call one day in advance in case of emergencies
8. Discipline for abusing sick
9. Close employee lounge
10. Fire employees at Will.

1. Make management offer retroactive
2. Grade Drug tests on a curve
3. Shorter hours—60 minutes are too long.
4. Switch to provide HBO in lounge.
5. Fee should depend on who we get to park with.
6. Give us a break!
7. Call one day later to schedule sick and in to schedule sick and emergencies.
8. Time off for good behavior. leave
9. replace with individual chaise lounges
10. **OK, if** Will is in upper management.

RES IPSA LOQUITUR (Humor)[209]

EVIDENTIARY RULES AT ADMINISTRATIVE HEARINGS: ARE THERE ANY?

Any article about evidentiary rules at administrative hearings will, perforce, be short. Before the State Administrative Procedure Act there were few, if any.[210] Indeed, there are those who claim that the topic of "evidentiary rules at administrative hearings" is an oxymoron[211]. Where there actually are rules, they are usually shorter than the World Wrestling Federation's Referee Handbook.

The State Administrative Procedure Act (SAPA)[212] § 306 provides that agencies need not observe the rules of evidence observed by courts, but shall give effect to the rules of privilege recognized by law. It also permits procedures to be adopted for submission of evidence is written form, adopting the logic of the ancient maxim "The truth will come out, even in an affidavit."

---

[209] This label required (by the editors) and by the Federal Truth in Labeling Act.

[210] The State Administrative Procedure Act § 100 provides: "The legislature hereby finds and declares that the administrative rule making, adjudicatory and licensing processes among the agencies of state government are inconsistent, lack uniformity and create misunderstanding by the public."

To the best of the author's knowledge, a contrary finding *after* the SAPA was enacted has never been made.

The section then concludes as follows: "Those agencies which will not have to conform to this act have been exempted from the act, either specifically by name or impliedly by definition." Those agencies are thus permitted by grace of the Legislature to be inconsistent, lack uniformity, and create misunderstanding in the public.

[211] An oxymoron is a contradiction in terms such as casual labor, spare change or justice court.

[212] Pronounced SAP-A with the accent of the first syllable.

Often a statute will be the starting point to determine what rules of evidence are applicable. Civil Service Law § 75 provides that the technical rules of evidence do not apply.[213] The same is true for Department of Motor Vehicle hearings.[214]

Which rules are technical? The rule of thumb is that if your opponent advocates the rule, it is technical, but if you advocate it the rule is fundamental to the evidentiary process.

Other Rules of Procedure.

Many hearing officers at administrative proceedings are not attorneys, and have little insight into the legal process because they do not watch Judge Wapner, Judge Judy, or L.A. Law. At administrative hearings the CPLR does not apply.[215] What rules do administrative judges apply? [216]

The Marquis of Queensberry Rules is one set employed. They include:

1. No hitting below the belt.
2. Go to neutral corners in the event of a knockdown.
3. The decision of the referee on a question of evidence is final.[217]

---

[213] At a hearing held by an administrative body, technical rules of evidence and procedure may be disregarded, *Rothkoff v. Ratner*, 104 Misc.2d 204 (1980).

[214] *Ries v. Adduci* 124 App. Div. 2d 923, app. dis. 69 NY2d 822, reconsid. den. 69 NY2d 985 (1986).

[215] *Fiedelman v. New York State Dept. of Health*, 58 NY2d 80 (1983).

[216] Contrary to popular belief, there is no rule that requires a *pro se* party to be represented by the hearing officer (for example, the police officer at a Department of Motor Vehicle hearing). However it happens, and the party so represented can have no complaint, since he is not entitled to effective assistance of counsel at an administrative hearing, *Walston v. Axelrod*, 103 App.Div. 2d 769 [11] (2nd. Dept. 1984).

[217] It has been said that it is useless to dispute the referee's ability to count to ten. That is one definition of the substantial evidence rule.

4. In the event of conflicting precedents, the brief with the earliest postmark wins.
5. A draw goes to the party paying the hearing officer's fee.

A different set of rules was authored by Robert Fulghum and is entitled *Everything I Need to Know about Evidence I Learned in Kindergarten*. These rules include:

1. Play fair—no hitting.
2. Share evidentiary rulings—Sustain about half for each party.
3. Always look both ways before ruling.
4. Always take a nap after lunch during a restful part of the case.
5. Say you're sorry.

Many hearing officers are retired judges who employ pre-CPLR rules ranging from the Civil Practice Act to the Code of Hammurabi. They precede evidence rulings with statements like, "Young man, I've forgotten more evidences rules than I'll ever know."

Some people believe that the only good evidence rule is no rule.[218] They believe in following experience rather than logical rules. They are in good company historically. Justice Holmes,[219] Stanley Baldwin,[220] Commodore Vanderbilt[221] and Judge Roy Bean agree.

The only law some hearing officers recognize is Murphy's Law. With no rules around it is amazing how often things do go wrong.

---

[218] "Rules! Hell, there ain't no rules around here. We're trying to accomplish sump'n," Thomas Edison quoted in Fischer, *Historians' Fallacies* p. xviii (New York, 1970).

[219] "The life of the law has not been logic: it has been experience." Holmes, *The Common Law* (Howe ed. 1963) p.3.

[220] "One of the reasons why our people are alive and flourishing and have avoided many troubles that have fallen to less happy nations is that we have never been guided by logic in anything we did," in Stebbing, *Thinking to Some Purpose*, (Baltimore, 1961). P. 17.

[221] "What do I care about the law? Hain't I got the power?" quoted in *Nobody Said it Better* p. 41.

Rules of Admissibility.

There is only one rule for the admissibility of evidence at an administrative hearing. It is inevitably expressed by the hearing officer as follows—"I'll take it for what it's worth." This is also known as the Rule of Getting Your Two Cents In. That's what its worth. Small Claims arbitrators follow the same rule.[222]

CONCLUSION

To paraphrase Mr. Dooley: The rules of evidence are applicable to those administrative proceedings to which they apply on account of their applicability.

---

[222] The topic of small claims arbitration is beyond the scope of this article. In other words, don't even get me started.

RES IPSA LOQUITUR (HUMOR)[223]

AN EMPLOYEE'S RIGHT TO
DRINK ALCOHOLIC BEVERAGES

by James M. Rose[224]

Mr. Ed[225] was suspected by his employer, the Census Bureau, of arriving at work under the influence of alcohol, although he denied it, and said that his clothes might smell of beer because he was wearing a shirt he had spilled beer on the previous night. As a consequence he was asked to attend the Employee Assistance Program (EAP)[226] for counseling and possible treatment, and he agreed in a written stipulation to cooperate in lieu of prosecution.

However, the EAP program insisted on randomly testing him. Mr. Ed once again did not oppose the test, but indicated that it would show that he had consumed alcohol off duty. EAP insisted the tests had to indicate that Mr. Ed was not consuming alcohol at all in order for them to certify to the employer that Mr. Ed was cooperating with them. Mr. Ed then refused to continue in the

---

[223] A label required by the editors. Humor is like a box of chocolates, it can be light or dark, or full of nuts. No, humor is like a bucket of fried chicken—it can be light or dark, greasy, unsatisfying, fast, cheap, bad for you—stop that metaphor, it's getting away!

[224] White Plains, New York. No photograph of Mr. Rose appears with this article because Bill Gates and Microsoft have acquired all rights to his image.

[225] A fictional name used for publication. There was no indication of the employee's fictional first name, although perhaps it was "Remedial." The employee's *real* first name was Horst.

[226] See the Mental Hygiene Law's § 41.54 captioned "Employee assistance programs." There are two sections numbered 41.54, the Legislature being inordinately fond of that number; but the one this article refers to is c. 819 Laws of 1992, and not c. 309 of Laws of 1992. Employees who drink alcohol to excess and search for EAP in the laws see double right from the start.

program. A disciplinary arbitration was commenced for violating the agreement to cooperate.[227]

Mr. Ed told the arbitrator, Jim Beam, "I know that I have to show up to work sober. I know that I cannot drink and drive. But no one has a right to demand that I stop drinking. Drinking is my hobby, and my legal and Constitutional right."

The arbitrator inquired as to the source of the legal right, and was directed by Mr. Ed to Labor Law § 201-d (1) (b) which defines "recreational activities" as: "any lawful, leisure-time activity, for which the employee receives no compensation and which is generally engaged in for recreational purposes, including but not limited to sports, games, hobbies, exercise, reading and the viewing of television, movies and similar material." The law prohibits an employer from discriminating against any employee who engages in such hobbies. Mr. Ed said that he drinks recreationally[228] and it is his hobby, along with rooting for the Milwaukee Brewers.

The Labor Law specifically provides that it is illegal for an employer to discharge from employment or otherwise discriminate against an employee because of "an individual's legal use of consumable products prior to the beginning or after the conclusion of the employee's work hours and off the employer's premises" at § 201-d (2)(b).[229]

---

[227] He refused to go to meetings of what he referred to as "alcoholics anomalous," because he said that he was a drunk, and not an alcoholic. When asked what the difference was, he said "Alcoholics have to go to meetings." This roughly approximates the views of the law on the subject—Mental Hygiene Law § 1.03 (subds. 13 and 14) defining "alcoholism" and "alcoholic," Mental Hygiene Law §§ 19.15 called "Programs of the Office of Alcohol and Substance Abuse;" and § 19.23 entitled "Education and Training."

[228] And in the past his drinking has led to his "re-creating" himself for posterity.

[229] Arguably that was the case law even before it became statutory law, see *Llano v. Levine,* 51 App. Div. 2d 630 (3rd Dept. 1976)—in which it was held that off duty drinking was a personal trait that was not misconduct on the part of an employee.

Further, Mr. Ed pointed to the repeal of prohibition as an indication that he has a constitutional right to drink. The Federal Government was put out of the prohibition business by the repeal of the Eighteenth Amendment to the Constitution,[230] and that includes his employer, the Census Bureau!

Further he indicated, the Declaration of Independence guaranteed the citizens the right to "life, liberty and the pursuit of happiness."[231] Each of us pursues happiness in his own way, he remarked. To celebrate the bicentennial, New York repealed its criminal sanctions against public intoxication,[232] an act which expresses the public policy that we are free to drink alcoholic beverages to excess.[233]

Doing so also could negate an element of a crime calling for a particular mental state, so drinking was recognized by the Legislature as beneficial in that it could provide a defense to a crime that would not be available to someone sober as a judge.[234] An entire law, the state's Alcoholic Beverage Control Law, is devoted

---

[230] The Twenty-first Amendment to the Constitution, effective on December 5, 1933.

[231] There is no truth to the rumor that in Jefferson's first draft it was "the happiness of pursuit."

[232] L. 1974, c. 1068 effective January 1, 1976. But, see Mental Hygiene Law § 21.09 (c)—"Emergency Services for Intoxicated persons." That law allows police to give emergency "services" (such as free rides to alcoholism facilities) to an intoxicated person "without his or her consent." Instead of "arresting" you and "throwing" you in jail, this law permits the police to render "emergency services" to you by involuntarily "placing" you in a treatment facility. The same end result is achieved. It is unclear if the Legislature meant to employ "services" in this statute as a noun (meaning "help"), or as a verb (as in the sentence "The stallion services the mare to produce a foal").

[233] Which was always the case as long as it occurred in private, *People v. Hook* 3 NY2d 485, 168 NYS2d 958 (1957).

[234] Penal Law § 15.25 indicates that intoxication is not a defense "as such," but implies that it could be a defense if the circumstances were right and one does not refer to it as "such."

to making sure that alcoholic beverages are available to the public conveniently.[235]

Moreover, beer plays an important part in Mr. Ed's religious beliefs, as it constitutes a sacrament in his religion, the Church of the Riteway. The Religious Freedom Restoration Act of 1993"[236] guarantees that the government cannot interfere with the religious beliefs of its citizens if some less restrictive manner would accomplish the same thing. An order simply not to be drunk on duty would suffice in this case, rather than banning the consuming of all alcohol, even off duty, Mister Ed argued.[237]

The arbitrator held that Mister Ed, A/K/A Horst, did not have to give up drinking off duty.

CONCLUSION

You can lead a Horst to EAP, but you can't make him stop drinking.

---

[235] See, Alcoholic Beverage Control Law § 2—"Policy of state and purpose of chapter."

[236] 42 U.S.C. § 2000bb, 107 Stat. 1488, P.L. 103-141, but since declared unconstitutional.

[237] For example, courts have often held that Native American religions that involve the use of peyote are true religions entitled to the protect of the first amendment. *People v. Woody*, 61 Cal. 2d 716 (1964) 35 ALR3d 939, but see *Montana v. Big Sheep*, 75 Mont. 219 (1926).

James M. Rose

LAW FIRM OF TUMMLER, SCHNORRER, PISCHER, & VERBLUNGENT, P.C.

September 5, 2001

Dear Government of Egypt:

Re: Reparations for slavery
September 9, 2001

It has come to my attention through media reports from the conference on racism in Durban, South Africa that the government of Egypt (hereinafter "You") advocate that former slaves receive reparations for back pay that they should have received from their slave masters, together with interest thereon.

I, (hereinafter "claimant") write to inform you of my claim based upon the Book of Exodus for wages that were never paid to my ancestors who were slaves in the land of Egypt.

By my calculation, wages ceased to be paid upon the death of Prime Minister and First Deputy Pharaoh Joseph (when a pharaoh who "knew him not" took the throne) until my ancestors were given exit visas (which Pharaoh later arbitrarily and capriciously attempted to revoke at the Red Sea when he raced after my ancestors (hereinafter "race based discrimination.") in 1312 B.C.E.

My ancestors were skilled construction workers who were forced to work on public works projects for You, constructing cities and forts along the frontier as part of a Strategic Defense Initiative (hereinafter "SDI"). Often they took jobs that native Egyptians would not.

They were not paid the prevailing wage rate for workers on public works projects. By that I do not mean zero (hereinafter "Gornisht")—the rate at which slaves were compensated, and which I understand you *are* willing to pay retroactively *and* with interest.)

My ancestors were not paid a living wage, and many provisions of the Egyptian Civil Service Law were ignored. They were not promoted by merit as in the time of Joseph, but were instead the victims of invidious discrimination in the terms and conditions of their employment. Disproportionately few became overseers or were appointed bureaucrats with cushy middle management "white tunic" jobs, despite their obvious skill in creative accounting. They received no paid vacations, no retirement or disability benefits, nor any uniform allowances. They were so overworked that they developed permanent congenital malformations of the upper spinal column and became widely known as a "stiff necked people" (Exod.33:5).

When Moses attempted to collectively bargain three days off to conduct religious observances, management retaliated on the rank and file by insisting that they collect their own straw for bricks (Exod. 5:11). They were never paid for the straw on a cost plus basis, as is customary on government defense contracts.

You benefited directly from the bricks that they made, and even a cursory examination of existing buildings in your country supports the conclusion that you are still using some of the bricks that they fabricated.

Claimant claims for back wages at $ 30,000 per year (the going rate for skilled union brick makers and allied trades) for a period of four hundred years (Exod. 12:40), which comes to $12,000,000.00. Simple interest at only 3% per annum for a period of three thousand three hundred and thirteen years on that claim comes to $ 39,756,000,000.00. The total of back wages and interest comes to $39,786,000,000.00.

In addition, Pharaoh's stubborn refusal to comply with Moses' reasonable requests caused approximately ten plagues (But who's counting?). My ancestors were inconvenienced, bothered and bodily vexed by the plagues, causing them to suffer property damage to their personal property as well as a diminution of their real property's resale value as a direct consequence of said negligent and tortious behavior. An itemized list will follow.

Because of your government's treatment of my ancestors they were required to eat the "bread of affliction," and claimant is still required to do so one week every year (not to mention bitter herbs!). Said "bread of affliction" has had a constipating effect on your claimant, and caused him to cry out at the end of a week, "Let my people go!"

Please remit a check for $39,768,000,000.00 by return mail, or I wouldn't want to be in your sandals.

Very truly yours,

Corner Office partner, for the firm.

THE HMO WAS A SUCCESS BUT THE PATIENT DIED[238]

One morning Katusha Rockette, the spouse of an employee of the Village of Nouveau Riche On Hudson, New York woke up with a bad sore throat at 3:00 AM. Her temperature was 103 degrees. She wanted to go to the emergency room because she suspected that she had the flu which was going around at work, but knew that she would first have to call the gatekeeper of the HMO[239] to which her employer had recently switched— Kevorkian Health Maintenance Organization and Upholstery Repair Co.

When she called, she reached the gatekeeper, Nurse St. Peter, the nurse[240] on duty.[241] Ms. Rockette was asked a series of questions explained in more detail below, and denied the right to go to the emergency room or see a non-plan doctor under her HMO plan. As a consequence, she was required to pay for the visit to her personal physician herself. All health care provided by the HMO was by video phone from Tijuana, because the HMO employed only Mexican doctors under the provisions of NAFTA (which stands for "Now Accented Foreigners do Tasks of Americans").

Ms. Rockette was irate, and filed for arbitration of the dispute, demanding reimbursement and "closure."[242]

---

[238] by James M. Rose, White Plains, New York. Mr. Rose is a potential County Court Judge, and always will be.

[239] HMO is an abbreviation which stands for Humungous Machiavellian Ogre.

[240] An impractical nurse.

[241] She had recently been hired. Although she had been selected as Miss Behavioral Science in Community College, she denied that in her interview, saying "Ain't Miss Behavioral." Her thesis had been "HMOs: Threat or Meance?"

[242] "Closure" is something that we all need. Like a digital cell phone, until recently we had never even *heard* of it, but now we all "need" it. If you sue for closure, then ask for a continuance, is that a waiver?

It came to be heard before arbitrator "Tab" U. LaRasa, a man so dull that his college subtracted credits for lack of life experience.[243] The Village was represented by an attorney from the HMO—Ms. Bessie Mae Kewlow.

During the arbitration it developed that the HMO was relying upon Nurse St. Peter's interpretation of several of the provisions of its plan described in the rather complex plan booklet, an interpretation that the arbitrator referred to in his decision as "the gospel according to St. Peter."

The first had to do with other insurance. The HMO indicated that a member would not be covered if the matter were covered by some other insurance, a usual provision for claims that would be covered because of Workers Compensation insurance, for example, or the health insurance of a spouse who had primary coverage.

Ms. Rockette said that night "I'm burning up! I've got a fever of 103," and St. Peter replied, "If it gets to 105 sell," but then said that was just a little HMO humor.[244] St. Peter asked Rockette if perhaps she had fire insurance for her primary coverage. Ms. Rockette said she had no fire insurance.

Ms. Rockette said "It's probably the flu. It's going around at work." St. Peter then suggested that the matter would be covered by worker's compensation if the flu was the result of an illness incurred at work. However, it was proved at the arbitration that Worker's Compensation[245] insurance covers only certain named illnesses, and influenza is not among them.

Nurse St. Peter asked if Ms. Rockette knew who had sneezed on her to give her the flu. Rockette asked why that was necessary information. She was told that, unlike automobile insurance, this HMO's insurance was not "no fault," and that the same rules of

---

[243] As for his personality, it was said that people preferred to talk to his answering machine because it had more warmth than he.
[244] very little.
[245] In this instance administered by Oracle Management of Delphi, New York.

law applied to this claim as would apply to any insurance. That is, Rockette would have to find, implead, and maintain an action against the person who got her sick, so that the HMO could seek contribution or indemnification.[246] "Someone who should have covered her mouth when she sneezed did not do so," Kewlow added, and then remarked, "I love the smell of negligence in the morning!"

"But," said Rockette, this is a world wide epidemic. It is sweeping the country like a plague. Would I be required to implead everyone who sneezed on everyone else until we get the first person who caught this flu from a pig in China?"

"Plagues," Cuelo replied, "are acts of God." She cited Exodus and the Passover story as proof of that proposition. Acts of God are excluded from all traditional insurance contracts, including this one she noted—pointing to small print in the exceptions clause; and, even if they are not, how could the HMO implead and get contribution from the Deity?

Nurse St. Peter then asked if Rockette had taken advantage of the free flu shot the HMO had offered to its members.[247] Ms. Rockette said she had intended to do so, but was out sick that day. Kewlow then indicated that Rockette was guilty of contributory negligence. By not staying home when everyone at work had the flu, she had violated the doctrine of the Last Clear Chance, a vestigial appendage of tort law which applies primarily on bar examinations.

The HMO then defended upon the ground that it was willing to send its usual "pre-approval" letter to Rockette in the mail. Rockette noted that she did not want to wait for five days until the letter came in the mail, and that the HMO's usual pre-approval letter was a "weasel letter" that said that the matter was approved—"Subject to further review by our staff to determine whether the

---

[246] Just like the Blue Crosses of several states that sued the tobacco companies for causing smoking related illnesses.

[247] Some neighborhood lads were employed by the HMO to offer "drive by" flu shots to all the HMO's customers.

matter is covered under the plan." In other words it was covered until it was decided that it was not covered.[248]

Ms. Rockette argued that she needed some antibiotics to fight the flu, and that is why she wanted to go to the emergency room or see a physician the next day. However, Ms. Kewlow argued that recent studies showed that there are some flu strains resistant to antibiotics, and thus the treatment would be experimental, which is also excluded under the plan's exclusions.

Ms. Rockette argued that at least she could get some prescription pain relievers for the sore throat and the headache if she could see a doctor, but Ms. Kewlow pointed out that the relief of pain would not *cure* the flu, and the exclusions from the plan included "maintenance, or any other treatment not meant to cure the illness."[249]

The arbitrator remarked that it seemed the HMO covered nothing, and that it was not a good plan. "On the contrary," Ms. Kewlow pointed out, "its stock was a star performer on Wall Street because it kept its costs down so well, and investment advisers considered it a star in the HMO market."[250] Ms. Rockette argued that the HMO, when it did pay her doctor's bills only paid some, and then often late and less than the amount by some random formula known only to the HMO. The formula, Ms. Kewlow replied, was based upon the "normal and customary fees" paid in the area,[251] a number arrived at magically, and shrouded in the cloak of trade secrecy which she refused to lift.

Arbitrator LaRasa wrote that both coverage and payment appeared to be arbitrary and random, in the same way getting

---

[248] If you think the author is making this one up, look at a pre approval letter from your HMO.

[249] If you think the author is making this one up, too, look at your HMO plan description booklet.

[250] Kevorkian Health Maintenance had offered the village an "exclusive deal" and was only fulfilling its promise by making sure the coverage was exclusive of most claims, Kewlow argued.

[251] by HMOs who decide what is normal and customary.

struck by lightening was random, to quote the words of Justice Stewart in *Furman v. Georgia* 408 U.S. 238 (1972).[252] Since Ms. Rockette's employer was a public entity, LaRasa declared the HMO to be in violation of the Eighth Amendment's ban on cruel and unusual treatment.

Now the HMO is in court seeking to upset the award on the grounds that (1) what they did to Ms. Rockette not unusual, but their usual response; and (2) it *refused* to treat Ms. Rockette, and the Eighth Amendment does not bar cruel *non*-treatment.

---

[252] He was describing how the death penalty was imposed by the states.

AN EMPLOYEE'S RIGHT TO HIBERNATE IN THE WINTER WITHOUT BEING FIRED

by James M. Rose[253]

A motion in a recent case brought to our attention an unusual claim that Federal statutes permitted an employee to hibernate in winter without being fired.

The employee, Chris Le Bair, worked for the Department of Defense (DOD). He claimed that he was suffering from Seasonal Affective Disorder (SAD). This is one of the "diseases" that have been newly discovered thanks to the miracles of modern science and the willingness of the health insurance industry to pay the claims of doctors who discover and treat the new disorders. The discovery of new diseases is in direct proportion to doctors' willingness to be paid extravagant sums of money to treat them, and to be expert[254] witnesses in court advocating the existence of diseases and disorders for which someone other than the plaintiff ought to be required to foot the bills.[255]

SAD is a disorder brought on by the change in the seasons. In the Northern Hemisphere as winter approaches and settles in, the days grow shorter and the nights grow longer. The lack of sunlight and warmth causes those who suffer from SAD to become depressed, surly, and to long for longer periods of sleep.[256] Scientists speculate that ancient man may have hibernated in caves like bears in winter when food was scarce. Those of us less descended from ancient

---

[253] White Plains, New York. The Federal Law in this article has be satirized for your protection.

[254] "Expert" has been defined as an ordinary person who testifies about his work more than one hundred miles away from his office. The word is made up of two components—"ex" meaning former, and "spurt" meaning drip under pressure.

[255] and thereafter should be recognized as disorders in the courts.

[256] B. Bowen,"Winter Depression," *Science News* July 25, 1992, p. 62.

man with more of a genetic memory of ancient habits may still long to sleep through winter.[257] SAD is recognized as a distinct disorder by the American Psychiatric Association[258] in its diagnostic manual, DSM-III.[259]

Chris Le Bair wrote a note to his employer that requested an unpaid leave of absence for the winter. His note began "Oh DOD, poor DOD, I'm feeling oh so SAD."

The basis of his request was the Family and Medical Leave Act of 1993 (29 U.S.C. §§ 2601 *et. seq.*).[260] While the public is aware that this law applies to leaves for pregnancy and illness of family members, it is less well known that it also allows for a medical leave by the full time employee[261] himself for up to twelve weeks[262] if he suffers from a "serious health condition."[263]

The expert witness, Sir Kay D. N. Writhem, submitted a certification to DOD,[264] and then said in an affidavit in support of the motion that, in his opinion, SAD comes within the purview of the statute because it is a "serious health condition." His conclusion is based upon that fact that "It's no joke" and "When someone suffers from depression he is too serious, and ought to lighten up."

---

[257] This article does not address whether the Americans With Disabilities Act 42 U.S.C. §§ 12101 et. seq. protects sufferers from SAD as disabled persons, ("the equinoctically challenged.").

[258] a group that is, by sheer coincidence, paid to treat it.

[259] R. N. Rosenthal, *Seasons of the Mind* (Bantam Books, 1989) p. 157.

[260] Effective August 8, 1993 (except for parts that are not).

[261] A full time employee is one who has been employed for more than twelve months (not necessarily consecutive) with that employer, and who worked more than 1250 hours in the previous year. The term is meant to exclude part time employees. If an employee takes twelve weeks off each year for his illness, three weeks vacation, and five sick days he is still (barely) a full time employee, but comes close to the 1250 hour minimum unless he works some overtime.

[262] 29 U.S.C. § 2612 (a)(1)(D).

[263] 29 U.S.C. § 2611 (11)(b).

[264] As required by 29 U.S.C. § 2613(b)(3).

He categorized Le Bair's SAD depression as bi-polar depression.[265] Therapy involving bright lights and tanning salons proved ineffective[266] because the plaintiff would then be required to travel through the cold and dark to go to and from work.[267]

Le Bair used to take the bus, but standing in the cold and dark caused him to become so depressed he often went home and did not even try coming to work.

What plaintiff needed as a medical treatment (to be paid for by his health insurance), Sir Kay opined, was to travel to a warm climate closer to the equator where the days are longer.[268] His mental condition would then "lighten up."[269]

The statute itself defines "serious health condition" as one that requires continuing treatment by a health care professional. The expert wrote that no health care provider worth a Medicare payment could not find a medical condition that does not require more than one treatment. Since SAD recurs each winter, it qualifies.

The case is still unresolved in court. Its report arose because of a motion to postpone a pre-trial deposition of Le Bair until "after the winter months."

Le Bair concluded that his condition was a handicap, because he was a person with a disability under the Vehicle and Traffic Law.[270] Vehicle and Traffic Law § 404-a provides that a mental disability which causes an unusual hardship in utilizing public transportation entitles a person to a handicapped license plate. Le Bair has now applied for one. The Commissioner of Motor Vehicles has asked DOD to transfer Le Bair to Hawaii.

---

[265] Specifically north polar and south polar. At the poles it is dark half the year, and SAD would be particularly devastating.

[266] and only alleviates the condition for about 60% of sufferers according to *Science News* September 23, 1989 at p. 198.

[267] And was not available because Le Bair's health insurance company, Indigo Cross, would not cover tanning salon bills.

[268] And possibly to take Sir Kay with him for therapy sessions on the beach.

[269] "He quoted Dr. Jimmy Buffet "Changes in latitudes, changes in attitudes."

[270] Vehicle and Traffic Law § 1203-c.

CHAPTER THREE

THIS LEGAL ADVICE IS ONLY GOOD ON A DAY THAT ENDS IN "WHY?"

WHAT IS THE APPEARANCE OF JUSTICE?[271]

Recently the Westchester County Attorney's Office changed its letterhead and added the county seal to it.[272] For the past several years it has used a stylized capital letter "W" on the top in dark blue (See Figure 1)

Westchester County

FIGURE 1

which apparently represented three baloneys or some other deli luncheon meat that comes stuffed into a tubular casing.[273] That

---

[271] The law in this article has been sealed for your protection. If the seal on this article has been broken you're on your own, Pandora.

[272] I have used the word "letterhead" since I still cannot remember whether to use "stationery" or "stationary" in this context.

[273] Or two misshapen extra strength pain relief capsules and a regular one. The "W" appeared during the Del Bello administration and the three stark vertical lines may be evocative of the three lower case letter "L"s in Del Bello's last name. Others suggest that the image represents a bunch of bananas—one of the county's leading exports.

logo, which appears on county vehicles and other property was never the official seal of the County. A search of the County charter and Administrative Code reveals no formal adoption of the tripartite symbol.[274] Unlike Gaul, Westchester is not divided into three parts, and why *this* "W" remains a mystery.

The new letterhead reflects the seal of the county which is described in the Administrative Code at § 205.11. That section provides:

The Seal of the County of Westchester shall consist of two (2) circles, one within the other, with the words "Westchester County, Seal"[275] around the outer circumference of the inner circle, and in the center of the inner circle the figure of Justice, standing, the dexter arm embowed, holding above her head her scales, in the sinister hand a straight sword, point downward, resting on the sinister foot."

The seal now being used is depicted in figure 2.

FIGURE 2

---

[274] The government is a bipartite one, consisting of the County Executive and the County Board of Legislators. It has no judicial arm. "Bipartite" should not be confused with "bipartisan"—nor will it be in this county. The County Board of Legislators has its own seal (Administrative Code § 209.61) which has no depiction of an allegorical figure on it. In its place is what is described as a "lozenge" inscribed with the numbers "1683." The numbers refer to the year in which the county was founded and not the number of Spanos and their relations currently employed by the County.

[275] Why does "The County of Westchester" have a seal that reads "Westchester County" instead of "The County of Westchester"? While this may appear

The County Executive is authorized to use a similar seal by Administrative Code § 213.11 except that his reads "County Executive of Westchester County, New York Seal." (See figure 3).[276]

FIGURE 3

Why does Justice appear as she does on these seals? Why is Justice not blindfolded?[277] Why does she appear to be throwing the scales of justice like a shot put or sniffing her armpit for freshness? Is she holding them behind her back like a contortionist? Are they held

---

to be nit picking, that is one of the functions of a scholarly publication. Apparently the County of Westchester is also known by the alias "Westchester County." It now appears to be in the process of changing its name to Westchestergov.com, as that phrase is beginning to appear on many of its documents.

[276] Why does the County Executive's seal have the words "New York" but the County's seal does not? Consider *that* another nit picked.

[277] Or, why *is* Justice blindfolded on other seals? The goddess Justice has been depicted as blindfolded only since the sixteenth century. The blindfold is now meant to depict impartiality, although Justice was supposed to have keen sight. In antiquity a blindfold was the symbol for lack of impartiality or randomness such as Cupid's blindfold.

Justice does not wear a blindfold because *she* is about to be executed. Rather, it is her *judgments* that get executed.

where she cannot see them because she is not concerned if they are in balance[278]

In the illustration (Figure 2) she appears to be balancing them on top of her head like a seal would. Is *that* why it says "SEAL" on the bottom?[279]

Justice is depicted a variety of ways on our seals. On the Westchester County Bar Association seal (figure 4)

FIGURE 4

---

[278] The Goddess Justice holds scales which are meant to depict the weighing of right and wrong. Her sword is intended to represent her power. Justice is one of the four cardinal virtues (along with Prudence, Fortitude and Temperance—(None of whom sound like a fun prom date.) The sword and scales are also attributes of Logic, one of the seven Liberal Arts. (J. Hall, *Dictionary of Subjects and Symbols in Art,* Harper & Row, New York 1974). The Greek name for Justice was *Themis*. That would make the Halls of Justice a *Themis* Park. Justice also appears on the state seal of Oklahoma (with her scales) and on the seal of the District of Columbia holding the Constitution. Five other states have seals involving swords. The seal of Arkansas contains a sword with the inscription "Justice" on it.

[279] And why is Justice always depicted in a long flowing robe that does not appear to resemble a judge's robe? Is it her nightgown—and, if so, has casual Friday finally gone too far?

she is blindfolded and holds much larger (heavy duty?) scales than in the County seal. On the County Bar Association seal Justice appears to be a blonde.[280]

What *is* the hair color of Justice?[281] It may depend on what day you inquire. The county seal depicted on the County Attorney's letterhead shows her with raven locks, but the County Executive's seal shows her wearing a blonde bun.[282] Yet on the great seal of the State of New York (See figure 5)[283]

FIGURE 5

---

[280] She is also a bit slimmer than the substantial figures on the other seals.
[281] Why is the allegorical figure of Justice depicted as a woman going back to the times when judges were exclusively male? In an 1885 toast to the Suffolk County (Mass.) Bar Association, Oliver Wendell Holmes Jr. said "To our mistress, the Law." Both Justice and The Law are apparently female. "Our mistress the Law" is a metaphor best left unvisualized.

William L. Prosser noted in *The Judicial Humorist*, "Justice has been described as a lady who has been subject to so many miscarriages as to cast serious reflections upon her virtue."
[282] Or has her hair been turned white by what Justice has seen in her Halls?
[283] The current Great Seal of New York is the fifth since 1777. This one dates from May 20, 1882. (Geo. Shankle, *State Flags, Seals, Songs, Birds, Flowers and other Symbols* (Wilson & Co., NY, NY) (1934) at 205.) The first

ORIGINAL NEW YORK STATE SEAL.
FIGURE 6

she has dark hair worn shoulder length and the size of her scales appears to be somewhere between the ones in the County Bar seal and the County Executive's seal.[284]

The sword position is another interesting difference. In the state seal the sword is pointed upward. In the words of State Law § 70:[285]

> ... Sinister. The figure of Justice proper, her hair disheveled and decorated with pearls, vested, or, above the waist a cincture azure, fringed gules, sandaled and mantled as Liberty,[286] bound about the eyes with a fillet proper, in the dexter hand a straight sword hilted or, erect, resting on the sinister chief point of the shield, the sinister arm embowed, holding before her her scales proper.

(Figure 6) was a smiley face. One hopes, along with fans of Ingmar Bergman, that New York does not get to a seventh seal. The current seal appears to be based upon the flag of the New York State Regiment during the Revolutionary War (Figure 7).

[284] We do not mean to judge the various depictions of Justice by the size of her pair of scales, of course. We would never do that, especially when she is armed with a sword.

[285] The Great Seal of the state is described in State Law § 73 as consisting of the device of arms of this state which is described in State Law § 70. The state does not have a "mediocre seal" because State Law § 72 provides that there be no other pictorial devices other than the arms of the state used in public offices.

[286] That's Liberty on the other side of the seal in Figure 5.

This definition raises several interesting questions. Why is Justice's hair disheveled? Is it because she put the blindfold on before she got dressed? Perhaps it is messed up from rushing from calendar call to calendar call, and court to court. Why are her eyes bound with a fillet—and a fillet of what? Beef? Sole?

Why is Justice on the sinister side of the seal?[287] Why does she have her sword in her right (dexter) hand while on the County's Seal she has her sword in her left (sinister) hand?[288]

Is Justice left handed in Westchester County, but right handed elsewhere—or even ambidextrous?[289]

Is the County of Westchester sinister handed?

Why is Justice depicted as having a belted waist in the County Bar and State seals, but having no belt[290] in the County's seals? Why does the County Seal depict her with a V neck robe, the state seal with a square neck, and the County Bar device with a lower cut bodice?[291]

---

[287] Why is she on the County seal at all, since there is no County judicial branch? Is it because the first Chief Justice of the United States (John Jay) was born in Westchester County? Is it because she is on the state's seal, and the state was born in this county on July 11, 1776?

[288] Why does Justice carry a sword if the pen is mightier than the sword? Perhaps because a sword does not leak in your pocket. Of course the County has a Pen as well as a sword. It has a jail, too. The author was given a T shirt that had the saying "The pen is mightier than the sword" on it. It shrunk unevenly when washed, causing the word "pen" and the word "is" to run together—resulting in the expression of an altogether different sentiment.

[289] i.e., even handed.

[290] or possibly an Empire waist robe.

[291] But never in skirts as short as those of Ally McBeal. When the Westchester County Bar Association Frolic Committee did a T-shirt with Justice's skirt billowing up (in the manner of Marilyn Monroe in *The Seven Year Itch*) (Figure 8) as a metaphor for Justice exposed in the Frolic, feminists complained.

What the length of Ally McBeal's skirts is supposed to depict is beyond the scope of this article.

NEW YORK STATE REGIMENTAL FLAG EMBLEM.

FIGURE 7

Obviously because Justice has an extensive wardrobe as befits a symbol of her stature.

But the most confusing problem is created by the feet.[292] The state Justice wears sandals,[293] but the County Bar's Justice appears to be barefoot. No Justice appears in six inch heels. Why would the County's Justice be required (by the Administrative Code) to rest her sword[294] on her sinister foot? What (or where) is the point?[295]

---

[292] "The time has come," the Walrus said, "To talk of many things: Of shoes—and ships—and sealing wax" . . . "Lewis Carroll, *Through the Looking Glass*, "The Walrus and the Carpenter." This quotation has nothing to do with the article except it does mention shoes and "seal" ing, but the relevancy is questionable at best. It's just appropriate to have quotations in scholarly articles.

[293] even in winter.

[294] Does her sword have a name like King Arthur's Excalibur or Prince Valiant's Singing Sword? Is it the sword with which King Solomon was going to impart justice by bifurcating a baby? Does Justice use her sword to bifurcate trials with a swift severance motion?

[295] Does the law *require* the County to stab itself in the foot? Is this an ancient way of avoiding the draft?

FIGURE 8

Please note that it was possible for *this* publication to write an entire article about Justice in Westchester County and women's hair styles, clothing and shoes without once referring to the incumbent District Attorney.[296]

---

[296] John Barrymore once compared having to read footnotes to getting out of bed and going downstairs to answer the doorbell on your wedding night.

SUICIDE AND HOMICIDE—ANOTHER SIDE?

by James M. Rose[297]

An attorney, "Mr. A"[298], and his wife "Bea"[299] were both told by their doctor[300] that they were suffering from a disease known to be fatal, and they could expect to die within a year. The disease had no known cure, and although the pain could be controlled with drugs, the debilitating effect on the sufferer and his family (who are fully conscious of the disease and its ravages) was terrifying to them.

They knew that suicide was illegal in New York,[301] and that no doctor would assist them in committing suicide.

Mr. A entered into a pact with his wife Bea, who signed a contract with him, in which she paid him one dollar in advance to kill her. He shot her to death. His religion permitted him to aide a person who requested she be killed, but did not let him take his own life with his own hand. He then wrote out a full confession, admitting to malice aforethought, had it notarized, waiving his rights under *Miranda v. Arizona*[302] and took it to the police along with the murder weapon with his fingerprints on it, and the contract and the dollar with fingerprints of both of them on it. He refused to have an attorney appointed to assist him, demanded to plead guilty to Murder in the First Degree, and he demanded the death penalty be imposed.

---

[297] White Plains, New York. Mr. Rose, a self proclaimed Vehicle and Traffic Law expert, currently represents a deer charged with not crossing at a deer crossing sign.

[298] a fictitious name for publication.

[299] *Ibid.*

[300] Who was not Dr. Kevorkian, a fictional name for publication.

[301] as Mr. A and his wife Bea were attorneys and the authors of many bar examination questions.

[302] A fictional case in which the name of the state has been changed for publication.

The District Attorney had engaged in a vigorous campaign recently in which she charged her opponent with being soft on the death penalty, and had pledged to employ it in the first case which arose where the statute appeared to support it. [303]

Mr. A pointed to Penal Law § 125.27 (1) (vi) which made it a capital offense to engage in a murder for hire. In this case the contract, the murder weapon, and even the dollar bill paid as consideration were in the possession of the police. The District Attorney felt compelled to fulfill her pledge and preferred charges of Murder in the First degree to which Mr. A immediately pleaded guilty.[304]

The public raised a hue and cry[305] that the man was obviously mentally disturbed, and that extreme emotional defense is a defense to the charge of murder in the first degree.[306]

The trial judge, Al Denti,[307] suggested it would be appropriate to assign an attorney to represent the accused, as he was not defending himself competently. However, Mr. A replied that he was a well known and well thought of criminal defense attorney himself, and tough judges like Judge Denti[308] had often commended him on the record for a job well done in murder cases. He said he was fully capable of defending himself. "Indeed,"

---

[303] Her slogan was "One man one volt."

[304] Bea's sister, Cici, was outraged and offered to pull the lever on the electric chair herself, but the state replied that she did not have the minimum requirements for the civil service title of executioner, and that the Governor's proposal to privatize executions in New York by hiring organized crime hit men who had been relocated under the witness protection program had failed in the Assembly.

[305] As to "hue and cry" see 23 Westchester *Bar Journal* No. 3 "The Law and the Hendiadys."

[306] See Penal Law 125.27 (2).

[307] who had been looking for a case to sink his teeth into.

[308] Judge Denti was notorious for not dismissing jurors for any reason. He had recently refused a request from the District Attorney to dismiss for cause a criminal trial attorney who had been called to serve on a jury in front of which he was to try the case!

he remarked, "in pleading guilty and demanding the death penalty I am accomplishing exactly what my client wishes."

The judge appointed an attorney to represent Mr. A nevertheless. The attorney was immediately discharged by Mr. A. The judge then reassigned the attorney, and told Mr. A that he was not permitting him to proceed *pro se*. Mr. A replied that as an officer of the court himself he would never disobey the court's directive, but that he was directing his attorney to seek the same result as he had been seeking *pro se*, and should the attorney refuse to do so he would file a complaint with the grievance committee that his directives were being ignored. All attorneys so warned declined to be appointed.

The judge then assigned to Mr. A a very experienced guardian *ad litem* instead under the Mental Hygiene Law. The guardian, Ms. Belle Vieux, was free to act as she felt appropriate despite her client's wishes, and moved to reopen the case.

She argued that Mr. A had a defense to the charges. His wife had been a clone of her mother. Penal Law § 125.05 reads: "(1) 'person,' when referring to the victim of a homicide, means a human being who has been born and is alive." Mrs. A was not "born"[309] the Law Guardian argued, and there was considerable debate as to whether she was a "human being" as that term is understood.[310]

Finally, she argued that the statute employs a curious tense. By definition a victim of a homicide is a person who *is* alive. The statute does not say "*was alive*" or "immediately prior to the homicide was alive." Thu,s it indicates that in order to violate

---

[309] She was grown outside of a womb.
[310] The argument being that human beings are the result of sexual reproduction involving the donation of one half of the chromosomes of a mother and one half of a father, and gestation within the womb of a female. Any clone not born in that manner may not be a human being, but simply a copy or extension of another already existing human being—in this case her mother who had predeceased her.

Mr. A "killed" the photocopy of someone who was already dead, Ms. Vieux argued.

New York homicide statutes the victim must be alive, and Bea was shot to death. Certainly, she argued, the Legislature knows the difference between the present and the past tense, and how to employ them. General Construction Law § 48[311] provides that "Words in the present tense include the future," but does not provide that they include the past, which must have been an intentional omission. We must give the language of the statute its only grammatical interpretation, she noted.[312]

The trial judge envisioned the headline in the Daily *News* the day after he accepted *that* argument—"**NUTTY JUDGE DECLARES MURDER IS LEGAL—UNLESS THE VICTIM IS STILL ALIVE!**" He was not about to throw out the homicide laws in New York. He denied the motion to re-open.

The guardian *ad Litem* then told the jury they were forbidden by law to impose the death penalty.

"He wants to die," Ms. Vieux said. "His whole scheme is an elaborate way of committing suicide. He cannot take his life with his own hand, so he is asking you to pull the switch for him. But Penal Law § 120.30 makes it a class E Felony for anyone, including you, to assist or intentionally aid another person to attempt (or commit) suicide. If you give him the death penalty you will not only give my client—this vicious wife murderer—what he wants, you will be committing a class E Felony."

As of this writing the jury has been hung, but Mr. A has *not*.

---

[311] How come there is no Specific Construction Law or General Deconstruction Law?

[312] c.f., Statutes § 94 "The legislative intent is to be ascertained from the words and language used, and the statutory language is generally construed according to its natural and most obvious sense, without resorting to an artificial or forced construction."

DOES A VOTER HAVE A RIGHT TO KNOW FOR WHOM HE IS VOTING?[313]

A young lawyer decided that she would run for the position of Village Justice in the Town of Nouveau Riche on Hudson. She filled out the questionnaire for the local judicial screening committee[314] last name first as it requested with her name, "Nye, Eve."

She went to all the local organizations that sought to screen candidates for judicial office to make sure that whatever the candidate believed comported with the particular bias or prejudice of the interest group. She went before the League of Women Voters, the League of Men Voters, the League of Androgynous Voters, the American Civil Libertines, the Council of Concerned Reactionaries, the America Firsters, the God Firsters, and the Me Firsters.

However when she spoke to them, she actually answered several of their questions concerning where she stood on the issues. Most of the other candidates declined to do so, and only discussed their education and experience.

The reason that they were reticent is Canon 7 of the Canons of Judicial Ethics. Specifically they were aware of the provisions of Canon 7 (B) (1) (c) which reads: "A candidate including an incumbent judge for a judicial office . . . (c) should not . . . announce his views on disputed legal or political issues . . ."[315]

As a result of her discussing the issues Nye was sent a caution by her local bar association and the screening committee rated her as unqualified. Its decision recited that it would have found her qualified but for her violation of the canon.[316]

---

[313] by James M. Rose, White Plains, New York, Chief Shop Steward, Union of Unconcerned Scientists and pollster for the Ornery Pollcats.

[314] A judicial screening committee is an organization named after a screen. A screen is a device used to keep pests out. Enough said.

[315] See New York State Ethics Opinion 73-283.

[316] Although one member said she was not qualified to be a judge because she was "too judgmental."

Eve Nye then sued the local bar association and the screening committee alleging that its position and the canon itself violated her first amendment freedom of speech and denied the voters a fundamental right.[317] "What good is it to be able to vote," she queried, "if the rules don't allow you to know for whom you're voting? Would the guarantee of the right to vote be fulfilled if you were blindfolded, spun around three times, and then allowed to pull random levers in the voting booth without knowing for whom you were voting?"

The rule literally prevents a candidate from running on the Right to Life line, or writing to that party to accept its nomination. Are the members of that party prevented from knowing if the candidates it wishes to nominate agree with its positions? Can't the members of the Socialist Workers Party know if they have nominated a candidate who supports or opposes capitalist punishment?

The case came before Judge Hugh De Mann. Ms. Nye represented herself and the screening committee was represented by the firm of Holden, Caufield, Chandler and Bing.

Ms. Nye argued that the First Amendment right to communicate with voters was recognized by the Supreme Court when it struck down legislation that prevented the distribution of anonymous election materials.[318]

But the Bar Association countered that the canon permits her to distribute materials and speak to groups. Her freedom to communicate was not being denied, it was only the contents of her speech that was being regulated. Freedom of speech is not

---

[317] She argued that the right to distribute electioneering pamphlets is a First Amendment freedom according to the United States Supreme Court in *Mills v. Alabama*, 384 U.S. 214, 86 S. Ct. 1434, 16 L Ed 2d 484 (1966).

This article was written before the Supreme Court's decision in *Republican Party of Minnesota v. White*, 536 U.S. 765 (2002). However, recent litigation in the courts has shown that extent the New York authorities will interpret that decision broadly is still in question.

[318] *McIntyre v. Ohio Election Comm'n*, 514 U.S. 334, 115 S. Ct. 1511.

absolute, and just as one may not shout fire in a crowded theater[319] or advocate the overthrow of the government by force and violence,[320]—it violates public policy if the voters were to know a judge's actual position on political issues. The authors of the canons were well aware of the prohibitions against "forum shopping"[321] for a judge friendly to one's cause. The Canon prevents voters who know a judge's political position from "forum shopping" at the polls by electing a judge with their own prejudices.[322]

The Bar Association screening committee asserted that there is no protected right to know who it is that you are voting for when you go to the polls. There is nothing in the Constitution that guarantees the right to knowledge about candidates. While the Fifteenth Amendment provides that the states cannot deny the right to vote based upon race, color or previous condition of servitude, it says nothing about denying the right to vote on some other basis—nor does it guarantee the right to know anything about the candidate. The Nineteenth Amendment guarantees the right to vote shall not be abridged on account of sex—but likewise does not provide that the voter be guaranteed a minimal amount of information about the candidate for which she votes. The Constitution does not say who has a right to vote[323]

New York State Constitution, Article II provides that every

---

[319] Justice Oliver Wendell Holmes wrote in *Schenck v. United States*, 249 U.S. 47 at 52, 39 S. Ct. 247, 63 L. Ed. 470 (1919).

[320] Penal Law § 240.15—Criminal Anarchy, ruled constitutional in *Samuels v. Mackell*, 285 F. Supp. 348, (EDNY, 1968) aff'd 401 U.S. 66, 91 S. Ct. 764, 77 L. Ed. 2d 688.

[321] A practice condemned by the courts and CPLR § 202; *Antone v. General Motors Corp.*, 64 NY2d 20, 484 NYS2d 514, 473 NE2d 742 (1964).

[322] When the screening committee was asked if knowledge of a judge's predisposition represented a "clear and present danger," they responded that "a little knowledge is a dangerous thing."

[323] Noted in *The Electoral Process*, A. Reitman and R B. Davidson, 2nd. Ed., 1980 (Oceana Pub Co.)

citizen shall be entitled to vote at every election for all officers elected by the people, but makes no guarantees a data bank concerning the candidates will be available, it was argued.

Ms. Nye remarked, "No wonder they call it *suffrage*."

Indeed, Judge De Mann pointed out, there is ample precedent for not knowing for whom you are voting. Election Law § 12-100 provides that the names of the candidates for president and vice-president appear on the ballot and they shall be deemed to be votes cast for the electors of the party.[324] However, the names of the electors themselves need not be on the ballot, and they need not be published before the election when the list of candidates is published by the Board of Elections according to Election Law § 4-122 (2).

And yet it is the electors, and not the candidates, who have the say as to who gets elected president and vice president. The electors themselves are not required to vote for the candidates for whom they are pledged and cannot be compelled to do so.[325] The voters are not entitled to know when they go into the booth to vote who the electors are or how they will vote.

So, by analogy, the voters are not entitled to "know" what the candidates in a judicial election believe in or stand for prior to their voting for them. "If voters are not given the power to know who is choosing the president—a person who has his hand on the nuclear trigger, can plunge the nation into war or recession, can double taxes or draft them or their sons into the military—how can they have a constitutional right to know the budget deficit position of the Village Justice who will determine their disorderly conduct charges and speeding tickets?" Judge De Mann wrote.

There is no constitutional right to know a candidate's positions on issues, he held. If there were, then campaign pledges might become enforceable contracts in court. A candidate who makes a promise is making an offer, and the voter who accepts it does so by

---

[324] L. 1988 c. 13 § 6; eff. March 11, 1988.

[325] *State v. Allbritton*, 251 Ala. 422, 37 So. 2d 640; *Opinion of the Justices*, 250 Ala. 399, 340 So. 2d 598 (1948) (when electors pledged to Harry S. Truman voted for Strom Thurmond in the 1948 presidential election.)

voting for the candidate and electing him or her. If the candidate later changes his mind and does not fulfill his promise, can a voter bring a contract lawsuit?

"Of course not," De Mann said, "because we know campaign rhetoric is only that, and the candidate is not expected to carry out his campaign promises.[326]

That being the case, it makes no difference what the candidate thinks before the election, since he or she will do whatever is felt to be appropriate or expedient after the election[327] regardless of campaign platforms."[328]

---

[326] c.f., *Harlow v. Fitzgerald*, 457 U.S. 800 (1982) in which it was held that a legislator has absolute immunity for actions taken as part of his legislative duties. If a legislator has absolute immunity, he cannot be sued for not fulfilling campaign promises to support or oppose specific legislation.

[327] C.f., *Brill v. Wagner*, 5 Misc 2d 768, 161 NYS2d 490 (S. Ct. Queens Co., 1957) in which it was held that a campaign promise to appoint the plaintiff if she worked for the candidate is *ultra vires*, illegal and unenforceable. The judge greeted with skepticism the proposition that campaign promises are enforceable in court. "The Court can only sympathize with the plaintiff and note that the number of those suffering from similar situations are legion all over the land." [Emphasis added].

Perhaps this is why voting call it "suffrage;" although it should be noted that the first definition for "suffrage" found in the *Oxford English Dictionary* is "prayers for the souls of the departed." In some precincts the souls of the departed are alleged to be voting still. Hughey Long is reported to have said that when he dies he wants to be buried in Louisiana, so that he can remain active in politics.

[328] He quoted William Butler Yeats' poem "The Old Stone Cross":

> A statesman is an easy man,
> He tells his lies by rote;
> A journalist makes up his lies
> And takes you by the throat;
> So stay at home and drink your beer
> And let the neighbor's vote."

Finally, Judge De Mann noted, "there is no more precious cornerstone of our democracy than the right to a secret ballot.[329] If you *really* knew who you were voting for, it wouldn't be a secret, would it?"

---

[329] New York has had the secret ballot since the Charter of Liberties and Privileges in 1863 according to M. Chute, *The First Liberty* p.66, (1969) (E.P. Dutton & Co.).

SGT. PRESTON, YOU CON: DO YOU ALWAYS GET YOUR LAND?

by James M. Rose[330]

In the 1950's Quaker Puffed Wheat and Quaker Puff Rice advertised they were "shot from guns." On your little black and white television you could see Gabby Hayes on NBC on Mondays and Fridays [331] firing the breakfast food out of a cannon (and you didn't want to be the janitor in the studio that had to sweep it up). At the time, no one worried about the environmental impact of shooting cannons full of cereal, or whether the Bureau of Alcohol, Tobacco and Firearms or the FCC, FDA, FTC would intercede for a variety of regulatory reasons.[332] But now it appears that "Gabby" and Sgt. Preston of the Yukon were involved in a fraudulent land swindle—so evocative of the true Wild West!

In 1955, the Quaker Oats Company placed on specially marked boxes of Quaker Puffed Oats and Quaker Puffed Rice offers to obtain a deed to one square inch of land[333] in the Yukon Territories. Quaker had paid $ 1,000 for 19.11 acres of frozen tundra in the Klondike.[334]

---

[330] White Plains, New York. Mr. Rose is not a cereal killer. The author gratefully acknowledges the assistance of Richard C. Feldman, Esq. of Evans, Feldman & Boyer, P.C. in New Haven, Connecticut who supplied a copy of the deed in question.

[331] *Hake's Americana and Collectibles Catalogue* # 114 (May 1991) at item 2493.

[332] Or some other "F" word agency» would make them verify the claim. Or hold that it was just "puffing." (See, *Gulf Oil Corp. v. Federal Trade Commission* 150 F. 2d 106, 109.

[333] These were not intended to be building lots, and the wilds of the Yukon did not have one acre minimum zoning (See, Territorial Lands Act c. 263 § 7 (1) which does require that transactions involving more than 160 acres be approved by the Governor.)

[334] according to an article entitled "Puffed-Cereal Eaters' High Hopes of Yelling 'Mush!' Are Groundless" the Wall Street *Journal* of December 12, 1991.

More than 20 million deeds went out. Romantic owners of one square inch of land wrote the company asking for a map. But the land was registered only in the name of Klondike Big Inch Land Co. Inc., an Illinois Corporation.[335] In 1965 the Canadian government seized it for non-payment of $ 37.20 (Canadian) in taxes.

And thereby hangs a tale. It seems that the estate of a homeless man whose identity could not be ascertained contained such a deed. The estate was probated recently. The man's property escheated to the state, and the Attorney General then attempted to perform his statutorily mandated duty of selling the property for the state.

Upon learning the truth concerning the fate of the deceased's land, he brought a class action on behalf of the decedent, John Dough,[336] and the other 19,999,999 deed holders similarly situated. Among the defendants were the Quaker Oats Company, Sgt. Preston of the Yukon,[337] The Royal Canadian Mounted Police, Klondike Big Inch Land Co., and Rutherford B. "Gabby" Hayes.[338] Sgt. Preston's dog, King a/k/a Yukon King, was named as a non-party defendant.[339]

They all denied the RICO claims[340] of land fraud, wire fraud,

---

[335] See Territorial Lands Act ch. 263 §5 (which governs land transactions in the Yukon and requires registration), and Land Titles Act c. 32 § 3 of the laws of Canada, formerly Ch. 162 of the Revised Statutes of Canada 1952.

[336] His staff picked the quixotic name because they believed the deceased man looked like he could have been a World War I doughboy. They decided not o pick the name "Pillsbury."

[337] Hence the bad pun in the title of this article.

[338] Gabby had his own premiums. His shot from guns rings with a swiveling cannon that shoots, and pictures on the bands of rice being shot from cannons now go for from $100 to $200 (See *Hake's, op. cit.* at 1417 and 1418).

[339] Perhaps because he would assert sovereign immunity applicable to kings.

[340] Among other frauds alleged to have been perpetrated by Sgt. Preston was the marketing of a cereal box premium non-functional "ore detector." According to *Hake's Americana and Collectibles* for May 1991 (# 114) at ¶ 2784. "Of the two or three we've had, none have worked."

mail fraud, false advertising, breach of trust, and failure to file a RESPA statement.[341]

The thrust of the action was that the defendants knew (or should have known) that cereal vendees to whom the offer was pitched were minors. Quaker, it was alleged, had a fiduciary duty to register the land in the name of each of the holders (who was too young to do so himself), so that each fee holder would receive a tax bill and have the opportunity to pay his own taxes.[342] Quaker answered that it was impractical to register square inch plots (or stake claims at the assay office in the method that such claims are staked in works of fiction).

But in reply, it was said that, at the very least, Quaker should have spoken up and told the children that it did not register the land in their own names, so that they or their real estate advisers could attempt to do so. It was argued that Quaker bore such a duty despite the traditional silence maintained by Quakers.

Quaker argued that the youth had not purchased the cereal, their parents had. No claims could be directly asserted by the youths, it posited. But that did not defeat their claims, the court held, since the cereal was purchased for the youths under the Uniform Gifts To Minors Act.

Value having been paid for the cereal, and a portion of the benefit of the bargain was the advertised deed for a square inch of the Yukon, Quaker and its subsidiary Big Inch could not ignore the promise it had made. They were under the duty to maintain the land free of liens while they held it in constructive trust for minors who could not hold property in their own names. When the cereal eaters came of age, the defendants did not put the property in the children's individual names, so they still held the land for the benefit of the class.

---

[341] Real Estate Settlement And Procedures Act, a/k/a the Redundant and Excessive Paperwork Act, 12 U.S.C. § 2602 *et. seq.*

[342] Each land owner's share of the back taxes at the time the land was seized was less than $ .0000018.

Quaker argued that the deeds were valid when given, and that they were under no obligation to register the title in the name of the tots, who could have done so themselves, or had a title company register their square inch. No one produced the map alleged to have been deposited at Klondike Big Inch's offices.[343] However, the court held that Quaker could be sued for a breech of a subsequent duty that rendered the land belonging to the class worthless. Quaker also offered to abate the default by remitting that portion of the purchase price of the box of cereal that represented the value of the land. Specific performance was out of the question, because, although Quaker could be made to repurchase the property to reconvey it, there were no metes and bounds[344] descriptions on the deeds to determine which piece was owned by whom. Some inches were land locked, while others had scenic views.[345]

The class was certified of all former owners of the property who obtained their deeds through cereal boxes, and the failure to pay the taxes on the land and to keep it free and clear of liens was held to be a fraud cognizable by RICO. Arguments were made about laches were made and rejected. The fact that the fraud was concealed, and the fact that the statute of limitations was tolled through the youth of the children led to a denial of a motion to dismiss.

Treble damages were assessed. The land was inaccessible and still frozen tundra. It was now the subject of claims made Indian tribes that it had been stolen from them by treaty violations. It was held not to have increased significantly in value since 1955, and the Canadian dollar having decreased, the total claim was held to be worth one thousand dollars (Canadien).

However, John Dough had not filled his name in on the deed where it says "fill in your name"

---

[343] How a map of one inch plots covering 19.11 acres could have been prepared that was not itself almost 19.11 acres was not adequately explained.
[344] or cereal and bounds.
[345] 19.11 acres would contain 119,870,150 square inches. Some of the land must have remained unsubdivided.

DEED OF LAND

This indenture made this 4th day of January, in the year of Our Lord One Thousand Nine Hundred and Fifty-five,

BETWEEN: **KLONDIKE BIG INCH LAND CO., INC.,**
DAWSON
a body corporate duly registered for the purposes of carrying on business in the Yukon Territory, having its head office for the said Territory in the City of Whitehorse, hereinafter called the "Grantor,"
OF THE FIRST PART

AND: _____ (fill in your name) _____ hereinafter called the "Grantee,"
OF THE SECOND PART.

WITNESSETH THAT the Grantor for good and valuable consideration now paid by the Grantee to the Grantor (the receipt whereof is hereby by it acknowledged) doth grant, bargain, sell, alien, enfeoff, release, remise, convey and confirm unto the Grantee, his heirs and assigns forever an estate in fee simple; WHITEHORSE

ALL AND SINGULAR that certain parcel or tract of land and premises situate, lying and being in the Yukon Territory more particularly known and described as follows: TRACT NUMBERED E 808858

comprising by admeasurement one square inch more or less as more particularly described in that certain subdivision plan, prepared and acknowledged by the Grantor under date the 15th day of December, A.D. 1954 and deposited at the registered office of the Grantor in the Yukon Territory, of the whole of Lot Two hundred forty-three (243) in Group Two (2) in Yukon Territory, as said lot is shown on a plan of survey of record in the Legal Surveys and Aeronautical Charts Division of the Department of Mines and Technical Surveys at Ottawa under number 6718, containing by admeasurement Nineteen and eleven hundredths (19.11) acres more or less; together with all and singular the easements, hereditaments and appurtenances to the same belonging or in any way appertaining with reversion and reversions, remainder and remainders, rents, issues and profits thereof and all the estate, right, title, interest, claim, property and demand both at law and in equity of the said Grantor of, in, to or out of the same or any part thereof;

TO HAVE AND TO HOLD the said lands and premises with the appurtenances and every part thereof unto the said Grantee, his heirs and assigns to his and their sole use, benefit and behoof forever; subject nevertheless to the reservations, limitations, provisos and conditions expressed in the original grant thereof from the Crown;
SEE OTHER SIDE

Since the Attorney General was unable to prove who the deceased was, he was unable to show that the deceased had registered his deed with Klondike Big Inch Land Co., Inc. or provided his name to Quaker. If he failed to register his name with them, they would have been under no duty to register his mini-parcel in the Yukon Territory. John Dough's estate could not exert a successful claim.

However since, the Attorney General prevailed upon claims made on behalf of other members of the class who were still living, he was entitled to Attorney's fees of $100,000 and went away happy.

DEED OF LAND

CONTINUED

AND the Grantor for itself, its successors and assigns doth hereby covenant, promise and agree to and with the Grantee, his heirs and assigns in manner following that is to say that it shall be lawful for the Grantee, his heirs and assigns from time to time and at all times hereafter peaceably and quietly to enter into the said lands and premises and to have, hold, occupy, possess and enjoy the same without the lawful suit, hindrance, eviction, denial or disturbance of, from or by the Grantor, and also that the Grantor has a good, sure and perfect estate in fee simple in the said land and premises and good right, full power and lawful authority to sell and convey the same in manner and form as they are hereby sold and conveyed and mentioned or intended so to be and the same are free from encumbrances, subject however to the provisions herein contained;

AND this conveyance and everything herein contained shall be wholly subject to a perpetual easement for ingress and egress, to, from, over and upon the tract herein conveyed for the use of the owner or owners of all other tracts of the land and premises herein described and further described and set forth in said subdivision plan hereinabove mentioned and without restricting the generality of the foregoing clause the same shall not in anywise be construed as a derogation from the grant hereby effected to the Grantee herein, and the Grantor hereby grants unto the Grantee a perpetual easement for ingress and egress, to, from, over and upon any or all of the tracts of land as described in the subdivision plan aforesaid as may from time to time remain vested in the Grantor;

AND the Grantor covenants with the Grantee that it has done no act to encumber the said lands;

AND the Grantor releases to the Grantee all its claims upon the said lands;

The provisions of the Land Titles Act being Ch. 162 of the Revised Statutes of Canada, 1952 and amendments thereto shall not apply to this Deed of Conveyance and in addition but not so as to limit the generality of the foregoing the Grantor shall not be obliged to do any acts or execute any instruments as may be necessary to better secure the title of the Grantee or to provide a transfer to the within described lands and premises registerable under the aforesaid Act nor to deliver or have registered a subdivision plan of the aforementioned Lot 243 or any portion thereof;

Wherever the singular or masculine are used throughout this Indenture the same shall be construed as meaning the plural or the feminine or body corporate or politic where the context or the parties hereto so require;

IN WITNESS WHEREOF the corporate seal of the Grantor has been hereunto affixed in the presence of its proper officers duly authorized in that behalf;

The Corporate seal of **KLONDIKE BIG INCH LAND CO. INC.** was hereunto affixed in the presence of:

[signature] PRESIDENT

[signature] SECRETARY-TREASURER

JAMES M. ROSE

MUCH SWEARING NECESSARY AT CLOSINGS

A title closing used to be a simple thing that required no more than an exchange of a deed for a check. The whole thing took about as long as a haircut, and involved about the same number of people. Now haircuts have become much more complicated, and so have closings.

First came the requirement to fill out a RESPA statement. RESPA is an acronym that stands for Redundant and Excessive Paperwork Act.[346] I wish I could enlighten you on where all the complete RESPA forms go, but I guess we should all rejoice that an army of clerks has not been hired to read them all and send them back for corrections.[347]

Next came the requirement for a certificate of occupancy,[348] the fire underwriter's certificate, and the termite inspection.[349]

Then came the requirement for a multitude of ever increasing affidavits. The FHA and VA have raised to an art form the necessity and array of swearing that must go on at a closing, such as the No Lead Paint affidavit, the House is Not in a Flood Plain Affidavit, and the like.

New York has expanded on the title company's lonely affidavit

---

[346] ERISA is an acronym too, but I don't know what it stands for or means. I used to think that FICA was an acronym, too. Then a found out that Tony Fica was a computer clerk for Congress. He wrote the FICA deduction into an obscure federal appropriations bill for the construction of sewage plants, and now he sits on the beach in Pago Pago collecting all of our FICA deductions.

[347] They disappear into that large file cabinet in the sky, and may actually constitute the "dark matter" that physicists claim is a large but unaccounted for proportion of the matter in the universe.

[348] Referred to as the "Sea of Oh" at closings. Neophyte attorneys who are asked where the Sea of Oh is should not start looking in a World Atlas.

[349] That is, an inspection *for* termites, not *by* them. It assures the buyers that termites have not be on the land openly and notoriously for so long that they can assert a claim to the title by adverse possession.

of no other name, and the occasional affidavit that the deponent is not the person who incurred some substantial judgment of record charging plaid sport coats at Sears. Now we have the no revolving credit affidavit and the gains tax affidavit—in which the seller swears that he bought the house for $60,000 and sold it for $120,000, and did not make more than $500,000 on the deal.

A recent unwelcome addition has been the Foreign Investors Real Property Tax Affidavit. Soon the buyer will be required to affirm that the money he is investing in he home is not proceeds from spying for a foreign government, or made as a traveling salesman selling of arms to a foreign government out of the White House Bargain Basement.

Now social policies have crept into the commercial transaction. General Business Law § 378 requires an affidavit that working smoke alarms are present. It is an admirable goal to protect our houses from fire, but we must ask what other social goals will creep into this formerly innocent exchange of deed and keys for a bank check. If we have to do this when we purchase a home, what will we have to do in the future when we purchase a car, or a bagel? An affidavit of no poppy seeds?[350] There is presently more swearing going on than at the scene of a traffic accident involving three truck drivers.

Perhaps we need an affidavit that the home has no bats in the belfry, squirrels in the attic, skeletons in the closet, and that no one besides those listed in the affidavit have keys to the premises.

Has the Assemblyman from Amityville introduced a bill which would require proof that the house is free of poltergeists, not built on an Indian burial ground, and that nothing in the house goes bump in the night except the furnace? Does the assemblyman from Orange County wish to introduce a bill declaring that mezzuzahs are fixtures that run with the land, and hence require a

---

[350] You could see the no poppy seed affidavit coming when defendants who failed drug tests began blaming it on poppy seed bagels, which reputedly cause positive drug tests.

certificate that they have not been removed from the gateposts of the house (or their functional equivalent).[351]

Wouldn't all prospective purchasers like to have a certification from the sellers that the house is not in a Bad Karma Zone (that there are no quarrelsome neighbors, no nearby religious cult, radical group or motorcycle gang in the neighborhood)? That the basement is certified as dry, and that a river does not run through it?

Shouldn't the Landmarks Preservation Commission certify that they do not consider the property worthy of designation, so that the buyer knows he can put aluminum siding on it or paint it garish colors? Should the Health Department certify that the house has been occupied by non-smokers? That the garden was grown without pesticides? That the owner's dog has not buried anything noxious on the property?

Westchester County has already required that a seller certify that the home has been tested for excessive radon readings on the premises. High radon readings have been found in northern Westchester County. Coincidently, that is the roughly the same area that deeds in Westchester recite reserves to the heirs of Philipse mining and mineral rights.[352] Perhaps the state or the county should just insist that the heirs of Philipse remove their dangerous minerals that are emitting radon. A flying squad of radon busters could be enlisted.

So when you next appear at a closing with the affidavit that the home is not in the glide path of an alien spacecraft clutched in your hand, remember all the other affidavits you need. Otherwise the title closer will have to request that you execute an affidavit of no other affidavits.

---

[351] That is in addition to the bill now pending that large apartment buildings, cooperatives and condominiums have a master muzzuzah on the roof.

[352] See, P. Shantz, Mining and Mineral Rights in the Heirs of Philipse," 11 Westchester *Bar Journal* 201. Your client buying that split level home in Cortlandt was always afraid that some prospector name Philipse would show up one day riding a burro, and start panning in his creek or sinking a shaft next to the rhododendrons.

THE LAW OF UNINTENDED CONSEQUENCES AND NICOTINE AS AN ADDICTIVE DRUG: ARE NON SMOKING STATUTES IN SCHOOLS NOW IN VIOLATION OF FEDERAL LAW?[353]

With a great deal of fanfare, the Federal Trade Commission recently announced that it had found that nicotine in cigarettes was an addictive drug[354] and it would therefore assert jurisdiction over its use.[355] One of the purposes of finding that nicotine was an addictive drug was to limit its availability to minors and to protect them from the harmful effects of smoking. Ironically, the announcement could have the opposite effect in New York because of the Law of Unintended Consequences.[356]

---

[353] by James M. Rose, White Plains, New York. The ideas expressed in this article are not those of the Westchester County Bar Association or even of Mr. Rose.

[354] There were 414 studies on this topic by researchers independent of the tobacco industry in the 20th century. In the Surgeon General's 1988 report the fourth chapter is entitled "Tobacco Use as Drug Dependence." See, "A Peace Plan for the Tobacco Wars," R. Kluger, New York *Times* Magazine April 7, 1996 p. 28 at 29.

[355] Or have the Consumer Product Safety Commission assert jurisdiction under the Federal Hazardous Substances Act of 1960 (15 U.S.C. §§ 1261 - 1277) for one (see a discussion in *Palmer v. Liggett Group,* 635 F. Supp. 392 (D. Mass 1989).

[356] The Law of Unintended Consequences is not a statute, nor a law of Nature. It is simply an expression used to indicate that there are more (unforeseen) consequences that often result when legislation intended to achieve one purpose sets off a chain reaction that frequently brings results quite different from those intended by its author. Examples of this phenomenon are infamous. They include (1) paying higher welfare benefits to families without a man in the family unit (apparently to compensate for the absence of a possible breadwinner), which resulted in men deserting their families so that higher welfare benefits could be obtained, which resulted in boys growing up without father figures and arguably resulted in them engaging

Public Health Law § 1399-o provides that smoking is not permitted in certain areas such as auditoriums[357], elevators, gymnasiums[358], etc. Then, in a redundant fashion, in Subd. 2 of §201399-o *all* indoor areas of schools are included, and penultimately in subdivision 8 outdoor areas of schools are added. It reads as follows:

> 8. Notwithstanding the provisions of any other law, rule or regulation, tobacco use shall not be permitted and no person shall use tobacco on school grounds; provided, however, that smoking by adult faculty[359] and staff members may be permitted in a designated smoking area during non-school hours. For purposes of this section, school hours shall include any student activity that is supervised by faculty or staff, or any officially sanctioned school event.

---

in anti-social behavior as a consequence; (2) the decision of Canadian provinces adjoining the United States to tax cigarettes heavily to discourage smoking, which led to the Canadian citizens coming across the borders to the United States to buy cigarettes and while here to purchase milk, bread and other necessities, thus driving small mom and pop Canadian convenience stores whose main business was selling cigarettes out of business; (3) the deregulation of the airlines to provide more competition and lower prices which has led to large airlines swallowing up smaller ones and monopolizing the air routes, thus providing less routes at higher prices.

While local legislators are required to consider the environmental impact of their laws by statute, and state legislators are required to estimate the fiscal impact of proposed legislation, no provision of law as yet requires them to consider the logical but unintended consequences that might ensue from their laws.

[357] (without first singing "Fee, fee, fie, fie, foe, foe, fum ?) Should the plural of this word be "auditoria?"
[358] See footnote 5. Should the plural be "gymnasia?"
[359] Is this a redundancy, too, or are there faculty members who are minors?

But, curiously, saying it three times is apparently not enough, as Education Law § 409 (2) reads as follows:

> 2. Notwithstanding the provisions of any other law, rule or regulation, tobacco use shall not be permitted and no person shall use tobacco on school grounds; provided, however, that smoking by adult faculty and staff members may be permitted in a designated smoking area during non-school hours. For purposes of this section, school hours shall include any student activity that is supervised by faculty or staff, or any officially sanctioned school event. "School grounds" means any building, structure and surrounding outdoor grounds contained within a public or private pre-school, nursery school, elementary or secondary school's legally defined property boundaries as registered in a county clerk's office.

This is obviously an important principle, since the Legislature had to say it at least twice [360] to make sure we got the point.[361]

Smoking is also a subject of instruction in schools, as the Commissioner of Education's regulations provide in part at §135.3. (a) "This program shall include, but shall not be limited to, instruction concerning the misuse of alcohol, tobacco and other drugs."[362]

---

[360] Once in 1975 and then again in 1994. The necessity of saying this twice is unclear. If there had been any variations in the words chosen to express the intentions of the legislature, one might divine the necessity for two statutory provisions. For example, see Statutes § 231 "In a construction of a statute, meaning and effect shall be given to all of its language, if possible, and words are not to be rejected as superfluous when it is practicable to give each a distinct and separate meaning."

[361] One is reminded of the apocryphal story of a young attorney arguing his first case before the Appellate Division. When asked from the bench "Do you realize you've said that three times?" he replied, "Yes, your Honor but there are five of you."

[362] One hopes this means that the students will be taught not to misuse tobacco rather than *how* to misuse it.

The Americans With Disabilities Act[363] and the New York State Human Rights Law (Executive Law § 296) require that individuals with disabilities be accommodated. Addictions to substances that are legal[364] are handicaps that must be accommodated in the workplace. Now, nicotine is such a legal and addictive drug. For teachers and non teaching school employees the workplace is the school. Neither Education Law § 409 (2) nor Public Health Law §1399-o may be a reasonable accommodation. They require the smoker not to smoke at all during his or her hours of employment anywhere on the school grounds. Moreover, those hours include times when student activities are occurring after school—which often will encompass the entire work day. The fact that the § 1399-o and § 409 (2) permit smoking in designated smoking areas only during non-school hours may not be enough to accommodate a truly addicted employee who would thus be prohibited from smoking during an eight hour period.[365]

The actual wisdom of the sections has been debated. What often happens is that teachers (and sometimes students) walk several feet past the boundaries of the school and smoke openly and notoriously across the street from the school in full view of the students. Thus, instead of smoking on break time and at lunch in a designated teacher's smoking lounge away from the curious eyes of the youths for whom they are supposed be role models to be emulated, the teachers smoke out in the open across the street where the students can see them. This is one unintended consequence of the present legislation.

Now, however, that nicotine has been declared an addictive but legal drug, and those who are addicted to it can be viewed as handicapped under the law, they may have to be reasonably

---

[363] 42 U.S. C. § 12182 et. seq.

[364] such as an obese person's addiction to food, see, *State Division of Human Rights v. Xerox Corp.*, 65 NY2d 213, 219; 491 NYS2d 106, 109 (1985).

[365] Is the result of declaring nicotine addictive the requirement to provide more frequent smoking breaks?

accommodated by setting aside a smoking room for them during school hours despite what the statute says, or it may be declared in conflict with the federal law against discrimination against the handicapped.

THE ANSWERS TO LIFE'S PERSISTENT QUESTIONS[366]

by James M. Rose[367]

Lawyers are in the business of providing answers to client's problems. In law school and when I took the Massachusetts Bar examination you got credit for recognizing what the problem was and the applicable doctrine (e.g.—the Rule in Shelley's Case), whether or not you came to the same conclusion as the examiners did concerning its application. Real life doesn't work that way. Clients don't care if you know the Rule in Shelley's case—they want answers. **Correct** answers.

After many years of practice, I now have more answers than I have questions. I know, for example, that an infinite number of monkeys sitting at an infinite number of typewriters for an infinite amount of time would produce not only the entire Federal Tax Code[368] but also a more intelligible version.[369] I know the sound that one hand clapping makes[370] and that it tastes just like chicken.[371]

---

[366] THIS ARTICLE IS ON A NEED TO KNOW BASIS ONLY. If you do not need to know the answers to life's persistent questions read no further.

[367] White Plains, New York. Mr. Rose was an Editor Demeritis of the Westchester *Bar Journal*.

[368] The probability as calculated by Dr. Math at http://mathforum.org/library/drmath/view/55871.htlm is 5 times 10 to the 818 power for the amount of keystrokes it would take.

[369] This calculation does not take into consideration what influence an infinite number of simian lobbyists with an infinite number of bananas would have on the revised edition.

[370] Like I'm going to tell you! Hint: It's not half a clap.

[371] The actual question as posed by Zen master Hakuin (1686-1769) in a koan was "In clapping both hands, a sound is heard. What is the sound of one hand?"

I know that Eros wrote the book of Love, but a large, multinational drug consortium currently holds the copyright.[372]

So here are the answers to life's persistent questions. (Like all important academic conundrums [373] they come with quibbling footnotes.)

1. The egg came first.[374]
2. The glass is half empty.[375]
3. A mature wood chuck could chuck 3/4 of a cord of wood per hour depending on the size of the woodchuck and whether it was hard or soft wood.[376]

---

[372] The Monotones asked this question in 1958, but never got past fifth place on the top ten hits list.

[373] I do not know if the plural should be "conundra" instead.

[374] Some people insist that this is just an instance of asking the wrong question—like who was the first person to speak French and did anyone understand him? French, like the chicken, is the result of a long series of small, incremental changes and did not leap into being (See, www.devhood.com/messages).

Some geneticists insist that the chicken is just the egg's way of producing another egg.

[375] Technically it is half full if you're filling it, and half empty if you're emptying it. Some people insist it is simply the wrong size glass (E.g. www.MIT.edu/people/drb).

[376] Reasonable persons may disagree about this one. The woodchuck (Marmota monax) a/k/a ground hog a/k/a whistlepig is a serious agricultural pest. No one asks how much ground a ground hog could hog if a ground hog could hog ground—an inquiry which is beyond the scope of this article.

The answer to this question depends on the size of the woodchuck, but one answer is the average is 328 butt cords and a median of 612 butt cords (except on Ground hog's Day)—see www.getodd.com/stuff/stupid/woodchuck.html.

Of course the question depends on what period of time the chucking is being done (See *www.madsci.org/posts/archives/may2000/958482443.zo.r.html.*)

For a calculation of the distance and velocity a woodchuck might chuck, see *www.maths.tdc.ie. ~ ~ 'icecube.cgi-bin/page=woodchuck.)*

The social implications of woodchucks chucking wood are discussed at home/earthlink.net-prejay2/fjw/x-chuck.html.

4. Of course it makes a sound—it's a tree![377]
5. No, auld acquaintance shouldn't.[378]
6. The peck of pickled peppers is for sale on Ebay.[379]
7. The soldiers have all gone to Iraq or Afghanistan.[380]
8. It's Memorex.

NEXT MONTH: The questions for life's persistent answers.

---

[377] If you left a tape recorder in the forest when the tree fell, it would record a sound, wouldn't it? If a judge writes an opinion and you are not there when it's written, isn't it still valid? It isn't all about *you*, you know?

If you need more information about the legal consequences of trees falling you can go to the website (I wouldn't dare make this up—look for yourself) www.treefalllawyers.com (the firm of Carley & Rabon in Charlotte, N.C.).

[378] A Scottish Folk song transcribed by Robbie Burns asked this question. Auld lang syne means old, long ago. There is some dispute concerning the actual words of other verses, although they have been painfully reassembled by musicologists using Scotch tape.

[379] This question (Mother Goose asked) is sometimes stated as "Where's the peck of pickled peppers", or in the alternative, "How many pickled peppers did Peter Piper pick?" This depends on the size of the peppers (Bell peppers are much bigger than chili peppers) and the size of the peck. An American peck is 537.605 cubic inches but an Imperial (British) peck is 554.84 cubic inches. (See—mathforum.org/library/drmath/view/58478.htm). The term "peck" is derived from the ancient French "pek" the size of which is unknown. (Not that I'm nit-pecking!)

[380] The soldiers had gone to Vietnam when the song "where Have all the Flowers Gone?" was sung by Judy Collins during the Chicago Seven trial. Judge Hoffman ruled that it had no place in a United States District Court.

See—www.law.umkc.edu/faculty/projects/ftrials/Chicago7/Collins.html.

BIGFOOT LOSES TEN POUNDS A DAY EATING ELVIS ON DIET SPACE ALIENS GAVE PRINCESS DI[381]
or
IAS, IOLA, AYE YI YI

This article will address three of the recent banes of lawyers existences, IAS, IOLA and mandatory pro bono work.[382]

Recently there has been unreported litigation concerning the new IAS (Individual Assignment System) and RJI (Request for Judicial Interference).[383] What happens when two parties to a case each buy an RJI unbeknownst to the other? As they used to say on the radio "The one with the earliest postmark wins."[384] Does the party who bought the later RJI get his money back because the case is already on the calendar, or does he get to keep the judge he got assigned with the RJI if he wants that jurist for some later case? Can he re-sell the RJI[385] which is only slightly used and has very little milage?

What happens when you check the "related case" box on the RJI? What is a related case? To what degree must it be related, and must it be related by blood or marriage? Consanguinity or affinity? Related to the experience some other judge had with some other case?[386]

If my recent experience is any guide, you don't have to lose any sleep pondering this weighty query since it doesn't matter. I

---

[381] The title has nothing to do with the actual contents of this article, and was meant only to be an attention grabber using all of the buzz words that the tabloid press uses to attract an audience.

[382] See, "Pro and Anti- Bono—Cher's Life Story," National *Inquirer*, June 13, 1988 p. 1.

[383] 22 NYCRR § 202.6.

[384] Maybe. Another court has held that the one with the earliest Index number wins.

[385] Nowadays you can sell anything on E bay.

[386] Does $E=MC^2$ and the Theory of Relativity have anything to do with this question?

recently had a case assigned to Judge West. I checked the box on the RJI when I filed a new case, indicating that Judge West had a related case. The new case was then assigned to Judge Nastasi. When I inquired why, since Judge West had the related case, I was told that the computer assigns cases automatically, and that Judge Nastasi will now decide if the cases are related. Of course he could have done that even if I hadn't checked the box—which was the old pre-RJI system. Judge West is obviously in a better position to determine if the cases are related, since he has already begun to deal with the first one. And what if Judge Nastasi doesn't think that the cases are related and Judge West does? After all, it's all relative.

Next we come to IOLA—who we all know was the Greek Goddess of Short Term Interest. She cruised the Aegean Sea on her yacht *The Overnight Float*. Actually, the courts use "IOLA" to refer to Interest on Lawyer's Accounts—which means that the Office of Court Administration is interested in making money from your escrow accounts, or what ever it is that you're supposed to be calling that account in which you hold other people's money. For about one year the Appellate Division's rules provided that it was not sufficient to call you escrow account an escrow account.[387] You were required to give it a different designation.[388] Just when you paid fifty bucks to get all of your checks that read "Attorney Escrow Account" reprinted to read "Attorney Trust Account," the rule was changed again,[389] and now it's O.K. to call your escrow account an escrow account. If the rule changes again, just get a rubber stamp

---

[387] This was apparently because people getting checks would not understand that the check they were getting was not from your personal funds . . . Perhaps they would think that your name was "Escrow."

[388] 22 NYCRR § 691.12., i.e., Attorney Trust Account. [Since this article was first written the rule has been relocated to § 1200.46 (b) ((2). Whether the numbering change reflects the fact that there are now about 400 more rules as there were fifteen years ago is beyond the scope of this article.]

[389] Perhaps in response to surveys that reflected that people usually didn't use the words "Attorney" and "Trust" next to one another.

to put the name of the account on your checks—it's cheaper than reprinting them every time the rule changes. And this time, call the account the "Other People's Money Account."

The IOLA money became a mandatory way to do charity. The OCA has been clamoring for another form of mandatory charity as well—mandatory pro bono work.[390] It is in keeping with the Thousand Points of Light philosophy that charity work is a moral obligation. Let us hope that the OCA does not want to get so much good publicity for the bar that pro bono lawyers will be required to wear candy stripes when in court-like the hospital volunteers. They may be mistaken for a dixieland band if they do.

Finally, I can report to my readers two new mortgage clauses that have come to my attention. They come from the law firm of Baker & Hostetler in Cleveland Ohio, who suggest them tongue in cheek only *after* a closing.

SECTION _____. *DEATH.*

Upon the death of any individual Mortgagor, the lien of this mortgage will extend to, and include, any cemetery plot, crypt, or other place of final internment of such deceased mortgagor, together with any rents, issues, incomes, and profits arising therefrom, and any and all renewals, replacements, accessions, improvements, and substitutions, and a prior perfected security interest in and to any and all affects, articles of personal adornment, gold fillings, and other things of value severed or capable of severance without material injury to the corpse of the deceased mortgagor. The foregoing lien and security interest may be enforced by an lawful procedure and will continue until whichever of the following first occurs: (i) full payment of the indebtedness, (ii) mortgagee is furnished with a substitute hostage of equal or better class or value, quality, usefulness, and value of the deceased mortgagor.

SECTION_____. *END OF THE WORLD.* Upon the occurrence of the end of the world before the full payment of the indebtedness, the Indebtedness, at the Morgagee's option, will

---

[390] "Wachtler Panel Votes Mandatory Pro Bono," New York *Law Journal*, January 13, 1989, p. 1 col. 3.

immediately become due and payable in full and may be enforced upon mortgagor by any available procedure. For remedial purposes, Mortgagee will be deemed aligned with the forces of light, and mortgagee will be deemed aligned with the forces of darkness, regardless of the parties' actual ultimate destination, unless and until Mortgagee elects otherwise in writing.

ASIDE[391]

THE LAW AND THE HENDIADYS

by James M. Rose[392]

In Volume 21 Issue Two of the Westchester *Bar Journal* we asked an apparently rhetorical question at page 169: Why do we say "arbitrary and capricious" when the definition of arbitrary is capricious and the definition of capricious is arbitrary?[393]

This aside will answer that question and others you may have asked—such as why do we say "cease and desist" when the definition of "cease" *is* "desist," and the definition of "desist" is "cease."

The answer is that each of those two phrases is an obscure figure of speech known as a hendiadys.[394] "Hendiadys"[395] is defined in the *Oxford English Dictionary* as a figure of speech in which a single complex idea is expressed by two words connected by a conjunction.

The example used by the *American Heritage Dictionary* is "grace and favor." The two words connected by the conjunction can be nouns or verbs, and sometimes they have the same or almost the same meaning, and sometimes they have different meanings but are meant to express a single concept when used together.

Shakespeare was fond of using hendiadys in which one word was logically subordinate to another such as "sound and fury" in Macbeth or "heat and flame" in Hamlet.

---

[391] The author is not quite sure what an "Aside" in a scholarly publication is, but his favorite is in 123 *U. Pa. Law Rev.* 1474 (1975) and is entitled "The Common Law Origins of the Infield Fly Rule." It compares the development of the common law to the development of the infield fly rule in baseball.

[392] White Pl ains, New York. Mr. Rose answers too many rhetorical questions.

[393] J. Rose, "How Arbitrary is the Definition of Arbitrary?" 21 *West. Bar Journal* 169 (Spring, 1994).

[394] The word ends in an "s," hence a (or "an" if you prefer) hendiadys. The plural is probably spelled the same way.

[395] From the Greek for "one by means of two" and pronounced "hen-die-uh-dis"

The *Concise Oxford Dictionary of Literary Terms*[396] defines the hendiadys as a figure of speech in which a single idea is expressed by means of two nouns joined by a conjunction. Examples given are "nice and warm," "house and home," and "law and order."[397]

However the two words do not necessarily have to be nouns, so that two adjectives "nice and juicy" are joined in a hendiadys. Similarly, "come and get it" are two verbs used as a hendiadys. Other hendiadys composed of verbs are "break down and cry," "rise and shine," and the recently popular "wake up and smell the coffee." We don't literally mean "wake up" or literally mean "sniff an aroma of roasted beans." We express the single idea that one should take notice of something that he or she should have been aware of before.[398]

One would think that attorneys would not be prone to use hendiadys because of Statutes §98 (a). That law provides: "All parts of a statute must be harmonized with each other as well as with the general intent of the whole statute, and effect and meaning must, if possible, be given to the entire statute and every part and word thereof."

That rule has been followed by courts which urge that every word in a statute be given meaning.[399] That is a rule for the writing of legislation, however, and is not one for interpretation of contracts or even every day speech. Therefore, the hendiadys "arbitrary and

---

[396] C. Baldick, *The Concise Oxford Dictionary of Literary Terms* (Oxford, 1990, p.97.

[397] The saying "big and fat" is my example of a hendiadys. "Big" and "fat" are probably used to convey the same or similar concepts, but are employed together to express a single idea.

[398] The plain language movement (now enacted by statute in New York as General Obligations Law § 5-702) had as one of its goals the simplification of contracts by the use of fewer words (see, 1990 Supplementary Practice Commentary to GOL § 5-702 by Richard Givens in *Mc Kinney's Consolidated Laws*). Hendiadys have the ironic effect of making something more comprehensible to the layman by using more words rather than less!

[399] *People v. Sheehy*, 204 Misc. 281, 123 NYS2d 720 (1953).

capricious" is a concept of case law, and each word need not have a separate and distinct meaning. The same is true for the concept of "cease and desist." Other examples of hendiadys used by lawyers are "given under my seal and hand" or "terms and conditions of employment." Look at any deed. Why does Blumberg Form No. A 291 Bargain and Sale deed say "to have and to hold" as if you could do one without the other? What is the difference between "a certain plot and a parcel of land"?

Lawyers have a reputation for being prolix. They never use only one word where they could use many.[400] The *Wall Street Journal* once published a humorous piece such in which an attorney gave a piece of fruit to someone in writing, and the gift took several hundred words of legalese to describe.

Thus, it is no surprise that lawyers routinely use three words together to express a single complex thought. Examples of these more than verbose hendiadys (or whatever the Greek would be for three words joined together to express a single concept or thought)[401] appear in wills—"I hereby give, devise and bequeath," and "the rest, residue and remainder," or when attorneys submit judgments starting each decretal paragraph (in the words of the form book)[402] "Ordered, Adjudicated and Decreed," or when they deed property "situate, lying, and being in."[403]

---

[400] Especially obscure or foreign words. It has been suggested by some that this is intentional—in order to make lawyers necessary, since only a lawyer understands terms that another lawyer uses (M. Odum, "If it Talks Like a Lawyer, There May Yet Be a Cure," New York *Times* June 5, 1992 B9.)

Hence the use of "ss.," in an affidavit. Professor Bryan Garner, the author of a style book for draftsmen of legal documents, suggests in that article that "ss.," does not mean "so sworn," but was actually a typographical error in which one scribe copied ancient paragraph marks, and the error crept into old form books.

[401] Would it be hen*tri*adys?

[402] *Carmody Wait 2d Cyclopedia of New York Practice with Forms*, § 63:33 (Rochester, 1990).

[403] Blumberg's Bargain and sale deed form No. A 291.

CONCLUSION

When reading court opinions, contracts or correspondence it may be helpful to keep in mind the concept of a hendiadys, and not try to give meaning to each and every word used.

FURTHER ASIDES

MORE ABOUT HENDIADYS

In Volume 23 Issue Three (Summer 1996) this publication contained an aside—"The Law and the Hendiadys." The author has received a variety of responses he wishes to share with his readers.

The article noted that a two word phrase such as "law and order" or null and void" is often used to express a meaning attributed to a single word. That figure of speech is called a hendiadys.

William Maker, Jr. wrote to advise us that we left out one of the most obvious of the hendidays used by lawyers and courts—null and void.[404]

Andrew Broadnick, Esq. called to say he had read some time ago an explanation for why lawyers may have used two words where one would do. He explained that after William the Conqueror won the battle of Hastings in 1066, the courts in England used what was then Norman French and came to be known as "Law French" in some of the courts.[405]

Other courts continued to use Latin, and English became the language of the courts in 1362. By then some pleaders were using words of both French and Latin origin that had passed into English in their pleadings.

For example, "null" which comes from the French "nulle" and "void" from the Latin "vacitum" were both used. "Arbitrary" from the Latin "arbitrare" and capricious from the French "capriceaux" were joined in pleadings.

"Cease" from the Latin "cessare" and "desist" from the French verb "desister" were employed.

One reason both words might be necessary was suggested by a reader, the late B. Anthony Morosco, Esq. At times in the

---

[404] Others added to our list of hendiadys "all well and good" and "forever and ever."

[405] Blackstone referred to "Law French" as a barbarous dialect.

history [406] of the English legal system, pleadings were parsed quite hyper technically. If "cease" were used it might have a different shade of meaning in the mind of a court than desist, the latter implying do no more while the former implied only stopping for a short period. The more words that were used the less the chance that it could be said that something had been left out.[407]

Although we no longer interpret pleadings in a hyper technical manner [408] such as that, we may use words of both French and Latin origin just to be on the safe side.

---

[406] Karl Marx said "History repeats itself, first as tragedy second as farce." What about the third time—as memorabilia on the Home Shopping Network? as nostalgia on Nick at Nite? As a rerun on the History Channel? Or unrecognizably as an Oliver Stone movie?

[407] He pointed out that indictments for murder in Texas used to include the fact that the victim was a human being, because someone once argued the indictment did not indicate whether the "Mary Brown" who had been killed was a human or a cow.

Judge Learned Hand once wrote "[T]here is no surer way to misread any document that to read it literally," *Guiseppi v. Walling*, 144 F. 2d 608 at 624.

[408] In a manner Chief Justice Breitel inveighed against (in a case involving the interpretation of a search warrant application) when he referred derogatorily to "like a year-book lawyer parsing a common law declaration" *People v Hansen* (1975) 38 NY2d 17 at 24, 377 NYS2d 461.

THE LAW OF MONKEY BUSINESS[409]

by James M. Rose[410]

Dr. Duelittle was a successful inventor[411] and investor. Among the indulgences that he bought for his scientific research foundation were four chimpanzees. He taught them American Sign Language[412] and then communicated with them. He taught them to use a computer, and the internet as well. Whatever his investment strategies and goals were, he "taught" them to the four chimpanzees when Dr. Duelittle "talked" to his animals.

When Duelittle died he left his whole estate and all of his investments to the four chimpanzees.[413] Although the law permits this to be done in trust,[414] he left his investments to them outright

---

[409] This essay was inspired by *Matter of Fouts et. al. as Trustee under the 1997 Chimpanzee Care Trust*, 176 Misc. 2d 521 (N. Y. Sur., 1998) That case dealt with the issue of whether chimpanzees who could communicate using American Sign Language could be considered persons with a disability and needed a guardian *ad litem* (with whom they could communicate), or were sufficiently protected by a trustee who controlled a trust for their benefit.

[410] White Plains, New York. Mr. Rose is more fun than a barrel of monkeys, and smells better, too.

[411] He invented and patented the refrigerator magnet, and as a consequence he became a magnet magnate.

[412] for the difference between American Sign Language, the signed English Language and spoken and written English see *People v. Ripic*, 182 App. Div. 2d 226, 587 NYS2d 776 (3rd Dept., 1992).

[413] Who he had named Greenspan, Buffet, Friedman, and Ruckheyser.

[414] See, Estates Powers and Trusts Law ("E.P.T.L." § 7-6.1. There are two sections both numbered "7-6.1" as the Legislature is inordinately fond of that number. The first is entitled "Honorary trusts for pets." The second is part of the Uniform Gifts to Minors act and is captioned "Definitions." The chimpanzees were adult chimps and not minors, at least in chimp years. Chimpanzees have an average lifespan of twenty years, and some live as long as forty-four years.

in his will, stating that he considered them colleagues and collaborators. An action was then commenced to declare a trust under the "Honorary trusts for pets"[415] provision of the E.P.T.L.

The chimpanzees were unhappy with the administrator assigned to the probate,[416] Hadley V. Backsendale, who was also the proposed trustee. He did not manage the trust funds using the theories of Dr. Duelittle, and he had not achieved the high return on investment that the chimps had when they were investing, and which they believed they were capable of obtaining if they managed their own money.

So, using the internet, the chimps located an attorney to represent them in Surrogate's Court. The attorney, Philo Phax, learned that the chimps were concerned that no investments be made in pharmaceutical companies using animals to test products,[417] or that were deleterious to the rain forest. When Backsendale argued that these ends should not be considered where investments are concerned, he was reminded that many universities had similar policies as a result of agitation from campus activists. He replied that the analogy of chimpanzees and undergraduate agitators was more than apt on several levels. He continued to disparage the abilities of chimpanzees.

The lawsuit drew a great deal of attention. The chimps were interviewed on television by Geraldo Rivera, who had invited them to stay in his home and to pick some stocks for him. On television they signed through a translator that the trustee did not have the sense that the creator give sponge, and disparaged his morals as well, noting that he was reported [418] to have a mistress, although he was married.

Backsendale then counterclaimed against the chimps for slander. A tangle of issues arose from the counterclaims. One had to do

---

[415] The section does not require the pets or animals prove that they are worthy of some honor.

[416] One of the chimps had been named as executor.

[417] See, e.g., *Immuno AG v. Moor-Jankowski*, 77 NY2d 235 (1991).

[418] On the internet by one Matthew Grunge.

with whether a chimp could be sued in court. Another concerned whether repeating something heard on the internet is *re*publishing, because if it is not there is a duty to investigate whether it is in fact true. If there *is* a duty is the standard to be applied that of how the "reasonable man," or "reasonable primate," or "reasonable chimp" would have acted?[419]

Another problem had to do with whether a counterclaim for slander lies in a Surrogate's action to impress a trust.[420] Yet another dealt with whether the Surrogate should disqualify himself since he was the one who had suggested his old acquaintance Backsendale. The issue of whether someone who signs something on television commits the tort of slander,[421] or libel [422] was certainly a question of first impression for Surrogate Maverick J. Holstein who got the case.

Finally, while there is a statute that makes it slander *per se* to "impute unchastity to a woman,"[423] there is no corresponding section that applies to men. Backsendale alleged that the statute was unconstitutional and illegal sexual discrimination.

Backsendale also sued Rivera for publishing the slander. In addition Backsendale pleaded that New York law was clear that chimpanzees are considered *ferae naturae*, that is wild by nature.[424] in contrast to domesticated animals. A court is entitled under case law to take judicial notice of the known nature of a monkey.[425]

---

[419] Is there such a thing as the reasonable chimp, since Backsendale appears to be arguing that the chimps lack the capacity to reason? If the chimps are recognized as wild animals, isn't the concept of "wild" antithetical to that of reason?

[420] The chimps signed that they were not impressed by Backsendale in the least.

[421] which is generally spoken.

[422] which can be committed by publishing a picture or drawing

[423] Civil Rights Law § 77.

[424] *Garelli v Sterling -Alaska Farms*, 25 Misc 2d 1032, 206 NYS2d 130 (S. Ct. Queens Co., 1960).

[425] *Gaccione v. State of New York*, 173 Misc. 367.

Therefore, Backsendale concluded, Rivera was liable for the slanders under the theory that there is absolute liability for the torts of wild animals by someone who keeps them in captivity on his property.[426]

The Judge opined that he did not believe the absolute liability for the torts of wild animals ran to slander by them, since that is not the kind of harm one foresees when keeping wild animals.[427] Moreover, the chimps were stating an opinion which is not actionable. Finally, he held that Backsendale failed to establish that the public places any faith in the judgment of another species of animal with a brain one third the size of a human brain.

On the issue of whether the chimps should control the trust, Backsendale argued that they should not be permitted to invest the money themselves because they are not human beings. They are concededly a different species—*chimpanzees pan troglodytes*. They are an endangered species listed in Appendix I of the Convention on International Trade in Endangered Species.[428]

The chimps replied that being another species did not mean that they could not make investments. After all, it was well known that an infinite number of them could write the entire works of William Shakespeare, which undoubtedly are far more elegant than the prosaic pleadings of Backsendale. They also pointed to a book of investment advice titled *The Idiot's Guide to Making Money in Wall Street*, which seemed to stand for the proposition that it did

---

[426] *Barrett v. State of New York*, 220 NY 423; see Prosser, *Law of Torts* § 57, p. 323, Restatement of Torts § 507 comment f.

[427] Since the chimps were free to come and go, they were not "in captivity," Rivera argued. One is not liable for the acts of wild animals in a forest he owns, but only the ones he keeps in cages, he noted.

[428] The chimps argued that Backsendale managed their trust so incompetently it was no wonder that they were endangered. If chimpanzees had been able to control investments so as to preserve their habitat, and had they been able to punish companies that captured them until their numbers diminished to the point where they were on the brink of extinction, they maintained, they never would have become endangered in the first instance.

not take much brain power to make money investing.[429] If there is a bull market, and a bear market, why couldn't there be a chimpanzee market, they reasoned.

Finally, Philo Phax directed the court's attention to the Random Walk Theory of investing. This theory provides that one cannot tell the direction of the market by simply reviewing charts or past history of a stock's price. At the bottom of this theory lurks the conclusion that no one can foretell the future movements of stocks, so one person's guesses, even random guesses, may be as good as that of any expert. The chimpanzees would not need to show any ability in order to be successful, Phax argued.

He noted that there are many contradictory theories of investment. Advise on being "contrarian" (that is choosing what the public is not choosing) is one strategy, while the opposite is often suggested by other investment professionals. There can surely never be any "science" to investing.

Backsendale admitted that the chimps had made money when they chose their own investments, but argued that it was merely by chance,[430] noting that a stopped clock is right twice a day, but that is by happenstance and not because of any ability to display the actual time. He asserted that the chimps should not be permitted to gamble the money away.

The chimps replied that investing is gambling whether it is done by humans or other species. Penal Law § 225.00 (2) states in relevant part "[a] person engages in gambling when he stakes or risks something of value upon the outcome of . . . a future

---

Backsendale disagreed, and argued that the opportunity for a quick buck never prevented most human investors from putting money into something that was harmful to their own environment, so why would monkeys be any different?

[429] The book *Guerrilla Guide to Investing* they conceded was not the same as the *Gorilla Guide to Investing*, a book that they were still busy "dictating" (i.e.,signing) to their stenographer.

[430] He argued that a rising tide floats all boats. The chimps pointed out, however, that Backsendale's investments sunk like a submarine.

contingent event not under his control or influence upon an agreement that he will receive something of value in the event of a certain outcome." The Legislature itself has defined gambling in a way that is indistinguishable from investments in a stock market.[431] The chimps must be permitted to succeed or fail on their own, and we must let the chimps fall where they may.

The chimpanzees argued although a court is entitled under case law to take judicial notice of the known nature of a monkey,[432] but what is now known about chimpanzees is quite different than what science knew about monkeys in the past. Chimpanzees are the animal with DNA that is the closest to that of human beings, and only one hundredth of the DNA of a human and a chimpanzee differs. If chimpanzees can sign well enough to communicate, who is to say they do not possess the ability[433] to invest their money?

Surrogate Holstein called Backsendale into chambers alone. No one knows what was said. A court officer later reported hearing something about "making a monkey out of you," but he could not identify the voice. Phax and the chimps were then called into chambers, and when they emerged the case was marked settled. The settlement is sealed, but it is reported that the chimps are active on the web buying and selling and doing quite well. The trustee of their trust, Backsendale, is reported to get a handsome fee for "managing" the trust.

---

[431] Similarly, he noted, the Legislature had difficulty in defining fortune telling in the Penal Law in a way that distinguishes it from investment advice, or defining organized crime in that same chapter in a way that distinguishes it from what the Legislature does.

[432] *Gaccione v. State of New York*, 173 Misc. 367.

[433] or intuition

CONCLUSION

If you could talk to the animals, what are the chances they would have something worth saying?

RES IPSA LOQUITUR (Humor)[434]

WHAT IS THE MEANING OF THIS?
or
WHEN IS IT NIGHT IN THE PENAL LAW BUT NOT IN THE CRIMINAL PROCEDURE LAW?[435]

"Divisible" and "indivisible" are opposites, but "flammable" and "inflammable" mean the same thing. While we're on this hot subject, "burn up" and "burn down" mean the same thing though "up" and "down" are opposites (and "blow up" and "blow down" are not synonymous).

Two words that are homonyms but at the same time antonyms are "raise" and "raze." If your stenographer hears you dictate "We [phonetic] 'ray-sed' the house," which one do you mean?[436]

If you tell people that your legal specialty is "private placements," what they think you do may depend on whether the audience you address consists of adoption attorneys or Wall Street securities gurus.

Lawyers must be careful using words, and we sometimes fall into erroneous ways. For example, we adjourn things "for all purposes" when we mean for any purpose.[437]

The law is a profession that specializes in wrestling with the meaning of words, and with drawing lines and putting things into categories. For example, the appellate courts have had to decide such weighty questions as whether hen's eggs are bird's eggs.[438]

---

[434] by James M. Rose, author of "They Execute Search Warrants, Don't They?"

[435] Reading this article is worth .005 Continuing Legal Education (CLE) credits, but understanding it is worth a whole lot more.

[436] If the DA asks for jail time after you argue for a monetary penalty, and the judge says "Fine," what does he mean?

[437] The adjournment is not both to plead guilty and try the case at the same time—it's for one or the other.

[438] Which no doubt required the testimony of an eggspert.

After all, hens do not fly.[439] The Supreme Court has pondered if a tomato[440] is a fruit or a vegetable.[441]

Reflective of the line drawing we are required to engage in is the question: When is it night? Is there a time when it is night but not nighttime?[442]

At common law before time pieces were common, "night" was defined not by the clock, but by the eyes. "Day time" was defined according to 4 *Blackstone's Com.* [Gavit ed] 844 if there be daylight or *crepusculum* [443] enough to discern a man's face at a reasonable distance.[444] Some courts have adhered to this definition.[445] Modern statutes prove that darkness has little to do with when night falls.[446] "Nightwork" is defined in Labor Law § 173 as from "twelve midnight or before six o'clock in the morning." The statute did

---

[439] On the other hand time flies like an arrow, and fruit flies like a banana. I have been unable to find such a case, although one is described in an anthologized piece Z. Chaffee, Jr. "The Disorderly Conduct of Words" in a collection by G. Rossman, *Advocacy and the King's English* 632 (1960). I have found a decision of the Second Circuit on whether duck's egg are "eggs of birds" (*Sun Kwok On v. United States* (2nd Cir. 1906) 143 Fed. 115). The distinction to be made was whether it was the egg of domesticated poultry or of a game bird.

[440] Whether the word is pronounced "Toe-mah-to" or "toe-may-to" is beyond the scope of this article.

[441] Although it is botanically a fruit of the vine, it is a vegetable for purposes of imposing a tariff, *Nix v. Heddon* 149 US 304 (1893); see, Z. Chaffee, Jr. "The Disorderly Conduct of Words" in G. Rossman, *Advocacy and the King's English* 632, (1960).

[442] Also spelled as "night time" (See General Construction Law § 51, and "night-time."

[443] Although this word sounds like something out of a Stephen King novel, it means twilight (see, *Black's Law Dictionary* 444).

[444] Hale's Pleas of the Crown i, 550-1.

[445] *Sasser v. United States* 227 F. 2d 358; *Moore v. United States*, 57 F.2d 840; *Atlanta Enterprises v. Crawford* 22 F. 2d 834.

[446] While night "falls," day "breaks". Things that fall often break (but not necessarily), whereas things break for reasons other than falls. Go figure.

not indicate why it was necessary to use "twelve" to modify midnight, as if there might be a mistake concerning which midnight the section was meant to define.[447] If those definitions make "night" fall too late for you, then try 19 U.S.C. §1401 which defines "night" as commencing at five PM and continuing until 8 AM for purposes of lading and unlading under the Tariff Act of 1930. If that is still too late for you, your night can begin at 3 PM, which is when a night differential kicks in under 5 U.S.C. § 5343 (f) if the hours of a shift fall primarily between 3 PM and 12 PM.[448]

Is the opposite of "nighttime" or "night" "day" or "daytime"? In *Distefano v. United States*, 58 F.2d 963 "daytime" was held to continue for some time after the sun set. In *United States v. Liebrich*, 55 F.2d 341 the time was extended to thirty minutes after sunset to thirty minutes before sun rise, while other courts have held that

---

[447] There are two midnights in each day according to *Leatherby Ins. Co. v. Villafana*, 82 Misc. 2d 144 at 146. However, the use of the term "midnight" in an insurance policy usually refers to the former when the policy commences and to the latter when it ends. Both of these midnights occur at twelve, and the author has not been able to find any "midnight" that does not. However Statutes § 231 is entitled "Every word to be given effect" and provides "In the construction of a statute, meaning and effect should be given to all its language, if possible, and words are not to be rejected as superfluous when it is practicable to give each a separate and distinct meaning." Therefore twelve must have some meaning as a modifier in this sentence to tell us which midnight.

A similar confusion exists when a statute refers to "moral turpitude" as in 31 U.S.C. § 703 (e) (1) (B) (v). "Turpitude" means base or shameful character, vileness or depravity. "Turpitude" would certainly imply bad morals, what other kind of turpitude is there? Is there an immoral turpitude? One court has held that "moral turpitude" means neither more or less than "turpitude," *In re Williams*, 64 Okla. 316, 167 P. 1149, 1152. It is not, therefore, logical, it is tautological *Hughes v. State Board of Medical Examiners*, 162 Ga. 246, 134 S.E. 42, 46.

[448] The mid-way between 3 PM and 12 PM is perhaps a "mid-night" that does not fall at twelve.

the daylight hours are the period from sunset to sunrise, *United States v. Martin*, 33 F. 2d 639.

"Overnight" should mean during the night and not when the night is over. However, one court has held that it is not a term that can be defined without knowing the context. The Supreme Court Schenectady County has opined: "The term "overnight" in the Zoning Ordinance of the City of Schenectady is not a technical term subject to absolute delineation by hours, minutes or seconds."[449] However, like pornography, the courts apparently know "overnight" parking when they see it.

Of course, we are concerned with the location where the law is to be applied, because it is always night and always day somewhere in the world. Take, for example, the Penal Law and the Criminal Procedure Law.

Penal Law § 140.00(4) defines "night" as the period between thirty minutes after sunset and thirty minutes before sunrise. "Night time" however, is defined in the General Construction Law § 51 as the time between sunset and sunrise.[450] Therefore, fifteen minutes after sunset is night time, but it is not night. It is *crepusculum!*

Criminal Procedure Law § 690.30 can be said to define "day" as 6 AM to 9 PM for the purposes of determining if a search warrant can be executed any time of the day or night. By process of elimination, night would be from 9 PM to 6 AM for purposes of that statute. Therefore, a burglary committed thirty-one minutes

---

[449] *Facci v. City of Schenectady*, 13 Misc. 2d 247, 250.

[450] So too, "night display" of the flag is defined as sunset to sunrise in 36 U.S.C. § 174. Other statutes that use the time from sunset to sunrise to require lighting are the Multiple Dwelling Law § 47 (hallways and stairwells), General Business Law § 245 (aircraft), Parks, Recreation and Historical Preservation Law § 25.03 (snowmobiles). One other uses that period to prohibit the serving of warrants of eviction, Real Property and Proceedings Law § 749. None of these laws defines when "sunset" or "sunrise" occurs, a proposition upon which reasonable scientists can and do differ.

No statutes use the term "dawn" which has no precise meaning, except, perhaps to Tony Orlando.

after sunset in December occurs "at night" according to the Penal Law; but a search warrant obtained to look for the proceeds of that burglary can be executed before 9 PM the same evening without being a day or night warrant because, although it is "night" in the Penal Law, it is not yet "night" in the Criminal Procedure Law!

IS IT TIME FOR A NEW STATE MOTTO FOR NEW YORK?

by James M. Rose[451]

Is there a word on your shingle that is not in English? [452] If you look at your certificate to practice law in New York issued by the Appellate Division in which you were admitted, can you spot a word that is not in English? The answer is an unequivocal maybe.

In the upper left hand corner is the motto of the State of New York. It appears there as part of the state arms and flag. State Law § 70[453] provides in part "On a scroll below the shield argent, in sable, Excelsior."

---

[451] White Plains, New York. Mr. Rose is the author of "Coping with a Co-Dependent Hard Disk."

[452] by English I mean modern American usage, and not the language spoken in England. see footnote 9, *infra*.

[453] Entitled "Description of the arms of the state and the flag."

In addition to the state flag the motto appears on the great seal of the state.[454] In 1778 the New York Senate adopted the motto.[455] What does it mean?

There are three meanings for "excelsior."

One meaning for the motto that would not be English is "Higher."[456] This is a comparative of the Latin *"excelsus"* for high. Does this motto describe New York State? Taxes in New York are the highest in the nation, so the motto "higher" or "ever upward" could refer to them, although it would be more accurate if it were "highest." If it refers to certain denizens of crack dens and other substance abusers it may be an accurate description of certain New Yorkers, but is that something that should be commemorated in a state motto?

New York's buildings were once the highest but are no longer, but how would the Senate know that in 1778? The same is true for prescient references to higher blood pressure or cholesterol counts.

One must exclude as a possibility that the motto refers to the poem of that name written by Henry Wadsworth Longfellow, the son of a lawyer, who was born in Maine and spent most of his adult life in Massachusetts. The poem was written in 1841, some sixty three years after the motto was adopted, and it the motto of New York that inspired the poem, and not the other way around. Longfellow saw the masthead of a New York newspaper with the

---

[454] State Law § 73.

[455] see, NY Senate 104th Session Doc. 61, Plate 1. When chapter 12 of the laws of 1778 was enacted, it did not refer to the motto, nor did it describe or illustrate the great seal (there was also a privy seal), but instead mentioned the seal having been devised that was to be deposited with the Secretary of State. A reference to a seal devised in 1777 (perhaps a different one?) appears in *New York Facts* p. 32, Clements Research Pub. Co. (1989).

[456] or "ever upward" according to *New York Facts, op. cit.*

state seal on it and was inspired to write the romantic and silly poem "Excelsior."[457]

The "inspiring" romantic poem is about a Swiss youth who takes the instruction to have loftier ambitions literally, and ventures into the mountains carrying "a banner with the strange device Excelsior!" in foolhardy disregard of the sensible warning not to go during a storm. As a result he is turned into a metaphorsicle for youth to emulate!

The poem was assailed for its Latinity by critics (as the New York motto can be), who felt the grammatically correct Latin would be either *excelsius* or *excelsiora*. Longfellow replied that it was excerpted from the sentence "*Scopus meus excelsior* est" ("My goal is higher") and was not an incorrect adverbial usage. (Longfellow, op. cit. at v. 1 p. 401.)

Henry Wadsworth Longfellow was advised in a letter that the poet George Sand had the same motto, (*Longfellow, op. cit.* at vol.1 p. 400) but there is no proof that the two of them ever got higher together.

The word "excelsior" is used by printers to describe three point type. Three point type is quite small and difficult to read. This line is printed in three point type. This, too, is probably not something for which New York wants to be celebrated. Would you like to introduce yourself as follows: "Hi, I'm from the small print state!" This meaning, while it is an American usage, probably post dates 1778, so it will not satisfy those people who are in search of the original meaning of the founding fathers.

Another meaning for "excelsior" is "slender curved wood shavings used for packing, stuffing and the like."[458] Here, at last, is a uniquely American word. The word "excelsior" is not found in

---

[457] according to Samuel Longfellow in his biography *Henry Wadsworth Longfellow*, vol. 1 p. 401 footnote 1 (1886) (Houghton Mifflin).

[458] *American Heritage Dictionary of the English Language* (New College Edition) 1981, p. 457.

the *Oxford English Dictionary*. That is because the English refer to this type of wood shaving as "wood wool."[459]

When the word "excelsior" came to mean wood shavings is not clear.[460]

One author mentions that it was the brand name of a particular wood shaving that has come to take on the meaning of the generic substance,[461] just as people refer to all gelatin desserts by the brand name "Jello," or all facial tissue by the brand name "Kleenex," or all photocopying as "xeroxing." Perhaps this brand name existed when the Senate adopted New York's motto in 1778. It had come to be used as a generic term as early as 1868. U.S. patent 75728 is for a machine for making excelsior to fill mattresses according to the 1869 Report of the Committee on Patents.[462] According to a Harper's magazine article in 1892 the primary usage of excelsior at that time was as a mattress stuffing. Do New Yorkers want to be known as mattress filling? It is highly unlikely. Moreover, most mattresses today are not filled with wood shavings, so the term refers to an obsolete practice.

Most packages today do not come stuffed with wood shavings, either. They are usually stuffed with polystyrene peanuts or plastic bubble wrap. Is it time to change the motto of New York to "Polystyrene peanuts" or "bubble wrap" to reflect the change?

Again the answer is "not likely." Polystyrene is also known as Styrofoam, or to chemists as $C_6H_5CHCH_2)_n$. Perhaps our state motto should be updated to "Styrofoam" because, like Excelsior, it is a brand name sometimes used to denote the generic, and is also

---

[459] H. L. Menken, *The American Language*, (Knopf, 1974) p. 280.

[460] *The Journal of Irreproducible Results*, Vol. 36 no. 6 reports at page 17 that excelsior was invented by "Ig" Ignatius Nobel, and that publication gives Ig Nobel Prizes in his honor. No proof of the existence of the inventor or his claim has been uncovered by this author, who by his revelation of this scandal, has no doubt insured that he will not receive such a prize in the future, and he will have to set his sights on the Pulitzer for this article.

[461] *Barnhart Dictionary of Etymology*, H. W. Wilson Co., (1988).

[462] In *A Dictionary of American English*, U. of Chicago Press Vol II, (1940).

is a packaging material. But plastic comes with its own baggage. It is beginning to be criticized as environmentally unsound because (unlike excelsior) it is not easily biodegradable.[463]

If we modernize our motto to "polystyrene peanut" or the more distinctive and scientific "$(C_6H_5CHCH_2)_n$", we are still employing a state motto connected with manufacturing. While New York could have been the Excelsior State when its economy was based primarily on manufacturing, in the 1990's and beyond New York will primarily be a service economy. A New York motto should reflect that service economy, something like "Please take a Number," "Do you want that with fries?" or "Temporarily out of Service." If New York's motto is not going to be in English, what language should be employed?

We invite your suggestions.

---

[463] Agoos and P. Savage, 141 *Chemical Week*, 24 (Dec. 9, 1987.)

James M. Rose

RELIGIOUS FREEDOM RESTORED IN 1993[464]

On November 16, 1993 religious freedom was restored in the United States of America. The chances are Americans did not notice it was missing, but on that date an act entitled the "Religious Freedom Restoration Act of 1993" went into effect.[465] It is in section 1 of the act that the short title of the Act is proclaimed to be no less than the "Religious Freedom Restoration Act of 1993."[466]

The purpose of the law was to overcome the Supreme Court decision in *Employment Division v. Smith*.[467] That case had established a new test in determining whether facially neutral statutes that allegedly burdened religious freedom should be held to violate the first amendment. Prior to *Employment Division v. Smith*, a government was required to show a compelling interest existed for whatever statute was being called into question as an invasion of religious freedom, a test established in such cases as *Sherbert v. Verner*[468] and *Wisconsin v. Yoder*[469]

The government may now substantially burden a person's exercise of[470] religion only if it demonstrates that the application of the burden to that person: (1) is in furtherance of a compelling

---

[464] The statutes and cases cited in this article are real. No names have been changed to protect the guilty. The statute parsed here was later declared unconstitutional in *City of Boerne v. Flores*, 117 S. Ct. 2157 (1997).

[465] 42 U.S.C. 2000bb, 107 Stat. 1488, P.L. 103-141.

[466] The act does not indicate what the long title is.

[467] 494 U.S. 872 (1990).

[468] 374 U.S. 398.

[469] 406 U.S. 205 (1972).

[470] According to the tests established in Section 3 of the Act.

governmental interest, and (2) is the least restrictive means of furthering that compelling governmental interest.[471] Despite the fact that the Act itself states in Section 3 (b) "Government may substantially burden a person's exercise of religion . . ." it states in section 6 (c) "Nothing in this Act shall be construed to authorize any government to burden any religious belief."[472]

What religious freedoms do you now have that you lacked between 1990 and November of 1993? *Employment Division v. Smith* dealt with the right of Native American employees to take peyote as part of a sacrament during a religious ceremony. They were fired for violating the state drug laws of Oregon, and then denied unemployment benefits. The United States Supreme Court held that the free exercise of religion clause in the first amendment did not prevent the State of Oregon from banning sacramental peyote in its general criminal laws prohibiting the ingestion of that drug.

One would assume that now Native Americans have the right to ingest peyote by virtue of the Restoration of Religious Freedom Act of 1993 by its very terms,[473] and yet Congress passed a separate bill a year later granting Native Americans

---

[471] This legislative codification of a prior judicially imposed test assumes that the test itself will pass muster in the eyes of future Supreme Court justices. If they should find that the test is too restrictive under the First Amendment, we could be faced with the ironic result that the Supreme Court would declare the Religious Freedom Restoration Act of 1993 in violation of the First Amendment's guarantee of freedom of religion!

[472] It is possible that the person who wrote both those sentences is the one legislator that promised to reduce your taxes and balance the budget at the same time.

[473] i.e., Section 2 (a)(4) specifically mentions the intention of reversing the effect of *Employment Division v. Smith*.

the right to engage in the traditional use of peyote for religious purposes.[474]

Since there is no Rastafarian Religious Freedom Act, can Rastafarians who claim they use marijuana as part of a religious ceremony claim the benefits of this bill? Similarly, can Christian and Jewish religious leaders give sacramental wine to their congregants' children as part of a religious ceremony without running afoul of laws prohibiting distributing intoxicating beverages to minors?[475]

Is the law meant to allow Mormons to engage in polygamy? In New York that is still a criminal offense.[476] We are not told in the Senate report[477] which appears to cite *Reynolds v. United States*, 98 U.S. 145 (1878) with approval as an example of a law where the government established that there was a compelling state interest in seeing that a male had only one spouse. Apparently Muslims whose religious beliefs allow them more than one wife may not have that privilege in this country.[478] Those religions that believe

---

[474] U.S. C. § 1996. In Section 2 of the act, *Employment Division v. Smith* is mentioned. Because this law was passed in addition to the Restoration of Religious Freedom Act does it mean that there are some religious freedoms that have not been restored to Native Americans in the 1993 Act? For example, what about the right to wear traditional long hair (see, *Rourke v. Correctional Services* 159 Misc. 2d 324, 603 NYS2d 647)?

You can be forgiven for missing the 1994 law, tucked between the one naming a federal post office in the Virgin Islands after Aubery C. Ottley, and technical corrections to the President John F. Kennedy Assassination Records Collection Extension Act of 1994 which require security clearances for review board personnel of that agency.

[475] For example, Penal Law § 260.20 (4). *Parents* can give children wine as a part of a religious celebration, but no law permits others to do so.

[476] Penal Law § 255.15.

[477] *U.S. Code Congressional & Administrative News*, January 1994 at 1892.

[478] And those who claim that they believe in ritual circumcision of females as part of Muslim ritual may not benefit from this law, either.

(or believed) in practices which we brand extreme will no doubt not benefit by the "restoration."[479]

Do Satanists who believe in the Black Mass and animal sacrifice come within the law's protection?[480] What about transfusions for Christian Scientists, or Orthodox Jews subject to autopsy[481]? The Hmong also object to autopsies on religious grounds, but based upon the *Employment Division v. Smith* case a court held that the government had a right to require them.[482] Must the Amish use fluorescent symbols on their slow moving vehicles operated on the highways?[483]

Quakers refused to obey portions of the immigration laws that required them not to employ illegal aliens, basing their refusal on the fact that their religion teaches them to help the strangers among them.[484] Does the law provide a defense to criminal charges for people who commit acts of violence against abortion clinics or persons who perform abortions? The Legislative history says that the law is not intended to affect the "issue of abortion"[485] but the law does not say so.

---

[479] "Ancient Mayans believed in child sacrifice for example.

[480] On the topic of the legitimacy of Satanism as a religion see a one paragraph note in the New York *Law Journal* of August 9, 1989 p. 1 col 2B. It indicates that a coven of witches won a tax exemption as a legitimate religious group from the state of Rhode Island. The state Tax Administrator found that the Rosengate Coven was entitled to a sale-tax exemption because it met the guidelines established in 1987 by the Supreme Court of Rhode Island. This case is an excellent example of why you want a wall of separation between your state and their church (*Everson v. Board of Education* 330 U.S. 1, 16).

[481] *Rotholz v. City of New York,* 151 Misc 2d 613.

[482] *You Vang Yang v. Sturner,* 750 F. Supp. 558 (Dist. Ct. R.I., 1990).

[483] *Minnesota v. Hersberger,* 462 NW2d 393 (Minn. 1990). As a safety measure the state's requirement was upheld.

[484] *American Friends Service Committee Corp. v. Thornburgh,* 951 F2d 957 (C. A. 9th Cir., 1991).

[485] Senate Report No. 113-11 at page 12. It is unclear what the "issue of abortion" means. Does it refer only to laws that permit or prohibit abortion, or is it intended to cover the issue of any civil disobedience from trespass to murder justified by a defendant's religious opposition to abortion as murder?

The courts have always had trouble with sincerely held beliefs of religions that they have concluded were genuine when those beliefs were in conflict with public policies. One issue in point is transfusions for Jehovah's Witnesses. When the case has dealt with the person himself or herself,[486] the courts have permitted the person to refuse a transfusion, but not where the belief has applied to that person's child.[487]

The courts have been able to see a compelling state interest in such things as preventing the carrying of swords on subway platforms,[488] in demanding blood tests be taken by driving while intoxicated suspects,[489] in intervening when a child tests positive for cocaine toxicology,[490] for the mandatory shaving of a beard for a prison photograph,[491] for prohibiting the selling of minister's credentials as part of a pyramid scheme,[492] and ordering a monk to work in order to support his former wife and child;[493] but not for requiring some one to carry a social security card if he has a sincerely held belief of theological origin that the card is the mark of the beast.[494]

---

[486] *Matter of Fosmica v. Nicoleau*, 75 NY2d 218, 551 NYS2d 876 (1990).

[487] *Jehovah's Witness v.King County Hospital Unit No. 1*, 390 U.S. 598 (1968); *Matter of Jamaica Hospital*, 128 Misc 2d 1006, 491 NYS2d 898 (S. Ct. Queens Co., 1985).

[488] *People v. Singh*, 135 Misc 2d 701, 516 NYS2d 412 (Crim. Ct. Queens 1987).

[489] *People v. Sukram*, 142 Misc 2d 957, 539 NYS2d 275 (Dist. Ct. Nassau Co. 1989.)

[490] *Fathima Ashanti K. J., a person alleged to be Neglected*, 147 Misc 2d 551, 558 NYS2d 447.

[491] *Overton v. Correctional Services*, 131 Misc 2d 295, 499 NYS2d 860 (S. Ct. Kings Co., 1986).

[492] *People v. Life Science Church*, 113 Misc 2d 952, 450 NYS2d 664 (N.Y. Co. S. Ct., 1982).

[493] *Matter of M.I. v. A.I.*, 107 Misc 2d 663, 435 NYS2d 928 (Fam. Ct. Kings Co., 1981).

[494] *Stevens v. Berger*, 428 F. Supp. 896 and *Matter of Martine S. v. Anthony D.*, 120 Misc 2d 567, 466 NYS2d 194 (Family Ct. Kings, 1983).

Senator Alan K. Simpson was concerned with the impact the Religious Freedom Restoration Act would have on suits by inmates. In 1992 inmates filed a total of 49,939 civil lawsuits—22% of all lawsuits filed in Federal court. They have alleged that religious freedom guarantees required the government to provide them with some unusual things such as a meal of Chateaubriand and Harveys Bristol Cream every other Friday night,[495] a special diet of organically grown produce washed in distilled water,[496] or that it allowed them the right to own and use nunchucks (a martial arts weapon).[497] They have argued that the first amendment requires that they be provided with the satanic bible[498] and the tools to practice witchcraft.[499] Now that their religious freedom has been restored, do they have the right to practice such religions, or practice more widely recognized religions at times that are in conflict with the normal functioning of the prison?[500] Is the solution to try these cases in some forum more appropriate than Federal Court, such as at the Galleria in the Food Court?

One problem with this law is that it forces the courts to determine if a religion is bona fide or not. For example, courts have often held that Native American religions that involve the use of peyote are true religions entitled to the protect of the first amendment.[501] But in

---

[495] *Theriault v. Silber*, 453 F. Supp. 254, 260 (W.D. Tex. 1978) appeal dismissed 579 F2d 302 (5th Cir. 1978).

[496] *Udey v. Kastner*, 805 F2d 1218 (5th Cir. 1986).

[497] *Abdool-Rashad v. Seiter*, No. 84-3816 (6th Cir. Aug. 8, 1985 unpublished case referred to in the Senate report.)

[498] *Mc Corkle v. Johnson*, 881 F2d 993 (11th Cir., 1989).

[499] *Dettmer v. Landon*, 799 F 2d 929 (4th Cir. 1986).

[500] Senator Simpson suggests that they do because the majority expresses its belief that the bill reverses *O'Lone v. Estate of Shabazz*, 482 U.S. 342 (1987).

[501] *People v. Woody*, 61 Ca. 2d 716 (1964) 35 ALR3d 939, but see *Montana v. Big Sheep*, 75 Mont. 219 (1926). Compare *People v. Mitchell*, 244 Cal. App. 2d 176 (1966) involving marijuana use that was not part of a bona fide religion and the argument that Timothy Leary made that he had formed a church with LSD as a sacrament *Leary v. United States*, 383 F2d 851 (5th Cir., 1967).

United States v. Kuch[502] the court was able to discern that the Neo-American church was not a bona fide religion and therefore not entitled to the first amendment's protections.[503]

Now that your religious freedom has been restored, is the next thing to be restored your faith in Congress?

---

[502] 288 F. Supp. 439 (Dist. Ct., 1968)
[503] The First Amendment does not allow the government to establish a religion, but apparently there is no problem with disestablishing one.

CHAPTER FOUR

SUPREMELY COURTING DISASTER
(BY AN ENGLISH TO LAW AND
LAW TO ENGLISH INTERPRETER)

DOES THE FDA HAVE JURISDICTION OVER MIRACLES?

Alexandros Chemedes, the owner of AlChemMe Pharmaceuticals Inc., had a dream one night. In it a complicated chemical formula appeared to him in a visual diagram. He heard a deep voice say "If you make it . . ." but he could not hear the rest. The substance in the diagram kept cracking open small spherical shells of some sort until the dream ended.

He was aware of the dream that led Elias Howe to invent the sewing machine,[504] and the divine inspiration that caused James Watson and Francis Crick to intuit that DNA took the form of a double helix. Al Chemedes believed his dream to be a divine inspiration (as he was a lay minister of the Church of God the Biochemist).[505] He set upon manufacturing the formula that he envisioned in his dream. After he had done so, he used it to try to crack open a variety of substances without success.[506]

One day, while he was suffering from a flu virus at work, he mistakenly inhaled a powdered version of the substance and felt better within hours.

Tests confirmed that his new concoction could destroy the tough outer protein shell, or capsid, of a single virion. The drug, which he named Miricol, could kill all foreign viruses in the body.

---

[504] In which Howe saw warriors carrying spears with holes in the spearheads. He used that configuration to formulate the sewing machine needle with a hole near the front in 1846.

[505] The pastor of his church was a pharmacist known as old Doctor Phil. His son Phil, Jr., was also a pharmacist and pastor, and was known as RePhil.

[506] He tried walnuts, a bowling ball and a stale bagel.

He tried it on mice, and found it to be an effective anti-viral agent.[507] This meant that Miricol could cure *any* disease caused by a virus—which includes warts, colds, flu, AIDS, rabies, polio, small pox, chicken pox, most sexually transmitted diseases, hanta virus, herpes and some cancers.

He began to develop a protocol to apply for testing rights from the Food and Drug Administration. Since 1938 new pharmaceuticals cannot simply be marketed without extensive tests to assure that they are safe and have no harmful side effects. After the 1962 thalidomide tragedy, the laws were tightened to provide a lengthy procedure for testing of new pharmaceuticals.[508]

AlChemMe Pharmaceuticals had on retainer a Washington D.C. law firm specializing in complying with complex FDA regulations and lobbying the government—Dross, Dross, Piffel, Arcana and Vestibuhl.[509] They were told to work on a plan to gain speedy approval of the drug.

Al Chemedes told his brother in law, Benny Fischel, an attorney, about the drug. Benny had a best friend, Will Ling, who was dying of a disease caused by a virus. Benny begged Al Chemedes to give the drug to his friend. But Dross² warned Chemedes that he must not. He could not sell it or even give it away—and no doctor could prescribe it without first obtaining FDA approval. No tests in which Ling could participate would be ready in time. If the drug were given away (and it worked) it would be readily apparent. The publicity that would follow such a violation of law would bring pressure to bear upon the FDA to civilly and perhaps criminally prosecute Chemedes, and might delay the approval of Miricol as well as land Chemedes in jail.

Al Chemedes thought he had a solution to the problem. He declared that the drug was divinely inspired because it appeared in a dream to him, just as many prophets and Biblical forefathers had been divinely inspired in their dreams. His Pastor, Dr. Phil, declared the drug to be a sacrament of his religion.

---

[507] The only side effect seemed to be that it increased their I.Q.'s ten percent.
[508] See 21 U.S.C. § 301-395 and 21 C.F.R. Part 866.
[509] Hereinafter "Dross²." Vestibuhl was the lobbyist.

However, a Dross[2] senior partner opined that a First Amendment defense to a food and drug act charge would not be successful because of previous case law involving the Church of Scientology's Hubbard Electrometer or E-meter.[510] As long as the food or drug or device was intend for use in the body it would fall within the jurisdiction of the federal watchdogs.[511]

Declaring the drug to be a sacrament did not mean it could be given administered with impunity under the First Amendment.

Chemedes explained his predicament to his brother in law. Benny's twin brother, Arty Fischel, practiced law with him. Together they represented numerous parking lot owners, and they ran the law firm started by their father, Oliver. That firm was known as the O. Fischel Law Firm of New York State. They advertised inexpensive litigation on television with the telephone number 1-800-CHEAP SUIT—and leave off the first "C" for contingency.[512] Arty came up with another remedy for the problem.[513]

---

[510] *Founding Church of Scientology v. United States* 409 F 2d 1146 (D. C. Cir. 1969) 13 ALR Fed. 747. That case mentioned in dicta that adulterated food used by a religion would fall within the jurisdiction of the FDA.

[511] For example, a tampon constitutes a medical device for purposes of regulation, and must be properly labeled with a warning about toxic shock syndrome, *Moore v. Kimberly-Clark Corp.* 867 F2d 243, (5th Cir.), rehearing den. 873 F2d 297.

[512] As a visual clue to remind viewers of the telephone number the announcer wore a tacky coat and pants.

[513] Arty had once come up with a creative solution for an importer who wished to bring expensive Italian shoes into this country and avoid paying the 100 % duty. He had the shipper send 10,000 left shoes only. When they arrived at customs the importer refused them, saying "What good are left shoes to me?" They were then auctioned off for a fraction of the import duty. He had a straw man purchase all of them.

Then, two weeks later when the 10,000 right shoes came, he refuse them again—saying they were of no value without the left shoes. Another straw man purchased them at a fraction of the import duty. Later several persons were paid minimum wage to match the pairs up, and the importer still made a tidy profit.

He simply modified the bailment language he used on the back of parking lot claim checks given out by his clients. Will Ling was told that the Church of God the Biochemist was hiring him to be a warehouseman. The valuable Miricol was a sacrament of the church, which he was to keep safely in his possession as a bailment. He was paid ten dollars by the church to act as a temporary warehouse for its product. The contract required him to keep the pills safe from all harm. He was strictly forbidden in the contract (because of FDA regulations) from consuming the pills. The contract explicitly provided that he was not permitted to take the pills three times a day with meals for two weeks nor operate heavy machinery for two hours thereafter—for example.

If Ling took the pills and violated the contract, exclusive jurisdiction to litigate the violation of the contract and impose damages was vested in an arbitrator. The arbitrator named in the contract was an attorney from The O. Fischel Law Firm of New York—Pete L. "Beetle" Baylor. The contract provided that, in the event of breach, liquidated damages would consist of the return of the ten dollars that the church had paid Will Ling to keep the pills safe and $100 damages—the amount that the church paid AlChemMe Pharmaceuticals for producing the pills.

Will Ling took the pills three times a day for two weeks and recovered from the disease. He cheerfully paid the liquidated damages to the church. When the FDA came calling, he told them that he was simply an untrustworthy bailee with whom one should not entrust anything valuable.

CONCLUSIONS

(Take your pick)

1. Where there's a Will, There's a way; or,
2. The flesh is Will Ling, when the Spirit speaks; or,
3. You're never sunk if you keep bailing; or
4. Anyone who thinks that a dog is man's best friend has never met a clever lawyer.
5. None of the above.

PARSING THE FEDERAL UNIFORM RESTROOM LABELING ACT OF 1986: THE LADY OR THE TIGER?[514]

Have you ever gone to the restroom of some aggressively cute theme restaurant and been unable to determine which one is intended for the accommodation of your sex? A Mexican restaurant may have wash rooms labeled "caballeros," or a western theme fast food chain will have a sign on its bathrooms for "stallions" and "fillies." A fast falafel eatery may have the rooms designated in Arabic, or in pictogram depicting figures in burkas and burnooses that are impossible to distinguish. And then there are the restaurants that cater to non-readers (i.e., the video generation) with confusing androgynous unisex shapes of its restroom doors.[515] Some congressmen and congresswomen have leap into the confusion, and have legislated our way out of the potentially embarrassing crisis with the Federal Uniform Restroom Labeling Act of 1986 (hereinafter "FURLA").

The law requires the use of the labels "MEN" and "WOMEN" on the doors of toilet facilities in lettering contrasting sufficiently with the color of the door at least two inches high to be conspicuously posted in places of public accommodation or facilities

---

[514] A cute title meant to signify a dilemma when asked to chose a door. The author is unaware of any restrooms actually so labeled. Rooms containing ladies and tigers (as in the famous story) do not come within the purview of this article if they are not restrooms. The tiger, however, may come within the ambit of laws related to labeling of furs to show the country of origin (15 U.S.C. § 69).

[515] Public Health Law § 1352-a requires restaurants with more than 20 seats to have "appropriately identified and maintained toilet facilities." It is a misdemeanor to fail to comply according to Public Health Law § 1353(1). Inappropriately labeled restrooms are therefore illegal. However, interpretation the word "appropriately" is certainly open for scholarly disagreement. Does it refer to the fact that the rooms must be labeled in a way that matches the theme of the restaurant? Does it mean appropriately to identify the sex using it, or does it merely require that the room be labeled to show that it contains a toilet?

that affect interstate commerce.[516] The Attorney General is empowered to seek injunctions against any establishments that fail to comply so that a citizen does not suffer an irreparable injury (to himself or his reputation). The jurisdiction to conduct appropriate inspections is allocated to the Department of Health and Human Services, apparently falling foursquare into the Human Services portion of its mandate. The Department is currently drafting a set of extensive regulations to clarify the intent and application of the statute, and they are expected in four years' time.

How does the statute comport with New York law? Labor Law § 381 requires restaurants to provide separate water closet compartments or toilet rooms for females. The section does not say whether the compartments have to be in a room set aside for females, or what they must be separate from. It does not require toilet rooms be set aside for men.

The General Construction Law provides that words of the masculine gender include the female,[517] and neuter.[518] Therefore, the term "MEN" on a men's room would include women and girls,[519] who could legally use the mens' room. The term "WOMEN"

---

[516] The law drew quick opposition from those who opposed making English the recognized national language, and challenges that this law discriminates against non-English speaking Americans are pending in the court.

[517] General Construction Law § 22.

[518] By "neuter" the statute may refer to corporations. The term "person" includes corporations (General Construction Law § 37, Executive Law § 292 (1)). A restroom in a place of public accommodation, and cannot be denied or withheld from a person on account of his or her sex (Executive Law § 296(2)(a)). Therefore, does the command in Public Health Law § 1352-a that there be "appropriately labeled and maintained toilet facilities" in restaurants requires a separate room for corporations? Since neuters are included in the masculine according to General Construction Law § 22, is it sufficient if the rooms reads "MEN AND CORPORATIONS" or "MEN AND NEUTERS" to appropriately identify the room?

[519] General Construction Law § 55.

does not include the masculine, so presumably men (which includes boys)[520] could not use the ladies' room.[521]

That, in turn, violates both state and federal sex discrimination statutes. While there is a rational distinction is permitting only men to use the mens' room and only women to use the womens' facilities, if ladies are permitted to use the mens' room and men are not reciprocally permitted to use the ladies' powder room, sexual discrimination has occurred.[522] The courts will no doubt order that men are entitled to the same relief as women are conferred under the statutes.

The Department of Health and Human Services where recently queried about the interpretation replied that FURLA has nothing to do with who actually *uses* the facilities, but deals only with how they are to be labeled.

However, Congress provided in § 153 of the Act that the states are required to pass all local laws required to implement the act,[523] or face the loss of Federal revenue sharing funds used to construct and maintain sewage treatment plants.

However, if courts rule that either sex can use either restroom, there is no reason why the rooms need be labeled at all. Does that mean that FURLA is unconstitutional for that reason? A law may be void if it is vague, or if it makes irrational distinctions. It is not unconstitutional simply because it is superfluous, or fails to achieve any purpose. Indeed, if a law which makes invidious distinctions is to be abhorred, then one which attempts to make distinctions but utterly fails would be a model of democratic constitutionality.

---

[520] General Construction Law § 29.

[521] Nor could neuters.

[522] If no *bona fide* considerations of public policy could be shown for the distinction. (Executive Law § 296 (2)(b)). But see, *City of Cleburne v. Cleburne Living Center*, 473 U.S. 432, 105 S. Ct. 3266, 3270 (1985) in which the court said: "A sign that says "MEN ONLY" looks different in a bathroom door than on a courthouse door." Part of the different appearance that the court has visually identified may come from the fact that one is viewed in indoor lighting, and the other by natural light.

[523] A power evidently reserved to the states under the Tenth Amendment.

James M. Rose

THE RIGHTS STUFF

It is a cherished cliche in modern America that the Bill of Rights would never pass Congress today because it would be too controversial. If the Constitution were put up to a vote, cynics say, it would be roundly defeated. Certain civil libertines insist that conservatives' reaction to the Bill of Rights is to pay it and be done with it, or add it to the National Debt.

There is a cry for a new Constitutional Convention to require a balanced budget, insure the rights of flags and other inanimate objects, and to give pro and anti abortion forces a battlefield on which to practice capital/Capitol punishment. What will result from such a convention is a new and radically different modern Bill of Rights. Here, in plain language of course, is the Bill of Rights that will emerge by consensus.

ANNOTATED BILL OF MODERN RIGHTS

1. Everyone has a right to his or her own space.
2. You have a right to sing the blues.
3. You have a right to chicken done right.
4. You have certain inalienable rights to life, liberty, and the happiness of pursuit (i.e., the right to future enjoyment.)
5. You have a right of redemption if you pay what's due (i.e., due process).
6. You have a right to wear sleeveless shirts (i.e., a right to bare arms.)
7. You have a right on red with caution (except where prohibited).
8. You have marital rights to one half of what you had the a right to all of before you were married.
9. Your government guarantees you the right of suffrage and will insure that you do suffer.
10. You have riparian rights in the Bronx River Parkway every time it rains.
11. You have a right to sue to determine who has the best lawyer.
12. All rights reserved.[524]

---

[524] Two wrongs do not make a right.

MUST DOGS WEAR SEAT BELTS?

Are dogs required to wear seat belts? Must they have driver's licenses if they operate motor vehicles ?[525] Those are questions that were posed recently in the wake of *Conyers v. Vinti*.[526] In that case, a nine year old dog was lying quietly on the floor in the front passenger's side of the defendant's vehicle. The vehicle was stopped at a traffic light. The dog suddenly jumped on the accelerator pedal, causing the vehicle to crash into the plaintiff's car, which was also stopped at the red light ahead of the defendant's vehicle.

The court discussed the liability of the dog's owner for its conduct, as well as the foreseeability of the accident, and concluded that the dog owner was liable because the car was an inherently dangerous instrumentality near which the dog was left unrestrained. The owner was liable because she should have put the dog in the back seat, the court concluded. The dissent noted that the dog had ridden in the vehicle many times before without incident.[527] Justice Mangano wrote in his dissent that the result ". . . represents, in my view, an affront to that particular species of the animal kingdom, i.e., the tame dog, 'which the law, guided by experience,

---

[525] Other questions posed to us recently but not answered in this article include how much testimony a witness could recant from a previous trial, put in the following way: "How much cant could a recanter recant if a recanter could recant cant (but can't)?"

[526] 107 App. Div. 2d 787 (2nd Dept 1985) app. dism., 64 NY2d 1040 (1985). See discussion in 12 Westchester *Bar Journal* 343.

[527] The case does not discuss the old rule of law that every dog is entitled to one bite, apparently feeling that a dog is *not* entitled to one joy ride. However, the concept that a dog is entitled to one bite is well established in New York law. Justice Dykeman noted in *Muller v. McKesson*, 10 Hun. 45, the propensity of the animal to misbehave must first be brought to the attention of the owner before he is liable in damages. *Smith v. Pehal*, 2 Strange 1264, stands for the proposition that every dog is entitled to one bite, a concept that can trace its origin to the 21st chapter of Exodus verse 28, although the courts in the United States generally confine themselves to precedent commencing with Chief Justice John Jay.

has always regarded as the friend and companion of man [citations omitted].'"[528]

Conyers v. Vinti arose in 1977, before the use of seat belts (referred to in the Vehicle and Traffic Law as "safety belts") became mandatory in New York. Vehicle and Traffic Law § 1229-c now requires that passengers in the front seat of automobiles be restrained by a safety belt or, if under four, in a safety seat.[529] Would the application of this law have required a different result if it had been in effect?

The answer is "no" for several reasons. Subdivision 8 of the section provides that ". . . non-compliance with the provisions of this section shall not be admissible in any civil action in a court of law with regard to liability." In addition, the dog was lying on the floor of the vehicle and was not riding on the seat. However, it is doubtful that a human passenger could escape application of the statute by saying he was riding on the floor of the vehicle. A child under four seated in the vehicle who is not restrained in a safety seat comes within the ambit of the statute, and a parent is not likely to evade liability by saying that the child was on the floor, not in the seat.

The statute does not limit its application to human beings in the vehicle. Rather it applies to all "passengers," so the question would revolve around whether the dog was a "passenger."

The word "passenger" is not define in the Vehicle and Traffic Law, nor in the Commissioner of Motor Vehicle's regulations. Why did the Legislature chose the word "passenger" rather than

---

[528] Justice Mangano did not discuss the fact that there are some friends and companions of man that most men he would not necessarily trust to operate a beloved vehicle.

[529] When this article first appeared there was no requirement that a shoulder safety harness also be worn, as there is today in the law. Sled dogs are more used to harnesses than safety belts, but the breed of the dog in the case is described as Scotch terrier. The case does not indicate how much scotch, if any, was in the scotch terrier, who was not charged with driving while intoxicated.

"occupant"? It obviously means something different than "occupant," since Vehicle and Traffic Law § 1213 (2) uses the words ". . . for each passenger *or* occupant in said front seat." If the words were synonymous then there would be no need to use them both nor the word "or."

Case law is enlightening. "Passenger" is defined in several cases such as *Garricott v. New York State R.R.*[530] and *Hopkins v. Long Island R.R.*[531] as a person who pays for his passage.[532] If the dog did not pay for its passage, then it is not a "passenger" under case law, and may be a mere "invitee" or guest.[533]

This still does not end our inquiry. When the dog hit the accelerator, it can be argued, it operated the motor vehicle, and hence was no longer a front seat passenger, guest or invitee. While "operates" is not defined in the Vehicle and Traffic Law, there is a substantial body of case law that has developed to define the word. Taking any step that alone, or in sequence that would move the vehicle forward constitutes operation.[534] At least one court has held that the operation must be intentional, and that releasing an emergency brake by mistake did not

---

[530] 233 N.Y. 9
[531] 21 App. Div. 2d 814 (2nd Dept. 1964)
[532] See also, New York Vehicle and Traffic Law § 1227 (2) which reads : "For purposes of this section, a passenger vehicle shall mean a vehicle designed to carry ten or more passengers and used to carry passengers for hire." However, the section governs consumption of alcoholic beverages in a vehicle, and it is not applicable to a situation when a dog is not also consuming alcohol in a vehicle. The dog was only nine years old, and nine year olds are forbidden to consume alcohol in New York. But in human years, the dog would be the equivalent of a sixty- three year old person.
[533] Vehicle and Traffic Law §§ 1238 and 2406 also use the word "passenger" in requiring passengers to wear helmets when riding on bicycles and all terrain vehicles respectively. Whether a dog must also wear a helmet under those circumstances is beyond the scope of this article.
[534] *People v. Marriott*, 37 App. Div. 2d 868, 325 NYS2d 133 (3rd Dept 1971).

constitute operation of a vehicle.[535] While a person is presumed to intend the natural consequences of his acts,[536] the same may not be said for dogs.

Justice W. F. Allen sitting in Oneida County Court in *Wiley v. Slater*[537] remarked in 1856: "[t]he courtesies and hospitalities of dog life cannot be well regulated by the judicial tribunals of the land." The same may be said for divining the intentions of canines.[538]

However, we need not tarry long over this puzzle, because Vehicle and Traffic Law § 1229-c refers to a *person* who operates a vehicle, and not an animal. "Person" is defined in the Vehicle and Traffic Law § 131 as "a natural person, firm, copartnership, association, or corporation, and there is no mention of animals. Applying the rule of Statutes § 240 "*expressio unis est exclusio alterius*"[539] it becomes clear that if the Legislature meant for animals to be required to use seat belts when operating or riding in vehicles, it would have so provided.

Nor would the dog need a license,[540] as Vehicle and Traffic Law § 509 only requires persons who operate vehicles be licensed.

---

[535] *People v. Marzulli*, 76 Misc. 2d 971, 351 NYS2d 775 (2nd Dept. 1973).

[536] *People v. Lieberman*, 3 NY2d 649, 652 (1958).

[537] 22 Barber 506 (1856).

[538] "The state of a man's mind, said Lord Bowen in *Edginton v. Fitzmaurice*, (29 L.R [Ch. D. 1885] 459 at 483 "is as much a fact as the state of his digestion." He did not speculate as to the state of a dog's mind. If children under a certain age cannot form the specific intent to commit a crime, what of animals? There are plenty of "reasonable man" cases, but try to find a "reasonable dog" case when you need one.

[539] Roughly, "the inclusion of one is the exclusion of the other," often used to mean that if the Legislature excluded something from a statute it did so intentionally. The state of the Legislature's collective mind may not be as easy to discover as the state of its collective digestion, thus requiring a whole volume of rules be applied to discern it.

[540] That is a driver's license. Of course, it would have needed a dog license by virtue of Agriculture and Markets Law § 109. That section fails to list the

CONCLUSION

The Legislature should address the loophole in our laws that allows animals to operate motor vehicles without proper harnesses and safety restraints.

SEX AND THE SINGLE FAMILY RESIDENTIAL ZONE

In the bucolic suburb of New Gomorrah, where the one family residential zoning requires two acre plots, The Church of Elvis the King[541] occupied a plot of land about ten feet higher than the old mansion behind it. That property was tied up for years in litigation,[542] but finally the heirs agreed to sell it to the state to be used as a group home for the mentally ill.

It is the State's policy to deinstitutionalize those with mental disabilities[543] and in so doing they have established group homes of up to eleven adult de-institutionalized persons unrelated to one another.

The neighbors attempted to resist it on the basis that the residents would not constitute a single family in this single family zoned area, and that their property values would plummet. However, the Padavan Law (Mental Hygiene Law § 41.34), which establishes site selection criteria for community residences, was held not to deprive neighboring homeowners of their property rights without due process, despite alleged reduction in neighbors' property value when such a residence was established, since a person cannot claim constitutionally-protected property interest in uses of neighboring property on ground that those uses may affect market value of his own property.[544] The fact that unrelated people would

---

privileges and immunities a dog obtains from being licensed, save for the immunity from rabies it receives from obtaining a rabies shot in order to be eligible for its license. In this regard the dog's license is similar to a marriage license, which also does not list the privileges and immunities its holder obtains (nor the obligations and duties), but operating a motor vehicle as a consequence of being married has never been numbered among them.

[541] which sat on the property of the former Church of the Cedars of Lebanon, so named for the cedar trees that graced the property before the church of Elvis the King removed them.

[542] see *Jarndice v. Jarndice*, 21 Dickens 431.

[543] see, *Crane Neck Assn. v New York City/Long Is. County Servs. Group*, 61 NY2d 154, 160, cert denied 469 U.S. 804; *Matter of Fisher v Webb*, 136 App. Div. 2d 806.

[544] *Mehta v Surles*, (1990, CA 2d Cir., NY) 905 F2d 595; *Little Neck Community*

be living together in a single family zone was also not a bar to a group home the court said.[545]

The congregants of the church were unhappily surprised by the eccentric behavior of the residents of the home. They made love in the backyard of the house within plain view of the windows of the church, which, because of the relative topography of the plots, looked down on the backyard of the group residence.

First the church members complained to the police, but to no avail. Because the properties were adjoining only at their backyards, the behavior was not "public," the police explained, since it could not be seen from the street.[546] Thus the residents could not be charged with any criminal offenses. Disorderly Conduct[547] requires an intent to cause public inconvenience, the creation of unreasonable noise,[548] or an act which intentionally disturbs a lawful assembly. As it could not be shown that the behavior was done with the intention of disrupting the church,[549] Disrupting a Religious Service and Criminal Nuisance charges could not be preferred, either.

The church wrote letters to the state complaining about the immoral behavior of its neighbors, and asked the state to have the group home supervisors stop the activity, or make the residents

---

Assoc. v. Working Organization for Retarded Children, 52 App. Div. 2d 90, 383 NYS2d 364 (1976, 2nd Dept).

[545] *Crane Neck Assn, Inc. v. NYC/Long Island County Services Group,* 92 App. Div. 2d 119, 460 NYS2d 69 (2nd Dept. 1983), affd 61 NY2d 154, 472 NYS2d 901, 460 NE2d 1336, app. dismd cert. den. 469 U.S. 804, 83 L. Ed 2d 11, 105 S. Ct. 60.

[546] Private annoyances, however exasperating or reprehensible, are insufficient where no breach of the peace has resulted, *People v Ludovici* (Co Ct., 1939) 13 NYS2d 88.

[547] Penal Law § 240.20.

[548] Apparently the noise created was reasonable for the specific activity.

[549] Indeed, since the residents of the group home lacked the legal capacity to form an intent to do anything criminal because of their mental disabilities, it would be impossible to charge them with any crime. However, they did have the capacity to consent to relations with someone else by virtue of 14 NYCRR § 624.20 (see footnote 14 *infra.*)

move it indoors. The state replied that while it sympathized with the sentiments of the congregation, but that the courts prohibited it from interfering in the sex lives of unmarried and consenting adults despite their lack of mental abilities.[550] The right is enshrined in the Mental Hygiene Law,[551] and Federal Law.[552] Were the state to interfere with the sex lives of patients, it could be sued for a deprivation of its wards' civil rights, it replied.[553] Therefore, its regulations guarantee such a right.[554]

---

[550] Our jurisprudence recognizes certain limitations on the ability of a legally incapacitated person to consent to participate in sexual relations. That limitation is an exercise of the State's *parens patriae* interest, invoked only where the individual is deemed unable to make a competent decision concerning a fundamental right (see, *Rivers v Katz*, 67 NY2d 485, 496).

[551] "§ 33.01. Protection of patients' rights

Notwithstanding any other provision of law, no person shall be deprived of any civil right, if in all other respects qualified and eligible, solely by reason of receipt of services for a mental disability nor shall the receipt of such services modify or vary any civil right of any such person, including but not limited to civil service ranking and appointment, the right to register for and to vote at elections, or rights relating to the granting, forfeiture, or denial of a license, permit, privilege, or benefit pursuant to any law."

[552] 42 U.S.C.A. § 10841 and § 9501.

[553] c.f., *Foy v. Greenblott*, 190 Cal. Reptr. 84, 141 C. A. 3rd l.

[554] 14 NYCRR § 633.4. Rights and responsibilities of persons receiving services. (a) Principles of compliance.

(3) The rights set forth in this section are intended to establish the living and/or program environment that protects individuals and contributes to providing an environment in keeping with the community at large, to the extent possible, given the degree of the disabilities of those individuals. *Rights that are self-initiated or involve privacy or sexuality issues* may need to be adapted to meet the needs of certain persons with the most severe handicaps and/or persons whose need for protection, safety and health care will justify such adaptation. *It is the responsibility of the agency/ facility or the sponsoring agency to ensure that rights are not arbitrarily denied.* Limitations of client rights must be on an individual basis, for a specific period of time, and for clinical purposes only.

The church could not prevent the activity, so it decided to construct a fence high enough to screen the offending activities. It applied to the Village of New Gomorrah Zoning Board of Appeals for a variance from the maximum six foot height restriction on fences. It proposed to make the fence twelve feet high on top of the ten foot high rear retaining wall between the properties—tall enough to screen the activities.

The church was aware that zoning ordinances *do* apply to religious institutions. Despite the First Amendment freedom of religion, the police power governing applications for special use variances[555] does apply. This was recently confirmed when the Religious Freedom Restoration Act of 1993[556] was declared

---

14 NYCRR § 624.4. "Reportable incidents, serious reportable incidents and abuse, defined." at (C) (2) provides "Any sexual contact between persons receiving services and others, or among persons receiving services, is considered to be sexual abuse unless the involved person(s) is a consenting adult."

In 14 NYCRR § 624.20. "Glossary." the definition of "Adult, capable." is:

For purposes of this Part, a person 18 years of age or older who is able to understand the nature and implication of an issue. The assessment of capability in relation to each issue as it arises will be made by the person's program planning team (see glossary). Capability, as stipulated by this definition, *does not mean legal competency*; nor does it necessarily relate to a person's capability to independently handle his or her own financial affairs; nor does it relate to the person's capacity to understand appropriate disclosures regarding proposed professional medical treatment. Whenever there is doubt on the part of any other party interested in the welfare of the person as to that person's ability to make decisions, as ascertained by the program planning team or others called upon by and agency, a determination of capability for a specific issue or issues may be made by a Capability Review board. [Emphasis added].

[555] *Matter of Westchester Reform Temple v. Brown,* 28 NY2d 488; *Holy Spirit Assn. for Unification Church v. Carle,* 90 App. Div. 2d 591, 456 NYS2d 195 (3rd Dept., 1982) a case involving a fence exceeding the maximum height.

[556] 42 U.S.C. § 2000bb, 107 Stat. 1488, P.L. 103-141.

to be unconstitutional when it conflicted with local zoning and police powers.[557] However, as Robert Frost said, "Something there is that doesn't love a wall."[558] The church was controversial with town residents who did not worship Elvis. The Town Zoning Board of Appeals, upon the urging of local residents who had objected to its cutting down the stately old cedars when it purchased the property, held that hardship to the church was "self-created" under Town Law § 267(b)(2)(b). In addition the zoning board of appeals denied the application because case law required the height of the wall to be added to the height of the fence, so that in total the combined height would be twenty-two feet—more than three times as high as the ordinance allowed.[559]

The matter came to be heard by Supreme Court Justice Hadley V. Baxendale. He found it ironic that he had before him an instance in which the wall between church and state had been ruled to be illegal. The United States Supreme Court had opined that there should be a wall between church and state,[560] and so has the New York Court of Appeals.[561] The State Liquor Authority has mandated a wall between a church and state licensed hotels serving liquor.[562]

How could something that the constitution requires be ruled to be illegal just because of a Village zoning ordinance? Can a Village Board of Trustees overrule the founding fathers? Can people

---

[557] *Borne, Texas v. Flores,* 117 S. Ct. 2157 (decided June 25, 1997).

[558] "Mending Wall," Robert Frost, *Selected Poems,* Grammercy Press, 1992, p. 87.

[559] see, *Matter of Perlman v Board of Appeals of Vil. of Great Neck Estates,* 73 App. Div. 2d 832, pp. 832 - 833, 570 NYS2d 656, (2nd Dept., 1981).

[560] *Everson v. Board of Education,* 330 US 1, *Mc Collum v. Board of Education,* 333 U.S. 203, *Zorach v. Clauson,* 343 U.S. 306, *Engle v. Vitale,* 370 U.S. 421.

[561] *Zorach v Clauson,* 303 NY 161 at 172.

[562] *Matter of Treadway Birmingham Co. v State Liquor Athy,* 62 Misc 2d 626, 310 NYS2d 565 (Broome Co. S. Ct., 1970), although because the method

who lack the capacity to commit a crime still have the capacity to consent to intercourse?[563]

The judge hastily called a conference in his robing room. When the State and church representatives emerged from his chambers, they each announced their intention to plant large cedar trees[564] on their respective sides of the property line. The Village attorney declared that landscaping was not governed by the zoning code, and was none of the Village's concern. The case was withdrawn.

CONCLUSION

Good trees make good neighbors, too.

---

of measuring the distance between them was not correct, the court reversed the S.L.A.

[563] See Penal Law § 40.15, which makes mental disease or defect an affirmative defense to any crime. Thus a male who is incapable of understanding the nature and consequences of his conduct would have a defense to a charge of statutory rape pursuant to Penal Law § 130.05 when the lack of consent is presumed because the female is mentally defective or mentally incapacitated. But it is a defense that needs to be pleaded and proved, and it does not mean that the police cannot attempt to intervene or prevent a presumed statutory rape of a female who appears to be "consenting" but does not have the capacity to do so.

[564] the church agreed to do so to honor its predecessor.

TOWARD A RECONCILIATION OF SEEMINGLY UNRELATED SUPREME COURT CASES—WARPING AND WOOFING IN THE SEAMLESS WEB[565]

It has been written that the law is a seamless web. Sometimes that requires those of us who are commentators to be deft spiders to weave the Big Picture. The following is an attempt to reconcile two cases some might not have realized were at odds and need reconciliation.[566]

In 1985 the Supreme Court gave us two remarkable precedents that appear unrelated. In the "Minimum Wage for State Employees Case" of *Garcia v. San Antonio Metropolitan Transportation Authority*,[567] the recent precedent of *National League of Cities v. Usury*[568] was overruled. The holding in Garcia may be summarized as follows: The municipal employees of the San Antonio MTA must be paid a minimum wage established by statute not withstanding the fact that the MTA is an intrastate operation,[569] and in spite of the provisions of the Tenth Amendment.

In *Tennessee v. Garner*,[570] the "Right to Flee Case,"[571] the

---

[565] Justice Oliver Wendell Holmes is credited with calling the law a seamless web, although it may have been Frederick Maitland who said it first according to Jeremy Miller, "Rico and the Bill of Rights: An Essay on a Crumbling Utopian Ideal," 104 Com. L. J. 336, 339 n. 13 (1999).

[566] The article that puts the "Silly" back into recon-silly-ation.

[567] 469 U.S. 528, 83 L. Ed. 2d 1016 (1985).

[568] 426 US 833 (1976). Editor's Note: The National League of Cities had different teams playing in when this piece first appeared. San Antonio was not one of them.

[569] But apparently affects interstate commerce if *Heart of Atlanta Motel v. United Sates*, 379 US 241 (1964) case has anything to say about it.

[570] 471 U.S. 1 (1983).

[571] The right to flee may be seen as a penumbra or emanation of the right to

Supreme Court ruled that an unarmed burglar who is fleeing from local the constabulary may not be shot by the local police.[572]

These seemingly unrelated cases suggest a statutory reconciliation. Since may older doctrines are being codified, from the clean hands doctrine[573] to the right to a speedy trial,[574] the solution to the problem is federal legislation.[575] All burglars who flee must necessarily affect interstate commerce, even if their flight is only intrastate. Therefore, all federal employees (The FBI, the CIA, the Secret Service, Postal Workers and clerks for the Social Security Administration) should be permitted to fire at them. An alternative would be to treat burglars as migratory animals under federal law,[576] but then burglars could only be shot when they are in season.

Our second untangling of the seamless web involves anti-trust cases. In the Cable TV Franchise Case[577] the Supreme court ruled

---

travel (which the court said in *Shapiro v. Thompson*, 394 U.S. 618 (1969) at 630 footnote 8 may itself be a penumbra of the Fifth or Fourteenth Amendment, or perhaps the Privileges and Immunities Clause, (Art. IV, Section 2). Then again, maybe it cannot. No one has yet suggested that there is a right to in private by combining the right to privacy with the right to travel. Tell it to a Federal Air Marshall, buddy.

[572] Regardless of how good their aim is.

[573] See New York Public Health Law and 10A NYCRR 14.1 *et. seq.* requiring food service workers to wash their hands.

[574] Criminal Procedure Law § 30.30. It was suggested by Chief Justice Rhenquist in an unreported decision in chambers that we have misinterpreted the Seventh Amendment. He suggested that it does not guarantee the right to a speedy trial. Rather since it reads "In all criminal prosecutions the accused **shall** enjoy the right to a speedy . . . trial . . ." it should be read literally as imposing a duty on the accused if and when he receives a speedy trial to appreciate it whether he likes it or not.

[575] This is wholly in keeping with other occasions upon which federal statutes were written to resolve problems that did not exist.

[576] Federal Migratory Birds Act of 1913, 37 Stat. 847.

[577] *Community Communications Co. v. City of Boulder,* 455 U.S. 40 (1982).

that a city could be sued for an anti-trust violation if it acts in an area where it's activities are essentially as a proprietor as opposed to governmental ones. The court previously ruled that lawyers cannot establish a suggested minimum fee schedule[578] without running afoul of the same anti-trust strictures. This suggests that when states set the fees for assigned counsel as they do under Article 18-b of the County Law they may violate anti-trust laws. They may be required to put each 18-b assignment up for competitive bidding at market rates, particularly where they monopolize the market in low income consumers of legal services in criminal defense work. In addition, since those lawyers are working for a government project, the government is required by Section 220 of the Labor Law to pay prevailing wage rates in the industry. However, the Bar Associations cannot even *suggest* what the prevailing rates are without running afoul of the anti-trust laws, can they?

---

[578] *Goldfrarb v. Virginia State Bar*, 421 US 773 (1975).

EVOLUTION STILL MAKES A TEACHER INTO A MONKEY'S UNCLE

by James M. Rose[579]

A disciplinary proceeding of a teacher which was reviewed by the New York Supreme Court, Appellate Division recently affirmed that a teacher may be prevented from teaching the theory of evolution in New York.[580]

John T. Scopes III is a middle school teacher who was disciplined for misconduct pursuant to New York Education Law §3020-a because he taught the theory of evolution to his class of 7th graders in the newly reconstituted Kiryas Joel Village Indian School. Several of the parents objected and then the Commissioner of Education commenced disciplinary proceedings.

After the United States Supreme Court ruled that a special district for the Satmar Hasidic sect could not be created,[581] Gov. Cuomo signed a bill that allowed the creation of a similar district.[582]

Evolution would normally be studied by the children of a school district as part of their science requirements. While Education Law § 3204 provides that students receive training in a list of subjects that includes science,[583] subdivision 5 of that section allows students to opt out of health related subjects for religious reasons with the approval of the Board of Regents. The bill creating this[584] exemption was passed at the urging of the Christian Science Church, which objected to teaching children about what scientists concluded were the causes and cures of diseases. Recently the Regents and some school districts have refused to permit such exemptions

---

[579] Shop Steward, Union of Unconcerned Scientists.
[580] The case referred to in this article is fictional—for the moment.
[581] *Board of Education of Kiryas Joel Village School District v. Grumet* 512 U.S. 587 (1994), decided June 27, 1994, 54 CCH S. Ct. Bull. B2985.
[582] See, New York *Law Journal*, July 19, 1994 p. 1 col. 2.
[583] Education Law § 3204(3) (a) (1).
[584] L. 1950, c.135.

concerning instruction about AIDS despite religious leaders' objections. The Appellate Division has upheld their exercise of discretion.[585]

The parents of all of the students in the School District in which Mr. Scopes taught had opted out of the health curriculum. They did so for religious reasons, believing that it was not proper to give sex education until the students were on the threshold of marriage.

Similarly, the denizens of the school district believed in the Bible literally.[586] They did not agree that man is descended from the lower animals, but rather they believe that he was created in the manner described in the book of Genesis.[587]

Mr. Scopes argued, however, that the subject of evolution was not health but science. Definitions of health in available dictionaries confirmed what he had asserted.[588] No section of the Education Law permitted opting out of science classes in general, as they formed a part of the required curriculum established by the Education Law.

However, the Commissioner of Education noted in his brief that the school district in which Mr. Scopes taught was not a normal one. It seems that the residents of school district had convinced the Commissioner that they believe they are Indians, because they are the descendants of the Two Unlost Tribes of Israel. The Bible is replete with references to the tribes that constituted the Jewish people.[589]

---

[585] *Ware v. Valley Stream High School District*, 150 App. Div. 2d 14, 545 NYS 2d 316 (2nd Dept., 1989).

[586] See 54 CCH S. Ct. Bull. at B2989.

[587] Kiryas Joel is no relation to Curious George—a fictional primate. "Kiryas" means "village" in the Yiddish dialect spoken by the Satmars. Thus the former name of the school district was a bit redundant, i.e., Joel Village Village School District.

[588] as did the Commissioner of Education's own regulation 8 NYCRR §135 (1) (j).

[589] For example, "You shall appoint magistrates and clerks for your tribes." Deut. 16:18-19.

The residents of the school district argued that Native Americans (referred to in the Education Law as "Indians") were the ten lost tribes of Israel,[590] and were their ethnic brothers, to whom they bore a facial resemblance in the nasal area.[591]

That would mean that the Ultra Orthodox Jewish community was itself an Indian tribe for purposes of the Education Law. Nowhere in that law is an Indian tribe defined.[592]

A separate curriculum for Indian schools is contained in the Education Law. While Education Law § 4105 refers to instruction of Indian children in "the common branches of reading, spelling, writing, arithmetic, English grammar and geography" conspicuous by its absence is any reference at all to science.

The Commissioner of Education concluded that there was no authorization for Mr. Scopes to teach evolution to Indian children. Mr. Scopes argued that although there was no authorization there was also no prohibition against teaching evolution, nor was it in violation of the public policy of the State of New York.[593] The Commissioner disagreed. The public policy of the state of New York is expressed in its statutes.[594] New York Statutes § 240 describes the doctrine of *expressio unius est exclusio alterius*.[595] Where the Legislature has chosen to include science in the list of subjects to be taught in the public schools in Education Law § 3204, and to exclude it from the list of subjects to be taught in Indian schools

---

[590] 2 Kings 17:6.

[591] *Types of Mankind*, Nott & Glidden, Phila. (1854) quoted at footnote 14 of *The Lost Tribes: A Myth*, Orlonsky, New York (1974).

[592] However, for purposes of student aid the term "New York State tribe" is defined in 8 NYCRR § 145-4.1 as any member of the six Iroquoian tribes, or a member of the Shinnecock tribe or Poospatuck tribe. The Satmars are apparently European Indians.

[593] He asked "How could it be improper to teach evolution when the state has adopted an official state fossil—the *Eurypterus remipes* (State Law § 83)?"

[594] *Matter of the Civil Service Employees Association v. Town of Harrison*, 48 NY2d 66, 421 NYS2d 839 (1979).

[595] The specific mention of one thing implies the exclusion of other things.

in Education Law § 4105, the omission must be viewed as intentional. It is thus the public policy of the state of New York that Indian children not be taught science.

The Appellate Division upheld Scopes' disciplinary conviction, but it vacated the penalty imposed because it was unauthorized by the Education Law. The punishment consisted of writing on the blackboard five hundred times "I will not teach that the Commissioner of Education is descended from monkeys."

THE ELECTORAL COLLEGE: ONE PERSON,[596] NO VOTE?

If you think that you have a right to select the president of the United States in the general election, you may be in for a surprise. You do not vote directly for the president and vice president, you vote for people who are designated as their electors. In creating electors to select a president, the framers of the constitution did not use the term "Electoral college" in Art. II § 1 cl. 2. The framers of the Articles of Confederation referred to a convention not a college. But 3 U.S.C. § 4 speaks of an electoral college, as does a case in 1876[597] and 1892.[598] The term found its origins in the debates of the Constitutional convention, and on September 4, 1787 the report of the Committee of Eleven spoke of a presidential election by a college of electors.[599]

In using the term "college" they did not mean an institution with a fight song, homecoming queen, a faculty,[600] and an anthropomorphic mascot[601], but rather a group of persons organized to perform a particular function.[602]

The Electoral College exists so that you will not have an unalienable right to select the next president.

---

[596] Although one hears the phrase "*one man*, one vote," it is not found in the leading case of *Baker v. Kerr* 369 U.S. 186, 82 S.Ct. 691, 7 L. Ed 2d 663 (1962) and shortly thereafter in 1967 the courts were referring to the decision as establishing "one person, one vote" *Penon v. Humphrey* 264 F. Supp. 250 (S.D. Miss. 1967) which is both politically and legally correct because of the passage of the 19th Amendment to the United States Constitution.

[597] *Case of Electoral College*, 8 Fed. Cases 4336, 1 Hughes 571, (Cir. Ct. S. Carolina).

[598] *Mc Pherson v. Blacker*, 146 US 1, 13 S. Ct. 3.

[599] *The Politics of Electoral College Reform*, C. D. Longley (Yale Univ. Press) 1972, p. 25.

[600] which is not to suggest that presidential electors have no faculties.

[601] If the electoral college had a basketball team, what would its nickname be? In a dissenting opinion in *Ray v. Blair*, 343 U.S. 214 (1952) Justice Jackson suggests it might be the Party Lackeys. "Go you Lackeys!"

[602] Bodies of electors for particular offices with which they would have been familiar would include the electors of the Emperor of Germany, such as The

The founding fathers did not trust their children to elect the president directly, and proposals at the Constitutional Convention to select the president by the largest popular vote nation wide were rejected.[603] Instead, the electoral college system was established so that the electors could use their judgment and discretion[604] as to who the best candidate for president would be, whether the voters chose that person or not. A number or electors for each state based upon the total of the state's senators and representatives is "appointed" by the states, in the words of the Constitution. Does this mean that the electors were to be elected themselves? Usually the word "appointed" does not mean elected.

The states were free to select the electors any way they wished. Initially they were selected in their state legislatures. In that way, a voter voted for president only by voting for a state legislator, who selected an elector, who may or may not vote as the voter or his legislator would.

In the first presidential election New York made appointments of electors by its legislature, Virginia divided into districts and the electors were chosen by a district wide rather than state wide election.

In the second presidential election, nine states chose electors by votes of their legislatures, three had at large voting, two had voting for electors by district, and North Carolina selected its electors by permitting only those representatives in the state legislature who represented a particular congressional district vote to for its district's electors.

On April 15, 1829 New York transferred the right to select the electors to the public. South Carolina did not do so until 1860.

Can the elector be compelled to vote for the individual to whom he is apparently pledged by serving as an elector? One court opined that the answer in New York is that the elector could be

---

Elector of Hanover, the prince who became George I; or the College of Cardinals who sound like they *are* an anthropomorphic mascot.

[603] For example on July 25, 1787 in the Constitutional Convention.

[604] See, *Opinion of Justices*, 250 Ala. 399, 34 So. 2d 598 (1948).

compelled by mandamus,[605] although the case stands for the narrower proposition that the names of the electors do not have to appear on the ballot with the candidate to whom they are pledged.

However, electors listed for President Truman who publicly indicated that they would vote for J. Strom Thurmond instead could not be compelled to vote for the candidate for whom they were initially pledged.[606] Because the very system was constructed to allow for the exercise of discretion it was impossible to enjoin that exercise, the court reasoned. The rationale for the Electoral College having receded into the mists of history, its demise would not have impressed Justice Jackson as a disaster, he remarked in *Ray v. Blair*.[607] That case also appears to stand for the proposition that the parties can require their electors to vote for their own candidate.

If the electoral college does not succeed in picking a candidate, the election is then thrown in to the House of Representatives. When this has happened in our past, the results have been potential disasters. And yet, one commentator concludes that the political compromise between direct election of the president and letting the Congress chose him which resulted in the Electoral College was only a temporary expedient because in the first presidential election it was assumed that Washington would gain a majority, and after that it was assumed that there would be no majority among independent electors, resulting in elections routinely being decided by the House.[608]

Procedures for the meeting of the electors are found in Election Law §§ 12-100 to 12-110. The electors are told when they can meet, how they can fill vacancies, elect a president and secretary of the college and when to vote. The get $ 15.00 per day and 13 cents a mile round trip.[609]

Their votes are transmitted in sets of two pursuant to 3 U.S.C. §§ 1 to 18. No fewer than four sets are delivered, showing that

---

[605] *Matter of Thomas v. Cohen*, 146 Misc. 836 (S. Ct., Kings Co. 1933).
[606] *State v. Allbritton*, 251 Ala. 422, 37 So. 2d 640, and *Opinion of Justices, supra*.
[607] *supra*.
[608] Roche, *The Founding Fathers*, p. 811.
[609] Election Law § 12-110.

Congress placed little trust in the mails or the messengers that would be employed. One set is delivered to the president of the U.S. Senate, one set to the secretary of state of the State, one set to the Archivist of the United States, and one set to the judge of the district court in the district where the electors met.

Very detailed procedures for counting the vote are found in 3 U.S.C. § 15 including the seating arrangement, and that the alphabetical order to be used in calling the states shall begin with the letter A.

"One person one vote" does not apply to the presidency[610] where only weighted voting is permitted. There is no right for persons to vote for president at all, as only the states select the president. Therefore, citizens of Guam, who are citizens of the United States have no say in the election of the President because they do not live in a state according to *Attorney General of Guam on Behalf of all U.S. Citizens Qualified to Vote Pursuant to the Organic Act v. United States*.[611]

If the vote for president is close in each state, a vote for a presidential elector in New York has more weight than one in Montana because it can mean the difference of many more electoral votes. On the other hand, if the election is decided by the House of Representatives then each state's delegation to the House of Representatives has one vote apiece. The vote of California's entire delegation can be counter balanced by the vote of the single Vermont congressman, a literal case of "one state, one vote."

---

[610] according to *Penton v. Humphrey, supra.*
[611] 738 F 2d 1017 (9th Cir. 1984); cert. den. 105 S. Ct. 1174, 84 L. Ed. 2d 323.

CHAPTER FIVE

FORMS FOR THE UNINFORMED

THE VERY MODEL OF A MODERN MAJOR GENERAL RELEASE[612]

This form was produced by the Multinational Corporation Protective Council, to protect heartless and bloodless corporations (which are creatures of statute without pride of ancestry or hope of posterity). It was written in cahoots with the Trilateral Commission, and crossed our desk recently with a paltry settlement check.

UNCONDITIONAL SURRENDER TO AND GENERAL RELEASE OF LARGE MULTINATIONAL CORPORATION

TO WHOM IT MAY CONCERN AND OTHERS WHO ARE JUST NOSY:

General Release[613] executed this day of, by Releasor _____ (hereinafter "Really Sore") whose address is 000 Northchester Drive, Nouveau Riche on Hudson, New York, and Humungous Multi National Corporation Inc. (hereinafter "Really Seize") of everywhere and anywhere (Internet address biglie@voracious.org), In consideration of the sum of What Seems Like A Lot To You but is Petty Cash to a Corporation Like Us ($00,000,000.00) less applicable withholding, and other deductions which greatly diminish it (hereinafter "Government's Cut") in (hot little) hand which nowadays is considered **FAIR**

---

[612] by James M. Rose, White Plains, New York. He is not associated with the Rose Law Firm, Little Rock, Arkansas. Use of this release or the words "general release" without the express consent of James M. Rose or Major League Baseball is prohibited.

[613] Release 4.1 3/4.

AND ADEQUATE VALUABLE CONSIDERATION, and other good and sufficient consideration too illegal to mention received from Really Seize, receipt of the legal portion of which is hereby acknowledged and the illegal portion of which is hereby denied, the Really Sore for himself, his alter egos, super ego, id, inner child, his clones, image, reputation, good name, his ghost, shadow, aliases, his A/K/A's, D/B/A's and IOUs, his C.B. handle, all his domain names, his various on line identities, all of his multiple personalities, his DNA or any mutation thereof, his immortal soul, his aura, and his heirs, his executors, administrators, children as yet unborn to the extent that guardians ad litem have not been named for them, his wife to the extent he is permitted to speak for her, his conservators, trustees, committee (including any sub committees), his proxies, his predecessors, closely held corporations, very limited partnerships, his assigns and Zodiac sign,

FOREVER RELEASES, DISCHARGES AND UNCONDITIONALLY SURRENDERS to the Really Seize, its parent corporation and sibling corporations (legitimate and illegitimate), and all of their present, former, and future subsidiaries and affiliates, partnerships, allied foreign entities in strange forms, hidden trusts and tax dodging mechanisms in tax havens, and foreign governments and/or politicians who are in their pockets; and each of them;

ALL OF THEIR PRESENT, former and future officers, directors, employees, agents, representatives, partners, successors, failures, flunkies, sycophants, yes men, henchmen, lackies, toadies, go-fers, toe kissers, brown nosers, apple polishers, boot lickers, lap dogs, myrmidons, spinmeisters, flacks, hacks, buttboys, briefcase carriers, scrubs, bench warmers, retainers, spear carriers, supernumeraries, subordinates, beasts of burden, office temps, per diems, menials, wannabees, hangers on, freeloaders, time servers, water cooler jockeys, clock watchers, photocopy machine romeos, wage slaves, pencil pushers, nit pickers, officious middle managers, bean counters, number crunchers, data processors, computer networkers, amanuenses, navel contemplators, interns, outterns, bureaucrats, wool gatherers, alibi Ikes, no shows, factotums, underlings, serfs, vassals, peons, pawns, indentured servants, pissants, varlets, valets, hirelings, puppets, quislings, parasites, fall guys, duffers, novices, greenhorns, schlemiels, sacrificial lambs, Judas goats, scapegoats, stooges, cannon fodder, straw men, drones, clones, schmoozers, snoozers, boozers, losers, receptionists, deceptionists, eye candy, mercenaries, goons, finks, scabs, operatives, informers, stool pigeons, jackals, hit men, condottieri, front men, tortfeasors, accomplices, co-conspirators, chums, cronies, retinues, poker buddies, entourages, posse, apologists, spinmeisters, caddies, astrologers, money launderers, shills, Swiss Bankers, mouthpieces, pettifogers, consigliari, scriveners, sophists, rogues, flotsam and jetsam, significant others, insignificant others, dependents, co-dependents, independent contractors including their undocumented aliens working off the books, and assigns, RICO, ERISA, OSHA, and each of them jointly and severally,

FROM AND AGAINST any and all claims, demands, causes of action, alleged dues and/or don'ts, obligations, onuses, requirements, mandates, accounts, extents, exposures, jeopardies, or liabilities of any kind whatsoever (whether legal or equitable, illegal or inequitable, moral or immoral); be they contractual, tortious or tortuous;

WHETHER (OR NOT) SUCH CLAIM IS PURSUANT TO common law, canon law, maritime law, case law, or federal, state, local, international, and interplanetary law (or anarchy) created by statute, Constitution, Administrative agency or Authority, regulation, rule, covenant, by law or by-law, charter, house rule, treaty, compact, concord, tontine, deal, pledge, perk, privilege, habit, custom, fashion, protocol, dogma, public opinion, prevailing style, usage, birthright, heritage, religion, societal norm or established pecking order, or because mom says so and she's your mom; no matter how they are alleged to have arisen which Really Sore now has or has ever had, or ever imagined to have against Really Seize by reason of any act, occurrence, omission, transaction, transgression, infraction, booboo, shakedown, rumor, insinuation, innuendo, thought, perceived slight (Real or imagined, conscious, subconscious or unconscious presently known or unknown, even if the memory of the same is presently psychologically repressed or known only to God), of Really Seize whether compensable or preposterous, from the time when the Universe was just a twinkling in the Creator's eyes up to and including the date of this release and until the cows come home and thereafter,

ARISING OUT OF OR RELATED TO the claim against Really Seize in a summons and complaint dated the day of 20__ or any claim which arises from, was made or could have been made, or could not have been made upon the facts related therein, or is in any way related to that claim by any stretch of the imagination; now and forever, to have and to hold (and to release), for better or for worse, in sickness and in health, for richer and for poorer,

AND FURTHER RELEASES AND WAIVES any claim concerning this agreement and the contents hereof, including but not limited to claims that this release was procured by fraud and deceit, overreaching, coercion, creative accounting, a media campaign, or because of the mental condition of the Really Sore (or lack thereof) that could be made in any forum including but not limited to in therapy or on a talk show. Really Sore is advised pursuant to the Older Workers Benefits Protection Act, the Age Discrimination in Employment Act (29 U.S.C.§ 621), and the Lawyer and Accountant Full Employment Act you have a right to consult with an attorney before signing this agreement. You have twenty one (21) days from the date of receipt of this agreement to consider your fate. If you sign this agreement you have seven (7) days in which to revoke this agreement, and if you do this agreement will be of no force and effect, and your attorney and Really Seize will descend upon you with both feet. No payments will be made to you until this seven (35) day period has expired. Really Sore affirmatively represents that before signing this agreement he has consulted an attorney, at least three legal advice websites, a physician, a psychiatrist, a substance abuse counselor, a spiritual leader, the Psychic Hotline, a guru, a palm reader, his know-it-all brother-in-law, the Oracle at Delphi, N.Y. and a registered Astrologer. Really Sore affirmatively asserts that he is not suffering from any condition that would prevent him from understanding what he is doing any more than any of the rest of us, and that he is not currently under the influence of any drug (legal or illegal), any alcoholic beverage, a sugar high, or any charlatan, guru, cult leader or radio waves generated by alien beings in a manner that prohibit him from comprehending in excruciating detail all the multi-layered nuances of this agreement.

Really Sore AGREES THAT this release is in Plain Language **AND BIG ENOUGH TYPE TO READ.** Really Sore represents he has read this agreement thoroughly and diligently, looking up all of the big words he did not understand in a dictionary approved by the American Librarian's Association, agrees with all the provisions of it, and is tickled pink to sign it just as it is. Really Sore affirmatively states that he has been told by an astrologer/chiropractor that Really Sore is signing on an auspicious day when the stars and his spinal column are properly aligned. Really Sore promises to think only kind thoughts about Really Seize. The parties agree that nothing contained herein is an admission of anything whatsoever by Really Seize, including but not limited to admissions that Really Seize exists at all, and anyone who says so is itching for a fight.

REALLY SORE agrees to cooperate fooly with REALLY SEIZE in its defense of any claim in any forum by perjury if necessary, and to hold REALLY SEIZE harmless for any and all claims. REALLY SORE AGREES that the terms of this settlement are CONFIDENTIAL and are on a need-to-know basis. Since there are some provisions of this general release that REALLY SEIZE believes REALLY SORE does not need to know, REALLY SORE has not been shown them. Should the terms of this agreement leak to the public even if it is not the fault of REALLY SORE, then REALLY SORE will forfeit the VALUABLE CONSIDERATION mentioned herein to Really Seize together with inflated costs and the exorbitant legal fees and unjustifiably padded expenses paid by Really Seize to several unctuous firms of attorneys.

THIS RELEASE may not be modified orally, in writing, electronically, telepathically or any other way. It shall be effective immediately upon its execution nunc pro tunc. WORDS USED in their singular sense shall also encompass the pluralistic and vice versa. Words of the male gender shall also include malefactors where appropriate, as well as refer to the female gender without gender neutering. Words used in the present tense shall also include the past and future tense, but not the conditional or subjunctive tense unless so interpreted by Really Seize. Rules of Grammar shall apply only where they are applicable. Rules of Punctuation and Capitalization shall apply RANDOMLY. There are no section headings in this release. If there were section headings, they would be illustrative only, and would not form a part of the agreement. The provisions of this agreement are severable (as is Really Sore). If any portion of this agreement is held to be unenforceable or invalid (or Really Sore is held to be an invalid) it will not affect the unconscionablity of the remaining portions thereof.

REALLY SEIZE may then pick and choose which portions of this agreement it will honor. Should Really Seize believe that Really Sore has violated, will violate, or is thinking of violating the terms of this release, Really Seize may commence an action. Venue for such action shall be the Court of the Star Chamber. The Laws of the Pack shall be the only law applicable to this agreement. Really Sore waives service of process in any such action, waives trial by jury and consents to trial by wombat,[614] the entry of an immediate default judgment in favor of Really Seize, and immediate execution of any judgment obtained therefrom by seizure of all of Really Sore's assets in the middle of the night by human waves of repo men.

{This space left unintentionally blank}

---

[614] Possibly a typographical error which should read "combat.".

IN WITNESS WHEREOF after profusely swearing an oath the REALLY SORE has hereto and thereto etcetera, etcetera, yatta yatta yatta set REALLY SORE'S hand and seal, made his mark and affixed his logo with the blood out of his veins this _____day of_____ in a manner notoriously public.
     I REALLY MEAN THIS:

_____

     REALLY SORE, his mark

Before me this____day of _____20 appeared_____, the REALLY SORE herein who showed me three (6) forms of photographic identification and left me a DNA sample and 25 cents (two bits) and who acknowledged that he is the REALLY SORE herein, and that he is absolutely thrilled with this settlement which I witnessed him sign.[615]

_____

Notary Public

INSTRUCTIONS TO REALLY SORE: Please execute yourself in front of a notary, and return to us in triplicate in this envelope.

---

[615] The author gratefully acknowledges the assistance of *Roget's Thesaurus* in the preparation of this release.

THE REVISED REQUEST FOR JUDICIAL INTERFERENCE FORM: BACK DESPITE POPULAR DEMAND[616]

Despite requests from the Office of Court Administration not to publish this form, as a public service to the bar, this publication has reproduced below the RJI (Request for Judicial Interference) form given to certain privileged attorneys who want the court to know the *important* information about their cases.

If you have to ask the fee for filing this form, you cannot afford it.

---

[616] by James M. Rose. Mr. Rose is in private practice in White Plains, New York. His practice is so private that he has an unlisted internet address. He is the author of "Reasonable Accommodations in the Workplace That Employers Must Afford Employees who call in Dead under the Americans With Disabilities Act."

REQUEST FOR JUDICIAL INTERFERENCE REV 1/00
         INDEX NO.
   COURT   COUNTY   DATE PURCHASED

PLAINTIFFS:

DEFENDANTS:

For Clerk's Eyes Only

[ ] File in circular file
[ ] E-Z Pay lane

IAS Entry Date

[ ] Date lost papers relocated

Judge Assigned
[ ] By Whom and How

R J I Date
[ ] Needs jury of lawyers
[ ] Needs jury from O.J. Simpson case

Date Retainer Agmt. Signed_____   Press Release Served (Y/N)_____.

NATURE OF JUDICIAL INTERFERENCE (check one box only and enter information)
[ ] Twist Plaintiff or Defendant's arm   [ ] Notice of golf outing_____
[ ] Yell at other side for daffy theory   [ ] Bar Ass'n business_____
[ ] Run up the Fee_____)   [ ] Complain about delays/business/clients
[ ] Review 10 lbs. of discovery demands   [ ] Young att'y needs practice
[ ] Order to show cause (clerk enter retirement date here_____) [ ] Chew the fat with other attys
[ ] Writ of habeas retainer   [ ] Pro Se Gibberish_____
[ ] Other ex parte application   [ ] Let trial judge know of juicy gossip

NATURE OF ACTION OR PROCEEDING (check ONE box only)
MATRIMONIAL   **TORTS**
[ ] Vicious Contested- VC   Malpractice   -%
[ ] Uncontested piece of cake-- POC   [ ] Religious   -REL
[ ] Contested Until money runs out--SEMI   [ ] Judicial   --JUD
                                              [ ] Botched Plastic Surgery -UGLI
COMMERCIAL   [ ] Faulty Breast and/or Penile Implant--SEX
[ ] Contract-Who on_____?--$$ [ ] Fiery Rear End Collision-- OUCH
[ ] Big Multi- Nat'l Corp --BMC   [ ] Carrier Won't Pay   00%
[ ] Corp. Small Mom & Pop-- SM&P   set forth % won't pay_____
[ ] Big Mother Class Action--PONZI   [ ] Environmental   -- TREE
[ ] No Class Action   --OCLAS   [ ] Imaginary   --IMG
[ ] Loan Company Collection --COLL   [ ] Id/Ego Bruise   --BOOBOO
                                            [ ] Libel/Slander   --PRIVL
[ ]* Other Commercial   OC   republish in this space_____
Indicate length of commercial_____   [ ] Other Tort (including
                                                Linzer)   YUM
REAL PROPERTY   **SPECIAL PROCEEDINGS**
[ ] Crazy/Greedy Landlord or tenant -CGL   [ ] Money Launder Scheme -- MLS
[ ] Violation of Plaintiff's Space--SV   [ ] Suit to impress Trust or Big Client--BIGC
OTHER MATTERS   [ ] Disinter Body for Tabloid TV Tests - BOD
[ ] Frivolous Lawsuit/Publicity Stunt--FRIV [ ] Election Law -- ULOSE
[ ] Penumbra of Bill of Rights--CIVLIB   [ ] Guardianship MHL Art. 81-- NUT
[ ] Post Hypnotic Trauma---PHT   [ ] Change Name and/or Baby --CHA
[ ] Declare Someone Legally Dead --DEAD   [ ] Revoke Gun Nut's Permit- BANG
[ ] OTHER_____ _____ - OTH   [ ] Claim of Govmt Entitlement-- TAX$
[ ] NOT OTHER__ _____ -ZILCH   [ ] Revoke Witness Protection--OHOH

Check "YES," "NO" or "MAYBE" for each of the following questions:

Is this an action/proceeding against a

YES	NO	MAYBE	YES	NO	MAYBE		
[ ]	[ ]	[ ] Deep Pocket	[ ]	[ ]	[ ] Public Figure?		Bankrupt:?
(specify_____)					specify if Tabloids will show up____)		[ ] No
[ ]	[ ]	[ ] Does the action /proceeding seek big bucks?					
[ ]	[ ]	[ ] Does the action /proceeding seek recovery for inner child's psychic trauma?					
[ ]	[ ]	[ ] Does the action /proceeding involve obstreperous attorneys?					
[ ]	[ ]	[ ] Does the action /proceeding require a judge with math or science skills?					

<u>All Cases Except Contested Matrimonials</u>

Estimated time period for case to be ready for trial (from filing of RJI to determination of frivolous appeals. Estimate with greater accuracy than a body shop does for insurance purposes)

[ ] 0-60 Months   [ ] Never   [ ] When current IAS judge retires

<u>Contested Matrimonials Only</u>: Check and make date with court clerk
     Have spouses cooled down?   [ ] No   [ ] Yes Date_____
     Have original attorneys been replaced yet? [ ] No [ ] Yes Date_____

<u>ATTORNEY (S) FOR PLAINTIFF (s): NAMES,   ADDRESSES   CELL PHONE NUMBERS</u>

<u>ATTORNEY (S) FOR DEFENDANTS (s): NAMES   ADDRESSES BEEPER NUMBERS/WEBSITE</u>

Parties appearing <u>pro se</u> should enter information in spaces provided above for foolish clients.

<u>INSURANCE OR DISEASE CARRIERS:</u>

PARTIES RELATED TO LITIGANTS PRESS SHOULD KNOW ABOUT: (IF NONE Write Newspaper "Help" column instead of entering info in space provided below)
     <u>Big Shot</u>   <u>Nature of Relationship</u>

I AFFIRM UNDER PENALTY OF PERJURY THAT, OTHER THAN AS NOTED ABOVE, TO THE BEST OF MY FAILING MEMORY AND UNDER THE PROTECTIONS AFFORDED ME BY THE FIFTH AMENDMENT AND <u>MIRANDA V. ARIZONA</u>, WITHOUT CHECKING MY FILES I REALLY CANNOT SAY THAT THE OPPOSITE MAY NOT ALSO BE TRUE.

Dated: _____
                                       (Signature)

                                       _____
                                       Partner with Corner Office

                                       _____
                                       Attorney for/against

Attach rider sheets if necessary to provide inadmissible evidence, hearsay, or ad hominem complaints about opposing counsel.

INSTRUCTIONS: **Please execute yourself in triplicate and return to the clerk in a sealed envelope. Then clerk will stamp.**

AGREEMENT FOR THE SALE OF BODY TO SCIENCE AND LEASE BACK FOR TAX PURPOSES

by James M. Rose[617]

Recently this form was faxed to us by a client. We share it with you since it is such a useful item.

WITNESSETH,[618].
AGREEMENT made this day of, 20 between:

1. Party of the fewer parts, LES E., (hereinafter "LES E.") and Party of the Greater parts, SCIENCE, INC., (Hereinafter occasionally referred to as "Less Sore"), For the good and sufficient consideration of $_____ in hand:

1. *CASH SALE OF BODY TO SCIENCE CLAUSE*[619]
LES E. hereby agrees to sell his body to Science, Inc.

1. *LEASE BACK OF BODY FOR FURTIVE PURPOSES CLAUSE*
LES E. hereby agrees to rent back his body (hereinafter "the Corpus") from SCIENCE, INC. for $_____ per month plus nominal service charges, usurious interest charges for overdue payments, state and local taxes, cost of lien filings, and dealer prep) and thereby obtain whatever taxes benefits he can obtain therefrom, including writing off his overhead to maintain the corpus and his monthly payments to rent the body back from SCIENCE for tax purposes.

1. *ALL RIGHTS RESERVED CLAUSE*
SCIENCE reserves all rights if any to depreciation on LES E.'s body as inventory of its Body Shoppe under applicable Internal

---

[617] White Plains, New York. Mr. Rose is a minor domo.
[618] Why is Seth always the witness on these things?
[619] Section headings are for purposes of misleading the authorities, and do not form a part of the agreement.

Revenue Code, regulations, rev rulings, and internal memoranda, including some known only to attorneys with LLM's in tax law. SCIENCE reserves to itself all the rights LES E. would have if he had still owned his body, such as the right to privacy, the right to publicity, all Constitutional rights including *habeas corpus* and the right to remain silent, any rights not yet spelled out by the United States Supreme Court under the penumbras of any amendment thereto, and to any conjugal rights enjoyed by LES E.

LESS SORE specifically reserves all gas, water and mineral rights in LES E., and the right to patent any valuable genes found in his DNA.

Should LES E. sell his blood for cash, SCIENCE shall be entitled to the money as estover.

Out of body experiences during the leasehold remain the property of Les E.

1. **SOUL PROPRIETOR CLAUSE**

LES E. retains the rights to his soul to sell separately to SCIENCE's subsidiary FAUST INDUSTRIES.

1. **POLICY STATEMENT CLAUSE**

LES E. agrees to keep the corpus insured for more than it's worth and SCIENCE, INC. shall be the beneficiary of any such insurance.

7. **WAIVER OF UNWAIVABLE RIGHTS CLAUSE.**

Les E. makes no warranties upon the sale of his body including but not limited to warranties of fitness (either physical or for a particular purpose) under the Uniform Commercial Code or any other law, including regulations of the Department of Agriculture governing the sale or lease of livestock.

Les E. hereby waives any and all statutory rights including unwaivable rights concerning unconscionability and other consumer protections passed by over intrusive governments.

8. **IT AIN'T THE INITIAL COST, IT'S THE UPKEEP CLAUSE**

Les E. makes no representations as to last year's maintenance charges for his body, and in disclosing the cost of food, shelter, medical charges and the like to LESS SORE prior to the sale and lease back makes no representations that the maintenance costs for this year will be similar to those for last year.

8. *BATTERIES NOT INCLUDED CLAUSE*

The corpus is leased "as is," subject to normal wear and tear and reasonable mileage. Les E. agrees not to place himself in stressful situations, nor take out of the ordinary risks that would imperil the corpus such as walking through Central Park after dark where the corpus would be subject to battery.

9. *A WAIST IS A TERRIBLE THING TO MIND CLAUSE*

Les E. agrees to limit his wild weekends to two (2) per year, and limit his intake of polysaturated fats. Consequently this contract shall not be governed by the Bulk Sales Act.

10. *UP A CREEK WITHOUT A PADDLE CLAUSE*

LESS SORE agrees not to sell this obligation or LES E.'s corpus up stream to any member of the opposite sex such as FANNY MAY, or to research institutions looking for spare parts for scientific experiments, or to rich celebrities looking for replacement livers, etc.

11. *WAIVER OF POSSESSORY SECURITY INTEREST BY LES E. AND ANY GHOSTS OR SPIRITS THAT MIGHT POSSESS HIM*

LES E. waives his rights (if any) to allege in any court of law that LESS SORE was required to maintain possession of LES E.'s body (corporeally or spiritually) to perfect a security interest therein, and agrees to hold his corpus in trust (Nevertheless) for SCIENCE, and hereby appoints the CEO of SCIENCE, INC., FRED DOPPELGANGER, as the sole trustee of said trust. The corpus of the trust shall be the corpus of LES E.

A separate trust indenture shall be executed on the corpus, however LES E. shall not be considered an indentured servant nor executed.

12. TERM LIMITS

This agreement shall last for better or worse, in sickness and in health, for richer or poor and for as long as LES E. shall live, so help him G-d.

13. SANTA CLAUSE

The law of the (ice) pack shall be the only law applicable to this agreement.

14. VENUE

Ven you get into town again, give me a call and we'll do lunch.

15. WHEREFORE CLAUSE

WHEREFORE, and therefore with pen in hand, etcetera, etcetera, and so forth, yattta, yatta, yatta, this agreement is hereby signed sealed and delivered.

_____

LES E.   LES SORE

If there is a problem with this fax transmission call us or AAMCO at 1-800-FIX TRAN

REALLY IMPORTANT CONFIDENTIALITY NOTICE

This fax transmission is intended only for the people we intended it for and not for you if you are not the person we intended it for—Ca-pish? It contains matters of client confidentiality and privileged information of the type people who can afford to retain attorneys who send faxes possess, and could go to jail for if that information ever came to light. If the reader of this message is not the person who it was intended for because our old failing eyes could not read the tiny type that fax numbers are printed in on the engraved letterhead of some pompous law firm to which we meant to send this stop reading it right now. Put it down. Why have you continued to read it after we told you not to?

YOU are hereby notified that disseminating this information in any way (such as placing it on your web site) or reproducing it in any form without the express permission of the sender and major league baseball is strictly prohibited. If you do we will sue you until you burst.

If you are the deli to which we fax our lunch order daily, please hustle it up and don't forget the napkins.

JAMES M. ROSE

STANDARD FORM SIDE LETTERS FOR OUTSIDE COUNSEL

by James M. Rose[620]

The opposite of "in house counsel" is not "out house counsel," but outside counsel. Outside counsel are often called upon to draft "Side Letters" to protect their client's side of the deal when the client needs to have a little something on the side. Without one, the client would have to worry about the parol evidence rule[621] which almost cost the Devil his deal with Shoeless Joe Hardy in *Damn Yankees*.

Portions of this piece of urban folklore come to us from an anonymous source by way of Cleveland, which seems to somehow enhance its hilarity.

STANDARD FORM SIDE LETTER

_____, 19____

To: _____
_____
_____

Re: Contract of Even Date
Ladies and Gentlemen:

In reference to the Contact of even date (Hereinafter referred to as the "Apparent Deal"), this letter sets forth the further understanding of the parties (Hereinafter referred to as the "Real Deal"). This Real Deal, is, of course, sincerely meant by the parties, but shall be enforceable in the manner indicated below (Check where appropriate):

---

[620] White Plains, New York. Because Mr. Rose is the author of *New York Vehicle and Traffic Law*, he refers to himself as a Roads Scholar.

[621] Not the parole evidence rule, which is Executive Law § 259-i (2)(c) and the Regulations of the State Division of Parole.

_____ Not at all.

_____ By the Same means as the Apparent Deal.

_____ By the withholding of future business.

_____ By strong, leather clad youths with sticks.

_____ By circumventing the parties mentioned in the non-circumvention provisions of the Apparent Deal.

_____ By revealing details of the Real Deal to various governmental investigating agencies.

_____ By notification to defaulting party's spouse of events occurring after signing ceremony.

_____ By unspecified means too hideous to mention.

Considering the parties have entered into the Apparent Deal without realizing the implications of the Worst Case, the parties now declare the Real Deal as follows: (Check one or more as appropriate):

_____ The Apparent Deal is off.

_____ Only the Apparent Deal will be publicly disclosed.

_____ Copies of this agreement will be signed, initialed and destroyed.

_____ All monetary amounts expressed in the Apparent Deal hereby are increased/decreased by a factor of _____.

_____ Expressions of mandatory commitments in the Apparent Deal hereby are declared to be only Best Efforts.

_____ The terms "Buyer" and "Seller" in the Apparent Deal are hereby reversed.

_____ Clauses_____ through_____ of the Apparent Deal are in there only to show to the Boards of Directors of the parties, but form no part of the Real Deal.

_____ Either party may cancel or assign any obligation in the Apparent Deal retroactively.

_____ Undisclosed personal fees and commissions

are payable to negotiators of the Apparent Deal as follows_____.

The above Real Deal is further subject to the provisions of the hereto attached Side Letter (the "True Real Deal") and the thereto attached Side Letter (the "Only True Real Deal"). The provisions of the Apparent Deal, the Real Deal, the True Real Deal, and the Only True Real Deal constitute the entire agreement of the parties, except as otherwise mutually understood and signified by a Wink and a Nod.

Very truly yours,

Firm:_____
By:_____
Title:_____

(Check One)

____ Agreed and accepted.
____ Read, but not understood.
____ Yes, but if asked I will deny.
____ Signed under duress.

Firm:_____ By:_____
Title_____
Firm:_____ By:_____
Title_____

CHAPTER SIX

"HOW LONG IS A TRIAL?"

"HOW LONG IS A PIECE OF STRING?"

CAN COURTS LEGISLATE POLITENESS FOR LAWYERS?

Chief Judge Kaye recently revealed her proposed code intended to make even litigators[622] polite in court.[623] The new set of rules is the Courtesy & Politeness Lawyer's Rules, or the C&PLR for short. It is modeled after the Code of Chivalry, which some of the current bar elders may recall was in force when they began practicing law back when they were citing the Code of Hammurabi. It takes some of its provisions, and a lot of inspiration, from the Geneva Convention for the Treatment of Prisoners of War, and other provisions from the Marquis of Queensbury Rules for Boxing, but it also draws inspiration from such diverse rules as the Infield Fly Rule, Newton's Third Law of Motion, and the Rule in Shelley's Case.

Getting lawyers to behave reminded some of what one wit said about a bear that is taught to ride a unicycle—what makes it an achievement is not that it is done *well*, but that it can be done at all.

The C&PLR is a first rather tentative step, like a peace treaty between warring Middle East nations. If lawyers can be made to

---

[622] "Litigator" is a word composed of two parts "Liti" from the Latin for "little;" and "Gator," short for alligator. In court these "small alligators" have displayed the manners of primitive reptiles at feeding time.

[623] "Thou Shalt not Disparage the Other Side's Lawyer," New York *Times*, July 13, 1997 p. 19 col. 4. The article reports that the code is to govern court clerks and other court personnel as well, the Chief Judge having determined that more is needed than placing the word "civil" in the job description of certain court clerks in order to achieve her goals of "courtliness."

cease hostilities, more ambitious steps will be undertaken later. So in additon to paying attention to Bar dues, lawyers will now have to pay attention to bar don'ts as well.

There have always been rules governing lawyer's conduct such as the Code of Professional Responsibility. Things like "tasteful" lawyer's advertising are mentioned in it. For example, lawyers should not print up bumper stickers that say "My lawyer [insert name here] can beat up your lawyer," or "Need a will? Leave it to me!" Television advertisements sponsoring "Baywatch" re-runs in which loud announcers in loud ties frantically urge the public to call "Discount Dick" Esq. at 1-800-CHEAP SUIT are frowned upon.

Federal and state court rules currently ban frivolous suits, but not frivolous ties, or ties with insulting hidden pictographs when read sideways.

The proposed code would prohibit lawyers from insulting their opponents in Latin phrases that they cannot spell. Statements in affidavits attacking the attorney on the other side will not be accepted by the courts unless accompanied by facts sworn to by someone with direct knowledge—and conclusory insults will be rejected.

If it becomes absolutely essential to say nasty things about the opposition, [624] do not do it in an undignified manner. Remember that "dig" is but the first syllable of dignity.

When holding the door for your opponent it is considered unacceptable to let it slip "accidently." The minority report believed it to be acceptable to throw your briefcase in a pre trial deposition to emphasize an objection, as long as you don't hit anyone with it. However intentional sneezing during your opponent's summation is frowned upon—unless done with a monogrammed handkerchief.

The code also defines burdensome discovery demands as those

---

[624] Remember the old saw you learned in law school, "If you have the facts on your side argue the facts, if you have the law on your side argue the law, and if you have neither argue *ad hominem*."

requiring the production of documents which exceed in weight the ability of the requesting attorney to clean and jerk or bench press the documents that comply.

Judge Kaye is known for previously instituting rules against attorneys having sex with their clients. That rule has been a hardship for attorneys who have been representing their spouses in various forums, not to mention what it has done to the sex lives of attorneys who have been appearing *pro se*.

Attorneys are required to answer telephone calls from clients promptly, even if it only means a tenth of a billable hour will result. Lawyers whose cell phones or beepers disrupt the court can be held *in communicado*. If they violate the rule a second time, the court can increase the power of their vibrating pagers to deliver a nasty electric shock.

At the end of the trial the parties are required to line up and shake hands in the manner of a Stanley Cup playoff. When you do, you had better check to see if your wedding ring is still there when you finish. Carrying the successful party around the courtroom overhead in the manner of the Stanley Cup is considered gauche, however.

Lawyers who violate these rules will be sent to try cases in the newly created Acrimonial Part, to be presided over by Judge May A. Culpa.[625] Attorneys who are impolite to their adversaries may be ordered to pick up their opponent's bar tab, or go to politeness indoctrination and re-education camp, or even perform community service by doing *pro bono* work. Prior to this, Justice Culpa dealt with an attorney[626] who disturbed a courtroom with his antics. She ordered him to enroll in a twelve step program to prove his "fitness to practice law." Unfortunately he entered a twelve "Step Aerobic" program to demonstrate his physical fitness, and while dancing up the courthouse steps to the tune of "Stairway to Heaven"

---

[625] When we asked what she was trying now, we were told "the patience of a saint."

[626] Described in the reports as a Mr. Toomler from the firm of Gonnif, Kvetch and Toomler.

he slipped a disc, and recently sent a notice of claim to the Office of Court Administration.

Opponents of the code[627] are mounting several legal challenges, claiming that the code discriminates against the courtesy impaired,[628] and certain older attorneys who have earned their living by creating chaos for many years and are "too old to learn new tricks" (or to give up their old ones).[629]

There is another problem that may delay the implementation of the rules. Although God had only Ten Commandments, there is already a thick pamphlet containing rules that govern the behavior of members of the bar. Volume Twenty-two of the New York Code of Rules and Regulations contains a multitude of provisions from a variety of sources, all of which a practicing attorney must comply with; including the Rules of the Chief Judge (22 NYCRR § 1.0 to 80.1);[630] Rules of the Chief Administrator of the Courts (22 NYCRR § 80.0 to 136.11), Uniform Rules for New York State Trial Courts (22 NYCRR § 200.1)[631] to Rules of the Court of Appeals (§§ 500.1 to 540.1), Rules of each Appellate Divisions (§§ 600.1 to 1100); Disciplinary Rules of the Code of Professional Responsibility (§§ 1200.1 to 1200.47); Special Rules for Procedure for Attorney's in Domestic Relations Matters (§§ 1400.1 to 1400.7), and Rules of the Ethics Commission for the Unified Court System (§7400 *et. seq.*) to name only more than a few. In addition

---

[627] Who say its is about as necessary as an appendix transplant.

[628] Who suffer from C.D.D., or "Courtesy Deficit Disorder."

[629] This is not to say that only older attorneys are discourteous. An attorney of the author's acquaintance has been writing a book to be titled *SOB's of the New York Bar* for two decades. Every time he thinks he is finished, he encounters another practitioner the exclusion of whom would make the work less than definitive.

[630] Which deal with such subjects as the color schemes suggested for courts (§ 34.1) and how often the ventilation system outlets must be cleaned § 34.1 (11)—showing that the Chief Judge's concerns encompass not only the Bar but also the grilles!

[631] These rules concern more than the topic of how uniforms are to be worn.

there are local court rules as well, such as the Uniform District, City, Civil and Criminal, and Justice Court Acts.

Until a spot opens up in the existing rules there appears to be no place to put the new rules!

WHY LAWYERS ARE ADVISING "TRESPASSERS MUST SHOOT RATS" SIGNS FOR CRACK HOUSES

by James M. Rose[632]

Of sex and drugs or hunting and real estate, the law clearly gives a preference to the latter pair as a case recently made clear.

John Di Generette,[633] the landlord and owner [634] of a notorious crack house in a dilapidated neighborhood was sued by Mr. John Smith.[635] The complaint alleged that Mr. Smith came onto the property to hunt for a notorious young lady named Jesse Belle[636] and join her in the pastimes for which the residence became infamous at the local precinct house. It developed in discovery that they included commercial sex, drugs, and shooting large rats that lived there.

John was injured when the stairwell he was standing in collapsed because of "poor"[637] maintenance. He cited in his motion for summary judgment all the usual law concerning the fact that he was on the premises (his status and that of Ms. Belle as invitees,

---

[632] White Plains, New York. I would like to thank my colleagues who were so generous with their suggestions after having read a draft of this piece. The errors and mistakes in this piece are attributable entirely to their meddling, and not to me.

[633] Of the real estate firm of Gow Jing & Di Generette.

[634] Through an intricate series of corporations, off shore trusts, and proxies. Men's Ray Inc. was a corporation in whose name the deed was registered. Men's Ray was a wholly owned subsidiary of Old Boy's Network, Inc. Old Boy's network had as its principal shareholder Men's Ray, Inc., which thus was a subsidiary of itself!

[635] A fictitious name for publication, although he often signed the guest register at sleazy motels with that very name.

[636] Also a fictitious name taken as a street name by a young woman with a Biblical bent.

[637] i.e., there was none.

licensees, or trespassers now making no difference in the eyes of the law),[638] that a duty was owned to him, and that through the negligence of the landlord and owner he was injured.

He alleged that stairways do not collapse of their own accord unless negligence is involved, and even cited the doctrine of *res ipsa loquitur*.[639] He noted that the owner made no attempt to bar people from the premises, and hence should be held liable for the consequences.

Di Jenerrete's attorney, Harry Ditament,[640] had a unique defense and so demurred to the complaint. It seems, he said, that Mr. John was engaging in what has become to be known as recreational sex and recreational drug use. The Courts of New York have recognized those terms. For example: "The mantle of constitutional protection surrounding personal intimacy is not, therefore, limited to married persons. It attaches to the individual not the relationship, and protects the individual's right to engage in nonprocreative, recreational sex."[641]

Sex for a fee is recreational, not procreational sex. Typically, it is the female participant who receives the fee. The arguments that prostitution harms the public health, safety or welfare do not withstand constitutional scrutiny. It may be that it is the fact that a woman is accepting a fee for recreational, sexual services that triggers the governmental intrusion upon this private consensual sexual conduct.[642]

The Appellate Division has noted "As for defendant's admitted "recreational" use of cocaine, it is settled that a witness may be

---

[638] *Sega v. State*, 89 App. Div 2d 412, 456 NYS2d 856, aff'd 60 NY2d 183, 469 NYS2d 51, 456 N.E.2d 1174, rearg. denied 61 NY2d 670, 472 NYS2d 1028, 460 N.E. 2d 232.

[639] Even though this column has copyrighted those words and they cannot be cited in motions without the express permission of the Westchester County Bar Association.

[640] of the law firm of Harry Ditament & Things.

[641] *Matter of P,* 92 Misc 2d 62, at 67, 400 NYS2d 455 (1977).

[642] *Id.,* at 81.

cross-examined with respect to specific immoral, vicious or criminal acts which have a bearing on the witness's credibility"[643] and "Claimant now admits that he began experimenting with cocaine at the time his work began to deteriorate, that he went from a recreational user to "becoming hooked", and went from "snorting" to "free basing," but never told his employer."[644]

Likewise the Legislature has recognized reluctantly the existence of this recreational activity when it said "The legislature does not encourage or condone the recreational use of marihuana or any other drug."[645]

Dating without sex or commercial sex, however has not been recognized by the Appellate Division as a recreational activity as defined by the Labor Law:[646]

"We are not at all persuaded by the Supreme Court's effort to force "a dating relationship" within the definition of "recreational activities" (Labor Law § 201-d [1] [b]) and accordingly reverse so much of its order as denied the motion to dismiss the first cause of action. Labor Law § 201-d (1) (b) defines "recreational activities" as meaning: "any lawful, leisure-time activity, for which the employee receives no compensation and which is generally engaged in for recreational purposes, including but not limited to sports, games, hobbies, exercise, reading and the viewing of television, movies and similar material".

The landlord then referred the court to *Iannotti v Consolidated Rail*[647] in which a statute to protect landlords, General Obligations Law § 9-103, is discussed. That law holds that landowners who allow persons to come onto their property for specified recreational

---

[643] in *Simon v Indursky*, 211 App. Div. 2d 404 (1st Department, 1995).
[644] *Matter of Kuehn (American Tel. & Communications Corp.-Hartnett)*, 174 App. Div. 2d 776, 570 NYS2d 722 (3rd Dept., 1981).
[645] Legislative findings and statement of purpose, (L 1977, ch 360, § 1.)
[646] See, *State v Wal-Mart Stores*, 207 App. Div. 2d 150, 621 NYS2d 158 (3rd Dept., 1995).
[647] 74 NY2d 39, 544 NYS2d 308 (1989).

purposes, one of which is hunting, owe them no duty of care.[648] The land can be in the city and be commercial property, for the Court of Appeals has noted, "There is no more reason to make a categorical exception from the scope of General Obligations Law § 9-103 for properties which are in active commercial use than for properties which are not located in remote, undeveloped or wilderness areas."

Thus, Judge Hawley S. Moote held that the very fact that the landowner made no attempt to bar hunting of recreational sex or drugs,[649] or hunting rats, made the property one which was covered by the law that establishes that there is no duty of care owed by a generous property owner[650] who allows recreation in our otherwise bleak inner cities. The demurrer was granted.

---

[648] There are exceptions in the law not relevant here, such as willful or malicious failure to guard or warn, and when the landlord charges a fee.

[649] And, on advice of counsel, had posted a "Trespassers Must Shoot Rats" sign.

[650] This statute is not in derogation of common law, but rather codifies what was the common law before the law with regard to invitees and licensees changed, the court said in *Rock v. Concrete Materials* 46 App. Div. 2d 300 at 302 (3rd Dept., 1974). That is, at common law no duty was owed to trespassers—going all the way back to the days when the General Obligations Law was still a Colonel.

A "SIMPLE" CASE OF DRIVING WITH AN EXPIRED REGISTRATION[651]

A common traffic infraction that a general practitioner has to deal with is driving a motor vehicle with an expired registration. Assume that your client owns a vehicle that he has insured in New York, and he has let his registration expire without renewing it.[652] Assume as well that he has been convicted of speeding within the past thirty six months.

Normally, he will be issued the summons portion of a uniform traffic ticket[653] alleging a violation of Vehicle and Traffic Law § 401 (1) (a). Let us assume he has also made a request for a supporting deposition, and received a deposition by the arresting officer which alleges that the driver drove his vehicle on a particular, date, time and place on the named streets of the jurisdiction in question with an expired registration as evidenced by a teletype from the Department of Motor Vehicles. The client asks you what he or you should do now. He is concerned with his driving "record" and his insurance rates.

Insurance Law § 2335 provides when insurance rates can be increased by insurance carriers. In a curious double negative way it prohibits increasing insurance rates for traffic infractions under the Vehicle and Traffic Law except for those mentioned in fourteen numbered subdivisions. Subdivision 13 provides that rates can be increased if a driver is convicted of "operating a motor vehicle insured under the policy without a valid license or registration in effect . . ."

Does this mean that the driver would have been better off if the car had not been insured under any policy, or that the statute

---

[651] by James M. Rose, White Plains, New York, author of *New York Vehicle and Traffic Law,* Second Edition (Lawyers Cooperative Pub. Co., 1992). This article is dedicated to proving that an "expert" can turn a simple case into something complex.

[652] The case presented is fictional and is an composite of real cases.

[653] 15 NYCRR § 91.3 (e, f, g).

would not apply if the vehicle were insured under someone else's policy (such as a relative, employer or wholly owned business) but your client had a current insurance policy in effect at the time for other vehicles he owned?

Then the section provides a curious escape. It continues "... except where the person convicted had a valid license or registration which had expired and was subsequently renewed." Because of the use of the words "had expired" one assumes that the driver can register the vehicle after the ticket is issued[654] and escape the fate of having his insurance rates increase. Why this curious turn of events would be permitted is unclear, unless it expresses a policy that the Legislature would rather see the State of New York get the registration renewal fee than the insurer get an insurance rate increase.

If the driver renews his registration, is he out of the woods as far as insurance consequences are concerned?

Subdivision 14 provides insurance rates can be increased when the driver commits "Two or more moving violations of any other provision of the vehicle and traffic law."[655] The use of the word "other" probably means other than the ones mentioned in subdivisions one through thirteen, so the mention of the registration violation in subdivision thirteen logically acts to eliminate its use for purposes of subdivision fourteen.

If it does not, is a Vehicle and Traffic Law § 401 (1)(a) registration violation a "moving violation"? Surprisingly, the often used term "moving violation" is not defined in the Vehicle and Traffic Law, the Insurance Law, the regulations of either Commissioner, or New York case law. Vehicle and Traffic Law § 401(1)(a) speaks of unregistered "operating or driving" as if operating could be accomplished without driving. The case law has held that indeed it can,[656] as operating can consist merely of

---

[654] Otherwise why would he have been convicted if he had a valid registration at the time the ticket was issued?

[655] In our example your client has a prior speeding conviction.

[656] *People v. Hakimi-Ford*, 137 Misc. 2d 116, 519 NYS2d 766 (Yonkers City Ct., 1987), a case involving steering a vehicle being towed.

turning the vehicle on without moving the wheels.[657] Therefore, it is technically possible to operate a motor vehicle without moving it, so the driver would not literally commit a "moving violation."

The only cases from other states (Ohio and Wisconsin) that define "moving violation" hold that driving with expired license plates[658] and with no registration[659] are not moving violations under those states laws and statutory definitions. Moving violations for those states are assumed to be those acts that have the potential to harm other drivers because of the manner in which a vehicle is operated on the roads, and so registration offenses do not fall within that concept.

As far as the driver's "record" is concerned, a registration offense earns no points.[660] It may still be endorsed upon his conviction stub unless he was driving a vehicle owned by his employer while working for the employer at the time of the violation.[661]

What should be done about the supporting deposition? It is insufficient on its face according to a recent case.[662]

The supporting deposition is supposed to state each element of the offense upon direct knowledge.[663] The police officer is not the repository of registration information and has provided no non-hearsay source for his statement that the vehicle was not registered. A written motion directed at the supporting deposition could be made, but is likely to be a waste of time and energy. The charges can refiled within the statute of limitations if they are dismissed for failure to file a supporting deposition.[664] There is no statutory

---

[657] *People v. Domagala*, 123 Misc. 757, 206 N. Y. Supp. 288 (1924).

[658] *City of Vandalia v. Walter,s* 43 Ohio App. 3d 35, 538 N.E. 2d 1096.

[659] *State v. Strassburg*, 120 Wisc. 2d 30, 352 NW2d 215.

[660] 15 NYCRR § 131.3(b)(7)(i).

[661] Vehicle and Traffic Law § 514 (2).

[662] *People v. Augusto Isabel*, New York *Law Journal*, June 7, 1993, p. 26 Col. 5 (Cr. Ct, New York Co., 1993).

[663] *People v. Cohen*, 131 Misc 2d 898, 502 NYS 2d 123 (1986).

[664] *People v. Nuccio*, 78 NY2d 102, 571 NYS2d 693, 575 NE 2d 111 (1991).

speedy trial time limit on refiling a traffic offense,[665] and the constitutional speedy trial guarantee will require the driver to show actual harm because of the delay.[666] At the trial of the matter, the police officer may have some problem showing that the car was not registered unless he gets his paperwork in order.[667] Perhaps he ought to have asked the driver to produce the registration and charged him with failure to carry it or a copy on his person as well to avoid the headache of proving this charge without it.[668]

Drivers who drive with an expired registration are often charged with violating Vehicle and Traffic Law § 401 (1) (a). The police officer's condensed chart he carries suggests it. [669] But the statute is a quasi-criminal one which must be strictly construed.[670]

If the car had been registered in New York when it was first operated on the streets and the registration was permitted to expire, has the driver violated the statute?

---

[665] *People v.Solomon,* 124 Misc 2d 33, 475 NYS2d 749 (Dist. Ct. Nassau Co.,1984).

[666] *People v. Taranovich,* 37 NY2d 442, 373 NYS2d 79, 335 NE2d 303 (1975).

[667] See, for example, *People v. Patterson,* 143 Misc 2d 592, 541 NYS2d 321 (City Ct, Rochester, 1989).

[668] Vehicle and Traffic Law § 401 (4). The failure to produce it creates a presumption that the vehicle is unregistered if it also has no window sticker indicating that the registration is currently in force.

[669] "Condensed Guide to Vehicle & Traffic Law of the State of New York," Looseleaf Law Publications Inc. 1992/93 Edition. This guide with plastic carrying pouch is meant to be carried by police officers along with their notebooks and to be used by them to determine what offenses drivers can be charged with. It is arranged in tabular form.

[670] Vehicle and Traffic Law § 155.

It reads:

"No motor vehicle shall be operated or driven upon the public highways of this state without first being registered in accordance with the provisions of this article except as expressly provided in this chapter."

RULES OF EVIDENCE AND PROCEDURE FOR TV COPS AND LAWYERS: A/K/A THE RULES IN TELLY'S CASES

by James M. Rose[671]

Lawyers are often frustrated when they see television shows depicting courtroom scenes unrealistically. They want to jump up and yell "Objection!" when a television lawyer asks a leading, prejudicial, plot summarizing question with several facts not in evidence embedded in it, and the actor playing the opposing counsel sits smiling at the jury.

Real lawyers[672] do not know that there is a different set of rules and procedure that apply to television drama which are contained in the FCCPLR.[673]

For example, anyone arrested has a right to a speedy trial, and usually goes to trial within a week or two of arrest, so as not to slow down the drama of the situation.

If a trial takes place in the beginning of any show in which the good guys are law enforcement officials, the charges must be dismissed for hyper technical reasons leading to a clearly guilty person going free.[674]

When clearly guilty persons are permitted to go free because of court rulings, any act of vigilantism is thereafter permissible by law enforcement officials. Indeed, in any show where the good guys are law enforcement officials, burglary of the defendant's premises without a warrant is encouraged as a means

---

[671] White Plains, New York. Mr. Rose watches too much television.

[672] This means attorneys admitted to practice, and includes all members of the bar, despite the views of the criminal defendant who said he did not want legal aid, he wanted a "real lawyer."

[673] Which stands for the Fictional Character's Code for Productions with Legal Rigmarole.

[674] If a trial takes place in the beginning of any show in which the good guys are defense counsel, an innocent man will be convicted.

of gathering evidence. This rule is known as "It's not on my *Mapp*."

Likewise, another rule requires that street punk informers be assaulted at will in order to obtain information. The only rights that they have is a right to have a right to the jaw. It's cheaper than bribing them and quicker than tedious police work.

Rogue cops on television may do as they please because they regularly resign from the force. Appeals by the prosecution from the suppression of evidence are not permitted. Rather the FCCPLR requires the resignation of police who disagree with pre-trial evidence suppression decisions. The FCCPLR (hereinafter "The Code") provides that once those cops are off "the force"[675] they may use whatever means of force they want, not because they are above the law, but because they are below it.

Most law and procedure exists to frustrate progress, the Code says. Any time a defendant is convicted after the actions of a rogue cop solve the case, the Code requires that the rogue cop be automatically reinstated no matter how egregious his actions were.

Police are encouraged (if not required) to entrap defendants. The more elaborate the scheme, the more it is encouraged. Drugs, money, contraband, henchmen and illegal items of all sorts should be provided to bad guys to assist them in breaking the law regardless of court decisions concerning entrapment. ("Entrapment" exists as a defense in TV land only in the beginning of a TV show to allow guilty persons to go free). Police acting undercover are encouraged to violate any and all laws in order to convince their criminal associates how "bad" they are.

Prosecutors and defense attorneys have no obligation to respect attorney client privilege. They are encouraged to blab their client's innermost secrets to innocent third parties so as to put those parties in danger.

Good guys who are mystery novelists, crime fighting priests, stand up comedians or other civilians in professions not related to

---

[675] Which is inappropriately named, since it seams the police department exists to inhibit the use of force on such TV shows.

law enforcement must be given total access to on going police investigations, autopsy findings, ballistic reports etc. without regard for confidentiality if they are the heroes of their own series.

Any judge may impose an arbitrary burden upon a good guy (prosecutor or defense attorney) in the first half hour of any show, i.e., "If you don't have that witness here in ten minutes I'm going to dismiss this case!" The judge must be "shown up" by the end of the program.

Evidentiary rules are different as well. An exception to the hearsay rule is any question that speeds the plot along. This is known as the "Rule Against Perpetuities." Argumentative questions containing plot summations are permissible, and in the second half of any show are encouraged. Near the end of any show an attorney may sum up during the questioning of any witness without objection.

Anyone bursting into court through the double doors[676] at the back is permitted (if not required) to interrupt direct or cross examination, summations or the jury charge.

On any show where the denouement will occur in court, no witness can be sequestered. Each *must* sit in court with all the others (regardless of who has or has not testified) awaiting the dramatic moment.

Questions concerning facts not in evidence are permitted at any time, and witnesses may be badgered in the interests of justice or expediency. Where the plot calls for it, the defendant goes first. Since no discovery is ever permitted (it would prevent the trials from being completed in an hour) trickery, deceit and surprise in court are encouraged.

Rules for sitcoms are somewhat different. All parties must represent themselves in court (i.e., must appear "*Amateur Se.*") No negligence doctrines apply, because in sitcoms there are no

---

[676] All courtrooms are required to have double doors at the back with court officers stationed inside them, who permit people to burst in without restraining the intruder, as they could do if they were standing outside where they should be . . .

reasonable men. The rule is: If characters want to be prudent, then they should suggest themselves to an author of a serious drama.

In a comedy, police must chase someone. They are required to be out of control, use excessive speed, and ignore the safety of bystanders. In a chase in a comedy at least one of the following is required to occur (and often more than once):

- Crashing into painters or sign hangers on tall ladders,
- Crashing into sheets of plate glass,
- Running over wet cement, particularly if it can be done at the same location more than once in a movie or TV show,
- Going the wrong way on a one way street or crowded intersection, causing cars to crash into one another,
- Just missing utility workers emerging from manholes,
- Getting some item such as a banner or paint to obscure the windshield of a vehicle in a chase (which vehicle must nevertheless continue the chase rather than pull over to remove the item), and
- Swerving in order to hit fruit stands. If a chase vehicle can hit either the business of a third generation WASP or a "foreign appearing" ethnic stereotype, the driver must crash into the business of the latter so that he or she will swear at the cops in his colorful native tongue.

Officers who engage in such behavior must be promoted and given new police cars to crash in following weeks.

No one may be hurt in such crashes, unless he can appear in a subsequent scene in cumbersome plaster casts that become the instrument of some other comic business.

CONCLUSION

Life Imitates Art, and Art's pretty mad about it.

BOOK REVIEW—
THE LAW OF VEGETABLE RIGHTS

by Professor Herb Barry
reviewed by James M. Rose[677]

In the 1960's and 1970's oil and gas lawyers made a fortune litigating mineral rights. In the 1980's advocates on behalf of whales and laboratory animals led to an explosion in the development of the law of animal rights.

Professor Herb Barry,[678] the occupant of the Luther Burbank Chair of Botanical Rights at Foraitch School of Law has now written the definitive text in the one logically remaining area to develop, and his premise is that the 90's will be the era of Vegetable Rights. After all, Professor Barry asks, what's left?[679]

Professor Barry, the president of the American Society for the Prevention of Cruelty to Vegetation has published this text as a guide through the yet to be charted wilderness of claims that relate to the plant kingdom, and it has been electronically published by Matthewmind Bender Co.

---

[677] White Plains, New York. Mr. Rose is a person who needs no introduction, but he could use a good conclusion and a few decent footnotes.

[678] Along with co Author Amber Waisoff Graine.

[679] This author, never one to let a rhetorical question go unanswered, replies that the answer is viruses. They are, in some scientists' views, not living things at all but rather chemicals, and yet they can replicate themselves and multiply. If they were guests on "What's My Line" and were asked if they were animal, vegetable, or mineral the answer would be that the jury's still out on that one.

The last vial of smallpox virus is secreted in a refrigerator controlled by the United States Government and a debate is raging about whether it should be destroyed or saved to be studied. The author suggests it may be protected under the Endangered Species Act (16 U.S.C. § 1532 *et. seq.*) if it is a species, which is defined in 16 USC § 1532 (16) inter alia as "wildlife." "Wildlife" is

Vegetables suffer from a negative image in the law. For example, in *Elbaum v. Grace Plaza*,[680] a comatose hospital patient had previously indicated she did not want to be sustained like a vegetable[681] or kept alive in the event she was ever in a "vegetable-like state."[682] In *Trio Distributors Corp. v. City of Albany*[683] the Court of Appeals' inability to say whether vegetables are "attractive to and popular with children" resulted in an ordinance being declared void for vagueness.[684]

The book treats such subjects as the Right to Compost, Germination Rights, and Discrimination against Hybrids. It takes the reader step by step through the litigation of a class action by lawns to enforce a Keep off the Grass ordinance.[685] Professor Barry has obtained his appointments by invoking New York State Constitution Article XIV § 5, which allows a suit by a citizen to enforce Article XIV, the Article that provides for the preservation of scenic beauty and conserving of natural resources.

---

in turn not defined, and, like pornography, judges may only know what wildlife is when we see it—or experience it!

For those who question whether vegetation can be wildlife, see a discussion of whether trees can be logged from New York's forest preserve in light of the State Constitution's provision that the area remain "forever wild," *Helms v. Reid*, 90 Misc 2d 394 NYS2d 987 at 586. Article XIV § 1 requires the area to "be forever kept as wild forest lands."

[680] 148 App. Div. 2d 244, 544 NYS2d 840 (1989)
[681] at 250.
[682] at 247-8. The Appellate Division, Second Department did not define "vegetable like state" in the decision, or indicate to what state the conservatee was referring. Perhaps it was California, where the lush valleys and year round growing seasons result in intensive vegetable cultivation.
[683] 2 NY2d 690, 163 NYS2d 585 (1957).
[684] at 696-7. In that case the City of Albany passed an ordinance that required vendors who sold from vehicles plying the streets to hire a second man to act as a lookout when the peddlers sold "products attractive to and popular with children."
[685] From the naming of a guardian *ad lawnum* right through to the appeal of the order for the guardian to pay a fine for instituting a frivolous action.

His recovery of damages for emotional distress suffered by an Adirondack Forest when nearby lakes were polluted by acid rain has become a landmark in this area, and brought him to the attention of societies dedicated to the rights of vegetation and other lunatic fringe groups such as "The Right to Plant Life Organization" and "Seeds have Needs."

Professor Barry has advocated using the Nuremberg trials as precedent for certain jungles that he represents that are seeking reparation for damage caused by Agent Orange defoliants. The Professor's career began when he won a draft deferment as a conscientious objector during the Viet Nam war on the ground that he was a Druid, and, as a worshiper of trees, he could not participate in any war in which defoliants were used to kill vegetation.

Many disagree with his controversial stand taken in the chapter "One Plant One Vote"[686] His argument that plants cannot be denied the basic necessities to flourish has been called "a pile of fertilizer." He has used the doctrine of adverse possession to argue that trees own the land under forests.[687] However, one case on adverse possession in New York, *Franzen v. Cassarino*,[688] has held that the person who planted vegetables obtained not only an easement, but adverse possession by the planting of a vegetable garden on a disputed parcel. Still, vegetable farms continue to be bought and sold without regard for the rights of the vegetables themselves.[689]

---

[686] For example, see the discussion in J. Winston Snide, "Law And the Lunatic Fringe—Publish or Perish as a Generator of Bizarre Legal Theories," 2 *Post Modern L. Rev.* 63.

[687] compare, O. Zone, "Air Rights and Remedies," 1 *Journal of Holistic Environmental Law* 333.

[688] 159 App. Div. 2d 950, 552 NYS2d 789 (4th Dept., 1990).

[689] See, for example, *Alger v. Alger*, 183 App. Div. 2d 1000, 583 NYS2d 321 (3rd Dept., 1992), a divorce in which ownership of a fruit and vegetable business was decided by the courts with no consideration given to the best interests or the custody wishes of the vegetables themselves.

Professor Barry has hoped to raise the consciousness of individuals concerning the rights of vegetables. Ironically, advocates of plants' rights favor all meat diets as well as totally synthetic furniture and clothes.

If you want to be in on the cutting edge of the law (a phrase that upsets Professor Barry's sensibilities) or just want to be trendy, this treatise is for you. (Available on line, on CD-ROM or animal skin parchment—this book is not printed on paper.

JAMES M. ROSE

IN PRAISE OF APPRAISAL[690]

A recent criminal case before Justice Shirley U. Jesstt in the Town Justice Court of New Gomorrah brought to light just how much the law favors alternate dispute resolution. The use of alternative dispute resolution in criminal courts has been taking place for a while. In 1988, over 20,000 cases were diverted to alternative dispute resolution from New York City Criminal Court.[691] The Office of Court Administration reports that in 1998 40,113 cases were referred to alternative dispute resolution. In all 22,834 decisions resulted from mediations, conciliations and arbitrations (other than statutory compulsory arbitration).[692] But this case put a new spin on that solution.

Mr. M.T. Nestor, a man whose sons used to mow his lawn for him before they moved away, borrowed an old lawn mower from his neighbor, Bill Hunker of the Hunker Down Parka Company. Nestor was not used to using a lawn mower. He paid little attention to what he was doing when he was going down a steep incline. As a consequence he drove the mower into a pond and ruined it.[693] Nestor offered to pay Hunker for the old mower, but neither could agree on the value of it. For several weeks they exchanged threats of violence on the internet. Then each charged the other with aggravated harassment in Town Court. When the case was called, they agreed to seek some resolution of the matter by submitting to alternate dispute resolution. They returned to their neighborhood, this time arguing vociferously about what form the resolution should take. They began making threatening gestures at one another with slats they removed from a picket fence that separated their homes, when their neighbor, Solomon King, happened by. He offered to help settle the matter, and they

---

[690] by James M. Rose, White Plains, New York, Chief Shop Steward, Union of Unconcerned Scientists.
[691] *People v. Benoit*, 152 Misc 2d 115, 575 NYS2d 750 (1991) at footnote 1.
[692] Per a telephone call to that source.
[693] The case referred to in this article is fictitious. No lawn mower was actually harmed in the creation of this story.

agreed to let him determine the old mower's value. When he indicated he was considering splitting the difference between the Hunker's and Nestor's figures,[694] Nestor and Hunker both threatened to strike *him*. King then threw up his hands and said in exasperation, "Well, why don't you fight over it and the winner takes all?" Hunker and Nestor began to pummel one another with hands, feet, and fence slats. The noise caused another neighbor, Ms. Ann Tropee, to call the police anonymously, but when they arrived the fighting had stopped. Nestor and Hunker each sent internet messages to the other claiming victory. Lacking other proof that the fight took place, the police then obtained a search warrant for the home computers of the two, and tried to get the stored files off their hard disks. When they applied for the search warrant the police told the judge "We're going to grab them by their two big hard drives and squeeze them good." However, when both Nestor and Hunker were arrested for assault in the second degree[695] and boxing without a license, they had an unusual defense and made an unusual motion. The motion to suppress the results of the search dealt with an intriguing question. The defendants argued that the police needed an *eavesdropping* warrant and not a search warrant. An eavesdropping warrant is needed to access an "electronic communication" according to Criminal Procedure Law § 700.05 (1). "Electronic communication" is defined in Penal Law § 250.00 (5) as an electronic transfer of data. Internet boasts that were sent as e-mail were such communications, the judge ruled. Since the entire hard disk was searched and the warrant contained no minimization provisions, [696] the results were suppressed.[697]

---

[694] The difference was one hundred dollars, and Solomon King said "Let's just split that baby down the middle!"

[695] Penal Law § 120.05.

[696] See Omnibus Crime Control and Safe Streets Act of 1968, 18 U.S.C. § 2510 and *People v. Floyd* 41 NY2d 245, 392 NYS2d 257 (1976) at p. 250. Have your streets seemed safe since this act passed in 1968?

[697] They were of no use on the charge under Unconsolidated Laws § 8933 (boxing without a license) in any event, since that is not one of the crimes

But the police then gave Solomon King immunity and proceeded to compel him to testify about what he saw. The District Attorney had charged the defendants with assault in the second degree, and with a violation of Unconsolidated Laws § 8933, which makes it illegal to engage in a boxing or wrestling contest without the approval of and licensing by the State Athletic Commission. Since the two had agreed to fight with King as the judge of the contest, the D.A. chose to prefer a charge which included engaging in an unsanctioned fight.[698]

The judge noted that the powers of the State Athletic Commission to oversee amateur and professional athletic contests are broad indeed,[699] but they are limited to boxing and wrestling matches. The jurisdiction of the Commission does not extend to fights with fence slats, which, if they can be categorized as any kind of sporting contest, most likely constitute jousting, or fencing with fencing. Normally when two people agree to fight one another both are guilty of assault, as combat by agreement is illegal.[700] The defense of Nestor and Hunker was that they had entered into an appraisal agreement, and that the fight was part of the agreement. Article 76 of the Civil Practice Law and Rules provides in § 7601 that a special proceeding can be brought to enforce an agreement to let a third person do an appraisal. The case law indicates that the appraisal procedure can be informal, and is, in essence, whatever the appraiser determines it to be. "The prevailing practice in appraisals is more informal and 'entirely different [from the]

---

enumerated for which an eavesdropping warrant can be obtained (See, CPL § 700.05.)

[698] The "prize" in the prize fight was the monetary difference in the alleged value of the lawn mower, although the Commission also has jurisdiction to sanction amateur bouts. (Unconsolidated Laws § 8905-6.)

[699] see *Matter of London Sporting Club v Helfand* 3 Misc 2d 431, 152 NYS2d 819 (S. Ct. N.Y. Co. 1956).

[700] *People ex. rel. Knight v. Eames* 115 NYS2d 248; c.f. *People v. Lewis*, 166 App.Div. 2d 238, 560 NYS2d 630 (1st Dept., 1990).

procedure governing arbitration.'[701] The result of the appraisal is final and binding, and can be confirmed as if it were an arbitrator's award. The defendants argued that the appraiser, Solomon King, chose trial by combat as his method of determining the appraisal. This is an ancient and little used procedure nowadays, but historically[702] it was a recognized method of resolving legal controversies.[703] It is, Justice Jesstt ruled, just another alternative form of dispute resolution that the courts consider so beneficial in relieving strains on the modern court system.[704] The bout will take place on ESPN 2 and Court TV next weekend. If it is successful ESPN and Court TV will fight over who gets the rights to broadcast future trials by combat.

---

[701] *Matter of Penn Central v. Con Rail*, 56 NY2d 120 at 127.

[702] See, R. Wormser, *The Story of the Law and the Men Who Made*, (New York, 1962) at p. 240.

[703] *Pando v. Fernandez*, 127 Misc. 2d 224, 485 NYS2d 162 (New York County S. Ct.1984) the court said "In Medieval law the demonstration of miracles in the courtroom and a show of divine intervention were grist for the judicial mill, and trial by combat and trial by ordeal constituted proof of God's will" at 231.

[704] (see, e.g., Evans & Bulman, Alternative Dispute Resolution Method Holds Out Promise of Great Utility, New York *Law Journal*, Jan. 24, 1980, p 25, col 2; Memorandum of Office of Court Administration in support of L. 1977, ch 165, McKinney's Session Laws of NY, 1977, p 2611). (See, e.g., Evans & Bulman, Alternative Dispute Resolution Method Holds Out Promise of Great Utility, New York *Law Journal*, January 24, 1980, p 25, col 2; Memorandum of Office of Court Administration in support of L 1977, ch 165, McKinney's Session Laws of NY, 1977, p 2611).

RES IPSA LOQUITUR (Humor)[705]

HOW ARBITRARY IS THE DEFINITION OF ARBITRARY?
or
READING THIS ARTICLE TO THE END MAY NOT GET YOU ANY CLE CREDITS, BUT IT COULD BE WORTH A FREE BEER

Courts deciding Article 78 petitions have applied the standard of whether an action is arbitrary and capricious for many years. Until recently courts looked upon "arbitrary" as an absolute, that is, as something without degrees. Just as one could not be a little pregnant, one could not be a little arbitrary.[706] This always made one wonder, though, why something had to be both arbitrary and capricious.[707] Are the terms not repetitive?[708]

Could something be arbitrary and not capricious, or *vice versa*?[709] The Court of Appeals has decided a case[710] which makes one

---

[705] by James M. Rose, whose is still accepting offers for the movie rights to his book *New York Vehicle and Traffic Law* and the sequel, *New York Vehicle and Traffic Law, 2nd Edition*.

[706] "Unique" is also an absolute, as it literally means "one of a kind," and something cannot be "very unique" (i.e., very one of a kind") as it is either unique or it is not, television announcers to the contrary.

[707] One of the definitions for "capriciously" given by the *Compact Edition of the Oxford English Dictionary* is "arbitrarily" (Oxford University Press, 1971), and one of the definitions of "arbitrary" is "capricious."

[708] Much like the young lawyer arguing before the Appellate Division who was reminded by the bench that he had said the same thing three times and who replied, "Yes, your honor, but there are five of you."

[709] Perhaps a lottery is an example of something that is arbitrary (that is why it is used) without being capricious. Can something be capricious without being arbitrary? How about a three year old's demands?

[710] *Matter of New York City Department of Environmental Protection v. New York City Civil Service Commission* 78 NY2d 318 (1991).

conclude that there are degrees of arbitrariness at law, because it speaks of "purely arbitrary" as being more arbitrary than "arbitrary" unmodified by an adjective and joined with "capricious."[711]

Is there an impure arbitrariness?

One of the definitions of "arbitrary" in the *American Heritage Dictionary* is "absolute."[712] How, then, could there be degrees of arbitrariness? Why does the decision say that if something is both arbitrary and capricious, then it is less arbitrary than "purely arbitrary," which means arbitrary[713] alone?

By "purely arbitrary" (unsullied by or diluted by capriciousness) the court means acting illegally, unconstitutionally, or in excess of an officer or body's jurisdiction.[714] Using that standard, and looking at some old statutes and recent case decisions, does it not seem that your rights themselves are a little bit arbitrary?[715]

A prisoner has a right to possess photographs of his naked girlfriend in his cell that amounts to a constitutional right, but a citizen cannot possess a cigarette lighter in his own home if it looks like a gun.[716]

On the other hand you apparently have no right to be shaved professionally on Sunday,[717] or to observe or participate in a professional sporting event on Sunday before 1:05 PM,[718] or to work for the Board of Elections if you are registered as an independent or a Liberal.[719]

---

[711] 78 NY2d at 323.

[712] *American Heritage Dictionary of the English Language*, Boston, 1980, p. 67.

[713] "arbitrary" and "arbitration" come from the same Latin root word, and if they don't they ought to.

[714] 78 NY2d at 323.

[715] If there are degrees of arbitrary, the author can say "a little bit arbitrary."

[716] General Business Law § 872.

[717] General Business Law §2016 prohibits it.

[718] General Business Law § 7. Why should it be illegal at 1:04 PM and legal at 1:06 PM?

[719] Election Law § 3-300.

You have a right to an out of state lawyer[720] or to a psychiatrist to help present your criminal defense in a murder case,[721] but not to help you defend a filiation claim even if you were temporarily insane to get involved with that child's mother.[722]

You have a constitutional right to beg,[723] and it's a good thing, too, because you have no right to earn a minimum wage if you work in prison.[724] But you do have a constitutional right to a smoke free cell there.[725]

You have a state constitutional due process right to use a private beach chair which a municipality cannot infringe upon by requiring you to rent one from their concessionaire[726] Your rights in this universe are ever expanding.[727] You have no right to misrepresent the name of the manufacturer of a frozen dessert,[728] or to operate on the tail of a horse,[729] or to mislead a consumer about the correct

---

[720] *Supreme Court of New Hampshire v. Piper*, 470 U.S. 274, 84 L.Ed 2d 205 at 212 (1985).

[721] *Ake v. Oklahoma*, 470 U.S. 68, 84 L. Ed 2d 53 (1985).

[722] Temporary insanity is apparently a defense to malicious wounding charges in the Virginia Penile Code, or to charges that you performed a sex change on your spouse without being a licensed physician in order to politically correct him, but temporary insanity is less likely to be a successful defense to speeding charges.

[723] *Loper v. New York City Police Dept.*, 999 F. 2d 699 (1993), see, New York Law Journal, August 16, 1993 P. 2, col. 1M.

[724] *Lavigne v. Sara* 424 So.2d 273 (La. App. 1st Cir., 1982); *Miller v. Dukakis* 961 F.2d 7 (1st. Cir., 1992).

[725] *Helling v. McKinney*, 509 U.S. 25 (1993).

[726] *People v. Buckley* 142 Misc 2d. 262 (Dist. Ct., 2nd Dist., Nassau Co., 1989).

[727] And like the ever expanding universe may be moving away from you at the speed of light.

[728] Agricultural and Markets Law § 71-i.

[729] Agricultural and Markets Law § § 308.

chemical composition of agricultural lime,[730] or to transport a bee colony without a license,[731] but citizens of New York have a statutory privilege to have their seeds tested by the New York state agricultural experiment station.[732]

Even inanimate objects have first amendment rights. An automated telephone machine has the constitutional right to call you in the middle of your dinner, because statutes banning them run afoul of free speech rights.[733]

Finally, the old saying that there is no such thing as a free lunch is passe as well. The time honored institution of Ladies Night at your local saloon[734] during which ladies are given one free drink is in violation of sex discrimination laws, a Wisconsin court has held.[735] Knowing this right may be worth a free drink to males who request one on ladies night at their local public house. They can cite this case if their place of public accommodation refuses to be accommodating.[736]

Not only is chivalry unconstitutional, maybe civilization as we know it is, too. But that conclusion is based upon a review of case law and statutes that was impurely arbitrary.

---

[730] Agricultural and Markets Law § 142-bb.

[731] Agricultural and Markets Law § 175.

[732] Agriculture and Markets Law § 140-a. "Seed" is defined in § 136 (2) of that law as a botanical structure used for planting purposes, so don't go trying to get them to do your sperm count. Besides, § 140 of that law allows the state to publish the results of the tests.

[733] *Moser v. Federal Communications Commission* __FS____ (Fed. Dist. Ct., Dist. Ore., May 21, 1993, 92 1408 RE), in *US Lawyer's Weekly January 3*, 1994 p. 6 col. 1.

[734] Which now has no right to have swinging doors (Alcoholic Beverage Law § 106 (9)(a)), but can call itself a saloon, as that prohibition has been repealed.

[735] *Novack v. Madison Motel Associates* (Dane Co. Wisconsin Cir. Ct.) 93 CIV 1005, in *US Lawyers Weekly*, January 3, 1994 P. 6, col. 2.

[736] Who says this isn't the most valuable column in the Westchester County Bar Journal?

STAMBOVSKY V. ACKLEY: WILL IT HAUNT GHOST WRITERS IN THE FIRST DEPARTMENT?

by James M. Rose[737]

In *Stambovsky v. Ackley*[738] the Appellate Division First Department was faced with a case involving an attempt to rescind a contract to buy a home in Nyack because the seller did not divulge to the buyer that the house was haunted by spirits.

Because the seller had written in *Reader's Digest*[739] in 1977 that the house was haunted, and told local papers in 1982 (as well as listed the house as a haunted one in a walking tour after the contract was signed) the Appellate Division wrote that "defendant is estopped to deny their [the spirits'] existence[740] and, as a matter of law the house is haunted."[741]

---

[737] White Plains, New York is Mr. Rose's usual haunt.

[738] 168 App.Div. 2d 254; 60 USLW 2070; New York *Law Journal,* July 22, 1991 p. 21 col. 4; see also Adams, "Haunted House Claim Restored", New York *Law Journal* July 19, 1991 p. 1 col 3.

[739] "Our Haunted House on the Hudson" by Helen Herdman Ackley, 110 *Reader's Digest* 217 (May, 1977).

[740] The court did not discuss whether the owner, Helen V. Ackley, could exercise her famous prerogative and change her mind. Could she just say the apparition was the result of a pepperoni pizza at bedtime, and she no longer believed it was a ghost? Once an Appellate Division judge writes something he may be bound by stare decisis not to change his mind, but is he estopped?

Why did he write such a thing? The judge later said, "I don't know. I felt compelled by some strange force to put that part in."

[741] Is this a question of law or parapsychology? The author was not able to find any questions of law on ghosts in reported cases going back to just after the Salem witchcraft trials. The indices of *McKinney's* and the United States Code are devoid of any reference to "ghost" or "haunted" or "poltergeist" although there is a definition of "spirit" in Section 3 of the Alcoholic Beverage Control Law.

This is a real case, and I did not make it up for this column,[742] although when one reads the opinion, somewhere about the fourth paragraph the reader expects that the Energizer bunny will come drumming his way through, or Candid Camera will appear.

What effect will this decision have on pending cases? Now that ghosts exist as a matter of law, will they be found bedeviling drivers who were alleged to have been negligent? Will their spirited intervention explain hitherto unknown behavior, and thus mean the end of the doctrine of *res ipsa loquitur*?[743]

Will there now be election redistricting cases based upon the one ghost, one vote rationale?[744] On the other hand, it may be much easier to determine the testator's intent in a will contest if you can examine him under oath him after he's dead.

ALR has no annotation about them, and nothing can be found in *Corpus Juris* nor is there a *Noncorpus Juris* in which to search. *Silva v. MacLaine*,697 F. Supp. 1423 is the only case tp describe something close. It is a case in which an author sued Shirley MacLaine for a copyright violation, alleging that her *Out on a Limb* was copied from his Date With the Gods. In the decision at 1425 the "spirit" was described as being composed of "ananas and anionites", the theoretical particles that exist in the spaces between neutrons, protons and electrons.

Can something be established as a matter of law that is not true as a matter of fact? How does one prove that ghosts exist? In 17 *Proof of Facts* 298, "ghost" is defined in Marine terminology as a false echo appearing in a position not corresponding to an actual object. Is that proof of the fact ghosts exist?

[742] Although I am considering an action against the Appellate Division for co-opting the premise often used in this column. Computer programmers say "Garbage in, garbage out," meaning that faulty data will lead to a faulty conclusion. This case demonstrates that a bizarre fact pattern will lead to bizarre legal conclusions, which has often been the comedic trick of this column.

[743] and with it the name of this column?

[744] Thus denying many ghosts in Philadelphia and Chicago their current practice, i.e., to vote early and vote often.

If a criminal defendant says he was possessed by spirits, should he be sent for a psychiatric examination, or is he just reaffirming what the Appellate Division already has written?

Can a seller now attempt to rescind a contract on the basis she was possessed at the time she signed, and it was not really her act but that of a spirit that channeled through her?

Will real estate attorneys now have to add a rider to contracts to contain a provision reciting that the house is devoid of ghosts,[745] poltergeists, spirits, things that go bump in the night (except the furnace) and other Amityville horrors?

What will title companies have to check before they can certify title? The Appellate Division noted that the ghosts' presence could mean the house was not "vacant." Will title companies have to check the *Reader's Guide to Periodical Literature* and the morgue of the local newspaper to be sure the house is free of ghosts? Ask the neighbors if they ever saw ghosts? Call a shaman as an expert to check out the house?[746] Indeed, if the ghosts "inhabit" the house enough for a court to say it is not vacant, is their presence substantial enough for them to have a claim on the house by adverse possession? If the title company wanted to clear the title by making sure the ghosts had no claim, what kind of very special proceeding does it bring?

How does it serve the ghosts with a notice to quit? By publication—and if so where? *Harper's Bizarre*? Where does jurisdiction lie (or float)? How do you get the ghosts to pay your retainer and with what?[747] How do you get them to obey the judgment?

Did the contract recite this was a one family home—and do the ghosts violate the zoning ordinances as well?

---

[745] The well known "ghost rider."

[746] In short, Who you gonna call? A riddle: Why does a shaman wear red suspenders? Answer: To keep his spirits up!

[747] Is this the kind of claim you want to take on a contingency—including the contingency that the court may rule that your client does not exist?

What the First Department was attempting to grapple with[748] was the limits of the doctrine of *caveat emptor*. It held that the defendant was not hesitant to tell the world the house was haunted, why was she very quiet with the seller?[749] Does the presence of the spirits mean the house is not worth as much haunted?[750] Did they bother the owner enough to make her sell after living in the house for more than ten years? The court did not go into why the seller decided to part with a house in which the ghosts were alleged to be "cheerful."[751] If ghosts can tell what the future will bring,[752] perhaps they whispered in the seller's ear that the residential real estate market was about to take a tumble, and it was time to get out—a sure way for a ghost to strike terror in the heart of a suburban New Yorker.[753]

The Appellate Division held that the buyer would not have to

---

[748] a difficult proposition when dealing with a ghost.

[749] Although the *Reader's Digest* article idicates that Ackley's seller did not warn *her* about the ghosts before she moved in.

[750] The Appellate Division recited that the rumors made the house worth less on resale. However, Ackley was fond of the ghosts in her *Reader's Digest* piece, noting that they left her presents like a silver tongs and a baby ring, and said she would miss them if she moved. Was the suit premature because the ghosts may have gone with her to haunt her new manse?

[751] New York *Law Journal* July 19, 1991 p. 1 col. 3. That would make them blithe spirits. They did wake up the Ackley children when it was time for school by shaking the beds, they threw open and slammed windows and doors (one assumes this violates a covenant of quiet enjoyment), and stopped swinging chandeliers in mid-flight.

[752] C.f., Macbeth. and Dickens's ghost of Christmases Yet to Be in "A Christmas Carol."

[753] If ghosts can forecast the future of the real estate market, the parties were certainly not on an equal footing, which might invoke the rule of *Mc Pherson v. Buick* and invalidate the contract for a completely different reason.

be familiar with local folklore, and thus was able to rescind when he found out the house had an infestation of spirits.[754]

The owner said it appeared that the spirits that inhabited the house were waiting for something.[755] Should he not have been wary? Sleepy Hollow is just across the river, and the house lies close to where Rip Van Winkle became a title insurance company's nightmare. In suburban Long Island the Amityville house is well known. According to one source, even the State Capitol in Albany is haunted.[756] Hadn't the buyer seen the movie "Ghost" which was so popular in 1990? Longfellow has written[757] "All houses wherein men have lived and died are haunted houses."

The Appellate Division was attempting to balance the doctrine of *caveat emptor* and the duty of fairness implicit in all contracts. It was a question not of the letter of the contract, but of the spirit.[758] Consequently the Appellate Division was able to exercise its equitable powers to order rescission because of the non-disclosure.

Why is *caveat emptor* the law of New York? In *Hargous v. Stone*[759] the Court of Appeals also mentions the doctrine of *caveat venditor*, a rule casting the responsibility for defects or deficiencies on the seller.[760] New houses have to be warrantied under General Business Law § 777,[761] certainly a departure from the doctrine. Do old house

---

[754] They were described as being in revolutionary war garb in a Victorian house. This anachronism was not explained.

[755] Perhaps a costume party, or Mrs. Muir.

[756] Auerbach, ESP, *Haunting and Poltergeists*, Warner Communications, 1986, P. 282. Supposedly the White House is haunted as well, and President Lincoln held seances there. The ghost of Abigail Adams appeared during the Taft administration, and the ghost of Lincoln is said to visit the Lincoln bedroom.

[757] in *Haunted Houses*.

[758] in several senses of the word.

[759] 5 NY 73. The Court was sitting in Elmira at the time.

[760] *Caveat emptor* is a rule of common law and *caveat venditor* is a rule of civil law.

buyers suffer a lack of due process because their homes are not required to carry warranties?

The dissenters saw the death of the doctrine of *caveat emptor* without seeing its ghost. Perhaps the dissenters should have summoned up a quotation from John Selden, who wrote in Table Talk "Equity in law is the same that the spirit is in religion, what everyone pleases to make of it!"

The decision of the Appellate Division was three to two, and it is not true as rumored that a mysterious opinion appeared which contained the phrase "over my dead body" and was signed "Cardozo, J.S.C."[762]

It appears that the doctrine of caveat emptor was intended to apply to merchants and business transactions where the seller would be familiar with the merchandise. (see 85 ALR 1224.) The doctrine of *caveat venditor* has mysteriously vanished into thin air.

[761] But are not required to be certified free of spirits.
[762] which stands for Justice's Spirit Concurs.

James M. Rose

LEGAL FICTIONS AND ILLEGAL ONES
or LIABLE FOR LIBEL?

Readers of good fiction value it because the ideas expressed in it are true and enduring, even if the characters in it are imaginary. Modern day critics have reasoned that a work of fiction is of more value if it represents the real world in a true and convincing fashion. However, the truer the fiction becomes, the more it may run afoul of our law of libel.

Fiction is supposed to be false, according to the law. A legal fiction is something known to be false but assumed to be true.[763] In *Landau v. Columbia Broadcasting System*[764] fiction was defined as "[t]he species of literature which is concerned with the narration of imaginary events and the portraiture of imaginary characters" (quoting from the *New English Dictionary*).

What happens when any similarity between persons living or dead is more than coincidental?

A recent California case reminds us. In *Bindrim v. Mitchell*[765] the plaintiff was a doctor and a promoter of nude marathon therapy who thought he saw an unflattering portrait of himself in Gwen Davis Mitchell's work of fiction *Touching*.

Although the name, appearance and academic degree of the character in the book were different from Dr. Bindrim's name, appearance and degree, nevertheless the court found overwhelming evidence that the plaintiff and the fictional character were one and the same.

Writers of a certain species of fiction that thinly veils real life became duly alarmed at the verdict in the doctor's favor, which was affirmed on appeal. Could they continue to write potboilers based upon world events?

The law of New York requires the same result as did the law of California. In *Corrigan v. Bobbs Merrill Co.*[766] (a decision that is

---
[763] *Ryan v. Motor Credit Co.*, 130 N. J. Eq. 531, 23 A.2d 607, 621.
[764] 205 Misc. 357, 128 NYS 2d 254 (Sup. Ct. N. Y. Co. 1954).
[765] 92 Cal. App. 3rd, 155 Cal. Rptr. 29, cert. Denied 444 U.S. 984 (197).
[766] 288 N.Y. 58 (1920).

captioned in volume 228 of New York Reports as "per Pound, J."—from back in the days when you could buy your law books by the Pound), a novel published by the defendants vilified a magistrate of the Jefferson Market Court named Cornigan. The plaintiff, a magistrate who sat in that court was named Corrigan. The defendants' author defamed the plaintiff, and the defendants were held liable, even though they did not know him or intend to injure him. The court determined that it was not who was aimed at, but who was hit that created liability.[767]

However, if the fiction is patently unbelievable the author may escape. The "Eloise case" is an example. In *Salamone v. Mac Millian Pub. Co.*[768] The plaintiff was the former manager of the Plaza Hotel, and subsequently a vice president of the Hilton Hotel Corp. He was described in a children's book, *Eloise*. The defendants published a parody of it called *Eloise Returns*. In the parody, Eloise, now a grown up, says that the Manager of the Plaza, Salamone, was a child molester. The defendants were shocked to learn that there was an actual person by the name of Salamone who had been the manager of the Plaza at the time the Eloise books were written, and who was embarrassed to see the description of him in the parody. The Appellate Division, First Department held that there no actual injury, because the plaintiff could produce no one who believed the story[769] or thought less of him because of it. Justice Kupferman concurred because the work was an obvious parody and not to be taken seriously. He did not discuss the theory held by many that parody can be a seriously aimed barb, or that

---

[767] Similarly, see, *Brown v. Paramount Publix Corp.*, 240 App. Div. 520, 270 N.Y. Supp. 544 (1st Dept. 1934). The film "An American Tragedy" portrayed the life of Chester Gillette, who murdered Grace Brown. Grace's mother sued, because the movie depicted her as neglecting Grace, even though her name was not used in the picture. The court held in her favor.

[768] 77 App. Div. 2d 501 (1st Dept. 1980).

[769] Did Magistrate Corrigan produce witnesses who testified that they *did* believe the vile tales concocted by the Bobbs Merrill author? If Paris Hilton grew up in a hotel, maybe the Eloise books explain a lot.

something said in jest can hurt the feelings of someone who hears it just as much as something said somberly.[770]

Along with parody, allegory is apparently a defense to liable as well. In *Silberman v. Georges*[771] the defendant painted an allegorical scene in which a young lady was being attacked by muggers with knives. The muggers were wearing masks, and the court concluded that there was no serious question that the masks depicted the plaintiffs, who were painters with whom the defendant had disagreements. The name of the work was "The Mugging of the Muse." The court concluded that the painting did not accuse plaintiffs of homicide, but was an allegorical expression of opinion that the plaintiffs damaged the arts. It was not meant to be taken literally. No one discussed whether damaging the arts was a more serious allegation in the plaintiffs' circle of acquaintances than homicide.[772]

The lesson of these case should be clear to perceptive fiction writers. If your fiction is too true or too believable you may be in trouble. If truth is stranger than fiction, then that is the fault of the fiction writers who put too much truth in their works. They must become more like the witness who, when asked if he would swear to tell the truth, the whole truth and nothing but the truth, replied, "Yes, and then some."

Many professional writers became nervous after the *Touching* decision. They demanded some legislation.[773] They wanted a typical dragnet bill with a myriad of regulations to tell them just what the law would permit them to do. Leading the fight was the National Association of Developers of Mini-Series for Television, who often base their potboilers on thinly veiled depictions of national events.

---

[770] No one discussed whether the author ought to have checked the easily discoverable information concerning the name of the manager of the Plaza before blithely calling him a child molester. Is there such a thing as reckless liable?

[771] 91 App. Div. 2d 520, 456 NYS2d 395 (1st Dept. 1982).

[772] The words "allegory" and "allegation" do not come from the same root.

[773] As an aside, the writers were concerned that they might be liable for placing a defective product on the market as well. A products liability theory that could

They wanted to know just how thick the veil must be. Script writers and rewriters complained through their newly organized PAC, the International Brotherhood of Word Processors and Reprocessors. Also heard from was the Association of Pulp Fiction Publishers, and the Gossip Magazine Trade Association. Among the concerned writers were Irving Wallace, Irving Stone, John Irving, Clifford Irving, and some other novelizers[774] not named Irving who fictionalized the lives of the famous for fortunes.[775]

Legislators responded, taking their lead from the Truth in Lending Act,[776] the Truth in Lending Simplification Act and Reform Act[777], the Truth in Negotiations Act[778], and the Truth in Securities Act.[779]

They proposed the Truth in Fiction Act. However, unlike the bills upon which it was modeled whose purpose was to insure the truth came out,[780] this bill seeks to limit the amount of truth that can be contained in any work of fiction to less than ten percent.[781]

---

be espoused by liabelees hit by the shrapnel of some author's tort might be asserted as a cause of action. Courts in New York have rejected that idea. When the book itself is used for the purpose for which it is intended, (i.e., to be read) no products liability claims have been successful. For example, in *Walter v. Bauer,* 109 Misc. 2d 189, mod. 88 App. Div. 2d 787 (4th Dept 1982), an allegedly defective science experiment was described in a book called *Discovering Science 4*. The publisher was not held liable, and arguments based upon a products liability theory was rejected.

[774] But not Washington Irving.
[775] Like Jackie and Joan Collins.
[776] 15 U.S.C. § 1601.
[777] 15 U.S. C. § 1601 et. seq.
[778] 10 U.S.C. 2304 (a).
[779] 15 U.S.C. § 77a.
[780] There is an old saying in the law: "The truth will out, even in an affidavit." But the saying has little relevance to this piece, so it is relegated to this footnote.
[781] However there is a debate whether the ten percent figure is meant to be ten percent of the ideas, or of the words, or merely of the weight (or gravitas) of the

The United States Department of Agriculture if the Department of Environmental Protection were considered as the agencies which would enforce the law.[782] The former keeps harmful additives out other substances.[783] The latter monitors our environment for harmful impurities. Who would keep "pure fiction" pure?[784]

The battle is now raging. Controversy also surrounds the issue of who would enforce the provisions requiring Fiction to be Stranger that Truth; and which agency will get to enforce the Truth in Non-Fiction Act, which would require that literature labeled as non-fiction be true.

---

article, to be measures per Pound, J. It is reminiscent of the controversy surrounding the .10 percent driving while intoxicated limits in Vehicle and Traffic Law § 1192 (2), and whether the reading of .10 percent alcohol in the blood is meant to be by weight of alcohol in volume of liquid blood, or by weight in weight of blood.

[782] No one seriously considered the National Council on the Arts to enforce the law because, well, no one considered it seriously.

[783] See 21 U.S.C. § 301 et. seq. and New York's equivalent, Agriculture and Markets Act § 200.

[784] "Pure fiction" is of course, a fiction, like "perfect stranger." No stranger is perfect, and no fiction is pure, the Bureau of Standards advises us. Into each fiction some truth must fall, apparently.

"Classical fiction" is maintained by the Bureau of Standards, which is charged with keeping the classics standard, or maybe just providing standards on which to place the classics.

RECENT DEVELOPMENTS IN THE LAW OF ETHNIC SLURS

by James M. Rose[785]

Recent developments have made it unclear whether calling someone who is prejudiced a bigot is a misdemeanor in New York.

In *People v. Dietze*,[786] the Court of Appeals declared that a portion of the harassment statute, Penal Law § 240.25 (2),[787] is unconstitutional. Its reasoning was that the statute was over broad, and prohibits a substantial amount of constitutionally protected expression. It thus violated the state (Article I Section 8) and federal (First and Fourteenth Amendments) constitutions.

This ruling must also call into question the misdemeanor penalties imposed by virtue of Civil Rights Law §§ 40-c and 40-d. The former section prohibited harassment as defined in section 240.25 because of "race, color, creed, national origin, sex, marital status or disability."[788]

Section 40-d made the penalty for violation of 40-c a misdemeanor.[789]

---

[785] White Plains, New York. Mr. Rose is the author of *Age Discrimination and the Right to Order Off a Children's Menu,* recently published by Fool Court Press.

[786] 75 NY2d 47 (1989)

[787] which read as follows:

"A person is guilty of harassment when, with intent to harass, annoy or alarm another person . . . (2) In a public place, he uses abusive or obscene language, or makes an obscene gesture . . ."

[788] Age is not in the list, so it is possible to call some an "old (expletive deleted)" without violating the Civil Rights Law.

Theoretically, nagging grandmothers who abusively annoy their granddaughters with requests to know when they will marry come within the prohibition against harassment based upon marital status (although the statute does require it be done with the intent to harass or annoy).

[789] The constitutionality of the statute was already is question because of the

While the statute no doubt expressed an admirable sentiment, the actual application of the statute would require the court to ban language that has passed into everyday usage.

"Race," "creed" or "national origin" become problematical when applied to language. Some of our everyday words have ancient, even Biblical origins. For example, the pejorative term "Philistine" is an ethnic slur on that fine, old biblical nation. When someone is described as a "good Samaritan" is it intended to distinguish him from other Samaritans who are not good?[790]

When a person who violates Penal Law § 145.00 by committing criminal mischief is spoken of as a "vandal," is that not an ethnic slur of an old German tribe? Is the Penal Law itself guilty of maligning all the innocent residents of Sodom (Penal Law §§ 130.38-130.50)?

When someone speaks of a "paddy wagon" he is referring to a police van that transports recently arrested criminals, but some believe the origin of the term was meant to be disparaging to the Irish, and to suggest that they were often found inside its confines.[791] The term "Dutch treat"[792] was meant to paint the Dutch as parsimonious. "To Welsh" on a bet is to default, and refers to that ethnic group. The term "Chinese fire drill" was intended to convey a lack of organization on the part of that race. "Indian giver" pictured Indians as untrustworthy when giving their word.[793] "Mongoloid" impugns an entire race.

"Puritanical" used to be a compliment, but in a world where we are urged by cartoon Ninja turtles to be open to new experiences

---

interpretation given to it in *Holy Spirit Assn. for the Unification of World Christianity v. New York State Congress of PTAs*. In that case Rev. Sun Myung Moon sued the state PTA for adopting a resolution critical of his religion, calling it a cult, and calling into question its status as a bona fide religion.

[790] See, Luke 10:30-34.

[791] Others believe that it referred to the police who drive the vans. Espy, Willard, *O Thou Improper, Thou Uncommon Noun* (1978), p. 196.

[792] i.e., where nobody is treated because everyone pays for himself.

[793] See also, "Honest injun." Ironic when one reviews the history of treaties with Washington to determine which party abrogated them.

some might view "puritan" as a scornful religious epithet. "Zealots" and "Pharisees" were ancient religious sects. "Cannibal" is derived from the Haitian tribe named the Canibas.

You could call people who use such words bigots—but not without violating the statute. The "Bigots" were a tribe in South Gaul in the 12th century.

Doubtless you can think of many other formerly "vulgar, derisive and abusive" phrases that have become part of our language.

Another curious problem with the Civil Rights statute was why the aggravating factors raised the penalty to a misdemeanor. It is offensive to a citizen to be abused in public. Is it worse if the person is harassed or annoyed because or race, color, creed etc.? Is it *more* offensive?[794] If so, is the statute still constitutional, or is the person who utters the statements nevertheless exercising freedom of expression permitted by the constitution even if it is acutely annoying to someone who hears it?

Perhaps the Court of Appeals missed the point of the harassment statute. While a person is permitted to express his opinions freely, his right to do so may end where he does it with the intent of annoying and harassing another person rather than to exercise his right to convey ideas. To call someone a Philistine while expressing your opinion may be permissible, but to call the same person a Philistine with the intent of harassing or annoying him may be a Penal Law violation.[795]

Does a civil complaint lie for intentional infliction of emotional distress for name calling after *Dietze*?[796]

---

[794] Than being called a "dog" or "bitch" as was the complainant in *People v. Dietze*.

[795] It is thus legal to ask the riddle "How many (insert ethnic group of your choice) does it take to change a light bulb?" unless it is done to annoy that ethnic group.

[796] Compare *Russo v. Iacono* 73 App. Div. 2d 913 (2nd Dept. 1980) [defendant alleged to have thrice used vile and obscene language] and *Halop v. Lurie* 15 App. Div. 2d 62 (2nd Dept. 1961) [defendant sent a taunting and insulting letter to a jilted ex-fiancee] with *Flamm v. Van Nierop* 56 Misc 2d

It is the intent of the speaker and not the contents of his speech that is regulated in the harassment statute. It is still legal to yell "Fire" in a crowed theater if there *is* a fire, after all, and illegal if there isn't one.[797]

The law still has the ability to determine the existence of "actual malice,"[798] a close relative of "with intent to annoy."

The state and federal constitutions permit the freedom to express ideas, and not the freedom to intentionally annoy neighbors.

1059 (S.Ct., Westchester Co. 1968) in which Justice Dillon wrote "On the other hand, offenses of a minor nature, such as name-calling or angry looks, are not actionable though they may wound the feelings of the victim and cause some degree of emotional upset. This is because the law has no cure for trifles" (at 1060).

[797] Modern law is increasing a series of acts of line drawing. Modern law knows few absolutes. When individuals' rights come into conflict, balancing tests become the way of determining the law. My right to speak is balanced against your freedom not to be annoyed by it. Law thus reflects what is appropriate as viewed by modern society, like the "pig in the parlor" cases. A pig is not offensive in the barnyard, but may be in the parlor. ("Nuisance may merely be a right thing in the wrong place—like a pig in the parlor instead of the barnyard." (Mr. Justice Sutherland in *Euclid v. Ambler Realty Co.* 272 U.S. 365, 388, 71 L.Ed. 2d 303, 47 S.Ct. 114) See, 16 Westchester Bar Journal 71, "Wry on Ham Hold the Huntley Notice"," at footnotes 2 and 3 on page 71.).Certain words are not offensive in certain contexts, but can be in the wrong context or the wrong place. For example "Bitch" is a perfectly good term when applied to a female dog, (although the University of Georgia women's basketball team insists on calling itself the Lady Bulldogs), but may be banned from public airwaves when used in another context.

[798] E.g., "It is incumbent upon plaintiff to prove at trial that the defendants published the subject issue of *Celebrity Skin* with actual malice, i.e., with knowledge that the nude photo did not depict plaintiff or with reckless disregard of that fact." *Davis v. High Society Magazine* 90 App. Div. 2d 374, 457 NYS2d 308 (2nd Dept, 1982).

THE NUTS AND BOLTS OF MENTAL HYGIENE PRACTICE:
Part I—The Nuts

by James M Rose[799]

CAUTION: The contents of this column may cause drowsiness. Do not operate the machinery of justice while thinking about this column. Take the contents of this column with a grain of salt. Do not mix the contents of this column with any reported case in your briefs or memoranda without the advice of counsel. This article may be harmful if swallowed whole. Do not bite off more than you can chew, chew slowly and repeat as necessary.

Do not read the contents of this column if you have been diagnosed with an imbalance of the four body humors, or if you have problems with an impaired respiratory or legal system. Do not read this column in a moving vehicle if you suffer from mal de mer, mal du pays, or mal de practice. Keep all law out of the reach of children. This article may contain or concern the fruits of the poisonous tree which are harmful to penumbras or emanations of rights.

Pregnant women should limit their intake of irony.

All warranties express or implied are disclaimed. The analogies in this column may be unconscionable. If irritation persists consult an analogist.

Do not mix law and public policy unless protected by a long black robe. Mix only on a high bench.[800]

WARNING: Obscure OSHA regulations require the wearing of gloves to avoid paper cuts when turning the pages. Some jokes in this warning may cause a feeling of *deja vu*.

WARNING: You have no right to remain ignorant. If you take Continuing Legal Education courses what you learn can, and

---
[799] White Plains, New York, This is a work of fiction. Any resemblance between James M. Rose and any person living or dead is the fault of genetics.
[800] Remember Emmanuel Kant, Elaine May, but Harold Wood.

will be held against you in a court of law. If you cannot afford continuing legal education the court will be disappointed in you. A little knowledge is a dangerous thing. Hard cases make bad law and *vice versa*.

WARNING: Some jokes in this in this warning may cause a feeling of *deja vu*.[801]

You must remember this: a kiss is still a kiss; assize is still assize. Keep away from firesides when a process server's due. Take good care of yourself if you want to sue.

The wheels of justice grind slowly, nevertheless you must wear a seat belt and eye protection when grinding.

That color shirt does not look good on you with your coloring and it makes you look fat.[802]

By turning the page of this article you agree to abide by all the terms of the Supreme Court, including but not limited to Special Term, IAS Term and the Appellate Term.[803]

DISCLAIMER: The opinions contained in the New York Reports are not those of the author, or of the Westchester County Bar Association, who are not responsible for them.[804]

SIDE EFFECTS: If verisimilitude occurs, you may experience lightheadedness such as a light going on over your head like in a cartoon. Aging may occur if you take a long time to read this article or spend a lot of time reading these warnings.

Death is generally considered the most undesirable side effect. Eyestrain may result from reading warnings in small print.

This column may alter your specific gravity or pH factor. One percent of readers reported having their retainer agreements converted to detainer agreements, but the same number report being abducted by alien spacecraft, so go figure.

---

[801] No, we did not say that before.

[802] In the Appellate Division there are no casual Fridays, and the court reserves the right not to serve patrons without shoes.

[803] The terms of those terms may not be altered orally.

[804] The Westchester County Bar Association is a registered trademark of the Westchester County Bar Association, and cannot be used by any bar or grill without permission.

This column has not been tested on humans, animals, vegetables or crash test dummies. This column has not been tested in court, and this is still the Beta version which may cause your justice system to crash, requiring you to reboot, or edit this run on sentence.

Mineral rights in this column are the property of the heirs of Phelpse. Only union labor has been used in the preparation of this column, however pursuant to the North American Free Trade Agreement (NAFTA) it was actually produced in Mexican unions[805] where index numbers and court costs are cheaper.

INSTRUCTIONS: For maximum *feng shui* effect read this column with a window behind you while facing a door.

Shake well before opening.[806]

This column may be read without first filing an RJI or submitting a photocopy of the index number application.

You are hereby advised to place all carry on luggage under your seat, return your seat back and tray table to their upright position, and securely fasten your seat belt pursuant to the requirements of the Plane Language Law.

WARNING: Do not mix the contents of these warnings with any other warnings least unforeseen interactions occur.

Don't say we didn't warn you.

CONCLUSION

Unfortunately, due to the length of the required warnings, the space allotted for the discussion of this subject has been entirely consumed.

In the Next Issue: Part II—The Bolts.[807]

---

[805] Where the work is assigned according to Señor Ity.

[806] The purpose of this warning is not to mix up the contents of this article, which are sufficiently mixed up as it is, but to give you some cardiovascular exercise.

[807] The author will write part Two by doing research, as he has never actually represented any on the Bolts.

James M. Rose

QUASI-EDITORIAL[808]

CLE-VER WAYS TO GET CLE CREDITS

The other day I took some time off from writing the screenplay for my autobiographical movie "A Homely Mind"[809] to look over the ream of advertisements that came in the mail in the previous fortnight hawking CLE [810] lecture credits. I quote now from an actual missive from Pace University School of Law which came on a light blue background (a color no doubt carefully selected using *feng shui* principles to entice me to part with some cash): "Feng Shui: An Essential to the Art of Business Management Especially for Lawyers [Sic]. 2.5 Credits Practice."[811]

It went on to introduce the instructor and course as follows:

"Shareane Baff, consultant and teacher of Feng Shui[812] since 1996 [813] will discuss how lawyers can make money and have an edge over their competitors using *Feng Shui*. *Feng Shui*[814] is the ancient Chinese art of maximizing the flow of energy called *Chi*.

---

[808] If you agree with this editorial you must be quasi.
[809] And sub-titled "A Face Made for Radio."
[810] CLE is an acronym which stands for confusing, lengthy and expensive.
[811] I am not making this up. I wouldn't have the nerve.
[812] *Feng Shui* is not pronounced as it is spelled.
[813] We are not given the academic credentials of Ms. Baff, who has dispensed ancient wisdom since the primordial year 1996. Does she have a doctorate in the divination of fortune cookies?
[814] *Feng shui* is actually pronounced "Fung Shu-way" according to several websites. It means "wind" and "water" in Chinese and has its origins in Taoist beliefs. They include the theory that the Earth is constructed upon the body a dragon and care must be taken not to erect any structures on its ... er ... sensitive parts. Modern adherants of *Feng Shui* believe that the dragon is just a metaphor for something—OCA perhaps.

* Learn *Feng Shui* principles to organize your interior office space
* Where to place your desk to gain control[815]
* How to attract success."

Now if you want to consult an interior decorator for business advice, I won't stand in your way.[816] The Reagans did well consulting astrologers before making important decisions on which compass heading to employ when steering the ship of state. But after I studied hours of cases in order to be knowledgeable enough to judge a moot court panel correctly and got *one* CLE credit, I take umbrage at the possibility of collecting two and one half credits for being told where to place my desk.

Since the OCA[817] ultimately has the say concerning the approval of CLE credits, does this course constitute some state endorsement of the principals of Taoism?[818] Has *Feng Shui* undergone the rigorous tests applied to expert opinion in *Frye* hearings? Has the reliability of the scientific principles upon which it is based been accepted in the scientific, legal or decorating communities?

As a person eager to learn new practice skills,[819] I want the *Chi* in my office to flow like the glib testimony of a $5,000 a day expert witness who has just been asked upon what he has based his opinion.

I'm not sure exactly what *Chi* is,[820] but I believe that if you step in a pile of it in an open field, it will stick to your shoes and impart a repugnant smell to your carpet.

---

[815] I hope the course doesn't overlook the possibility of placing it in the center of your opponent's sternum.

[816] Do you want your office to reflect the design aesthetics and decor of a Chinese take-out restaurant? A Chinese laundry?

[817] An acronym for Office of Continuing Aggravation.

[818] Will next semester's course be "Optimum Placement and Decoration of the Wall between Church and State"? Taoism is also not pronounced like it's spelled.

[819] I try to keep an open mind but I have posted a "No Dumping" sign there.

[820] When I was growing up "Chi" was a scoreboard abbreviation for the White Sox or Cubs.

Have these experts advised OCA on the correct way to arrange a jury box, which door the plaintiffs and defendants should enter or exit, and what color the judge's robes ought to be? Does Chi *flow* in courtrooms as well, or does it just roll down hill?

Are there other CLE courses we can take that will impart equally as arcane theories of the most auspicious moment to take a plea? Are CLE credits available for studying the auguries in the entrails of animals sacrificed by oracles in Delphi, New York? Can numerologists advise us (in return for handsome remuneration) which index numbers are unlucky for plaintiffs, and, if they can, how many CLE credits is it worth?

The difficult CLE credits to get are those ethics ones. I have envisioned a marathon ethics seminar for the same people who take legal advice from interior decorators. I believe there's a large pool of them out there—Barnum said that there's one born every minute.

The seminar consists of a panel of celebrities who have had recent brushes with ethical dilemmas and can tell us about what hard knocks taught them. Enron's Kenneth Lay would teach the ethics of corporate marketing, Michael Milken could address International Finance, Leona Helmsley could discourse on the ethics of state taxation avoidance, Arthur Anderson could hold forth under the snappy caption "There's no accounting for Accounting", and Westchester's own Bill Clinton could address the ethics of Grand Jury testimony and the definition of irregular and intransitive verbs in the present tense.

My problem with this panel is that some entrepreneurially minded member would no doubt get the bright idea that it is easier to simply *sell* the CLE credit certificates than it is to actually teach the course.

This will give rise to the necessity of a CLE course that addresses the ethics of buying and selling CLE ethics credits on the Web.

However, I have an even more ingenious way of making money than teaching interior decoration to aesthetically challenged lawyers under the ADA.[821]

---

[821] The ADA is *not* an acronym for Attorneys With Dysfunctional Antechambers.

I plan to copyright or trademark the terms "plaintiff" and "defendant"—terms I have used for years in *my* legal papers. Then anyone who brings a lawsuit in the English speaking world will have to pay *me* a small fee.

James M. Rose

SUING THE DEVIL IN NEW YORK[822]

In *United States ex. re. Mayo v. Satan and His Staff*[823] Federal District Court Judge Weber was faced with a civil rights lawsuit by a prisoner[824] who alleged that Satan and his staff were deliberating placing obstacles in plaintiff's path and causing his downfall. Judge Weber rises[825] to the occasion by looking at procedural jurisdictional issues.[826]

This article asks: What if such a case were brought in New York? Judge Weber first looks at the issue of personal jurisdiction over the defendant. There were no cases in which the devil had been successfully sued in his judicial district. There were none in which the Devil appeared voluntarily as a plaintiff, although the judge alluded to one in which the Devil appeared a long time ago in New Hampshire and faced off against Daniel Webster.

---

[822] by James M. Rose, White Plains, New York, This column was tested on humans so as not to injure laboratory animals.

[823] 54 F.R.D. 282 (Dist. Ct., W.D. Pa., 1971).

[824] Or so it appears because the action is brought in the form of a habeas corpus petition. The case does not indicate if Mayo was a prisoner, and if he was it does not indicate whether it was a state or federal government that had a court commitment to "hold the Mayo" corpus. Neither does the report reveal why the suit was brought in the form of a habeas corpus although it was a civil rights suit. The most likely answer is that it was a *pro se* action by a prisoner who used whatever forms were available in the prison law library. When it comes to lawsuits, one size does not fit all—hence the need for litigation boutiques.

[825] or perhaps descends.

[826] The court does not deal with the substantive jurisdictional questions. For example, even if Satan was interfering with Mayo, the complaint fails to state a civil rights cause of action unless the Devil was doing so in conjunction with a municipal defendant under color of law. The decision does not recite whether Mayo alleged that a government was in league with Satan. What color is color of law? Most law suits attorneys own are either navy blue or gray flannel (see footnote 3, supra.).

While Judge Weber could find no evidence of the work of the devil in the Western District of Pennsylvania, the result could be very different if one were to look around New York.

In the New Hampshire case the devil was referred to as a "foreign prince." We do not know if he would assert the defense of sovereign immunity in New York, or that New York would recognize such a claim.[827] Trying a case on the Devil's home turf[828] would be an extreme example of *forum non conveniens*.[829]

Finally, Judge Weber noted that Mayo did not include any directions for accomplishing the service of process.[830]

That, too, would not be a problem in New York. Long arm jurisdiction would be available even if the devil did not physically travel to New York, as long as he transacted some business sufficient

---

[827] see *People v. Coumatos*, 32 Misc 2d 1085, 224 NYS2d 507 (Ct. Gen. Sessions 1962) in which a United Nations employee was not immune from prosecution. There is no treaty between the United States and Hell (we hope) granting immunity to American diplomats in Hell. This absence of reciprocity may result in denial of diplomatic immunity to the Devil here. The purpose of sovereign immunity is to allow the Executive Department of the Federal Government to deal with foreign governments without embarrassment by other branches of government, the Supreme Court, Westchester County told us in *Weilamann v. Chase Manhattan Bank,* 21 Misc. 2d. 1086, 192 NYS2d 469 (1959)—but there is no proof that the State Department considers the Devil a foreign prince under the Foreign Sovereign Immunity Act (28 U.S.C.§ 1330.)

[828] A true home court advantage.

[829] Any appeal would certainly involve a "hot bench."

[830] Details are important in the law. Ludwig Mies Van Der Rohe once said "God is in the details." Is the opposite true as well, that is that "The Devil is in the General Propositions"? Ludwig Mies Van Der Rohe also said "less is more"--a statement which applied to his architecture, but not his five part name.

to grant New York jurisdiction over him.[831] Service on any satanic cult will do.[832]

It would take a New York lawyer to want to get in a battle with the Devil, but how does one prove that the Devil exists as a matter of law and transacts business in New York?[833] The answer is found in the decisions of the Appellate Division and the Court of Appeals in the Unification Church taxation case, *Matter of Holy Spirit Association for the Unification of World Christianity v. Tax Commission.*[834] The state tax commission alleged that the church's activity were primarily political, and that, as such, it was not entitled to a tax exemption as a religious institution. During the course of a hearing, a transcribed book call *Divine Principles* was introduced as an exhibit.[835] It recited

---

[831] CPLR § 302(a)(1) provides that "a court may exercise personal jurisdiction over any non-domiciliary***who in person or through an agent***transacts any business within the state."

[832] See a one paragraph note in the New York *Law Journal* of August 9, 1989 p. 1 col 2B that indicates that a coven of witches won a tax exemption as a legitimate religious group from the state of Rhode Island. The state Tax Administrator found that the Rosengate Coven was entitled to a sale-tax exemption because it met the guidelines for religious organizations established in 1987 by the Supreme Court of Rhode Island.

[833] Why one would want to do so is another question entirely. An enterprising attorney might believe that the Devil has deep pockets, despite the fact he is so often depicted as having no pockets at all.

People try to make a connection between evil and money when they say "Money is the root of all evil." However, the correct quotation is "It has been said that the love of money is the root of all evil. The want of money is so quite as truly." (Samuel Butler, *Erewhon* XX)[Emphasis added]

Although it may be possible to sue the Devil in New York, collecting a judgment would be much harder—See, R. Cutler, "Executing Judgments Under FSIA [Foreign Sovereign Immunities Act]: Winning Isn't Everything," New York *Law Journal*, August 17, 1995, p. 1.

[834] 55 NY2d 512, 450 NYS2d 292 (1982) reversing 81 App. Div. 2d 64 at 81 App.Div. 2d 74. Therefore, advocates of the principles of tripartite government are doing Satan's work.

the principles of the group's beliefs, and was the scripture upon which the organization was founded. Among the things that it recited was that in World War II some of the nations served Satan (p. 475 of the book) and that the doctrine of separation of powers is a satanic principle which Satan exploits to accomplish evil *(Principles* at 468.)[836] The book was admitted into evidence as a church record, and the court ultimately held that the Church was, in fact, a business. The book was, therefore, a business record. As every fledgling law student knows, a business record is not only admissible, it is prima facie evidence of the information contained in it. It is therefore evidence of the doings of Satan in, *inter alia*, New York.

A possible defense for the Devil suggests itself. When disasters happen in New York we seldom blame the Devil, and those who *have* blamed the Devil for their problems in reported cases have often been placed in mental institutions as a result of their beliefs.[837]

Rather, we refer to calamities as "acts of God".[838] When a court renders a declaratory judgment that some disaster was an act of God[839] it allocates responsibility among parties and establishes causation. If it finds the cause of the disaster is attributable to an

---

[835] 81 App.Div. 2d at 89.

[836] 81 App. Div. 2d 74. Therefore, advocates of the principles of tripartite government are doing Satan's work.

[837] For example, *In the Matter of Nathaniel T.*, 112 App. Div. 2d 692, 492 NYS2d 311 (4th Dept., 1985); *People v. Kittle*, 154 App. Div. 2d 782 (3rd Dept., 1989); *Matter of Mental Hygiene Legal Services v. Wack*, 75 NY2d 751, 551 NYS2d 894 (1989); *Mental Hygiene Legal Services on relation of Angel Cruz*, 148 App. Div. 2d 341, 538 NYS2d 554 (1st Dept., 1989); *Thomas J.D. v. Catherine J. D.*, 79 App. Div. 2d 1015, 435 NYS2d 338 (2nd Dept., 1981); *Bell v. NYC Heath and Hospital Corp.*, 90 App. Div. 2d 270, 456 NYS2d 787 (2nd Dept., 1982).

Has the Devil (or his attorney—the Devil's Advocate) been crafty enough to convince judges he doesn't exist, and therefore anyone who says he does is crazy? That is the ultimate defense, and better than immunity!

[838] or "*vis divina*" (Rhymes with misdemeanor—if you're Ogden Nash).

[839] "The Lord has given and the Lord has taken away," Job 1:2.

act of God,[840] is the issue of the Devil as a cause of the loss precluded by *res judicata*?[841]

And what will the damages be if you prevail? In the Book of Job the Devil tempts God to wrongfully ruin Job. At the end of the Book of Job his "relief" is that he is restored twofold by God.[842]

CONCLUSION

Most law journal type articles need conclusions, and this one is no exception.

---

[840] God is not made a party to those actions for declaratory judgments. It would not be wise to sue God, the Ultimate Deep Pocket. When Job sought to question God concerning a perceived injustice, Job lost his house, flocks, all his possessions, and his family as a result. He was reduced to sitting naked and scratching a tormenting disease. And you thought Federal Court discovery sanctions were tough!

[841] Or can liability be apportioned among God and others under *Dole v. Dow Chemical Co.*, 30 NY2d 143, 331 NYS2d 382, 282 NE2d 288 (1972)? What ever happened to "Guilty as Hell?"

[842] Job 42:10.

DISORDERS IN THE COURT—ALL RISE

by James M. Rose[843]

Mental disorders are finding their way into court more and more in our complex society.[844] With the advent of the Americans With Disabilities Act,[845] the Family and Medical Leave Act,[846] and similar state legislation, more and more the courts are involved with the subject of disorders either by those who are affirmatively seeking relief, or those who are defending their own actions and using disorders to excuse or explain them.

The most recent and extreme example of that was an insanity defense asserted in *People v. Ralph Cramdown* in Supreme Court, Westchester County before Justice Apocraphya. The defendant Cramdown, a bankruptcy attorney with the firm of Skratch & Snif, in a fit of rage, killed a client who was described as a slimy slumlord who owned twin tenements,[847] and who was a corporate raider who had systematically raped and pillaged a corporation,[848] destroyed the lives of its employees, and reduced the value of the shares so much that they went from being traded over the counter to being traded under the counter. The client had consistently lied to Cramdown, had not paid him, and was often late to court.[849]

---

[843] White Plains, New York, and author of *Protecting the Judas Goat and the Skeet Under the Endangered Species Act.*

[844] By that the author means that mental and physical disorders are the lynch pin of cases in many fields, and means to cast no aspersions on the advocates, witnesses, jurors or judiciary.

[845] Americans With Disabilities Act, 42 U.S.C. §§ 12101 *et. seq.*

[846] Family and Medical Leave Act of 1993 (29 U.S.C. §§ 2601 et. seq.) effective August 8, 1993 (except for parts that are not).

[847] The press called him the lessor of two evils.

[848] who prided himself on the fact that there was nothing lower than his bottom line.

[849] A defense suggested by sympathetic members of the local bar was justifiable homicide.

His initial defense was that he had just gone blank and acted in a fit of rage. This classical insanity defense was referred to in the press as "blank rage."

Although "disorders" have been used before as part of an insanity defense,[850] this case took a bizarre twist. Mr. Cramdown, a lay preacher for a modern religion called the Ethical Humanist Society [851] pleaded a First Amendment defense as well. A psychiatrist was appointed to examine Mr. Cramdown. They had many long and delightful philosophical conversations at the expense of the taxpayers. When the psychiatrist was asked in court if Mr. Cramdown knew and appreciated the difference between right and wrong,[852] he replied that Mr. Cramdown had convinced him that there is no difference.

---

[850] For example, "Personality disorder" *People v. Kasten*, (191) 175 App. Div. 2d 884, 573 NYS2d 731; "schitzo-affective disorder" *People v. Markowitz* (1987) 133 App. Div. 2d 379, 519 NYS2d 376; "isolated explosive disorder" *People v. Enchautegui* (1989) 156 App. Div. 2d 461, 548 NYS2d 461, appeal denied 76 NY2d 787, 559 NYS2d 992, 559 NE2d 686; "Post traumatic stress syndrome" *People v. Santana* 80 NY2d 92 (1992) and *People v. Rodriguez* 192 App. Div. 2d 465 (1993); "thought disorder" *People v. Gensler* 72 NY2d 239; "temporary functional psychosis" *People v. Diaz* 51 NY2d 841, 433 NYs2d 751 (1980); "adjustment disorder" *People v. Ryklin* 150 App. Div. 2d 509, 541 NYS2d 103 (2nd Dept., 1989); *People v. Maula* 138 App. Div. 2d 307, 526 NYS2d 441 (1st Dept., 1988); "dissociative disorder" *People v. Bruetsch* 137 App. Div. 2d 823, 527 NYS2d 287 (1st Dept., 1988) and *People v. Mendez*, 1 NY 3d 15 (2003); "hystronic personality disorder" *People v. Vozzo*, 283 App. Div. 2d 310 (1st Dept., 2001); and "episodic dyscontrol paroxysm" *People v. Roudabush* 123 App. Div. 2d 649 (2nd Dept., 1986). At the time this article is being written, Joel Rifkin's attorney has announced that he will rely on the "adopted child syndrome" as a defense.

[851] He used to be a devout coward, but then he lapsed.

[852] The ancient and debated standard known as the *M'Naghten* test was modified by the passage of the revised Penal Law in New York. The current test found in Penal Law § 40.15 requires (inter alia) a defendant to lack the

Mr. Cramdown had convinced him that all ethics are situational, and that therefore one had to make his own decisions based only upon the situation as he knew and understood it. Right and wrong as absolutes do not exist, he concluded in either ethics or the law.

Mr. Cramdown's attorney, John De Jennerette, of the law firm of Loess, Swift, Moore, Caustic & De Jennerette, convinced the judge that the psychiatrist's views should prevail.[853] The judge noted that killing could not be considered "wrong" if the several states and the Federal government authorized it under their capital crimes statutes.

Extortion is something the state practices as well when it makes you pay taxes under threat of imprisonment (which itself is akin to kidnaping, or the crime of unlawful imprisonment.) The state forbids gambling, and yet it runs its own numbers game, lotteries, video poker, OTB parlors, and various gambling schemes. The state profits from the taxes on cigarettes and alcoholic beverages, which are known to cause a variety of diseases. The state was therefore estopped to argue that there were moral "rights and wrongs" if the state itself practiced the very acts it forbid to its citizens as "wrong," and had no moral compass of its own.

The taking of a life is merely prohibited,[854] and not morally wrong,[855] the judge concluded, or else the states and the Federal government would not be permitted to do it either. This is in keeping with a trend in the United States Supreme Court to view all constitutional rights (and wrongs) as situational rather than absolute so that rights have to be balanced.[856]

"substantial capacity to know or appreciate . . . (2) That such conduct is wrong."

[853] Justice Apochraphya wrote that he hesitated to say the psychiatrist was right or wrong since there was no right or wrong, and that he would therefore rule only that this view should prevail.

[854] *malum prohibitum.*

[855] *malum in se.*

[856] My right to speak is balanced against your freedom not to be annoyed by it. Law thus reflects what is appropriate as viewed by modern society, like

Then Mr. Cramdown's First Amendment freedom argument was addressed. He believed as a religious belief (as modern society apparently believes in a secular context) that what is "right" in a situation requires each individual to consider the context of his act and determine by balancing the rights of the many and the rights of the individual what is "right" or "wrong." He killed a useless and lawless outlaw who had ruined many peoples' lives, and whose absence improves the world. His act was not forbidden by his own religion, which taught to seek the greatest good for the greatest number, and was therefore not "wrong," since there is no "wrong" in any absolute sense, but only in a comparative one.[857] His religion was not a First Amendment bar to his prosecution because it did not teach that one should kill. However, it was a defense in that, if he sincerely believed that there is no right and wrong, he could hardly be held to appreciate the difference.[858] The accepted charge to the jury on insanity is that a defendant know that his act was "contrary to the laws of God[859] and man."[860] The laws of man include the state killing, the judge held, and a jury determining what the laws of God are requires the state to impose a state theology at variance with that of the defendant, and hence in violation of his First Amendment rights.

While he was in jail, Mr. Cramdown sued because his cell was declared by the county to be in a no smoking area. Mr. Cramdown

---

the "pig in the parlor" cases. A pig is not offensive in the barnyard, but may be in the parlor. ("Nuisance may merely be a right thing in the wrong place—like a pig in the parlor instead of the barnyard." (Mr. Justice Sutherland said in *Euclid v. Ambler Realty Co,*. 272 U.S. 365, 388, 71 L. Ed. 2d 303, 47 S. Ct. 114).

[857] This is sometimes referred to as the disability defense of the "differently moralled," and should not be referred to as the "morally impaired" which expresses a value judgment that someone else's beliefs are incorrect.

[858] Indeed, Mr. Cramdown said he did not appreciate being told to appreciate the difference by politicians in the Legislature.

[859] "Whose God?" Justice Apochraphya inquired, anticipating a battle between the ten amendments and the ten commandments.

[860] (*People v. Wood* 12 NY2d 69 at 67).

argued that nicotine was an addictive drug, as congressional hearings showed. Since cigarettes are legal drugs, his addiction is like a food addiction of an obese person,[861] and requires that he be reasonably accommodated[862] like that person—but unlike someone who is currently addicted to an illegal drug.[863] The government was required to accommodate the disability by permitting him to smoke inside his cell which is a place of public accommodation,[864] he argued.[865]

He further argued that making the jail a smoke free zone and requiring people to go outside the building to smoke in the courtyard was an act that had a deleterious effect on the environment. Therefore it could not be undertaken by a governmental entity without a full environmental impact study in which the effects of secondary smoke (which would now be released into the environment instead of being contained within a building) had to be considered.

While the study was pending the judge dismissed the charges against him.

---

[861] *State Division of Human Rights v. Xerox Corp.* (1985) 65 NY2d 213 at 219, 491 NYS2d 106, 480 NE2d 695.

[862] See The Americans With Disabilities Act, 42 U.S.C. § 12182 (b)(2)(A)(ii).

[863] Although nicotine is an addictive drug he denied he was addicted, and said that he could quit ten times a day and, often did.

[864] as a lodging (42 U.S.C. § 12181 (7)(A)). The government pointed out his cell was not very accommodating.

[865] Individuals with breathing problems or allergies have to be accommodated by limiting the amount of cigarette smoke they inhale, but are not entitled to an absolutely smoke free workplace as an accommodation if they can function with less accommodation *Harmer v. Virginia Electric Power Co.*, 831 F. Supp. 1300 (E.D. Va. 1993). The case implies that they may have to be accommodated with a smoke free environment if necessary. Who gets accommodated in a one cell jail when someone with an allergy requiring a smoke free environment and someone with a nicotine addiction are placed in the same cell is anyone's guess.

[866] Take this article with a grain of salt and don't call us in the morning, Dr. Dixit advises.

RES IPSA LOQUITUR (Humor)[866]

DR. IPSIE DIXIT'S ADVICE TO THE LAW LORN: "BE UPSTANDING IN COURT"[867]

by Dr. Ipse Dixit, Doctor of Ettiqutology[868]

Anyone can tell you what the law is. Your clients frequently do. A small percentage even get it right. With the advent of LEXIS and WESTLAW, even inanimate objects can advise you about its changes.

More subtle, and perhaps more important to attorneys, are answering the problems of etiquette in the courtroom. This will be increasingly true in courts in the nineties, where Gresham's Law dictates that style drives out substance in any public forum. To slash that Gordian Knot, we sought the counsel of Dr. Ipse Dixit, occupant of the Ann Landers Chair of Forensic Decorum and Gratuitous Advice at the PostModern School of Law in Entropee, Mass.,[869] where he holds the title of Assistant Maven.

We have asked him to discuss several controversies that have appeared in the popular press recently.[870] The first raged for a while in the New York *Law Journal,* and concerned how one addresses an ex-judge while in court as an adversary of the former jurist. The other deals with whether one should laugh at the jokes told by a presiding judge.

---

[867] Clever pun based upon what is said when the judges enters the courtroom in England.

[868] as told to James M. Rose over a lime and bottled water in White Plains, New York. The views expressed in this article are not those of the Westchester County Bar Association, who have requested Dr. Dixit to present proof of his degree which he describes as an EmilyPost-Doctorate.

[869] Obscure pun for physics majors. Dr. Dixit used to be a cosmetologist, but he is now a cosmologist, because his dentist advised him to eliminate the "t," as it stains teeth.

[870] As this is a quarterly publication, "recently" is always a relative term. "Permanent" is a relative term in life and in law, Judge Fuchsberg reminded

Dr. Dixit knows that an adversary would like to show respect for his opponent—but not *too much*. Therefore, for either the bench or an opponent to refer to a litigating attorney as "Judge" may give that person an unfair advantage in the eyes of a jury. Dr. Dixit has suggested that he be referred to as "The Formerly Honorable."

To laugh or not to laugh, that is the question[871] next addressed by Dr. Dixit. Alan Dershowitz, peripatetic mouthpiece of the rich and famous, told *New York* Magazine, arbiter of modern megalopolis morals, that he makes it a point never to laugh at jokes told by judges. What should the practitioner who may *actually* have to appear in that court again do?

This problem requires a complex response. Asking Mr. Dershowitz' advice on matters of courtroom seemliness may be like getting your tax advice from Leona Helmsley. Dr. Dixit has a more judicial temperament—his best subject in school was recess.

He notes that many of our customs in court are merely ways of assuring politeness in a confrontational situation which is often fraught with tension and unpleasantness. The more formal the setting, the less likely chaos will reign. That is why we call the judge "your honor,"[872] and why the most powerful person in the courtroom is the one who, regardless of sex, is wearing a black dress.[873] It is a symbol of his power, and is meant to promote decorum and to defuse the volatile situation. Lawyers as well must dress somberly, because a judge can fine them for wearing a frivolous suit.[874]

---

us in *Dutchess Sanitation Service v. Town of Plattekill,* 51 NY2d 670 at 673-4.

[871] Literary allusion.

[872] Regardless of what he or she did before ascending to the bench.

[873] If you look at the portrait of John Jay that hangs in Court of Appeals Hall in Albany, you will see our first Chief Judge wore a red robe. His successors chose black (perhaps because red did nothing for their complexions), but the reason for this chromatic change is lost in the mists of history, See *Revlon on Forensic Couture.*

[874] It's in the Federal Rules. You may not be able to find it, but trust me, it's in there somewhere.

You must always be polite to judges if you want to have any *amicus* in *curiae*. Dr. Dixit reminds you that, if the judge reacts to your argument by asking, "How stupid do you think I am?" it is *always* a rhetorical question.

Likewise Rumpole's "By now it should be clear even to your honor . . ." is literary fiction.

Therefore, one should laugh politely at the judge's jokes. They, too, are sometimes told to lighten the atmosphere of a sensitive situation.[875] Judges are not permitted to tell bad jokes,[876] so, as a matter of (administrative) law the joke is deemed to be funny. This provision is *not* known as the "Gag rule," which is something else.[877] However, judges are not permitted to tell very funny jokes because of a state regulation which is often known as the Law of "Gravity."[878]

Therefore, Dr. Dixit reminds the attorney not only to stand up in court when the judge comes in,[879] but also to be upstanding.

---

[875] Or to "entertain" a motion.

[876] See, 22 NYCRR § 100.1 which requires a judge to observe high standards of conduct.

[877] If the judge indicates that he will invoke the "gag rule," it is not polite to suggest that your opponent's mouth requires an extra large size gag.

[878] See 22 NYCRR § 100.3 (a) (2) "A judge shall maintain order and decorum in proceedings before him or her." A joke which is so funny that it upsets decorum would appear to violate this regulation.

[879] This is not a court rule, but a custom. It should be done even if the judge does not tell jokes, as it has nothing to do with the term "stand up comedian." Mr. Dershowitz did not indicate that he also flaunts his independence from the judiciary by not standing up when the judge comes into the courtroom. One is reminded of the attorney who did not stand up when a judge entered court. The judge then remained standing. When the seated attorney asked him why he was standing, the judge replied, "Because it is customary when I come into court that one of us stands."

CHAPTER SEVEN

ON A SCALE FROM EXCELLENT TO POOR, ALL'S FAIR IN LOVE, WAR AND TAXES

"DON'T LOOK FOR TRUTH IN MY COURTROOM, IT'S NOT A LOST AND FOUND"[880]

When mutual fund mogul Wes Tosterone[881] married super model Esther Ginn,[882] their friends said it wouldn't last. It didn't.

All the tabloids were interested in obtaining the details of their divorce cross complaints. But Domestic Relations Law § 235 makes the contents of the County Clerk's file confidential.[883] Nevertheless, gossip monger Bjorn Otto Wettloch[884] published what he said were the allegations in their complaints in his Sunday column "Wicked Gossip" in the tabloid New York Voyeur. She was supposed

---

[880] by James M. Rose. Mr. Rose is the author of "Seven Daily Habits of Highly Defective Lawyers."

[881] He is the founder of NoLoad Contendre, a mutual fund that invests in companies that the Anti-trust division of the Justice Department is currently investigating.

[882] Known for her conviction for investing in Colombian extra-legal pharmaceutical futures.

[883] Section 235 - which replaced Rule 278 of the Rules of Civil Practice in 1962- insofar as pertinent, recited:

"Information as to details of matrimonial actions.

"An officer of the court with whom the proceedings in an action to annul a marriage or for divorce or separation are filed, or before whom the testimony is taken, or his clerk, either before or after the termination of the suit, shall not permit a copy of any of the pleadings or testimony, or any examination or perusal thereof, to be taken by any other person than a party, or the attorney or counsel of a party who had appeared in the cause, except by order of the court."

[884] who went by his nickname "The Bastard."

to have alleged to friends that his mutual fund performed a lot better last year than he did, and he is reported to have told people that she was "surgically enhanced."[885]

Esther Ginn publicly denied to the Wall Street *Scoop* that Wettloch was correct about the pleadings, and called him a liar. The *Voyeur* and Wettloch then sued Ginn for libel, and insisted they had a right to print true reports of court cases.[886] She counterclaimed for an invasion of privacy. She told the morning talk shows that a *tabloid* suing a *public figure* for libel was like a dagger—ironic and very sharp.

Esther Ginn was represented by Marie Dunn Dant of Werdie, Prolix and Verbose. Wettloch chose for his lawyer Harry Kopp of Bagadonitz & Coffey. The case came before Judge Izzy Rantinov in the discovery stage when Wettloch refuse to reveal his source[887]

---

[885] "Esther Ginn's lawyers were alleged not to have directly denied it, but to have replied that "all's fair in love and war." (Quoting Francis Edward Smedley in *Frank Fairlegh* (1850)). The judge pointed out that such was not the case, since in war there *are* rules such as the Geneva Convention. Don Quixote said that Love and War are the same thing (Pt. II Book III, Ch 21), and the Babylonian goddess Ishtar is the Goddess of both love and war.

[886] Section 74 of the Civil Rights Law reads as follows:

"Privileges in action for libel.

"A civil action cannot be maintained against any person, firm or corporation, for the publication of a fair and true report of any judicial proceeding, legislative proceeding or other official proceeding, or for any heading of the report which is a fair and true headnote of the statement published.

"This section does not apply to a libel contained in any other matter added by any person concerned in the publication; or in the report of anything said or done at the time and place of such a proceeding which was not a part thereof."

[887] Citing his privilege to keep confidential his journalist's source (section 79-h of the Civil Rights Law, the so-called "Shield Law"), the State Constitution's guarantee of freedom of the press (N.Y. Const, art I, §8), and *Matter of*

and Ginn refused to produce the two matrimonial complaints as part of a discovery demand because in an invasion of privacy suit truth is not a defense, it's an offense.[888]

Mr. Kopp insisted that he was entitled to see the complaints because his client was called a liar—a libel. He had to show the truth of his client's statement. He said that Wettloch chose to sue for libel because a court is the proper forum to search for the truth.[889] The Judge scoffed.

"Don't look for truth in my courtroom, it's not a lost and found. If you want to look for truth go to a university and become a scientist,"[890] he said. He noted that many universities had mottoes that referred to truth,[891] "but courts are concerned with more important things."[892]

Beach v Shanley, 62 NY2d 241, 476 NYS2d 765. The privilege is important to maintain a free press he noted, although the Judge remarked that the Sunday edition of the *Voyeur* was not free, but $1.75.

[888] "Nor, where no public figure is involved, may truth be pleaded as a defense to the causes of action for invasion of privacy. The very nature of that tort is the publication and exploitation of a person's private life and activities in such a manner as to cause him embarrassment and mental suffering. Since such injury may result even if the material published is entirely accurate, it follows that truth is irrelevant to a charge of invasion of privacy." *Shiles v. News Syndicate Co.* 27 NY 2d 9, 313 NYS2d 104 (1970).

[889] Kopp quoted the often heard statement that "Truth will out—even in an affidavit." When Mr. Kopp embellished his rhetorical flourishes with references to the Gospel According to Saint John (8:32) "the truth shall make you free," the Judge reminded the expensive Mr. Kopp that far from making *him* free, it didn't even make him inexpensive.

[890] "Science is a search for the truth," wrote Linus Pauling in *No More War* (1958).

[891] Harvard ("*Veritas*"), Yale ("*Veritas et Lux*") and Brandeis ("Truth Even Unto its innermost Parts") for example.

[892] He noted that in Wall Street and in the fashion modeling business, good impressions (or "image") were more important than the actual truth—since image is what attracts buyers and not reality.

He then proceeded to enumerate situations where the courts will ignore truth for one reason or another. "Finality or predictability is considered more important than truth to the court system, "he first noted. Thus there are statutes of limitations that prevent the truth from coming out if it involves a stale claim. Notice of claim requirements[893] which prevent the courts from considering the truth are clear indications that there are other more important things than truth to the courts.

Newly discovered evidence is often barred by the doctrine of *res judicata*. If truth were paramount in the courts, old controversies would be reopened again and again—"More often than the press revisits the Kennedy assassination," his honor noted. However, the courts have wisely held that *"Res judicata facit ex albo negrum, ex negro album, ex curvo rectum, ex recto curvum."*[894]

That is because courts prize finality above truth. "Wisely," Judge Rantinov noted, "*resolutions* of conflicts are preferred to deciding the conflicts correctly.[895] Otherwise, I would never get my calendar clear, which is the one thing that is of the utmost importance to the Office of Court Administration. They actually don't care *how* I dispose of cases as long as I do. The losing litigants will always criticize me no matter how long I take, so swiftness is wisely elevated in the law above a prolonged search for truth."[896]

"Look at *Miranda v. Arizona*[897] and at *Mapp v. Ohio*.[898] Are

---

[893] which are conditions precedent to commencing a lawsuit.

[894] "*Res judicata* makes white black, black white, the crooked straight and the straight crooked." *People ex. rel. Watchtower Bible Tract Society v. Haring*, 286 App. Div. 676, 683.

[895] Juries may not impeach their verdicts, for example, even if they later conclude that they misunderstood the court's charge, *Labov v. New York*, 15 App. Div. 2d 348, 545 NYS2d 826 (1989).

[896] Thus it is said by some wags that the public is always sure that an accused is guilty right up to the moment of the guilty verdict, after which they are convinced of his innocence.

[897] 384 U.S. 436.

[898] 367 U.S. 643.

they concerned about the truth? No, because perfectly true confessions are suppressed for the failure to warn a defendant of the glaringly obvious—that if he tells the police that he is guilty, his confession can be used as evidence against him at his trial! Physical evidence of a crime such as the murder weapon, which is the best evidence of guilt, can be suppressed for the failure to obtain a valid search warrant. The "truth" of the existence of the evidence is kept from a jury because a constable blundered. We value the rights contained in the Fourth and Fifth Amendment to the Constitution more than we do truth.[899]

If someone confesses to his priest, his social worker, his doctor or attorney, that evidence, although obviously true, is not admissible.[900] Why? Because privacy and the confidentiality of those relationships are more important than whether a jury hears the truth. Individual rights, finality, privacy, and other public concerns are all prized by courts above a quest for the truth.

A trial is not a search for the truth,[901] it is a search for a solution to a conflict within a set of complex rules."

---

[899] The rationale for suppressing evidence to enforce the Fourth and Fifth Amendments has been expressed as follows—As between the criminals and the police, it is our preference that the *criminals* be the ones who do wrong, so we punish the police when they do wrong, or at least we do not reward the police with convictions because they violated the constitution. If the police were indistinguishable from the criminals, the system would break down.

[900] See the spousal, attorney-client, physician-patient, clergy, psychologist, and social worker privileges (Civil Practice Law and Rules §§ 4502-4505, 4507, 4508).

[901] And he noted that prosecutors have been criticized by the Appellate Division, Second Department for telling the jury that a trial was a "search for the truth," (*People v. Sepulveda,* 105 App. Div. 2d 854, 857 [43] 1984; and "You are here to search for the truth" *People v. Robinson,* 83 App. Div. 2d 887 (1981). The court's rationale was that the statement tended to mislead the jury on a question of law, thus usurping the judge's function to do so.

Pointing to the sign in the back of the courtroom reminding occupants to "watch their hats, coats and other personal belongings,"[902] Judge Rantinov noted that frequently more is lost in courtrooms than is found.[903]

One of those situations where truth is disregarded is a suit for invasion of privacy, he remarked. As Warren and Brandeis declared in their seminal article, "The Right to Privacy" (4 Harv. *L. Rev.*, at p. 218):

"The truth of the matter published does not afford a defense [to an action for invasion of privacy]. Obviously this branch of the law should have no concern with the truth or falsehood of the matters published. It is not for injury to the individual's character that redress or prevention is sought, but for injury to the right of privacy. For the former the law of slander and libel provides perhaps a sufficient safeguard. The latter implies the right not merely to prevent inaccurate portrayal of private life, but to prevent its being depicted at all."

Wettloch did not have to reveal his source, the Judge ruled, because the Shield Law considers freedom of the press more important than the truth. Esther Ginn did not have to reveal the contents of matrimonial pleadings because the privacy afforded to matrimonial proceedings was more important than the truth.

Judge Rantinov then addressed the merits of the cases. He remarked that no one believed anything he read in a column labeled "Gossip,"[904] or much of anything the *Voyeur* printed

---

[902] "Are there such things as impersonal belongings?" he mused.
[903] Some people have lost not only coats, but whole suits there.
[904] He quoted *Goelet v. Confidential, Inc.*, 5 App. Div. 2d 226 at 229-230, 171 NYS2d 223 (1st Dept., 1958), a case in which the court held its nose concerning a report about Robert Goulet in *Confidential* magazine and said:

> We are not unmindful of the daily content of our current newspapers and periodicals. In addition to the vast growth of the gossip columns, we find therein detailed reports of the

anyway;[905] and that it would be hard to defame a scavenger who reveled in his nickname "the Bastard."[906] Similarly, Judge Rantinov expressed skepticism about the privacy "rights" of two very public figures[907] who kept several firms of publicity agents on both coasts busy seeking press coverage of the intimate details of their lives.

The case was quietly settled in chambers, and it quickly disappeared from his busy calendar. We cannot reveal the terms of the settlement because the file was sealed, and the truth may never be known.

---

piquant facts in matrimonial litigation and the colorful escapades and didoes of well-known persons which are not unlike those in the article about which plaintiffs complain. Even a cursory examination of the contents of some of our daily newspapers makes evident that such stories are part and parcel of the reading habits of the American public. We cannot undertake to pass judgment on those reading tastes. The increased circulation of magazines such as "Confidential" is mute testimony that the public is interested in the kind of news those magazines purvey.

[905] He pointed to its motto: "The truth, the whole truth, nothing but the truth, and then some."
[906] Despite the provisions of General Construction Law § 59 which banned the terms "bastard" and "illegitimate child" from "public papers."
[907] "Isn't being a fashion model about exhibiting your figure to the public?" he queried.

DEEP IN THE HEART OF TAXES;
OR FEW HAPPY RETURNS

by James M. Rose[908]

If the confusing nature of New York State Department of Taxation forms have you swearing oaths[909] (or if you are an attorney swearing affirmations instead),[910] you may resort to oaths more frequently[911] when you attempt to interpret the State Tax Law itself.

Recently a charge of computer fraud and felony failure to file tax returns in *People v. Dorothy Kahm a/k/a "Dot" Kahm* raised an issue of tax law that had lawyers and judges flummoxed.

Appropriately for a case in which an issue involving the filing of tax returns electronically and computer fraud[912] was raised, "Dot" Kahm was arraigned electronically pursuant to Criminal Procedure Law § 182.20 (1).[913]

---

[908] White Plains, New York. Mr. Rose is the champion of fairness who heard recently that the weather forecast was for partial clearing, and sued to demand impartial clearing.

[909] see, CPLR § 2309 for the form of oaths you can swear.

[910] CPLR § 2106. That section applies to physicians, osteopaths and dentists as well, acknowledging as it does the need for such professionals to engage in frequent swearing.

[911] You have a constitutional right to swear an oath, and shall not be rendered incompetent to do so because of your religious beliefs according to the provisions of New York State Constitution Art. I § 3, although if you start swearing oaths too frequently or in inappropriate places *that might* cause a court to render a determination you are incompetent.

[912] Certain frauds that used to be "done with mirrors" are now done with computers. Ultimately her attorney, E. Coli (who together with his brother Al Coli (nicknamed "Salty") form the Coli Firm), suggested that the appropriate punishment for computer fraud would be virtual imprisonment.

[913] You can see these arraignments on Channel 87—on the Arraignment/Entertainment Network.

She was charged with a failure to file her tax returns for three consecutive taxable years under Tax Law § 1802 which reads:

Repeated failure to file; personal income and earnings taxes

(a) Any person who, with intent to evade payment of any tax imposed under article twenty-two or any related income or earnings tax statute, fails to file a return for three consecutive taxable years shall be guilty of a class E felony, provided that such person had an unpaid tax liability with respect to each of the three consecutive taxable years.

(b) In any prosecution for a violation of subdivision (a) of this section, it shall be a defense that the defendant had no unpaid tax liability for any of the three consecutive taxable years.[914]

In the middle of the three years 1990-1992, Ms. Kahm had enough withheld from her income to cover her taxes. Justice Dee Nyde was faced with a statute that was at best confusing and at worst contradictory.

If, in order to commit the offense, one needs to have an unpaid tax liability for each of three years, the prosecution was missing an essential element of the case. That was true because they could not prove liability for "each" of the years, nor would the years be "consecutive."[915]

But what, then, is the meaning of subdivision (b)? It is an element of the offense that there be three consecutive years of liability, so it is redundant to say it is a *defense* if there was no liability for any of the years.

Why is "any" used in subdivision (b) rather than "each?" E. Coli argued that it is a defense if taxes were not owed for any *one* of the years, and 1991 was such a year. The prosecutor argued that it was only a defense if there was no tax liability for any of the three years at all, and that there was tax liability for two of the three years.

---

[914] That's really what it says. We couldn't make this stuff up—you need to be elected to the Legislature to write laws like this.

[915] The District Attorney's argument was that *all* tax years are consecutive. To District Attorneys the opposite of consecutive is concurrent (as in the kind of sentences Justice Nyde usually imposed).

What is the need for the language defining a defense in subdivision (b), Justice Nyde pondered, when the prosecution has to prove three consecutive years of unpaid tax liability as an element of the crime? If an element of the crime is missing there is no *prima facie* case, and no need for the Legislature to enact subdivision (b) making it a defense if the prosecution cannot prove each element of its case.

She remarked that it appears the state Department of Taxation has found a way to tax our mental abilities to interpret statutes in addition to our income!

Indeed, she queried, isn't the last clause in subdivision (a) beginning "provided that . . ." redundant as well? An element of the offense is the *intent to evade* the payment of taxes. If one has no unpaid tax liability in any of the three years, how can she intend to evade payment of taxes she has *already* paid or *never owed?*[916]

In order to avoid (or was it evade?) the problem, the District Attorney preferred a charge of not filing her taxes on time[917] in violation of Tax Law §1801 [918] because Dot Kahm had not filed her taxes yet for 1995[919] and it was already May 20, 1996. Her

---

[916] The taxes would not be "unpaid" or a "liability."

[917] He could not reduce the felony charges concerning 1990-2 to misdemeanors because of the statute of limitations.

[918] § 1801. Failure to file a return or report; supply information; or supplying false information

> (a) Any person who, with intent to evade any tax imposed under article twenty-two of this chapter or any related income or earnings tax statute, or any requirement thereof or any lawful requirement of the tax commission thereunder, shall fail to make, render, sign, certify or file any return, or to supply any information within the time required by or under the provisions of such article or any such statute, or who, with like intent, shall supply any false or fraudulent information, shall be guilty of a misdemeanor.

taxes must be filed by April 15 (four months and fifteen days after the close of her tax year because she had no extension) he argued.[920] But the Colis had an unusual defense. The New York State Budget is due to be in place by law on April 1.[921] But it was not yet in

> (b) Any person who, with intent to evade any tax imposed under article nine, nine-a, thirteen, thirty-two or thirty-three of this chapter or any requirement thereof or any lawful requirement of the commissioner of taxation and finance thereunder, shall fail to make, render, sign, certify or file any return or report, or to supply any information within the time required by or under the provisions of any such article, or who, with like intent, shall supply any false or fraudulent information, shall be guilty of a misdemeanor.

[919] Tax Law Article 22 (Specifically § 652) indicates that returns must be filed when the commissioner's regulations require unless there is an extension or a form is filed requesting that the commissioner calculate the tax due. Requests for extensions cannot exceed 6 months (§ 657).

The regulations (20 NYCRR § 152.1) state:

The New York State income tax returns of individuals, trusts, estates or partnerships required to be made under this Subchapter must be filed on or before the 15th day of the fourth month following the close of the taxable year (April 15th in the case of a calendar year taxpayer). The words close of the taxable year referred to in the previous sentence have the same meaning for New York State income tax purposes as when used for Federal income tax purposes.

[920] New York months are presumed to be the same length as the rest of the nation's months, despite the expression "in a New York minute." There is no expression "In a New York Month."

A "New York Minute" is one of the New York Times.

[921] State Finance Law §203 (1). After 1943 the first day of New York's fiscal year is (appropriately) April Fool's Day. In 1942 the fiscal year was only eight months (it ran from July 1, 1942 to March 31, 1943—see State Finance Law § 3) probably due to war shortages.

place when this misdemeanor charge was filed, so in Albany it was not yet April 1—much less April 15!

While the case was pending Dot Kahm pleaded guilty to a class B misdemeanor—the *attempt* to violate Tax Law § 1801. That is, she pleaded guilty to an attempted failure to file tax returns,[922] and she paid a virtual fine.[923]

---

[922] Under the theory that she had intended not to file her return electronically, but had inadvertently E-mailed the returns to the state, anyway.

[923] The computer fraud charge was reduced to the violation of endorsing a check below the line that reads "Do not endorse below this line."

A FINE LEGAL MESS YOU'VE GOTTEN US INTO NOW, OVIE!"[924]

A court recently wrestled with several thorny issues, which is an event likely to draw blood. It then produced a flowery opinion[925] which blooms[926] in Miscellaneous Reports. It concerned a husband and wife who left sperm and ova at an *in vitro* fertilization clinic with written directions that the ova be fertilized. Several months later the couple separated and sued to determine "custody."

The fertilization clinic, known as "Extra Ventre Sa Mere," was located within the jurisdiction of the court, at the intersection of Great Birnam Woods and Dunsinane Hill Ave.[927]

The *in vitro* fertilization clinic had offered to deposit the items into court (CPLR § 2602), in order to meet its obligations to "deliver"[928] the goods as a bailee,[929] but the court had no practical place to put them, and refused to use the refrigerator in the judge's lounge.[930] The court searched for a "depository" as the term is used in Rule 2605 of the CPLR. It ultimately held that a sperm bank [931]did not qualify as a "depository."

The husband referred to pseudonomically in the opinion as John Dough,[932] had deposited sperm with the clinic. The wife,

---

[924] By James M. Rose. Mr. Rose is the author of the Country and Western song "You think you put the "Fun" in "Fundamentalist," but I know you put the "Mental" in instead.

[925] Literary illusion.

[926] Continued horticultural imagery.

[927] See footnote 3.

[928] By "deliver" the judge found the UCC envisioned only a deposit of goods, and did not use the term in the obstetrical sense.

[929] UCC § 7-303 and New York annotations.

[930] The court held that it might have a an unconstitutional "chilling effect" *Gooding v. Wilson*, 405 US 518 at 521.

[931] Specifically Gamete Federal Savings & Loan.

[932] Thanks to the judge's stenographer's overzealous spell checker.

Tae Kwon Dough, left several ova in the hopes that fertilization could take place, and the result implanted in the wife, who was having difficulty conceiving. The written instructions claimed they were irrevocable.

While the logical thing to do would be to return the wife's ova to her and the husband's sperm to him, the court found it was faced with a legal problem and not a logical one.[933] The issue arose in a divorce case, so the parties argued that principles of equitable distribution must prevail. Applying Domestic Relations Law § 236 (B) (1) (c), they posited that the sperm and ova were considered "marital property" since they were acquired during the marriage, and not separate property. The court could thus award either party all or some portion of the property.

Moreover, until one or both parties withdrew the instructions to the lab, the court held it could not interfere with a conception decision made by the parties without violating their constitutional rights to privacy.[934]

The court was unable to determine whether the action should have been commenced as a replevin, or a habeas corpus, or a custody case, or a motion *in limine*.[935]

The Department of Social Services intervened, seeking an order of protection for the potential fetuses under the Family Court Act,

---

[933] "'The life of the law has not been logic,' Holmes wrote in *The Common Law* (Howe, 3rd ed., 1963, p.3); and logic has had little to do with the courts' decisions on these types of matters," the judge wrote.

[934] "In the wake of *Roe v. Wade* (410 US 113) and *Eisenstadt v. Baird* (405 US 438), it cannot seriously be doubted that the protection of the due process clause of the Fourteenth Amendment extends to matters involving whether or not to have children (see also, *Doe v. Bolton* 410 US 179; *Loving v. Virginia* 388 U.S. 1, *Griswold v. Connecticut* 381 U.S. 479; *Skinner v. Oklahoma* 316 US 535." Judge Wachtler dissenting in *Schulman v. N.Y. Health and Hospitals Corp.* 38 NY2d 234 at 245.

[935] *"In limine"* means "in the beginning," and the Lawyer's Bible commences: "*In limine*, God created Heaven and Earth."

and suggested that the normal standard would be "the best interests of the child," if, indeed, there were a child.

The judge then determined it was necessary to appoint a guardian *ad litem* to litigate the preliminary questions. That procedure had been followed before for unborn children.[936] Unborn children have certain statutory rights.[937] He reasoned that the sperm and ova, if united, would form a child, and the parties had given express directions to the clinic to unite them. No further actions were apparently needed by the parents to form a potential child, and thus the potential child had the right to be heard in court, as well as to due process of law under Family Court Act Article 10. As the Supreme Court remarked in *Roe v. Wade*, the state has an "important and legitimate interest in protecting the potentiality of human life" ([emphasis added] (410 US 113 at 162).[938] In any event, a guardian *ad litem* was needed to litigate the issue of whether a guardian *ad litem* was needed.

However, since some of the potential fetuses might have interests at odds with others, he ordered that each potential combination of sperm and ovum be assigned separate counsel—and the case is now awaiting the assignment of a hundred million attorneys.

---

[936] *In The Matter of Smith* 128 Misc 2d 976, 492 NYS2d 331, 334; *Matter of Gloria C. v. William C.* 124 Misc 2d 313.

[937] Such as the right to inherit (Estate Powers and Trusts Law § 2-1.3 (a) (2)), and to give informed consent through a parent (Public Health Law § 2805 (d)), or sue if it was not given (*Hughson v. St. Francis Hospital*, 92 App. Div. 2d 131.)

[938] see, also, *Harris v.McRae*, 448 U.S. 297 at 325.

AGREEMENTS BETWEEN A HUSBAND AND WIFE TO ENGAGE IN SEXUAL INTERCOURSE MUST BE IN WRITING TO BE BINDING

A curious mixture of statute, case law and common law have led a court to conclude recently that husbands and wives must agree in writing to have sexual intercourse for the agreement to escape the application of the statute of frauds.

The issue arose in a divorce case[939] in which the grounds for divorce were stated as a refusal of the wife on numerous occasions to have sexual intercourse with the husband.[940] The wife demurred on the grounds that there were no agreements in writing that the wife be required to engage in sexual intercourse with the husband, and that the Statute of Frauds[941] required all such agreements to be in writing.

The wife's attorney cited an unusual precedent for this unusual claim. In *People v. Liberta*[942] the Court of Appeals held that the statutory scheme which defined "female" as someone other than the accused's wife denied equal protection to women. The result of the case was that a husband could be charged with raping his wife if she did not consent to intercourse. The court in that case discussed in scholarly detail the origin of the "the marital rape exemption" from the time of Lord Hale in the 17th century to the 1881 Penal Law and beyond. It concluded "We find that there is no rational basis for distinguishing between marital rape and non marital rape . . . We therefore declare the marital exemption for rape in the New York Statute to be unconstitutional." The conclusion

---

[939] *Doe v. Doe* (unreported Supreme Court, Westchester County 1990). The names of the parties have not been changed for purposes of publication, they were named Doe (i.e., John and Tae-Kwon Doe.)

[940] This ground may be cruel and inhuman treatment, but used to be deemed abandonment as well, see *Diemer v. Diemer*, 8 NY2d 208 (1960) at 209.

[941] General Obligations Law § 5-701 (3).

[942] 64 NY2d 152, 485 NYS2d 207, 474 NE2d 567 (1984), *cert. den.* 105 S.Ct. 2029, 471 US 1020, 85 L. Ed 2d 310.

that can be drawn from *Liberta* is that sexual intercourse between a husband and wife must be by mutual consent, and that it is not a incident or component of the marriage license.

The wife then turned to the General Obligations Law, and noted that subdivision three of the statutory codification of what used to be known as the Statute of Frauds requires that certain agreements be in writing. One of those species of agreement that the statute requires be in writing is one that "is made in consideration of marriage."

An agreement to engage in sexual intercourse between a person who is married and someone else must certainly take into consideration the fact that one of the parties is married. For a husband to enter into intercourse with someone other than his wife is the criminal offense of adultery in New York.[943]

"Sexual relations between man and woman are given a socially and legally sanctioned status only when they take place in marriage and, in turn, marriage is itself distinguished from all other social relationships by the role sexual intercourse between the parties plays in it."[944]

The dictionary[945] defines "in consideration of" as "because of." Dictionary definitions are useful in determining the sense in which a word is used in a statute.[946] Therefore, legal intercourse between a husband and wife takes place in consideration of (that is "because of") the marriage.[947]

---

[943] Penal Law § 255.17.

[944] *Diemer v. Diemer Id.* at 210.

[945] *Webster's New World Dictionary of the American Language,* College Edition at 313 (1959).

[946] *McKinney's* Statutes § 234.

[947] At common law a husband and wife were considered one (Blackstone's Commentaries [1966 Edition] p. 430. An agreement to engage in sex with one's wife would, therefore, be an agreement to have sex with one's self. The legal implications of an agreement to engage in sex with one's self are beyond the scope of this article. The legality of loudly advising a police officer to do so used to depends upon whether it was done with the intention of harassing or

At common law written agreements between a husband and wife were void. Now, however, many aspects of the marital relationship are governed by antenuptial agreements. In the case at bar the husband did not produce an antenuptial agreement indicating that the wife was required to engage in sexual intercourse with him any particular number of times a year, nor proof that the agreement was violated.

Neither did he produce any written agreement between them that she agreed to sexual intercourse on the occasions mentioned in the divorce complaint. Oral agreements to enter into sexual intercourse, being in violation of the Statute of Frauds, were not enough and the husband's proceeding was dismissed with costs.

CONCLUSION

What a wife may elect not to do to her husband, a court can.

---

annoying him, compare *People v. Bacon,* 37 NY 2d 830 (1975) and *People v. Caine,* 70 Misc 2d 178 (1972) at 179 with *People v. Dietze,* 75 NY2d 48; and is likewise beyond the scope of this piece.

TAX CONSEQUENCES OF ACQUIRING A TROPHY SPOUSE[948]

Marla Maypole was the "trophy wife"[949] of real estate Developer Ronald Sump. But unlike wine, cheese or beef she did not get better with age and Sump divorced her. However, he agreed to pay her alimony, which because of clever tax planning under IRS § 1041,[950] was not taxable.[951] The IRS was annoyed.

No one expected the IRS to take notice years later when four people who were famous for being famous on such tabloid TV shows as Hard Edition and Inside Copy got married. All four had been married before. The two men, Don Yuan and Chad Jigeleau were famous for dating rich women, although they themselves had no means of support—visible or invisible.

The two youngish women, Charlotte Anne Czachkow and Marla Maypole, had been what the tabloids call "trophy wives" of older and quite rich men. Their only means of support was payments from their first husbands. Charlotte Ann had married Chad Jigeleau, and Don Yuan had married Maypole. But after a longish party (the beginning and ending date of which no one could quite recall) they got quickie divorces and married each other's spouses.

The men joked that the women were "two of a kind" and "very much alike." When the tabloid New York *Voyeur* alleged that the remarriage was a stunt to gain publicity, free meals and free lodging from businesses that sought publicity, the parties did not deny it.

---

[948] by James M. Rose, White Plains, New York, whose autobiography was recently released in its own recognizance.

[949] "She won her trophy from the Las Vegas Bar Association, which voted her "Miss Trial of 1990."

[950] 26 U.S.C. § 1041, the Internal Revenue Code of 1954 as amended.

[951] See, G. C. Lepow, "Tax Policy for Lovers and Cynics: How Divorce Settlement Became the Last Tax Shelter," 62 *Notre Dame L. Rev.* 32 at 58 (1986).

Chad thought he got the better of the deal, as his new wife, Ms. Maypole, received a million dollars a year in alimony, whereas his former wife got only a half that amount.

But the IRS had been lurking, and it determined that the marriage was a taxable event. It argued that he had acquired a capital asset that produced a large yearly income which resulted in a recognized capital gain of a half million dollars in the process.

Normally a *wife* is not a taxable asset, and as a result a marriage is not usually a taxable event. But IRS noted that the tax code *does* allow depreciation of professional athletes' contracts with sports franchises.[952] Thus wives held for investment can be treated as assets in the same way, it argued. Since Chad's "business" was marrying well, he had acquired a valuable asset analogous to an athlete's contract.

But Chad countered that, if the IRS was correct about his wife being an asset, he had made a unique arrangement under an obscure and poorly understood statute. As aging professional fortune hunters themselves, the only asset Chad and Don Yuan had was their wives, who kept them in the public eye and noteworthy. As they were all in the "business" of being famous, and their wives were "assets" used in that business, they argued that property of a like kind had been exchanged under IRS Code § 1031. That section provides that assets of a like kind held in a business may be exchanged without a recognition of gain or loss on the exchange of property.

Another strange provision of I.R.S. Code. § 1031 came into play as well. Subdivision (e) provides "for purposes of this section livestock of different sexes are not property of a like kind."[953] Why this was added to the section is anyone's guess. Indeed, the public policy behind the section **itself** is probably anyone's guess. Senator

---

[952] 26 U.S.C. § 1245.
[953] Livestock of different sexes are apparently not alike enough to be "like kind." As the French say, "Vive la Difference!" For a longer discussion of the differences between the sexes see *Men are from Mars Women are from Venus*.

Hitchcock, in the course of the 1921 debates on § 1031, said, "This is like all these other amendments; it might just as well be written in Greek, as far as I'm concerned."[954]

President Harding remarked of it, "I can't make a damn thing out of this tax problem. I listen to one side and they seem right, and then—God!—I talk to the other side, and they seem just as right."[955]

The wording of the statue clearly required the conclusion that an exchange of livestock of the *same sex* could be an exchange of assets of a like kind,[956] since the inclusion of one is deemed the exclusion of all others by rules of statutory interpretation.[957]

We do not usually consider that humans are livestock. But in this case we are dealing with the interpretation of something as arcane as a federal tax statute, and words used in those monstrosities could be defined in unusual ways[958] because they are employed as "terms of art."[959]

---

[954] 61 Cong. Rec. 6564 (Oct. 21 1921) quoted in M. Kornhauser, "We Don't Need Another Hero," 60 *U. So. Cal. L. Rev.* 397 at 441.

[955] R. Murray, *The Politics of Normalcy*, 54-55 (1973) quoted at footnote 116 of Kornhauser, *supra*.

[956] Perhaps the legislators had simply confused it with a swap of like *kine*.

[957] See Statutes § 240, "*Expressio unius est exclusio alterius*"—the specific mention of one thing implies the exclusion of other things.

[958] For example, a swap of a male horse for a bull is an exchange of livestock of a like kind, but a trade of a female pig for a male pig apparently is not "like kind" under the statute. Go figure.

Another example is the definition of "sell" under the Penal Law includes giving away (*People v Milom*, 75 App. Div. 2d 68, 71); and an illegal parking lot may be an educational institution, *In the Matter of Syracuse University*, 59 Misc 2d 684, 300 NYS2d 129 (S. Ct. Onondaga County, 1969)

[959] A "term of art" is essentially the arcane jargon of some profession, and we may never learn exactly who Art is, nor why he has the power to define words in such peculiar ways.

"Livestock" is not defined anywhere in the Internal Revenue Code. However, 7 U.S.C. § 6502 (11) defines it as "any cattle, sheep, goats, swine, poultry . . . or other non plant life." Humans are clearly alive and are not plants, so they fall within the definition of livestock. A trophy wife held for the purpose of an investment[960] could thus be exchanged without any tax consequence to the parties.

The exchange of a Czachkow for a Maypole for publicity purposes does not result in a taxable event.

CONCLUSION

With careful tax planning, perhaps only death is certain.

---

[960] The parties submitted affidavits swearing under oath that the exchange of wives was a business deal, and that "love" was a term they only understood in the context of tennis.

CHAPTER EIGHT

CRIMINAL PRACTICE NEVER MADE PERFECT

LEGAL STATUS OF COMBATANTS IN
THE WAR ON DRUGS[961]

The legal implications of declaring and prosecuting a war on drugs became an issue recently when what appeared to be a routine weapons and drug possession case was called before Judge Amanda B. Rekkonwitt, a Court of Claims Judge sitting in a Supreme Court Drug Part.

The prisoner, Marshall Lawless, would give only his name, and refused to answer any other pedigree questions when asked by the clerk. When Judge Rekkonwitt directed him to answer, he invoked the protections of the Geneva Convention, and claimed to be a prisoner of war in the frequently mentioned War on Drugs.

His attorney, I. Phil Tower of the law firm of Maughum & Popp, noted in his argument that the United States would spend $19.2 billion in the War on Drugs this year, and state and local governments another twenty billion in the effort. This "mobilization" has been referred to as a war since the 1970's, when it was declared by President Nixon with the concurrence of Congress.

He argued that the jails in this country have been filled by "prisoners" of the war. He noted that 1,579,566 people will be incarcerated in 2003 for drug related offenses, and that, as a result, the incarceration rate in the United States of 690 per 100,000 is second only to war torn Rwanda.

"If it's a war we've declared," Tower noted, "then we have to treat those that fight in it as prisoners of war under the

---

[961] by James M. Rose, White Plains, New York. This is Mr. Rose's mind, and Mr. Rose's mind on the War on Drugs.

Geneva Convention."[962] He argued that the weapons charges must be dismissed as Lawless was a soldier in a war on drugs[963] and entitled to carry arms. (The war is only on illicit drugs, as it is clear that prescription drugs have already won great victories—establishing beachheads in the evening news broadcasts of all major networks.)[964]

Judge Rekkonwitt had to decide whether the War on Drugs meant that soldiers in it could carry arms. While at first the proposition appeared to be absurd, so does much of what emerges from our *nisi prius* benches today, so she directed her attention to parsing the issue, and burned a great deal of midnight electricity[965]

---

[962] The Geneva Convention is not the Swiss equivalent of the Tailhook Convention and does not involve middle aged Swiss businessmen with large expense accounts looking for a good time. By all reports, the delegates to the convention did not wear funny hats, or run through the corridors of the hotel looking for alcoholic beverages and members of the opposite sex. The Geneva Convention relative to the Treatment of Prisoners of War was adopted August 12, 1949 by the Diplomatic Conference for the Establishment of International Conventions for the Protection of Victims of War held in Geneva April 21 to August 12, 1949, and went into effect October 21, 1950. The United States is a signatory.

[963] By all accounts drugs appear to be winning the war, or at the very least have established a tactical advantage. To paraphrase the Commander in Chief "We are closer to the beginning of the war than the end." Every day we appear to get closer to the beginning and further from the end.

[964] If anyone doubts the ubiquitous presence of prescription drugs simply watch any evening news program, and watch General Claritin, the purple pill, pills for hair or potency loss, bone loss, social anxiety, gas, allergies and the like. If we were to ask our doctors about the pills each time a commercial inveigled us to do so, the poor physicians would be so swamped with phone calls they would hardly have an opportunity to golf.

[965] It is Con Edison that burns the oil to make the electricity, and its customers who consume the kilowatts.

in so doing. "The Law is a Jealous Mistress" she noted, oblivious to the gender issues the statement presents for sitting female judges.[966]

The Geneva convention applies to declared wars [967] which this armed conflict has been since the 1970's. It applies whether or not both parties acknowledge the conflict. Prisoners of War are defined, inter alia, in Article 4 (2)(C) as persons carrying arms openly, as Marshall Lawless acknowledged he did.[968] He also conducted operations in accordance with the laws and customs of war, attacking law enforcement when necessary.

In any event, Article 5 states that if there is any doubt as to the status of a person falling into the hands of the enemy after committing a belligerent act, he is entitled to be treated as a prisoner of war until his status has been adjudicated by a competent tribunal.[969] Lawless pointed out there was no one in court more belligerent that he, and that the jurisdiction of the Court of Claims or a judge sitting by designation in the Supreme Court Drug Part did not extend to determining whether individuals were prisoners of War. Judge Rekkonwitt (who frequently referred to herself as "the court") asked whether the convention required that the judge, rather than the defendant, be sent for a competency determination. "Just because this tribunal has the word "court" in its name does not mean it has jurisdiction any more than does the Galleria Food Court," Lawless argued.

---

[966] We know that we live under the Rule of Law in this country, and that the Law is a Jealous Mistress. What is the correct description of this condition? Rule by a king is Monarchy (not Kingology), and rule by religious persons is a Theocracy (not priestology). Rule by the rich is plutocracy (not richology). Should rule by Jealous Mistresses be called Fatal Attractology?

[967] Part I Article 2.

[968] See Also Article 43 of Additional Protocol I.

[969] The British *Weekly Telegraph* of February 4, 2003 reports that at the very least, the "competent tribunal" must be recognized by the International Committee of the Red Cross and Red Crescent.

He also argued that his confession should be suppressed because he could only be asked his name rank and serial number. However, the Judge ruled that while he could be required to give no more than name, rank,[970] and serial number he could be asked other questions. Since Article 22 prohibited internment in penitentiaries for prisoners of war, and so many drug related convicts are interned there now, if Judge Rekkonwitt declared that Lawless was a prisoner of war it would result in wholesale gaol delivery. She declared that Lawless was not a prisoner of war. "The War on Drugs was meant to be a metaphor, and not meant to be taken literally like the War on Poverty, or Warren Berger. If it were not a metaphor, the War on Poverty would require us to reinstate debtor's prisons," she ruled.

Lawless then moved to suppress his confession on another unusual ground. It seems that at the end of it next to his name he placed a small letter "c" in a circle. He claimed that the work was thus copyrighted by him under the Copyright Act of 1976,[971] and could not be quoted in court to the judge or jury without his express permission—which he was declining to give. He had made application to register it at the Copyright Office as required.[972]

The court required I. Phil Tower to produce the application and the document from the government acknowledging the copyright. When he did, the Judge admitted it into evidence under the business records rule.[973] She then ruled that since it was a document on file with a government, it could be admitted into evidence under CPLR § 4520, which permits such filed documents to go into evidence as *prima facie* evidence of the facts therein. If the copyright law meant it could not be read out loud at the trial, the CPLR allowed it to be shown to the jury, just as a copyrighted

---

[970] He claimed that his name was Marshall, and his rank was Field Marshall (see, for example, Major Major in Catch-22).
[971] 17 U.S.C. § 501 et seq.
[972] by 17 U.S.C. § 411(a).
[973] CPLR § 4518.

book could not be quoted without permission, but could be circulated by a library that bought it. The motion was denied.

Lawless was convicted and sentenced to house arrest. However, he lived in a mobile home, and was last seen driving it off into the sunset.

James M. Rose

OGLING RECENT BARE BREAST CASES: PROHIBITIONS IN SEARCH OF A RATIONALE?

by James M. Rose[974]

Since this is sweeps week in the scholarly law journal field, we have chosen to discuss several recent cases dealing with bare breasts. We begin by comparing the topic of Federal regulation of information about abortion at federally funded clinics.[975] and the nude dancing case.[976]

Justice Scalia found in the nude dancing case that topless dancing was an action, and not speech that was protected by the First Amendment. Thus it became clear that abortion was something you could do but not talk about, and topless dancing was something you could talk about but not do. Are there other things we can do but not talk about and talk about but may not do?[977]

Perhaps the Supreme Court will not reverse *Roe v. Wade*, but will continue to write other opinions making it more difficult for those seeking abortions. After the nude dancing case it may rule that abortions must be performed with all participants fully clothed.

Justice Scalia was revealed as someone who reads the Constitution literally, and does not consider an action to be symbolic speech.

What does this group of cases tell us about the constitutional philosophy of Justice Souter? He is apparently a strict constuctionist, looking for the actual intent of the founding fathers. We are told

---

[974] White Plains, New York. Author of *Everything I Learned in Kindergarten Was on Fire When I Was Lying during Nap time.*
[975] *Rust v. Sullivan*, 500 U.S. 173, 111 S. Ct 1759 (1991).
[976] *Barnes v. Glen Theater Inc.*, 501 U.S. 560, 111 S. Ct. 2456 (1991).
[977] One must keep in mind the old grammar school distinction between "can" and "may." A politician may talk about balancing the budget but cannot do it.

that he looked for any evidence that the Founding Mothers actually danced nude, but he could find none.[978] If the Founding Fathers were free to talk about topless dancing they did not do so.[979]

Justice Souter filed a concurring opinion in which he rejected "society's moral views" as a basis for limiting topless dancing, but rested his decision on the police power to control "the secondary effects of adult entertainment establishments."[980]

Thus the court was free to consider assertions nude dancing encourages prostitution, increases sexual assaults and attracts[981]

---

[978] In colonial New England women got married in the nude (or in their shifts) on the King's Highway because, according to an old English tradition, if a woman married that way her husband would not be responsible for her premarital debts. Earle, *Customs and Fashions in Old New England* (Scribners, 1893) pp. 77-79.

There was no indication whether dancing was part of the ceremony. That portion of the common law has not been continued in the Debtor and Creditor or Domestic Relations Law. Indeed, it appears the Penal Law would prohibit it, Compare Penal Law § 245.00 and 245.01 and *People v. Hollman* (1968) 68 NY2d 202, with New York State Constitution Article I Sec. 14 and In *re Carnegie Trust Co.*, 206 NY 390.

[979] That is there is no reference to it in their diaries. Of course no one is still living who engaged in small talk with them around a blazing fire on a cold winter night over a few hard ciders, so we don't know what they talked about in private.

There is no reference to nude dancing in their diaries. However, like Samuel Pepys they may have kept their diaries in code. They could have written in the kind of code one often hears government witnesses testify about when they review wiretap transcripts in organized crime trials. If "How is your crazy Aunt Sophie?" can be code for the consignment of a kilo of heroin, then "We must hang together or surely we will all hang separately" may be code for "Abigail was shaking her bare booty."

[980] 111 S. Ct. 2468-9.

[981] Although there was no proof the dancer said "Hey, Big Boy, Wanna see my crime magnets?"

criminal activity,[982] although the court did not address nudity unconnected with dancing.

In *Barnes* the concurring opinion of Justice Scalia notes that public nudity was an offense at common law. Was it? In addition to footnote 5 *supra.*, see *Rex v. Gallard*[983] in which an indictment of a woman running on the common wearing nothing above her waist was dismissed because the conduct was not immodest or unlawful.[984]

In New York, our review of the case law starts with *People v. O'Gorman*,[985] in which the Court of Appeals interpreted a Yonkers city ordinance requiring people to appear in "customary street attire." The case involved a woman dressed in short pants, a halter covered by a jacket and no stockings or hat. The man involved had short pants and a polo shirt. The arresting officer described them as hikers, and contended that the woman was required to wear a skirt to conform to the ordinance which read:

"No person over the age of sixteen (16) years shall be permitted to appear in bathing costume or in any other than ordinary street attire upon an public street or thoroughfare of Yonkers."

What does ordinary street attire consisted of in Yonkers, and does it differ from ordinary street attire in other cities?[986]

---

[982] 111 S. Ct. at 2469. Is it possible that the court is confusing cause and effect—that is through zoning restrictions the topless bars have been relegated to high crime areas (cf., *Renton v. Playtime Theater, Inc.*, 475 U.S. 41, 105 S. Ct. 925, 89 L. Ed. 2d 29 (1986), or even that the proprietors of such establishments know where their best customers are? If so, isn't there an interest in keeping crime confined to one area of the city, rather than let it infiltrate all neighborhoods?

[983] 25 Eng. Reprint 547 (1733).

[984] (See 93 ALR 996).

[985] 274 NY 284 (1937).

[986] Would a bride and groom on the sidewalk in formal attire violate the statute? Would a visiting African or Indian in a full robe? A judge in his robe? Someone retrieving a morning newspaper in a bathrobe?

The court found nothing wrong with the intentions of the statute and stated at 286:

> The law of the proper thing to do is not written in a book but rules most of our living. To meet the cases of persons who insist on being conspicuous by exposing too much of their anatomy, it may well be reasonable to prescribe that men and women shall cover themselves, at least when on the street.

The court held, however, that the language of the statute was too broad because it prohibited citizens from wearing unusual clothing that was decent. "The constitution still leaves some opportunity for people to be foolish if they so desire."[987]

The vagueness of the statute was its undoing. A female companion in long white pants was not arrested although she was not wearing a skirt.

However, what was not "the proper thing to do" in Yonkers at that time may be a proper thing to do now.[988] Behavior has changed, and what was forbidden before is now protected by the Constitution.[989] These cases deal more with the *improper* thing *not* to do. Is there anything that we should not do or wear on the street of Yonkers today? In earlier decades men did not wear earrings on the streets of Yonkers (unless they were pirates), but now they do. In the middle of this century a properly dressed woman would not go downtown without a hat and gloves on, but by the late sixties some of them would go there without shirts.

---

[987] *Id.* at 287. That quotation could be motto of this column!

[988] In 1956 a woman from Kansas was prosecuted in White Plains City Court for wearing her shorts too short on the street. (See *Reporter Dispatch* June 27, 1956 p. 1, and July 2, 1956, p. 16). About that time high school students polled believed it was improper to wear shorts to school, and one student was sent home for being so attired, *Reporter Dispatch*, June 20, 1956, p. 14.

[989] c.f., *People v. Onofre,* 51 NY2d 476 declaring Penal Law §130.38 (the consentual sodomy statute) unconstitutional.

In *People v. Price*[990] the female defendant wore a fishnet top with no undergarments through which her breasts were visible. Although this was not customary attire, the court dismissed the charge of indecent exposure (Penal Law § 245.01) noting that the statute was intended to forbid commercial exploitation of nudity and not casual nudity. Despite the court's statement, it later held the statute had been correctly applied to nude sun bathers who are not commercially exploiting anything,[991] and despite the court's admonition that the statute was also meant to prohibit nudity that was likely to create public disorder, it is found not in the Article of the Penal Law (Article 240) captioned "Offenses Against Public Order," but in one (Article 245)[992] entitled "Offenses Against Public Sensibilities."[993] Later, however, in *People v. Santorelli*[994] the court held that the revised statute did not forbid topless sunbathing that was not accompanied by lewd behavior.

In 1937 there was a more homogeneous society with more "understood" rules, and the Common Council of Yonkers assumed the average citizen knew what could and could not be worn as customary attire. Even the Court of Appeals acknowledged there was a "proper thing to do."[995]

---

[990] 33 NY2d 831 (1973).

[991] *People v. Hollman*, 68 NY2d 202. (1986).

[992] The Article contains prohibitions against public lewdness as well as marathon dancing and cycling. The section also forbids exhibitions in which one voluntarily submits to indignities such as permitting objects to be thrown at his head. All of these are apparently not forms of expression protected by the constitution.

[993] "Public sensibilities are cast aside when baring breasts is a political statement, it appears, *People v. Craft*, 134 Misc 2d 121.

[994] 80 NY 2d 875 (1992).

[995] "The proper thing to do" sounds like the "politically correct" thing to do, a phrase now much in the news. The proper way to dress is "sartorially correct" and probably we have to read the Style Section of the Sunday New York *Times* to avoid being gauche.

Now, however, there is no universally accepted Miss Manners or Emily Post to tell us what the rules are. Now who will tell us "the proper thing to do"?

One answer might be found in *People v. David*.[996] The court looked for some basis upon which to uphold the constitutionality of Penal Law § 245.01 (now entitled "Exposure of a Person") which bans public nudity.

Although the court gave a bow to the origin of our traditional morality by quoting Genesis 3:6-11,[997] our new "God" emerges—the expert. Modern trials are now the battle of the scientific expert, and this issue proved to be no exception. A developmental psychiatrist testified that the female breast is a primary sexual characteristic in today's society. In the United States today the female breast possesses the erotic proprieties of a primary sexual organ, she concluded, and therefore should not be bared because of its effect on the psychological development of impressionable male youth.[998] Does this run contrary to a Court of Appeals decision in *People v. Muller*[999] which noted at 411:

---

[996] 146 Misc 2d 115 (1989) a decision of the City Court of Rochester.

[997] In which Adam and Eve are embarrassed by their nakedness after eating the forbidden fruit.

[998] She did concede that the culture and not nature determines what body part has such an effect, and that in other cultures other body parts also have such a function and in them the female breast does not. She admitted that if the female breast were routinely exposed it would lose that effect, and there would be no need for such a statute. So did the experts that testified in *People v. Santorelli* (see 80 NY2d 883 at footnote 3) who testified that enforced concealment reinforces the cultural obsession with the female breast.

[999] 96 NY 408 (1884). This is another case in which the court said it was not necessary to define what is indecent because everyone knows indecency when they see it. It was cited with approval in a dissent in *People v. Tylkoff* 212 NY 197 at 206 which would have upheld the an indictment for offending public decency for calling a woman a whore. As late as 305 NY 336, 345 in *Matter of Commercial Pictures Corp. v. Board of Regents* the Court of Appeals

It is evident that mere nudity in painting or sculpture is not obscenity. Some of the great works in painting or sculpture as all know represent nude human forms. It is false delicacy and mere prudery which would condemn and banish from sight all such objects as obscene simply on account of their nudity . . . . The presence of a woman of the purest character and of the most modest behavior and bearing may suggest to a prurient imagination images of lust, and excite impure desires, and so may a picture or statute not in fact indecent or obscene.

But in the same volume of Miscellaneous reports as *People v. David* there is a case which upholds a statute forbidding topless males from appearing on the streets as well. *People v. Duyck*[1000]dealt with the constitutionality of an ordinance forbidding topless persons.[1001]

The court noted that ordinances based solely upon esthetics have been upheld by our courts, quoting from *People v. O'Gorman*.[1002]

Thus in 146 Misc 2d there are two differing rationales for statutes forbidding bare breasts, scientific and esthetic (at about the same time the United States Supreme Court issued a concurring

---

was defending similar language against vagueness charges by noting "It is not a valid criticism that such general moral standards may vary slightly from generation to generation."

[1000] 146 Misc 2d 629 (App. Term, 9th and 10th Jud'l Dists.)

[1001] The ordinance in question read:

"No person shall appear in a public street in said Village clothed or costumed in such manner that the portion or his or her breast below the top or the areola is not covered with a fully opaque cover."

[1002] But see *People v. Craft*, 134 Misc 2d 121, in which the court states at 127 the male breast is not so offensive as to require prohibition, and the concurring opinion in *People v. Santorelli* 80 NY 2d at 881 which suggests that the female breast is no more a sexual organ that the male breast.

opinion using a "crime magnet" theory.) None is based upon morality.[1003] All may leave the nagging question in the mind of the practitioner "what else can be banned on an "esthetic,"[1004] "scientific" or "crime magnet" basis?

Laws against exposure of the female breast at rest or in motion are statutes in search of a rationale, and this article describes points which we shall have to grasp and examine closely in the future.

[1003] The concurring opinion in *People v. Santorelli* suggests at 80 NY2d 881 the particular public sensibility against exposure of female breasts is a commonly held bias, and is based upon archaic and stereotypic notions and therefore no legitimate governmental objective is behind it. If the commonly held bias is common to enough of the population so that the exposure of a breast would be offensive to a vast majority of them, would that public sensibility then be a legitimate governmental interest? What has happened to the law of the proper thing to do?

JAMES M. ROSE

RES IPSA LOQUITUR[1005]

THE CONSTITUTIONAL RIGHT OF MINORS TO KEEP AND BEAR SQUIRT GUNS,
or
ARMS AND THE CHILD

by James M. Rose[1006]

Mother Goose, being duly sworn deposes and says, Once upon a time there was a school district that seized from a minor a squirt gun, and was pursued in court doggedly. And thereby hangs a tail.

The Grande Central School District had a rule prohibiting weapons from being brought into its buildings. A.Nononymous[1007] brought in his backpack a SooperSoak squirt gun of neon green plastic, a toy in great favor among the pre-adolescent set. While he evinced no intention of using it to start any altercation, he testified that it was necessary to use in defense of his person against other individuals who were so armed outside the school grounds on his way home[1008]

When the SooperSoak was discovered it was immediately confiscated by a playground monitor. With the aid of the National Rifle Association, the child then sued to replevy the item and for a

---

[1004] "Can we now bar ugly people, too? What about ill fitting clothing? Will we deputize fashion police? Can the law be ahead of or should it reflect "public sensibilities?"

[1005] A paper previously delivered to the Express Mail counter of the White Plains Post Office.

[1006] White Plains, New York; Moe Stappi Undistinguished Fellow, Nappa Valley Law School, and Executive Director of the Federal Witless Assistance Program.

[1007] Not his real name, A fictional name for publication to protect the identity of the minor.

[1008] The escalating arms race among eight year olds required him to possess this squirt rifle, as a mere squirt gun (pistol) lacked sufficient range for effective defense.

declaratory judgment that he had a constitutional and statutory right to keep and bear the armament.

The allegation was that the Second Amendment to the United States Constitution, and New York Civil Rights Law § 4 which are identically worded authorized the child to keep and bear the item.[1009] Civil Rights Law § 4 reads: "A well regulated militia being necessary to the security of a free state, the right of the people to keep and bear arms cannot be infringed."

The judge was faced with the issue of whether a squirt gun is an "arm." Arms has been defined by one court as "Anything that a man wears for his defense, takes in his hands or uses in his anger, to cast at or strike another."[1010] Under this definition even a snowball would qualify. The judge held the squirt gun was an "arm".

It was then argued that the school district, acting *in loco parentis,* [1011] had the right to seize the weapon because the child was only eight years old. The court easily disposed of the argument, as the Amendment and the Civil Rights law speak of "people" and eight year olds are people. Even unborn children have statutory and constitutional rights.[1012] "People" means the same thing as "persons."[1013] Penal Law §265.05 is entitled "Unlawful Possession of Weapons by persons under sixteen." But in the definitions of weapons that persons under sixteen cannot possess squirt guns, are not found unless they are powered by carbon dioxide.[1014]

[1009] The Second Amendment is a limitation on the Congress and National government, and has no application to the states, *Moore v. Gallup,* 267 App. Div. 64, 45 NYS2d 63, aff'd 294 NY 846, 59 NE 2d 439.

[1010] *State v. Buzzard,* 4 Ark. 18.

[1011] A legal term from the Latin roughly meaning "like a crazy parent."

[1012] Such as the right to inherit (EPTL § 2-1.3 (a) (2)) and to give informed consent through a parent (PHL § 2805 (d)), or sue if it was not given (*Hughson v. St. Francis Hospital* 92 App. Div. 2d 131.)

[1013] But not the same thing as "person," as a court has held that bearing arms is a collective and not an individual right, *United States v. Warin* 530 F2d 103 (6th Cir, 1976), cert. den. 426 US 948, 96 S. Ct. 3168, 49 L. Ed 2d 1185.

[1014] See, *Adamowicz v. Schafer,* 155 Misc 2d 695, 589 NYS2d 61 (1992).

A discussion of definitions is in order. "Firearm" is defined in Penal Law § 265.00 (3) and "deadly weapon" in § 10.00 (11). Nowhere is "weapon" or "arms" defined, although descriptions of specific types of weapons are. For example, § 265.10 is entitled "Manufacture, transportation, disposition and defacement of weapons, dangerous instruments and appliances." It contains no specific definition of "weapons" and leaves to the imagination whether a dishwasher with a short circuit is a "dangerous appliance." In any event, it does not appear that a squirt gun is actually defined anywhere as a "weapon" that the law prohibits youths from possessing.

Case law interpreting Civil Rights Law § 4 has held that there is no right to carry a concealed pistol or handgun, because "the people" are allowed to keep only those weapons suitable for use by a militia in wartime for the general defense of the community.[1015] Thus, the people could not keep pistols or brass knuckles, but could keep and bear stinger missiles or short range tactical nuclear weapons.[1016] The right to keep and bear weapons not mentioned in Article 265 is thus preserved. Ancient weapons such as maces, lances or halberds are probably legal as a consequence, and squirt guns are not on the prohibited list.[1017]

[1015] *Matter of Guida v. Dier,* 84 Misc. 2d 110, 375 NYS2d 826, modified on other grounds 54 App. Div. 2d 86, 387 NYS2d 720. (S.Ct., Saratoga Co., 1974); See *English v. State,* 35 Tex.476 (1872).

[1016] European countries have not found long range nuclear weapons to be practical, and Ukraine, for example, has agreed to turn in 1500 nuclear weapons in return for $1,000,000,000.00 in gift certificates to toy stores. Other countries are considering the feasibility of swapping their nuclear weapons for majority participation in a farm implement factory. It would be owned by a corporation that would be established by Western governments and would be called Plow, Inc. The Ukrainians are considering turning their nuclear weapons into Plow shares.

[1017] If not actually use! The court noted that there is no constitutional right to keep and bear ammunition. However, squirt guns use water as ammunition, and there is an extensive body of law concerning water rights.

Although the school district argued that it could have a policy to dissuade students from using weapons, the NRA pointed to §2-a of the Education Law requiring the district to permit the militia to recruit on school campuses, and Education Law § 809-a authorizing school districts to devote hours of public school instruction to the safe use of firearms! It is logically inconsistent, the judge found, to dissuade a student from doing what the schools are permitted to teach him.[1018]

However, every word or phrase in a statute is to be given effect.[1019] The right of the people to keep and bear arms must be read *in pari materia* with the modifying phrase "A well regulated militia being necessary for the security of a free state." Therefore, the arms may only be kept and borne if they are in connection with a well regulated militia. The court found no proof that the militia in New York was well regulated,[1020] and it distinguished "regulated" from "subject to a multitude of regulations by government."[1021]

On the issue of whether New York is a "free state" the same multitude of federal, state, county, city, town, village and municipal corporation charters, local laws, ordinances, statutes, and regulations prevent such a conclusion.

The court searched history to find instances of the militia employing squirt guns. It held that water cannons used to quell riots were similar. A gun is a gun, and having found that the squirt gun was a weapon, the court held that it was seized by the School District prior to the expiration of the mandatory five day waiting period created by the Brady Handgun Violence Protection Act of

---

[1018] The district argued that school teachers are also authorized to teach sex education classes, but can still dissuade students from practicing what they teach.

[1019] Statutes § 230.

[1020] Rejecting the proffered testimony of some older officers that they consumed much bran and hence were "astonishingly regular."

[1021] What one court has called a rat's nest of local, state, and federal regulation. *People v. Studfin*, 132 Misc 2d. 326 at 333.

333

1993,[1022] and that the district could not possess the gun until the backgrounds of the Board's members could be examined!

EDITOR'S NOTE: After the publication of this article, the Illinois Bar Association based a moot court question on the issues raised in it with the author's permission.

[1022] 18 U.S.C. § 922(s)(1).

RES IPSA LOQUITUR[1023] (Humor)

THE EFFECTS OF GRAVITY ON THE LAW AND VICE VERSA[1024]

What the Constitution of the State of New York has to do with bathroom odors is uncertain, Justice Heisenberg wrote in a case he decided in state Supreme Court recently.

The way the issue came about was that Mr. Strawman, an owner of an apartment building, was accused by a tenant, Mr. Javert, under Multiple Residence Law § 171.[1025]

That section, as you are undoubtably aware, provides that in Multiple Residences, bathrooms containing water closets must have a window or skylight, or, if they do not, they must be ventilated by mechanical or gravity ventilation. A gravity ventilation system must be capable of four changes of the volume of the air in the room per hour.[1026]

Mr. Javert, a sewer inspector and sometime author, tested the air in his rented multiple residence bathroom by placing into it a noxious gas of some sort. He did not reveal the exact gas nor the method he used in disseminating it. He then "measured" the rate that the smell dissipated by coming into the room after a quarter

---

[1023] *Res ipsa loquitur* is a registered trademark of the *Westchester County Bar Journal*, and anyone caught using those words, even in motion papers, will owe the Bar Journal a large fee.

[1024] by James M. Rose, White Plains, New York. Mr. Rose is the man who put the "fun" in fungible.

[1025] Not to be confused with the Multiple Dwelling Law, although it is not clear just why, or why there is a need for two laws on the subject. It is possible that "Multiple" modifies "Law" and not "dwelling" or "residence" in each.

[1026] § 171 (6) provides "In lieu of a required window or skylight, it shall be lawful to install a system of mechanical or gravity ventilation for water-closet compartments or bathrooms in any portion of a dwelling. Such system of ventilation shall be constructed, arranged and maintained continuously to

of an hour and claimed to be able to still detect the odor.[1027] This he claimed to do on three separate days, and when he could still detect the odor filed this complaint.

Strawman's attorney, S. Crowe Czashajeck,[1028] first argued that the air in the room had in fact changed, but the smell (not in itself air) did not. The specific gravity of the smell could have been heavier than the air and lingered near the floor in the towels, while the air that had been in the room before the smell turned over.[1029]

He then argued that gravity ventilation works by the weight of air.[1030] While it was conceded that on some occasions the air in the room was, in fact, replaced more than four times an hour, when the wind was blowing strongly at right angles to the soffit vent opening (like a person blowing over the mouth of a glass beer bottle) it acted like a lid that prevented outside air from entering the opening, and thus was an exception to the laws of gravity.[1031]

It was argued that on average this occurred one tenth of the time, and thus, by the law of averages, nine tenths of the time all the air in the water closet room was replenished more than four times an hour.

Judge Heisenberg admitted that there were indeed laws of physics, but he was uncertain of their principles. He was concerned

---

provide at least four changes per hour of the air volume of each such water-closet compartment or bathroom."

[1027] While there is a speed of light and a speed of sound there is no specific speed of smell.

[1028] Of the firm of Czashajeck & Splitt.

[1029] The law did not say four *total* changes of air, he argued. However, the judge inquired what the purpose of the law was, if not to get the smell out.

[1030] for a description of gravity ventilation see, Carl and Barbara Giles, *Ventilation: Your Secret Key to an Energy Efficient Home* (Tab Books, 1984) at p. 43.

[1031] Also referred to as Newton's Laws in the motion papers. It refers to the laws of Sir Isaac Newton, and not his cousin Figaro Ishmael Newton, also known as "Fig" Newton. While Isaac was sitting under apple trees, Fig conducted many experiments blowing across the tops of beer bottles, and even formed

that he would need to learn the laws of physics[1032] in order to deal with this case. An apartment owner attempting to comply with this law one would have to obtain a physics expert, he mused, perhaps by looking in the yellow pages under "Mechanic, Quantum."

Javert's lawyer, Peck Sniff,[1033] argued that the volume of air in the room must always be capable of replacement four times an hour, rather than on average four times an hour. Czashajeck asked the court to apply the law of averages.[1034] Concepts from high school math such as median, mean, mode, average and percentile swirled uncomfortably in the judge's head.[1035]

Sniff argued that "average" numbers were inapplicable because they were imaginary, and the statute dealt with the real world. If the average person has two point five children he does not have a Nancy, Fred and Bi...." He said, "On this jury of six men and six women, the "average" juror has one breast and one testicle, but if any jurors were so configured I could not address them as ladies and gentlemen of the jury!"

The judge inquired how Javert selected the days he ran the tests, and was told they were chosen randomly. "You mean arbitrarily?" he asked. When the answer came back in the affirmative, the judge ruled that if the law of averages required something be done in an arbitrary and capricious manner it denied due process

---

a jug band, the Newton Ramblers. It is believe that he assisted Sir Isaac in his studies of inertia (because a fragment of a research paper in the hand of Sir Isaac contained the notation "See Fig I.")

Fig's death is considered to be his most successful proof of Newton's first law, that is that a body at rest tends to remain at rest unless acted upon by some outside force.

[1032] Something he was not able to conquer in high school before turning to the law.

[1033] Of the firm of Skratch & Sniff.

[1034] The judge admitted he knew little about the law of averages, except for its unsavory reputation for "catching up to you" like a mugger in a dark alley.

[1035] He was a schoolboy in the days before "new math" and now wondered if he

of law[1036]—so he declared the law of averages to be unconstitutional. Therefore, he ruled that the bathroom would have to pass a test conducted at *any* time.

But Strawman's attorney argued that no case or statute defined "gravity ventilation."[1037] The statute imported into the law concepts of the weight of air and the operation of Newton's Laws of Motion.[1038] Having to know the weight of air and the operation and exceptions to the law of gravity bothered the judge.[1039] Strawman's attorney urged him to invoke New York State Constitution Article III § 16.[1040] That section prohibits the legislature from passing acts that incorporate by reference any existing law "except by inserting it in such act."

Judge Heisenberg remarked that the Court of Appeals has written, "The purpose of the constitutional prohibition against incorporation by reference is to prevent the Legislature from incorporating into its acts the provisions of other statutes or regulations which affect public or private interests in ways not

---

would have to learn it for this case. What was wrong with the old math, he wondered, wasn't it hard enough to learn?

[1036] c.f., *American Ins. Assn. v. Lewis*, 50 NY2d 617, 431 NYS2d 350 (1980).

[1037] Since one attorney was arguing for the laws of gravity and the other for the law of averages, the judge was concerned he would have to apply choice of laws doctrine. Since the demise of the *lex loci* test, New York has replaced it with the "center of gravity" test. But that brought him back to the laws of gravity again! Like death and taxes, "gravity" too seems inescapable, he remarked.

[1038] Judge Heisenberg was barely able to understand the Civil Practice Law and Rules' laws for motions, he joked.

[1039] The press, who called this the "odor in the court" case, noted of the once athletic but now portly Judge, that gravity had not been kind to him, and this was his chance at revenge.

[1040] Article III, § 16 provides: "No act shall be passed which shall provide that any existing law, or any part thereof, shall be made or deemed a part of said act, or which shall enact that any existing law, or part thereof, shall be applicable, except by inserting it in such act".

disclosed upon the face of the act, and which would not have received the sanction of the Legislature if fully understood by it, *People ex rel. Board of Commrs. v Banks*, 67 NY 568, 576; see, *People ex rel. Everson v Lorillard*, 135 NY 2." [1041] Judge Heisenberg doubted whether, like himself, the members of the Legislature fully understood the effects of the laws of gravity when they incorporated Newton's Laws[1042] in the Multiple Residence Law without fully setting forth the laws of gravity. He noted that even the Court of Appeals was unwilling to recognize Newton's Laws of centrifugal force in a tort case.[1043]

He ruled that the statute was unconstitutional. As Javert was leaving the court room he was arrested for violating Environmental Conservation Law § 71-2105 and 6 NYCRR § 201.2 [b] for operating an air contamination source without a certificate and § 211.6 for creating air pollution. Javert was taken away muttering under his breath that "the whole thing stinks."

A report of the case in the New York *Daily Voyeur* the next day appeared under the headline "Author Voids Where Prohibitted by Law."

[1041] *Matter of Medical Society v. Doh*, 83 NY2d 447 at 452-3, 611 NYS2d 114 (1994).

[1042] "The laws of Newton are not the laws of New York," Judge Heisenberg proclaimed, perhaps confusing Sir Isaac with the town in Massachusetts.

[1043] *In Matter of Smith (Great Amer. Ins. Co.)*, 29 NY 2d 116, 324 NYS2d 15 the court refused to accept as "physical contact" by one vehicle with another the snow and ice thrown off a truck by centrifugal force, stating: "Unfocused forces, whether produced by centrifugal force or ricochet, set off by a moving vehicle do not provide the kind of physical nexus contemplated by the statute nor understood in common parlance to constitute physical contact with the vehicle itself." at 121.

James M. Rose

"WHEN THE BILL OF RIGHTS COMES—DON'T PAY IT!"[1044]

Law of the late twenty-first century appears on the author's fax machine from time to time because of a software problem in a time travel program that will occur with the Y10K bug.[1045]

One such report deals with what happened when the candidate of the New Millennium Party—a party of conservative ideology that described itself as consisting of Laissez Faire Internet capitalists—nominated its presidential candidate Phil S. Stein.[1046]

In the traditional manner of presidential candidates, he promised a platform that would be tough on crime, cut taxes, make it easier to prosecute tax cheats, and be more capitalistic. He, unlike, the other candidates, had a grand unified theory of how to accomplish it all with one bill. Other candidates had been criticized for lacking "the vision thing"—i.e., a Grand Unifying Theory Syllogism (GUTS). Candidates who lacked GUTS had image problems. But Stein was elected enthusiastically[1047] and proceeded to put his plan in place.

He cracked down on crime by eliminating the pesky limitations on police actions imposed by the Fourth and Fifth Amendments to the Constitution. He knew that the voters would never agree to repeal anything that had the public relations savvy name "The Bill of Rights." Instead, he complained that protections which could

---

[1044] by James M. Rose, White Plains, New York. Mr. Rose is fully Y2K complacent.

[1045] It will develop in 9999 that software will have to be adjusted for yet another digit. Software geeks will gesture with their middle finger "Sure—here's your extra digit." They will admit that they had not been concerned with the year 10K problem because geeks have never been good on dates of any kind.

[1046] He was the initial party offering (IPO).

[1047] Each year fewer and fewer people vote because of the Law of Diminishing Returns.

be enjoyed only by criminals guilty of anti-social acts [1048] were outmoded 18th century concepts that were as inappropriate in the late 21st century as Sunday Blue Laws, child labor laws, and anti-trust law enforcement. He proposed to bargain with the taxpayers about their rights.

Voters used to bargaining about the price of groceries and mortgages on the internet were willing to sell their constitutional rights back to the government.[1049] The government began a campaign that the Bill of Rights *costs* the taxpayers by increasing crime, and used the slogan "The Bill of Rights—don't pay it!" An analogy was made to collectively bargaining, in which unions waive certain statutory protections in return for salary increases.

Phil S. Stein's plan was for the government to offer a 7% tax reduction of taxable income on the 1040 tax form each year in exchange for a waiver of the taxpayer's Fourth Amendment rights; a 7% reduction for waiving the Fifth Amendment rights, and a total of 15% for waiving them both at the same time. The average taxpayer believes that he will never need the Fifth or Fourth Amendment protections in his lifetime, so they became costly luxuries when compared to immediate cash to use on internet shopping,[1050] the latest infomercial offerings of Ron Popiel III, and the miracle spot remover D'oxy-Klean.[1051]

In case law, such as *Johnson v. Zerbst*,[1052] the United States Supreme Court has ruled that an individual is free to waive his constitutional protections if the waiver is knowing and intelligent.

[1048] He reasoned that innocent people had no need to assert their right against self incrimination because they had nothing to fear from the truth, and individuals with nothing to hide had no reason to object to searches which would come up empty handed.

[1049] A few taxpayers prudently leased them back again, despite a public outcry that they were "lessors of two evils."

[1050] He even suggested re-naming the IRS the "Internet Revenue Supplement."

[1051] A spot remover so powerful that fast talking infomercial hucksters apply it to dalmatians and convert them to short haired samoyeds.

[1052] 304 U.S. 458.

Lawyers were skeptical, and advised their clients to be careful selling their birthrights to the government for a mess of pottage if they might owe a lot of back taxes, because the 15% bargain may not be economically sound. Indeed, the lost revenue from the 15% reduction to honest taxpayers was more than compensated for with the revenue from dishonest taxpayers who had waived their protections against self incrimination and the search and seizure of their records.

IRS scrutinized with great care the returns of the people who would not waive their rights. The ironic result was that the people who refused to waive their Fifth Amendment rights were treated as if the refusal itself were incriminating.

Soon wealthy taxpayers were dissatisfied with a mere 15% tax reduction, and bargained an even bigger reduction on the theory that they were risking more without the constitutional protection, so it was more valuable to them. Graduated tax rates remained, but new graduated tax reductions that increased as income increased resulted in the inversion of the old graduated taxes.

The case that appeared on the author's fax machine was an unreported Second Circuit decision about the tax plan. The Second Circuit has instituted a plan where some of its decisions are not released or published. Since knowledge is power in the information age, the courts are unwilling to share their power with mere mortals. Their decree was expanded in the 21st century to prohibit even attorneys involved in the cases from knowing the reasoning by which a decision was reached. Decisions would be on a need to know basis, and the attorneys in the case did not need to know. The court determined that it was not necessary for attorneys who do an appeal to actually know the law applicable to the case.

The unreported case involved a taxpayer, Bill O. Wright, who waived his constitutional protections on his income tax return. He was then prosecuted by the government after a random search of his computer discovered he was actually in the business of fixing DNA tests in paternity cases.[1053] He brought a habeas corpus petition against the sheriff *(People ex. rel. of Wright v. Hrong)* alleging that his waiver was not a knowing one. His learning specialist opined that he is easily distracted, and his train of thought not only can be easily derailed,[1054] it often crashes into a bridge abutment.[1055]

Wright said he checked the wrong box. He had intended to check the box on the tax return contributing one dollar to the party of his choice.[1056]

Wright alleged that he had been drinking heavily when he filled out his taxes, and he was too drunk to understand the legal consequences of what he was doing. The court rejected that argument summarily. It noted that people had often alleged they were too drunk to understand their *Miranda* warnings or Driving While Intoxicated breath test warnings when they were arrested.[1057] The courts have held as a matter of law that one need not be sober to make legal decisions, a point illustrated in reported decisions.[1058]

Finally, he argued that his waiver was not an intelligent one, either. The court took one look at him and agreed.

[1053] He did it on a contingency for men paying a lot for child support. His motto was "If you're broke, we'll fix it!"

He became a suspect when he inadvertently "fixed" the wrong DNA sample, and proved that a birth mother could not have been the parent of her child.

[1054] He was obsessed with money, and putting a penny on the rails of his train of thought was enough to derail him.

[1055] Wright said that when tax time came around he was "Busier than a one-armed paperhanger after they passed the Americans With Disabilities Act."

[1056] He wanted to contribute to the party because, he said, if everyone in America "kicked in a buck" we could all have "one hell of a party!"

[1057] See, for example *People v. Rafferty,* 148 Misc 2d 494, 560 NYS2d 741 (Dist. Ct. Nassau Co., 1991).

[1058] *Matter of Carey v. Melton,* 64 App. Div. 2d 983, 408 NYS2d 817 (2nd Dept. 1978).

RES IPSA LOQUITUR (Humor)[1059]

NEW DEFENSES FOR NEW CAUSES OF ACTION

by James M. Rose[1060]

Those of us who labor in the vineyards of the law making its fine wines[1061] have noticed that there are newly popular causes of action emerging.[1062] They have led to the law business allegedly picking up, although it still appears lackadaisical.[1063] Where there are new causes of action there are new defenses to cope with them.[1064] Continuing the oenological images, this is new wine for new bottles. This article tastes some of them.[1065]

Money Laundering Control Act of 1986 (18 U.S.C. § 1956-7).

One of the emerging crimes most popular with United States Attorneys is money laundering. It has been proclaimed the "white collar crime of the 90's."[1066] According to an article in the New York

---

[1059] "For things said false and never meant, Do oft prove true by accident."
—Samuel Butler.
[1060] White Plains, New York. Mr. Rose is the author of "First Aid for Sound Bites."
[1061] And its sparkling wines, too, until our case of athlete's foot cleared up.
[1062] The number of new kinds of law suits being created is an indication of economic health tracked in the Index of Misleading Economic Indicators.
[1063] The FDA has not yet established the minimum daily requirement for daisical.
[1064] And no doubt seminars will quickly follow, and then frequent mailings about audio and video tapes of them.
[1065] But refrains from an awful pun about wine and Roses.
[1066] "Money Laundering—The Crime of the 90's" G. Richard Strafer, 27 *Am. Crim. L. Rev.* 149 (1989).

Law Journal it has become more favored among federal prosecutors than was RICO in the 1980's,[1067] or conspiracy prosecutions prior to that.[1068] The civil forfeiture provisions have led to the confiscation of entire businesses and much personal property.

Defense attorneys are afraid that any item their client purchases will be confiscated—like that $4000 stair climbing fitness device that your client uses before he takes the elevator to the 27th floor of his office building. One litigation boutique[1069] has come up with the defense—entrapment.

Since it is the government that prints United States currency[1070] it has provided an essential element of the crime. If there were no United States currency no one would be able to launder it. Without this vital element supplied by an agent of the United States Government the commission of the crime would be impossible—and the courts have held that government agents supplying a vital

---

[1067] E. Abramowitz, "Money Laundering: The New RICO?" New York *Law Journal*, September 1, 1992, p. 4 col. 1.

[1068] *United States v. Certain Funds on Deposit in Account No. 01-0-71417 Located at Bank of New York* 769 F. Supp. 80 (EDNY, 1991).

[1069] A litigation boutique is where you go to get a custom law suit, instead of the places that do volume business off the rack.

[1070] 31 U.S.C. § 5114. "The Secretary of the Treasury shall engrave and print United States currency and bonds of the United States Government and currency bonds of United States Territories and possessions from intaglio plates on plate printing presses the Secretary selects." This is the same section that limits the portraits on currency and securities to deceased individuals, although portraiture of living persons has been permitted on revenue stamps; and is the section that requires "In God We Trust" to appear on currency and coins (which the courts have held is not the establishment of religion, *Aronow v. United States,* 432 F.2d 242 and does not violate the free exercise clause, *O'Hair v. Blumenthal,* 462 F. Supp. 19, affd 588 F.2d 1144, cert. denied 442 US 930, 61 L. Ed. 2d 298, 99 S. Ct. 2862 (1978)) or the separation of church and state.

element of the offense the lack of which would make the crime impossible is the essence of entrapment.[1071]

Employer Liability for Sexual Harassment in the Work Place

A variety of state, federal and local laws, regulations, administrative orders and collective bargaining agreements now prohibit sexual harassment.[1072] Conduct between the sexes in the workplace which previously went unreported or unprosecuted has formed the basis for lawsuits—and places management in a position of potential liability for permitting such conduct to occur on its premises.

A new defense to such conduct is found in, of all places, the Americans With Disabilities Act of 1990 (42 U.S.C. § 12111 et. seq.) (the "ADA") as well as in the same statutes that prohibit discrimination against persons on the basis of sex and, inter alia., disabilities.[1073] The ADA is closely modeled after the Federal Rehabilitation Act of 1973, which prohibited discrimination by the Federal government and its grantees. Thus government grantees

---

The New York *Law Journal* reported in August 9, 1989 at page 1 col. 2 B that a coven of witches was granted a tax exempt status, although it is "church" you would want to separate from your state. As far as federal tax exemptions for religious groups are concerned (26 U.S.C. § 501 (c) (3)) atheists are not entitled to them because they do not believe in the church, anarchists are not entitled to them because they do not believe in the state, and agnostics do not get them because they are unsure of whether to apply.

[1071] Compare *United States v. West* 511 F. 2d 1083 (3rd Cir. 1975), *United States v. Bueno*, 447 F. 2d 903 (5th Cir., 1971) with *United States v. Russell*, 411 US 423; *Hampton v. United States* 425 US 484, 48 L. Ed 2d 113, 96 S. Ct. 1646; *United States v. Pardue* 765 F. Supp. 513 (1991).

[1072] And protect both sexes from harassment not just women. Therefore, one should not refer to the statutes as providing "broad protection"—a description that is too narrow.

[1073] The New York State Human Rights Law (Executive Law §290-301) prohibits discrimination based on sex as well as disability. The definition of disability is contained in Executive Law Section 292 (21) and is quite wide ranging. It has defined disabilities ranging from obesity to AIDS. Employers were prevented from discriminating against former alcoholics and drug addicts[1074] who now claim to be rehabilitated.[1075]

A handicapped person is defined as somebody with a physical or mental impairment (which is later defined) or is regarded as having such an impairment (Section 84.3(j)(iii)).

The term physical or mental impairment includes any physiological disorder or condition. Section 84.11 states that no qualified handicapped person shall, on the basis of handicap, be subject to discrimination in employment under any program or activity to which this part applies. Specifically, hiring, upgrading, promotion, tenure, demotion, transfer, layoff or termination are mentioned in subdivision (b) of that section. The only exclusion in that regard are individuals who are alcohol or drug abusers whose current use of alcohol or drugs prevents such individuals from performing the duties of the job in question or whose employment by reason of such current alcohol or drug abuse would constitute a direct threat to property or the safety of others 29 U.S. Code §706(8)(B).

However, among the disabilities are also mental (i.e., psychological) ones. What happens when an employee claims to have suffered from a psychological disability (i.e., the inability to keep his or her hands off a fellow worker of the opposite sex because of a mania) for which he now claims that he is cured?[1076]

The employer who permits an employee to remain on the payroll and seek rehabilitation may well have to offer the employee

---

are prohibited from discriminating on the basis of handicap or disability (Executive Law Section 296(1)(b)). It includes alcoholism and drugs, see *Doe v. Roe* Inc. 143 Misc. 2d 156.

[1074] Drug testing is permitted by the Drug-Free Workplace Act of 1988 (41 U.S.C. § 701); and despite popular belief the Americans With Disabilities Act does not require that drug tests be graded on a curve.

[1075] Section 504 of the Federal Rehabilitation Act of 1973 (Public Law 93-1112, 87 Statutes 394, 29 U.S.C. § 794). Regulations defining who comes within the ambit of Section 504 are found in the Federal Register, Volume 42, number 86. The definitions are found in Section 84.3.

[1076] The defense of the "differently moralled" or "morality impaired" individual as a handicapped person.

more than one chance. In *Callicotte v. Carlucci* 698 F. Supp. 944 (D.D.C., 1988) the Court found that alcoholism is a recurrent problem requiring federal agencies [and grantees] to accommodate it as a handicap. The Court cited with approval the conclusion of Judge Gerhardt Gesell in *Whitlock v. Donovan*.[1077] Judge Gesell wrote that permitting a person only one attempt to rid himself of alcoholism is not a reasonable accommodation.

"Since it is recognized that relapse is predictable in treatment of alcoholics, an agency is not justified in automatically giving up on an employee who enters treatment but who subsequently relapses."

Relapses are just as likely to occur in people suffering from intractable mental illnesses which we are only dimly aware of how to identify and treat.

Therefore, is it a defense to the charge that an employer permitted sexual harassment to occur on his premises when he was aware that such conduct had occurred in the past that he was required to retain the offending employee and was only complying with the requirements of the Americans With Disabilities Act? Stay tuned.

Resource Conservation and Recovery Act of 1976

As fast as the new defenses are invented, the prosecutors find new crimes. Take for example the state prosecution of certain police officers who were charged with shooting at inner city motorists they believed were speeding. In the infamous Rodney Prince case, several police officers were prosecuted for assault and attempted murder when the District Attorney argued it was inappropriate to fire deadly weapons at speeders. The officers' defense was that these motorists asked to be let off with a warning, so they were firing warning shots across their bows. They were acquitted.

Federal prosecutors then brought criminal charges against them alleging a violation of the Resource Conservation and Recovery

---

[1077] 598 F. Supp. 126 (Dist. D.C.), *aff'd. sub. nom. Whitlock v. Brock*, 790 F2d 964 (D.C. Cir.)

Act of 1976, 42 U.S.C. § 6928 (d) (2). In *Connecticut Coastal Fisherman's Assn. v. Remington Arms Co.*[1078] the Second Circuit found that a gun club was liable for pollution it caused when lead (a hazardous waste) contained in buckshot got into land it owned. The police officers were charged with knowingly disposing of hazardous waste without a permit because of the lead in their bullets. The Environmental Protection Administration is now looking into whether police must file an environmental impact statement before each discharge of a weapon.

[1078] 989 F. 2d 1305, (2nd Cir, 1993), New York *Law Journal* April 19, 1993 p. 5.

James M. Rose

CAN THE COURTS FASHION A REMEDY FOR DODGE BALL?

by James M. Rose[1079]

The courts were recently asked to remedy yet another bane of childhood that threatens the happy and healthy development of our children—the scourge of dodge ball.

It began when a child who was forced by his gym teacher to play in a dodge ball game called the Child Abuse Hotline in Albany.[1080]

The New York State Department of Social Services maintains a toll-free telephone hotline to receive reports of abuse and maltreatment (see, Social Services Law § 422 [2] [a]). Upon receipt of a complaint, it must be determined whether the acts alleged, if true, "could reasonably constitute a report of child abuse or maltreatment" *(ibid.)* and, if so, the matter must be referred to the appropriate local agency for an investigation (see, ibid.), which must determine within 60 days whether the report is "'indicated'" or "'unfounded'" (Social Services Law § 424 [7]).

In this instance the child reported that his physical education instructor, "Jungle" Jim Machismo, required him to participate in a game of dodge ball or flunk the course. As a result the child was hit by a ball and his arm was slightly bruised.

Dodge ball is a "game" in which a ball of some kind[1081] is thrown by one child at another with the intention of hitting the other child with the ball.[1082]

[1079] White Plains, New York, and Undistinguished Fellow at the Johnnie Cochran Institute of Theoretical Forensics and author of "How Many Billable Hours does it take to Change a Light bulb?

[1080] 1-800-342 3720.

[1081] A soccer, volley or rubber kick ball usually, but see footnote 7 *infra*.

[1082] If the ball is caught the thrower is out, but if it hits the target child without being caught the target is out. See, A. Arnold, *World Book of Children's Games* p. 38, (World, 1972); S. Hunt, *Games and Sports Around the World*, p. 219, Ronald Press, 1964). In England the same

Under Family Court Act § 1046 (a) (ii), a prima facie case of child abuse or neglect may be established by evidence of an injury to a child which would ordinarily not occur absent an act or omission of respondents, and that respondents were the caretakers of the child at the time the injury occurred.

The investigating child protective worker, herself traumatized in childhood by being struck by balls thrown by bigger children in dodge ball contests, found that there was indeed child abuse or neglect occurring.[1083] A complaint against the instructor who had insisted the game be played and that the child [1084] participate in it was then lodged in Family Court.[1085] If found guilty, Machismo could be fired, criminally prosecuted, and required to comply with public notification provisions contained in New York's version of "Megan's Law."[1086]

The case was assigned to Family Court Judge Vernelle E. Quinn-Ochs[1087] who examined the coach's argument that dodge ball was a universal and time tested game of unknown origin, and hence a tradition in the public schools. Extensive research yielded nothing on the origins of the game. One term paper, written by a football player majoring in Recreational Studies at an Associated Press Football Poll Top Ten school, postulated it was invented by Col. Richard I. Dodge—the founder of Dodge City, Kansas. That frontier city was known for its violent gunfights in the streets, and

---

game is called "tig" I. and P. Upie, *Children's Games in Street and Playground*, p. 99, Oxford Press, 1969.

[1083] For a description of injuries in a dodge ball game that led to a negligence complaint see, *Feder v Board of Educ.* 147 A.D. 2d 526, 537 NYS2d 828 (2nd Dept., 1987).

[1084] Whose name was reported in the traditional Family Court manner only by first name and last initial as "Wim P."

[1085] In order to alleviate the situation described in this article, some schools specified that the game be played with a Nerf ball, until hunting and emasculating Nerfs was outlawed.

[1086] The statute requires that convicted child abusers wear a scarlet letter "A".

[1087] Observers in her court reported that she was "no spring chicken."

it was theorized that Colonel Dodge invented dodge ball[1088] to substitute as a less lethal outlet for aggressive gunfighters.[1089]

The judge was not impressed by an argument that would exclude from the definition of child abuse anything that was traditional, noting that corporal punishment in the schools had been traditional but was now abolished.[1090]

However, a problem was encountered when the teacher requested that the child who complained be examined by a doctor or psychiatrist. The potential trauma that can be suffered by child abuse victims has been widely discussed and documented (see generally, Parker, The Rights of Child Witnesses: Is the Court a Protector or Perpetrator?, 17 *New Eng L Rev* 643, 648-656; Note, Videotaping Children's Testimony: An Empirical View, 85 *Mich L Rev* 809). The "validation process requires that the child establish a relationship with the expert. It necessitates the child's recounting and reliving the traumatic incidents suffered. She must overcome fear, guilt and embarrassment. Multiple validations would subject a truthful child to another form of child abuse . . . [and] a child fabricating such abuse must be severely emotionally disturbed and

---

[1088] Various versions of the game exist. The trial judge noted that one which employs more than one ball is called "Bombardment." The name alone conjures up a vicious attack with explosives intended to maim and murder.

[1089] A kind of corollary to Frederic Jackson Turner's famous thesis of the frontier as a safety valve. The paper received an "A"—but then so did all the papers in the class (History of Frontier Recreation 1840-1888), which was taken exclusively by students on athletic scholarships. Their success in the class no doubt confirmed the wisdom of giving them the scholarships.

[1090] It has been noted that one generation's reforms are a subsequent generation's problems. The Progressives insisted on municipal ownership of things like transportation and electricity, only to have this generation of politicians see municipal ownership as a problem. A generation that replaced the spoils system with the civil service system would surely be unhappy to see the contracting out of public jobs now going to political supporters of recently elected politicians. So replacing bullets with Dodge ball may now result in

could be seriously traumatized by continuous probing."[1091] Therefore, Judge Quinn-Ochs ruled that the child could not be examined prior to trial as it might cause further trauma.

But permitting the child to testify in court would also constitute child abuse, the gym teacher argued. If Judge Quinn-Ochs ruled that the child could testify despite her ruling prohibiting pre-trial examination, Mr. Machismo threatened to call the child abuse hotline and report the judge.

A long adjournment was then taken to consider this new turn of events.

---

dodge ball being declared child abuse. This Hegelian cycle may see corporal punishment return with capital punishment. The reform in which the abolition of corporal punishment took place may now itself require reform because it created so may behavioral problems in schools.

[1091] *Matter of Tara H.*, 129 Misc 2d 508, 509, 494 NYS2d 953.

JAMES M. ROSE

LEGAL FOLKLORE: HOW MANY GRAND JURORS DOES IT TAKE TO INDICT A HAM SANDWICH?

Folklore is a traditional belief or legend. Ancient folklore believed that the sun traveled across the sky on the back of a turtle. But just because we no longer believe that bit of wisdom does not mean that we don't have our own modern folklore.

On example of a modern equivalent was recently given by Chief Judge Wachtler, who is reported to have said that an insensitive prosecutor if he were so inclined could "indict a ham sandwich."[1092]

It is not reported *where* he is alleged to have made the remark, although it is likely that such a statement may have been made about a *certain* ham sandwich at a *certain* Albany diner.

Also not revealed is what offense a ham sandwich could be indicted for committing. No doubt you could indict it for violating Agricultural and Markets Law § 201-a and 201-d if it dared to call itself kosher.[1093]

Perhaps you could indict it for even showing up in a kosher deli. While there may be a proper place for ham sandwiches, that is an improper one. This doctrine is in keeping with the Supreme Court's language in *City of Newport v. Iacobucci*: "[A]s long as people who like pigs keep them in secluded barnyards, they do not offend the sensibilities of the general public."[1094]

This is the "pig in the parlor" doctrine first pronounced by Mr. Justice Sutherland in *Euclid v. Ambler Realty Co.*, "Nuisance may be merely a right thing in the wrong place—like a pig in the parlor instead of the barnyard."[1095]

[1092] Abrovsky, "Grand Juries, New York *Law Journal*, January 16, 1987, p. 1, at p. 24 col 3 note 4.

[1093] The author does not know how it could call itself anything unless the ham was mixed with tongue in the sandwich.

[1094] 479 U.S. 92, 101 note 4 (1986) (Stevens, J. dissenting).

[1095] 272 U.S. 365, 388 (1926). See, *Federal Communications Commission v. Pacifica Foundation*, 438 U.S. 726, 750 (1978)—The Seven Dirty Words Case" so frequently referred to by comedian George Carlin. The "Makin' Bacon Case"

Perhaps you could indict it for Assault in the Second Degree[1096] if it causes a stupor and is a preparation capable of causing the same.

I suppose you *did* indict a ham sandwich in Westchester County it would receive an alibi notice, a form which is automatically attached to the back of all indictments. Then the ham sandwich could say, as do so many defendants faced with an alibi notice, that it could not possibly have committed the offense charged as it was home in the parlor with its mother at the time of the crime.[1097]

If it made certain statements, it would also be "served"[1098] with a notice of an intention to offer certain oral admissions.

How many grand jurors it would take to indict the ham sandwich seems to have been answered by the case *People v. Infante*.[1099] It would take twelve as a minimum to hear all the evidence, but sixteen to be a quorum. While the twelve must hear all of the evidence, be charged,[1100] and deliberate, the other four are along for the ride. It takes twelve grand jurors to indict a ham sandwich but sixteen to return a true bill. How much should a true bill for a ham sandwich cost? That is a "charge" that is passed along to the defendant when he is "charged" with a crime. If he is

---

is another name for the *FCC v. Pacifica* Case, because it refers to a song with that name.

[1096] Penal Law § 120.05 (5).

[1097] The pig in the parlor defense, see note 4, *supra*.

[1098] *People v Huntley*, 15 NY 2d 72, 225 (1965). This notice is known to a generation of older attorneys as the "Huntley notice," and to younger attorneys as a "§ 710.30 notice" because their collective experience is post 1971, when that section of the Criminal Procedure Law went into effect. This test is more effective for determining the age of an attorney than carbon dating.

[1099] 124 App. Div. 2d 86 (2nd Dept., 1987).

[1100] This is in keeping with the restaurant theme of "serving" subpoenas, "charging" the grand jury, and having it return a true "bill." Consider also the "role" of the prosecutor at note 1, *supra*.

convicted, he must pay a mandatory surcharge,[1101] it is clear that the Legislature believes that criminals must pay even if crime doesn't.

Of course you can't really indict a ham sandwich because it isn't a person. All offenses described in the Penal Law begin with the language "A person is guilty of . . ." The definition of "person" is found in Penal Law § 10.00(7) [1102] and would exclude a ham sandwich unless it is a governmental instrumentality. Some governments may work in strange and mysterious ways, but few are known to deputize sandwiches. If the ham sandwich were a "person" it would still have to be over sixteen years old to be charged with a crime,[1103] and a sandwich that is sixteen years old *sounds* criminal.[1104]

The belief that you could indict a ham sandwich tells us much about modern legal folklore. It illustrates what people are willing to believe about the present legal system.

I recently met a layman who told me that a state trooper must wear his hat when he writes you a speeding ticket or the ticket can be "thrown out."[1105] Of course, whether the trooper was wearing his hat or not has nothing to do with whether the law was violated, or whether the driver is guilty, but people are willing to believe that the legal system is so taken up with technicalities and so

---

[1101] Penal Law § 60.35. What charge is the "surcharge" on top of in order to be "sur"? The original crime charged, I suppose.

[1102] "Person" means a human being, and where appropriate, a public or private corporation, an unincorporated association, a partnership, a government of a governmental instrumentality.

[1103] Penal Law § 30.00 (1).

[1104] Judge Wachtler did not say where you could try the ham sandwich. One appropriate venue would be the local shopping mall's Food Court.

[1105] Perhaps the argument as framed by a layman would go like this:

A regulation of the state police requires all troopers to be in full uniform while on traffic duty. The hat is a part of the uniform. If the trooper is not wearing the hat he is out of uniform. If he is out of uniform he cannot perform the duties of a police officer. (This is the part of the argument that seems to leap a large canyon in two small bounds.) If he cannot perform the duties

unconcerned with guilt or innocence that it would not punish a speeder if the trooper issuing him a ticket did not wear a hat.[1106]

There are other instances of legal folklore that we have heard. Some involve strange rulings or strange verdicts. It makes you wonder what the public perception of the legal system as a method of obtaining a determination is; and whether the system is perceived as a method of finding the truth, of just of disposing of cases in some random manner.

---

of a police officer, he cannot write a simplified traffic information. Criminal Procedure Law § 100.10 (2)(a) defines a simplified traffic information as an accusation written ". . . by a police officer . . . authorized to write the same." He is not authorized to write same (c.f., People v. Shapiro 61 NY2d 880 (1984) unless he complies with the directives of his superiors.

[1106] The mirrored sunglasses are optional.

RES IPSA LOQUITUR (Humor)[1107]

ARE STREET GANGS INDIAN TRIBES?

by James M. Rose[1108]

A recent case has determined if what we call a street gang could decide murder charges in a way that would bind a New York court.

The defendant, Blackfoot "Doe,"[1109] was indicted for the murder of a rival gang member. He pleaded former jeopardy, and moved to dismiss the indictment on the basis that he previously had been acquitted by a court of competent jurisdiction.

The facts discussed by the court in its decision revealed that the defendant was member of the Native Bloods, a well known street gang in New York City. This group has existed for several generations in the inner cities. In so doing, it was alleged, it took on all the *indicia* of, and thus became an Indian tribe. It conducted initiation ceremonies into the group. Members were born into, died, and were buried according to the customs of the group. It developed its own folklore, legends, songs, tribal government and rules, and its own court system to deal with disputes. It had its own "colors" or tribal dress, its members sometimes sporting Mohawk haircuts, and to an extent, developed its own tribal language understood only by other tribe members.

The group was active in defending its own territory[1110] from other similar groups. On occasion, like Indian tribes did before America was settled, they met with their rivals and signed "peace treaties." The government of the city acting through its police department arranged and participated in the peace treaties, and

---

[1107] Or, for the purposes of this article "Race Ipsa."
[1108] White Plains, New York. The movie rights to Mr. Rose's *New York Vehicle and Traffic Law* are still available.
[1109] A fictitious name for purposes of publication.
[1110] Ironically these "Indians" were from the area of Columbus Circle.

attempted to enforce them. All of this activity, it was argued, meant that the Native Bloods were acting as an Indian tribe, and were even acknowledged as a *de facto* tribe in their dealing with the police, who came to the gangs' chiefs and councils when there were disturbances in the communities.

When faced with this argument in state Supreme Court, the Assistant District Attorney argued that the gangs were not Indians, but merely vandals. However, the court pointed out that the Vandals were also a tribe, but Germanic in origin. Like the Native Blood tribe, they had rules and customs of their own that governed their relationships and lives.

Blackfoot Doe had shot and killed a rival gang member[1111] after a peace treaty had collapsed.[1112] A Native Bloods investigation was conducted. A "trial" was then held at which witnesses testified before the Bloods tribunal on the issue of whether Blackfoot had murdered the other gang member. It was concluded that he killed an enemy combatant of another tribe in a battle in time of war. Doe had been acting as a "soldier". He was acquitted by the Native Bloods tribunal.

Thereafter he was indicted in New York County, and the New York State Supreme Court was required to consider if it had jurisdiction over the alleged offense. Plenary jurisdiction over Indian matters resides in the Federal government[1113] However, the federal government "has lawfully delegated a portion of its control over New York Indians to the State of New York by enacting section 232 of title 25 of the United States Code."[1114]

[1111] The rival gang was called the Canarsies, possibly related to the tribe that sold Manhattan to Peter Minuit for twenty four dollars. It was clear profit as they did not own it at the time. The Raritans sold Staten Island six times, *(Manna-hatin: The Story of New York,* (Manhattan Co., NY, NY 1929), p. 20.)

[1112] A witness said that the two behaved "like wild Indians."

[1113] *Matter of Heff* 197 U.S. 488 [1905], *United States v. Kagama* 118 U.S. 375 [1886].

[1114] *People v. Cook* 81 Misc.2d 235 at 242.

New York State Constitution Article VI Section 31 provides "This Article [the Judiciary Article of the State Constitution] does not apply to peacemakers courts or other Indian Courts, the existence and operation of which shall continue as provided by law."

18 U.S.C. § 1152 provides that criminal jurisdiction of offenses committed by one Indian against the person of another Indian may be punished by the law of the tribe. The court in *People v. Boots*[1115] concluded that New York courts have jurisdiction concurrent with that of Indian courts.[1116] It was alleged by the defendant Blackfoot Doe that the acquittal by an Indian court is entitled to *res judicata* effect, and thus double jeopardy protections must apply. Doe alleged that he could not now be tried by New York courts, which must give full faith and credit to a judgment of an Indian court. As was said in *Bennett v. Fink Construction Co.*,[1117] the Indian nations are not subservient to New York courts. Decisions of peacemaker Indian courts are final and conclusive on New York courts, *Application of Jimerson*.[1118]

The prosecution argued that it was ludicrous to find that Doe was an Indian. However, the defendant argued that there is no definition in state or federal law of "Indian" or "Indian tribe" which is applicable to the specific issue of court jurisdiction.[1119] "Book 25 of the McKinney's New York statutes is entitled the "Indian Law." (See, Indian Law § 1.) Nowhere in that law is there a definition of "Indian."

The District Attorney argued that the Native Bloods were not ethnically Native Americans, but by color and genetics African

---

[1115] 106 Misc 2d 522 at 536 (Franklin Co., Ct. 1980.)
[1116] See chapter 671 of the Laws of 1962, and *Mohawk v. Longfinger*, 1 Misc 2d 509.
[1117] 47 Misc 2d 283.
[1118] 44 Misc 2d 1028, aff'd 22 App. Div. 2d 417.
[1119] There are several definitions used for purposes of federal laws unrelated to the situation at bar. They include 25 U.S.C. § 450b, which defines "Indian" as a person who is a member of an Indian tribe. An "Indian tribe" is defined as any nation, or other organized group

Americans[1120] However, the law does not define Indian" or "Indian Tribe" by color, or even country of origin. A tribe can choose to initiate new members. Historically, Indian tribes have initiated people into the tribe who were not genetically identical to them. If the Native Bloods were a transplanted African tribe, who is to say that they are not "Indian" if they chose to be, the court asked.[1121]

In *Baciarelli v. Morton* 481 F. 2d 610 the court determined that under Federal Law a tribe has the sole authority to determine its membership. In *Bennett v. Fink*, supra., then Supreme Court Justice Matthew Jasen said:

> It is not for this court to determine what shall be qualifications of membership in the Seneca or any other Indian Nation . . . It is for the Seneca Nation to determine who are the Senecas according to their laws, usages and customs." at 47 Misc. 2d 285.

The Native Bloods, having declared themselves a tribe and Blackfoot Doe a member of the tribe, leave the court powerless to find otherwise.[1122]

Such a determination is left to the sensibilities of the tribe itself, and is as much beyond the law as a determination of who is or is not a member of a religion.

Finally, the District Attorney argued that the Native Blood "tribe" has no reservation, and hence could not be a tribe. But the court noted that Supreme Court said: "[t]he relation of the Indian tribes living within the borders of the United States * * * [is] an anomalous one and of a complex character * * * They were, and

---

[1120] Hence the defendant's tribal name "Blackfoot."

[1121] If "Native American" tribes are descended from Asian wanderers that crossed a land bridge, who is to say how much traffic there was on the bridge and in what direction it flowed?

[1122] The District Attorney then argued that if the Native Bloods could be considered a tribe, the same argument could be advanced by some organized crime "families" with historical customs, membership procedures, and councils. The court declined to reach that issue, which was not before it.

always have been, regarded as having a semi-independent position when they preserved their tribal relations: not as States, not as nations, not as possessed of the full attributes of sovereignty, but as a separate people, with the power of regulating their internal and social relations * * *[1123]

The court then asked if a tribe was any less a tribe because it was driven from its reservation and deprived of its turf? Besides, it remarked that the police acknowledged that the Bloods had a "turf" by mediating peace treaties with other gangs.

The court ruled that it was bound by the determination of the Native Blood tribe, and of the tribe's courts. The indictment was dismissed.

[1123] *United States v. Kagama,* 118 U.S. at 381-382 quoted in *People v. Cook,* 81 Misc 2d at 250.

INEVITABLE ISSUES AT INEVITABILITY DISCOVERY HEARINGS

In the case *Nix v. Williams*[1124] the United States Supreme Court carved out an exception to the exclusionary rule when it held that evidence which would "inevitably" have been discovered by law enforcement officials need not be suppressed by the courts. This decision will give rise to a plethora of cases (inevitably to be called "progeny") involving issues created by the new doctrine. Therefore, this article was inevitable.[1125]

First, how "inevitable" must something be to qualify? On a scale from death and taxes at the top, to winning the Lotto three weeks' running on the bottom, there are some things that are quite likely (i.e., that case you've been avoiding trying all year will be reached the week you plan to take vacation), and not very likely (that motion you made to inspect the grand jury minutes and dismiss for the failure to make out a *prima facie* case will be granted). Where does the likelihood that a police officer would have found something sooner or later fit in? If you've been looking for that other brown sock you need to make a pair and your spouse says, "Oh, it'll turn up some day" how likely is that? When you say to your associate, "I know that somewhere there is a case I've seen that's exactly on point" and you hunt for it, you know that an infinite number of hackers at an infinite number of Lexis or Westlaw computer terminals can't find it before you need it. Therefore, the only thing that is clear is how unclear the "inevitability" standard is as a standard.

The result must be "inevitability" hearings in order to determine how inevitable an event would be. (That much is inevitable.)

A likely witness at an inevitability hearing will be a mathematics professor who specializes in the study of probability using arcane

---

[1124] 467 U. S. 431
[1125] i.e., necessary. The Surrogate of Westchester County equated "inevitable" with "necessary" in *In Re Flewwellin's Will,* 123 Misc. 256, 202 NYS2d 496 (1924).

computer formulas even he cannot understand.[1126] Through the aid of such devices he can tell you the corner on which the next big personal injury case will occur. After all, the hearing will not be much different that predicting future earning in personal injury cases since they both involve prognostication.[1127] What must the prognostician consider?

Police departments have varying reputations for ability in executing constabulary duties. Certainly the equation must contain some multiplier (or divisor) based upon the competency of the department involved, ranging from the Sherlock Holmsian to the Keystone Cop like. As with radar and driving while intoxicated breath testing devices, will there be some presumption of competence based upon the possession of a certificate indicative of the police officer's matriculation from the Municipal Police Training Academy? If the officer cannot find the court house in order to testify, is there a presumption that he or she would not have found that heroin secreted in your client's daughter's teddy bear? If the police officer cannot find the police report he claims to have filed about how he inevitably lighted upon the evidence in question, is that evidence that he would not have found the contraband in question inevitably; or that *if* he had found the evidence he would inevitably have misplaced it before the trial?

Inevitably, we are told, the sun will burn out and all life on this planet will cease. The chances of that happening before your next monthly mortgage payment becoming due are remote, however. Therefore, the next expert witness who must testify is an actuary. What are the odds that the police officer would have found the incriminating evidence within the statute of limitations (or

---

[1126] It has been said that any quantum leap in technology is indistinguishable from witchcraft.

[1127] Prognostication is the province of highly remunerated experts with many degrees. Fortune telling (Penal Law §165.35) is the scheme of poorly compensated scam artists with many convictions. Other than that, there is little difference. The work is the same whether described euphemistically or pejoratively.

before the Supreme Court does away with the exclusionary rule altogether by creating so many exceptions to it that they swallow up the rule?)

What is the evidentiary standard by which inevitability must be determined? Must an event be inevitable beyond a reasonable doubt (Doubtlessly Inevitable), merely more likely than not (Probably Inevitable), or inevitable beyond all doubt (Inevitably Inevitable)? Does the burden of proof lie with the burden of going forward? Does it ever shift back and forth like a bored juror during a judge's charge on circumstantial evidence?

It will "inevitably" be decided that the issue is one of fact and not of law. Therefore, jurors, who are particularly suited to determine such things, will be charged that they are required to decide what would have happened if something other than what did happen had happened. Jurors have been doing that in trials for years, even when they were not charged that it was their duty to do so. However, if they are required to predict what would have happened in the future, is their verdict in violation of Penal Law § 165.35 which makes it a class B misdemeanor to tell fortunes for a fee?[1128]

[1128] EDITOR'S NOTE: That is not likely, since the jurors will not be asked to determine what *will* happen in the future, but what *would have* happened. There is no Penal Law offense of Fortune Telling in An Alternate Universe.

RES IPSA LOQUITUR (Humor)[1129]

GULLIBUL'S TRAVAILS

by James M. Rose[1130]

Daniel D. Gullibul, (born of the cusp of Capricorn), who once suffered from the delusion that Elvis was impersonating *him*, called a 900 area code telephone number he saw on cable television for the purpose of obtaining a personal horoscope from Claire Voiant of The Psychic Boiler Room, a show on the Phrenology, Astrology, Tarot, and Spiritualism Information and Entertainment (PATSIE) Network.

He gave his birth time, date and place and was told, "Venus conjoins Uranus, and your stars are favorable for romance. Approach a person who has previously rejected you, and she will be more favorably inclined towards you romantically."

Gullibul followed this advice, although his boss had previously told him that his fellow worker Priscilla "Prissy" Victoria did not want him within fifty feet of her, and if he upset her again he would be fired. Armed with the knowledge from his astrologer that she would not reject him this time, he asked her to join him in his apartment for dinner and gave her a present of lingerie. Victoria was not amused.[1131] She had Gullibul fired, and filed a multi-million dollar sexual harassment suit against him and his employer for turning her workplace into a hostile sexual environment.

Gullibul call Voiant back, and she opined that he must have approached a Virgo who had rejected him, and her advice would only have been valid of he had approached a Moon Child.

He went to the local district attorney's office and angrily demanded that Claire Voiant be charged with the misdemeanor of

---

[1129] This column is not a prediction of the future. Do not try to predict the future yourself without the aid of a trained professional—although what else is there to predict?

[1130] Mr. Rose is the author of "The Right to Counsel During Bar Examinations."

[1131] Victoria's secret was that she was scared to death Gullibul was a stalker.

fortune telling.[1132] In addition, he requested that the District Attorney seek a sentence that provided for restitution from Claire Voiant[1133] for the cost of his call, and indemnification for any damages Victoria may obtain from him in her sexual harassment suit.

Voiant hired the immense Wall Street law firm of Rock, Paper & Scissors who attacked the misdemeanor information in human waves of young associates directed by partner with a corner office—Charles Evans Huge (a Taurus).

Their first assault on the information involved freedom of religion. Claire Voiant said that it was her religious belief that she had the ability to predict the future based upon her interpretation of the stars. Since this was a good faith belief, the state could not interfere with it. The case came before part time Village Justice and health food store entrepreneur Millie Tonin Neuage (an Aquarius) who expressed skepticism. She noted that horoscopes in newspapers appeared not on the religion page, but most often with the cartoons. However, it was pointed out to the judge that she had often remarked that the local newspaper, which she referred to as the *Distorter Repatch*, seemed to get things that went on in her court backwards, and that she would not take notice that what appeared in it was accurate.

C. E. Huge directed the court to *People v. Ballard* [1134] (where a defendant was charged with five counts of fortune telling) in which

---

[1132] Penal Law § 165.35 reads as follows

Fortune telling:

A person is guilty of fortune telling when, for a fee or compensation which he directly or indirectly solicits or receives, he claims or pretends to tell fortunes, or holds himself out as being able, by claimed or pretended use of occult powers, to answer questions or give advice on personal matters or to exorcise, influence or affect evil spirits or curses; except that this section does not apply to a person who engages in the aforedescribed conduct as part of a show or exhibition solely for the purpose of entertainment or amusement.

[1133] Under Penal Law § 260.27.

[1134] *People v. Ballard*, 143 App.Div. 2d 919, 533 NYS2d 558 (2nd Dept, 1981).

the Appellate Division said "The defendant argues that the application of these criminal statutes to him infringes upon his constitutional right to freely practice his religion (US Const 1st, 14th Amends; NY Const, art I, §3). However, as we noted above, the jury properly rejected the view that the defendant's repeated promises to his victims to the effect that he could influence evil spirits were sincere, and instead found that the defendant's promises were deliberate lies, made with fraudulent intent."

The *Ballard* case stands for the proposition that the question of whether the defendant could influence evil spirits[1135] was a factual one for the jury to decide, and not a legal one! Sincerity in one's religious beliefs was therefore a defense.[1136]

However, the court reject that argument, indicating that Ms. Voiant was free to divine the future and draw horoscopes to her heart's content as long as she did not do it on a 900 telephone number requiring the caller to foot the bill. The First Amendment guarantees the right to practice a religion, but not to profit from it.[1137] The statute does not prevent fortune telling—it only prevents fortune telling for a fee.

Huge and associates then argued that the statute infringed upon freedom of speech. Horoscopes were a protected form of commercial speech. *In New York City v. Learning Annex*[1138] New York City was prevented from banning commercial speech which involved distribution of flyers advertising courses in Astrology.

[1135] Spirits such as ghosts were held to exist as a matter of law in *Stambovsky v. Ackley*, 169 App. Div. 2d 264 (1ˢᵗ Dept, 1991).

[1136] If the Legislature concluded that any assertion that a defendant could predict the future was illegal as a matter of law, it would not be a question for the jury.

[1137] Which is why the Not-For-Profit Corporations Law applies to religious corporations, see *Rector, Church Warden and Vestrymen of St. Bartholomew's Church in City of New York v. Committee to Preserve St. Bartholomew's Church, Inc.*, 84 App. Div. 2d 309, 445 NYS2d 975.

[1138] 150 Misc 2d 791, 571 NYS2d 380.

This statute, they argued, simply could not prohibit the distribution of predictions of the future for a fee because, a great deal of the economy of the United States involves people who earn their living doing just that. Does the fortune telling statute apply to any stockbroker or market newsletter that offers advice or predictions to the bulls and bears of the stock market? Does it apply to government or bank economists who read the harbingers of retail sales to predict interest rates and employment, to futures traders who buy and sell options on commodities, mortgage brokers who try to predict interest rates, or weather forecasters? Is fortune telling practiced by government agricultural agents who do crop forecasts, or the Farmer's Almanac, by odds makers, by epidemiologists, or doctors who advise special diets for illness, or the Harris Pollsters[1139] when they do their job?

Did the judge herself violate the statute when she sentenced the previous defendant and said, "If you violate the terms of your probation I'll send you to jail?"

Justice Neuage held that the statute required more than just a statement about what *might* happen in the future, it required a detailed one with the pretense it would be the fate or fortune of the customer. The predecessor to this statute, was interpreted in 1914 in *People ex. rel. Priess v. Adams.*[1140] The judge in that case wrote: "I believe that there is a line of distinction between the person who pretends to be able to read the future and tell with positiveness what will or shall happen; and the one who merely reads a sign as indicating what ought to happen but is particular to make it plain that he is not attempting to predict future events."

Judge Neuage then noted the same distinction was made in *People v. Malcolm.*[1141] The defendant in that case was convicted

---

[1139] Who often start reports with "If the election were held today . . ." (but seldom follow that phrase with "no one would vote because everyone thinks it's going to be the second Tuesday in November.")

[1140] 32 Crim. Rep. 326.

[1141] 90 Misc. 517, 154 NYS2d 919 (Ct. of Gen. Sessions, 1915).

because, rather than just attempting to give general advice as to the future, she predicted a particular marriage. In this case Voiant gave particularized advice that would bring her within the ambit of the language.

But Rock, Papers & Scissors was not finished. It noted the long history of Astrology, dating back to 3000 B.C. in Babylon, Assyria and Egypt.[1142] Some scientific basis for astrology has always been asserted. In People ex. rel. Priess the defendant argued that she studied the science of Astrology. "In the reading of the horoscope the defendant went through an absolutely mechanical, mathematical process to get at her conclusions. She claims that astrology never makes a mistake and that if the figures are correct the information given is correct."[1143]

The defendant's brief in that case argued that:

> "Astrology is the science which describes the influence of the heavenly bodies upon mundane affairs and upon human character and life. It is a mathematical or exact science as it is based upon astronomy which describes the heavenly bodies and explains their motions, etc. It is an applied science in that it takes the established principles of astronomy as its guide in delineating human character, and all its judgments are based upon mathematical calculations. It is an empirical science, because its deductions are based upon accurate data gathered for thousands of years. Astrology is the oldest science in existence. It is not only pre-historical but pre-traditional, and must not be classed with fortune-telling . . . Astrology is the science of the effects of the Solar Currents on the living things on Earth including human life."

The D. A. scoffed. Any theory that solar currents affected human events was crackpot pseudoscience, he said.

[1142] See, Paulson-Howe, "Is Astrology Fortune-telling?" 64 *American Astrology* 27.

[1143] 32 N.Y. Cim. Reports at 339.

However, Justice Neuage pointed out that many current theories in physics sound like only crackpots[1144] would believe them. Quantum physics says that a particle can go from point A to point B without traveling across the space in between, that a positron is an electron traveling backwards in time, and that someone who traveled close to the speed of light would age slower than someone who did not. Non-scientists are skeptical of those theories, but that does not mean they are not correct.

The present statute adopts a concept from its predecessor, in that it contains the phrase "he claims or pretends to tell fortunes." The court held that elements of the offense of fortune telling that the District Attorney was required to prove beyond a reasonable doubt were that Astrology did not have a scientific basis, and that Claire Voiant could not actually predict the future.

The case was adjourned for the parties to line up their experts.

[1144] The scientific term for "crackpot" is "psychoceramic."

PETTY THOUGHTS AND GRAND ILLUSIONS; THE VALUE OF MONEY

Grand larceny is not stealing something worth a "grand," despite what I was once told by a client who specialized in selling pre-owned items he had liberated. People who believe that have been fixated by quantification. They want to define "gross negligence as 144 times as negligent as ordinary negligence because that is how a gross is defined.

Grand larceny is defined, *inter alia*, as stealing property when the value of that property exceeds $250.[1145] That seemed simple enough—until lawyers got involved. Here is a colloquy that took place recently at a felony hearing in the Village of Nouveau Riche On Hudson before Judge Apocrypha. For the defendant is the young attorney Perry Materia.

Defense Counsel: The people have failed to prove that the value of the property taken exceeds the statutory $250, you honor.
The Court: But there was testimony that he retail value of items taken exceeded $400 in value, counselor.
Defense counsel: But that's in today's currency, your honor, not in Penal Law money.
The Court: In what?
Defense Counsel: Grand Larceny in the Third Degree is a statute that became effective in September 1967. While it did represent an increase from the former figure of $100, it's obvious that $250 bought a lot more in 1967 than it does today. Gasoline was 27cents a gallon. The value of money has declined since then. It's easy to determine just how much because, by coincidence, 1967 is the base year used by the Federal Government to determine the consumer price index. In June

---

[1145] Since the publication of this article in Volume 12 of the Westchester Bar Topics in 1985, the Legislature followed the lead recommended by this article and increased the distinction between petty and grand larceny to a grand in P.L. §155.30 in 1986.

1985 the purchasing power of the 1985 dollar was reported as 31.9 cents in 1967 dollars.

The value of the dollar is measured against a lot of things, such as gold. Penal Law Section 155.00 [1] defines property as "*any* money . . . or article, substance of thing of value." The use of "any" money indicates that the value of the property is determined independently from the value of United States currency, since property has an intrinsic value while the value of money can fluctuate.

Every day in the newspapers the dollar is valued against a grab bag of foreign currencies—shekels, yen, drachma, rupees and sols.

But since the larceny provisions of the Penal Law were written in 1967, we have to measure the value of the stolen property in 1967 United States dollars. Therefore, the items taken should be worth, in 1967 dollars over 319% what they would be worth in 1985 dollars in order to constitute grand larceny.

District Attorney: That's ridiculous. Besides, some items have increased in value since 1967 and some have decreased.

Defense Counsel: Exactly. That's why I mentioned the *value* of the money and not the value of the goods. The value of stolen property is measured by the market value at the time they are stolen according to Penal Law Section 155.20.[1146] In this case a video disk was one of the items allegedly stolen. That wouldn't be worth anything in 1967 since there would not have been any video disk players to play it on. A pocket calculator was taken as well. Those things cost a lot more in 1967 when they were relatively novel and the technology was not mass produced as it is today. We're not after the value that today's property would have in 1967, we have too look at the value of the property today, but in 1967 dollars. My point is not so outrageous—it's merely that we have to draw the same line that the Legislature drew in 1967 to be faithful to the legislative

---

[1146] See, *People v. Appedu*, 11 App. Div. 2d 761, (2nd Dept., 1985).

intent embodied in the statute. If we don't, crimes that would be petty larcenies in 1967 become grand larcenies in 1985 by the mere passage of time.

The Court: But then we would have to determine the intrinsic value of each item taken as well, counselor. Some defense contractors charge $ 637 for an ashtray.

Defense Counsel: That's not larceny, that's highway robbery.

District Attorney: But Judge, the Legislature is not unaware of inflation. It's raised the cost of index numbers and notes of issue several times since 1967. It's raised its own pay, too. It increased the monetary jurisdiction of this court. Every year that the Legislature does not change the larceny statute, it amends the statute by its inaction to move the line lower.

It changes the line between where petit and grand larceny is drawn by choosing not to redraw it. The Federal government has chosen not to redraw the line by changing its definition since 1930.[1147]

(The female Assistant District Attorney then turned to Mr. Materia and said):

"And, in conclusion, my response to Mr. Materia can be summed up in one word: Lunch."

Defense Counsel: *Lunch?* What *about* lunch?

District Attorney: I thought you'd never ask.

The Court: Decision reserved.

[1147] See *People v. Cruz,* New York *Law Journal,* July 30, 1985, p. 7 col. 4.

MONEY SPEAKS, BUT IS IT WORTH LISTENING TO?

We suggested in "Petty Thoughts and Grand Illusions: The Value of Money" that the line between petty larceny and grand larceny needs redrawing. Readers have reacted.

One reader who frequently represents landlords who petition to have their rent controls raised, suggested a Grand Larceny Guidelines Board to take testimony and make findings about where the line should be drawn. He suggests that it be composed of one assistant district attorney, one member of the general public chosen mysteriously but with political connections to the party in power, and one thief. The board's findings would be subject to the inevitable court review. One drawback is that the process will mean that the results will not be final until years later, but if landlords and tenants can put up with it, so can thieves. If the line is ultimately redrawn where the board set it, thieves can be given refunds on their sentences, or credit on the next one.

There would be objections to applying the government's cost of living adjustments (COLA). Modern lifestyles call for expenditures not contemplated or conceived of in 1967. It does not take into consideration the cost of cable television, for example. Many people feel that life without cable television is not worth living. Then there's the cost of IRA's, now necessary to supplement what is universally considered as inadequate Social Security (which in 1967 we all planned to retire on). And what about the cost of computer hardware and software? Therefore the Classic COLA should be replaced by New Cola, it is argued.

Another reader questioned whether United States currency is the standard by which theft of services can be measured. That reader attempted to give a bus driver a twenty dollar bill. The driver pointed to a sign that said "DRIVER IS NOT REQUIRED TO CASH BILLS LARGER THAN $10.00." The reader referred him to the upper left hand corner of his federal reserve note which read: "This note is legal tender for all debts, public and private." Why was the bill not acceptable? Perhaps the driver would accept the bill for the fare, but would not be required to make change for it?

Another reader suggests that possession of most federal currency in the Miami Federal Reserve District is illegal. The Miami *Herald* for February 19, 1985 page 1 c reported that cocaine is so pervasive in Southern Florida that traces of it were found on ten of eleven $20 bills tested by them. Another test run by a Miami defense attorney found cocaine on every $50 and $100 bill taken in a sample from seven banks. Since it may be argued that possession of any amount of cocaine is illegal according to Penal Law 220.03, is possession of currency with the knowledge that it is almost certainly tainted and illegal?

Money for our court system is the final topic. The Chief Judge suggested higher fees for index numbers and the establishment of one for the RJI (Request for Judicial Interference). The motto of New York is "*Excelsior*" which means "higher."[1148] Court costs will live up to the state motto. Therefore, we unveil the *Res Ipsa* court financing plan for court repairs:

Hold a session of the Appellate Division in every ailing court room in the Judicial District. Appellate Division terms can be held anywhere (Judiciary Law Section 75). Section 76 provides that the Appellate Division may enforce performance of the duties of the sheriff to provide the room in which the court is held be properly heated, ventilated, lighted and kept comfortably clean and in order (Judiciary Law Section 402). Suppose that the Sheriff cannot physically accomplish those tasks, or that the court house belongs to a city, town or village? No problem. The Sheriff can round up a posse (Judiciary Law Section 400) of city, town or village workers to do it. Finally, judges and court personnel can file OSHA complaints (Labor Law Section 27-a) about their unsafe or unhealthy conditions. New laws are not needed until the old ones are used.

[1148] It also means wood shavings as another article on the state motto in this volume examines in detail.

"*E Pluribus Unum*" means "one out of many" which is a good description of the devaluation of a single bill ln our currency.

Another reader has suggested that Court TV gets its raw materials too cheaply. Important trials should be put up for bid, and the networks should be made to pay for them like they do for the Olympics, the NBA of the NFL. How much do you think they would have paid for the exclusive rights to the O. J. Simpson or Martha Stewart trial?

CHAPTER NINE

GRIMM & BARRETT, ESQS.
A FANTASY DREAM TEAM

RES IPSA LOQUITUR[1149]

THE STORY OF THE
THREE LITTLE PIGGS, LTD.

by James M. Rose[1150]

Once upon a time,[1151] there was a Three Little Piggs Limited Partnership. It consisted of three brothers named Pigg who planned to develop a certain cornfield in Kansas with low cost summer cabins. They secured the proper permits, filed the correct environmental impact statements, attended the public hearings, secured the financing documents, filed and got approval from the local building departments for the site plans, checked for radon and Indian graveyards, searched title, attended an often adjourned closing and swore out the appropriate affidavits for the Internal Revenue Service, and commenced to construct the cabins.

The first house was made by a revolutionary new process which turned straw (an environmentally responsible renewable resource) into siding. The second house was constructed by the same experimental process, but used sticks. When the surveyor checked the lot lines after construction however, he found that there was a

---

[1149] Ingredients: Humor, (from concentrate), Law (from headnotes), natural and artificial puns, partially hydrogenated statutes, fluff, traces of irony, inert filler, and sodium benzoate as a preservative.

[1150] White Plains, New York. When the next judicial nominating conventions occur, Mr. Rose will change his name to "negotiable instrument" in an effort to get endorsed.

[1151] Traditional way of starting a scholarly legal article.

problem. Someone had read the site plan upside down, and the houses were being built in the wrong locations. It was necessary to put the cabins on flat bed trucks and move them. Then the trouble began.

The Chief Federal Inspector from the Department of Housing and Urban Development, B. B. Wolff, appeared in the cornfield and declared "If you build it, I will come." He alleged that since the houses had been moved they were "manufactured houses" even though they were not pre-fabricated. How moving a house makes it "manufactured," and the bizarre consequences of that determination follow.

The National Housing Act § 308(c)(1) (Pub. L. 97-35) provides that all references to "mobile homes" in the statutes of the United States should be changed to "manufactured homes," and thus in one pen stroke legislation wiped out more mobile homes than any tornado.

A "manufactured home" is defined under 42 U.S.C. § 5402 (6) ("The National Manufactured Housing Construction and Safety Standards Act of 1974") as one that is transportable. Because the home is transportable, it must comply with the Manufactured Home Construction and Safety standards of § 5403. B.B. Wolff was not impressed with the Three Little Piggs construction standards, and stated in an affidavit that he could "huff and puff and blow the house in."

The Piggs' responsive pleading conceded that Wolff was a blowhard, but replied that the house was not a mobile home, but had only fortuitously been placed on moving equipment to relocate it. It was never *intended* to be mobile and thus, it was never intended to be "manufactured."

Judge Madonna Goose ruled that the *reason* why the house moved was none of her concern, as the statute was not concerned with the house's motivation, but only its locomotion. The statute does not require a specific intent on the part of the builder or the home, so the house's actions in moving were *malum prohibitum* and not *malum in se.*

When the Pigg's attorney described the government's theory as being based upon flawed premises, the Judge replied, "Yes, the gravamen of the case is constructing flawed premises."

She declined to answer the Piggs' attorney's query whether the house would become "manufactured" (i.e., "mobile") if a tornado picked it up from the farm and deposited it somewhere "not in Kansas anymore" as "nonsensical *in toto*."

The Three Little Pigg Limited Partnership had refused to let Chief Inspector B. B. Wolff in to inspect the premises pursuant to 42 U.S.C. § 5413 (a). They did so because their attorney had advised them to "beware of a Wolff in Chief's clothing." The pleadings alleged that Inspector Wolff and his deputy V. Ed Armis had knocked and announced their purpose, stating "Let me in," and repeated, "Let me in." The Piggs replied "Not by the power of your imperium."[1152] Wolff threatened a prosecution of the Three Little Pigg Limited Partnership, and said that the cost of defending it will "eat you all up." Indeed, the Piggs defaulted on the bank loan for the house built of hay. The bank officer sent them a scolding letter that concluded "People who live in grass houses shouldn't blow loans."

Next, the Pigg's attorney argued that the cabins were not homes or residences at all, as they were only for the use of campers in summer. The judge pointed out that the § 5402 definition says "'manufactured home' means a structure transportable in one or more sections." A cabin is a "structure" and the section does not apply to houses only. "A house many not be a home," she noted, referring to an old song, "but it certainly is a structure."

The judge ruled that the Piggs were required to comply with the manufactured housing law.

However, § 5403 (d) allows a manufacturer to file with the Secretary a form prescribed by him stating that, to the manufacturer's

---

[1152] The Judge rejected the defense that Wolff needed a warrant to inspect as "a fairy tale." See *Wolf v. Colorado* 338 US 25 (1949) overruled by *Mapp v. Ohio* 367 US 643 (1961).

knowledge, the structure is not intended to be used other than on a site built permanent foundation. The statute does not say *when* the form must be filed, so the judge let the Piggs file it after the case was over.

When last seen, B.B. Wolff was in Minnesota on a frozen lake looking at an ice fishing hut that had been trucked out there and had no permanent foundation.

CONCLUSION

The job is not over until the paper work is completed.

THE DEFENSE OF HANSEL AND GRETEL

by James M. Rose [1153]

The trial of those notorious children Hansel and Gretel concluded in Clinton County Family Court recently. This article will review the legal issues that arose. As you no doubt recall, Hansel and Gretel were prosecuted for the murder of the elderly Ms. Coven who they described as a witch. She was found stuffed in an oven and cooked in a particularly grizzly manner. The case drew constant attention from the tabloid television shows Hard Edition and Inside Copy.

At first their attorneys, the brothers Grimm,[1154] defended Hansel and Gretel Menendez by alleging that they were not responsible for their acts by reason of the fact that they had been victims of abuse by their parents.

Their father, a wood chopper by trade, had twice intentionally abandoned them in the woods at the insistence of their wicked stepmother in an effort to kill them, they maintained. This abuse excuse[1155] was rejected by the trial judge, D. Bertha DiBlooze [1156] and the siblings were forced to defend on the merits.

[1153] White Plains, New York. Mr. Rose recently sold his body to science and then leased it back for tax purposes.

[1154] Les and Mo Grimm of the law firm of Grimm, Grimm and Barrett.

[1155] What abuse as a child causes a person to do later is the subject of some dispute. Compare *Matter of Glenn G.*, 154 Misc 2d 677, 587 NYS2d 464 (Family Ct., Kings Co., 1992) footnote 6 which reads "See, for example, Hurtado, Child Abuse Case Tests New Defense: Lawyer to argue mom's inaction caused by being battered herself, *Newsday*, May 15, 1989 at 5, col 1 (city ed)." with *People v. Ciervo* 123 App. Div. 2d 393, 506 NYS2d 462 (2nd Dept. 1986) in which it was argued that a battered woman's inappropriately violent reaction was based upon her perception she needed to defend her children from what she saw as the beginning of abuse.

[1156] Citing case law she had recently learned at the Judicial College in Reno, Nevada where she took a course in Defenses in Criminal Cases in the first semester, and one in Remedial Defenses in Criminal cases in the second semester.

The first set of charges against them included trespass, larceny and malicious mischief. Ms. Coven was a member of a radical militia[1157] that lived in the remote woods and concealed its unorthodox religious beliefs (that the tabloids alleged included witchcraft and child sacrifice) from prying eyes. She lived in a home constructed entirely of gingerbread,[1158] sheet rock candy, fruitcake and icing. Her cabin was in violation of all known building codes. She had constructed it in a remote area to avoid building inspectors.

It was Ms. Coven's belief that stale gingerbread and old fruitcake are the hardest substances known to womankind, and that they are impervious to all known harm including a direct nuclear strike. She believed such an attack would be launched imminently by the United Nations.[1159]

Hansel and Gretel had wandered around in the forest with nothing to eat for three days after being abandoned by their father. When they happened upon the cottage they set upon it ravenously stating "I'm so hungry I could eat a house."[1160]

Their defense to the trespass and malicious mischief charges was justification because of the existence of an emergency. They were starving to death and trespassed on the land of Coven to eat the cabin to save their lives. Justification is a defense under the Penal Law.[1161]

[1157] called the Jeffrey Dahmer Brigade.

[1158] She bragged that she lived in a cabin she had baked with her own hands. She was known for her curious insistence (on the Internet) that Abraham Lincoln grew up in a log cabin made from jelly rolls and French desserts known as "bouche de Noel"—in English "Yule logs."

[1159] which she believed coveted this country's confectionery supplies.

[1160] It was unclear whether they had heard about the location of the candy home on the internet and were lured to it by Ms. Coven in violation of the Helms Purification of the Internet Act of 1995, which has as its premise that children should neither be obscene nor heard.

[1161] See Article 35 and in particular § 35.00 and 35.05.

The Penal Law provides that conduct is criminal but excused when it is "necessary as an emergency measure to avoid an imminent public or private injury".[1162] Thus in *People v. Padgett*[1163] the emergency defense was asserted when a defendant broke a door in order to escape being assaulted. Interestingly, the commentator to the Penal Law [1164] uses as an example of the defense of emergency breaking into a rural house to make a telephone call to save a person's life, but says nothing about eating the house.[1165]

Hansel and Gretel were then imprisoned by the lady they called a witch.[1166] The children testified that Coven threatened to cook them for dinner. To that end, she fed both of them cookies, candy and cake for two weeks to fatten them up. She then invited Hansel to get in the oven.[1167]

[1162] See Penal Law § 35.05 (2).

[1163] 60 NY2d 142, 468 NYS2d 854, 456 N.E. 2d 796 (1983).

[1164] William C. Donnino in *McKinney's Consolidated Laws of New York* Annotated Book 39 (1987) at 91.

[1165] Can the state pass laws which allow someone to eat your house without a warrant? Article I § 12 of the New York State Constitution speaks of "the right of the people to be secure in their . . . houses . . . against unreasonable seizures."

Is a candy house an attractive nuisance—particularly if it attracts mice and ants?

[1166] Her militia friends denied Hansel and Gretel were unlawfully imprisoned nor held as prisoners of war. They alleged that the children were the subject of a citizen's arrest and were being held to await trial, and that their nabbing was justified in defense of Ms. Coven's property.

[1167] Her friends (after obtaining a hefty fee to appear on television) insisted to Geraldo Rivera (on the show entitled "People Who Eat Flesh and Recipes from Those Who Cook for Them") that it was all a mistake. They say that Ms. Coven simply said that the children looked "so cute I could just eat you up" that they "looked good enough to eat," that she was going to "have them for dinner" that they were "sweet young things" of "tender years" were made of sugar and Spice" and needed some carbohydrate loading. They insisted that

He resisted, and said he would not fit since it was a large microwave and not a conventional oven. He insisted that it would not accommodate him, and so Coven attempted to show him that it could contain her. Then Gretel pushed Coven into the microwave.[1168] The defense then contended that both Hansel and Gretel were suffering from a sugar induced condition[1169] that affected their judgment. However, no contemporaneous tests were performed to ascertain hyperglycemia, and they were unable to show sugar intoxication that overcame their judgment.[1170]

They said that they were so happy to have stuffed the old lady in the oven and to be able to escape that they did a high five[1171] and accidentally fell against the "start" button on the microwave which Coven had set. The jury acquitted them of homicide charges.

The siblings were also prosecuted for theft because they found gold and gems in the strange house which they took with them when they left. They were arrested while wandering in the woods for a week. However, they claimed that they had planned to turn the loot in to the government to see if anyone would claim it, and hence had not committed larceny.

The prosecution could not show that they had intended to deprive the heirs of Coven of the money permanently.[1172]

The police were suspicious what an old lady with no known means of support and no history of inheritance was doing with a fortune in untraceable valuables easily convertible to cash stashed

---

the Menendez children misinterpreted and overreacted; and that Coven wanted Hansel to climb into the oven to help her clean it.

[1168] Gretel alleged that she only used the force necessary in her own defense in so doing. How much force is necessary for self defense is measured by what the beholder perceives and not what is actually necessary, *People v. Goetz*, 68 NY2d 96, 506 NYS2d 18, 497 N.E. 2d 41.

[1169] or sugar high sometimes referred to as the "Twinkie Defense."

[1170] Intoxication is not a defense as such, but evidence of it can be offered to negate elements of the crime such as intent (Penal Law. § 15.25).

[1171] A traditional ceremony to celebrate a "stuff."

[1172] See Penal Law Article 155.

in a hideout in the woods. Civil suits are now exploring who is entitled to the treasure—the estate of Coven, her militia buddies (who claim it is their treasury), Hansel and Gretel Menendez, or the state by escheat.

Meanwhile, Hansel and Gretel are appearing daily on television talk shows, have sold their story to the supermarket tabloids such as the National *Voyeur*, and have sold the rights to a mini-series about their ordeal in order to pay their legal bills to the law firm of Grimm, Grimm & Barrett.

JAMES M. ROSE

THE LEGAL CONSEQUENCES OF BUILDING A BETTER MOUSETRAP

by James M. Rose[1173]

Accepted wisdom has it that "If a man make a better mousetrap, the world will beat a path[1174] to his door."[1175] Whether he seeks out the world or it seeks him out, he had best be prepared for the legal consequences, according to a recent unreported case.

It appears that the Pied Piper Exterminators (a one man D/B/A hereinafter "Piper") contracted with the town fathers of the hamlet of Hamlin (in Orange County) to rid the entire environs of rats and mice. The contact was entered into, and the pied piper "performed" in several senses of the word. He dressed distinctively in a "queer long coat" of half yellow and half red; danced, and piped on a device of his own making until all the rodents in the area were led into a nearby stream where they were unexpectedly drowned. Administrative agencies of all sorts and descriptions then descended upon Piper.

The first litigation dealt with whether he was required by the New York Environmental Conservation Law to register with the department as an exterminator as allegedly provided for in Environmental Conservation Law § 33-0907. The extermination of rodents is an area that is pervasively regulated and licenses are required of professional exterminators.

[1173] White Plains, New York. Mr. Rose is the author of *New York Vehicle and Traffic Law* and asks this question: New York Vehicle and Traffic Law § 375 (2) (a) requires headlights be turned on whenever windshield wipers are turned on. When wipers are on intermittent, must you turn your hazard lights on so that your headlights blink intermittently?

[1174] The consequences of the world beating a path to one's door, including the environmental consequences, and whether an easement would be created are beyond the scope of this article.

[1175] This statement is attributed to Ralph Waldo Emerson but is not found in his writings. A similar quotation is found in his essay "Common Fame" (1885), but it contains no reference to better mousetraps.

There was no doubt that rats and mice are defined as "pests" in the law (ECL § 33-0101 (34)). They are less welcome than almost any living mammal, even out of town lawyers.[1176]

Piper argued however, that he need not register because he rid the town of mice by a curious combination of his dress, music, and movements and hence used no "pesticide" as that term is defined in ECL § 33-0101 (35). He sold or applied no "substance or mixture of substances" and therefore need not register, he noted.

However, that was not the end of the inquiry. The Federal Insecticide, Fungicide and Rodenticide Act, (FIFRA), 7 U.S.C. § 136 to 136y applies not only to pesticides but also regulates the use of "devices." That term is defined in § 136 (h) as "any . . . contrivance . . . which is intended for trapping, destroying, repelling or mitigating any pest." Section 136j makes it unlawful to sell or distribute any misbranded device. Section 136w(c)(3) allows the federal government to require labels for such devices and those standards are contained in 40 C.F.R. § 165.1 et. seq.[1177] It was conceded that when the piper performed his acts he wore no labels of any kind.

He argued however, that a person is not a "contrivance." He used a pipe of some kind, the exact nature of which he refused to reveal as a trade secret. The government maintained that the pipe also required a label and that it required a child resistant package. However, Piper maintained that the pipe itself was not a device but a musical instrument, and that the whole of his actions (but

---

[1176] In *Supreme Court of New Hampshire v. Piper* 84 L.Ed. 2d 205 at 212 the Supreme Court recognizes the necessity of out of town lawyers as the only means to vindicate federal rights in some areas. "The lawyer who champions unpopular causes surely is as important to the 'maintenance or well being of the Union' *Baldwin*, as was the shrimp fisherman in *Toomer, supra*. or the pipeline worker in *Hicklin*" and may even smell better, too. This unwelcome Piper was not related to the Pied Piper as far as the record shows.

[1177] The government argued that the piper and his pipe were pesticides because they made claims that they could get rid of pests, *United States v. 681 Cases containing Kitchen Klenzer*, 63 F. Supp. 286 (D.C. E.D. Mo. 1945).

particularly the tune he played) are what ridded the town of mice, and tunes are not devices. The law does not require every piccolo to be licensed just because it catches a rodent's fancy, the judge concluded.[1178] The tune did not "repel" the pests, it attracted them. That is the opposite of what the law forbids.

When Piper argued that he did not repel the rodents, he attracted them, the government countered that he "possessed" the rodents, and that the rodents themselves were not properly labeled. The curious argument went as follows: Rats were fur bearing animals in the possession of Piper, and thus their skins are required to be labeled to show their country of origin under 15 U.S.C.§ 69. Piper replied that the law only applied to the skins of dead fur bearing animals, but the government countered that the statute does not make any distinction whether the fur possessed is on a living or dead animal (see 15 U.S.C. 69 (b)!), and that after they drowned they were dead. However, that law only applies to imported fur, Piper countered, and there was no showing that the rats in question were anything but domestic. The court inquired if the government's interpretation would require an exterminator to label all rodents after exterminating them.

Piper was then charged with polluting the stream with dead carcasses of the rodents. The Environmental Control Law prohibits the polluting of streams (ECL § 15-0503). Piper pointed out that the rats were defined as "wildlife" in ECL § 11-0103 (6) (a) because they were among ". . . all other animal life existing in a wild state except fish, shellfish and crustacea." They were certainly not tame or domestic animals, and as such belong to no living person.[1179] Piper noted that if wildlife takes a swim in a stream that cannot be said to be "pollution". In nature wildlife is commonly found swimming in streams, and pollution is the placement of items in

---

[1178] but see, *United States v. 95 Barrels of Alleged Apple Cider Vinegar,* 265 U.S. 438 (1924). "A deception may result from the use of statements not technically false or which may be literally true" at 443.

[1179] But see ECL § 11-0105, which provides that all wildlife is the property of the State.

streams that are not naturally found there. On occasion even dead wildlife is found in streams.

Piper proved that rats can swim, and are well known for deserting ships in times of peril. He had no foreknowledge that these rats would mysteriously drown, and had thus not caused "pollution."

The government countered that if the rats were a rare species with a natural range only in Hamlin they might well be protected under the Federal Endangered Species Act 16 U.S.C. § 1533 and ECL § 11-0535.[1180] Since rats generally are strong swimmers and these rats were not, the Government argued that they must have been a new species of non-swimming rat deserving of protection. The judge rejected the argument, noting that he did not swim but that obviously did not make him a different species.

The state argued that Piper should have taken measures to see that the rats did not die within the stream and thereby cause a nuisance. However, he pointed that to do so he would have needed a permit because ECL § 11-0507 (3) requires a person to have a permit to willfully liberate wildlife within the state. Moreover he could not trap the rats alive because ECL § 11-1101 (3) prohibits trapping wildlife in the season in question.

The state argued that Piper could be required to remove the dead rats from the river before they became a health hazard. Piper replied that the state owned the them even after they were dead. "Any person who takes . . . wildlife . . . thereby consents that title thereto shall remain in the state for the purpose of regulating their control and disposition." (ECL § 11-0105).

Piper filed no environmental impact statement prior to ridding the hamlet of rodents, and hence the Town argued that he violated that Environmental Conservation Law, in that a draft environmental impact statement was required to be circulated among potentially concerned agencies before this drastic action which effected the environment could be undertaken.

[1180] See, *Sierra Club of Ireland on Behalf of 453,398 Snakes v. St. Patrick* 143 All Ireland Rpts. 298.

The court held that Piper merely played a tune and danced and the curious animals followed him. If someone must file an environmental impact statement every time it was possible that he would be followed down the street by a curious cat, dog or other animal, the court ruled, then the bureaucrats have finally succeeded in bringing life as we know it to a standstill.[1181]

The town argued that the rats were "wildlife" which belongs to the state by definition. Their wanton destruction by Piper was criminal mischief for which he could be prosecuted. However the judged ruled that such an argument required the state to prove that the rats had some value. As they were conclusively labeled "pests" in the Environmental Conservation Law they could not be said to have any value at all, and the Town had been willing to pay for their destruction.

Piper successfully defeated charges that he conducted a parade without permit. A parade, he noted, contains more than one person. While domestic animals like horses are often found in a parade, wildlife without cages or leashes is not. A movement of unrestrained wildlife (*ferae naturae*) is not a parade, the court held, but rather is known as a migration. One man walking in front of a migration is not a parade, it concluded.

Similarly, Piper did not disturb the peace or commit disorderly conduct. The music he played was not offensive or overly loud, and no ordinance prohibits the playing of a flute in a public place.

Piper was charged in a lawsuit by the Town with creating a civil nuisance. The court held that he did not create the nuisance—which existed before he got there. Rather he rid the town of what the law defines as a "pest." Eliminating pests as called for in a contract is not a nuisance. The court asked rhetorically if citizens were to be charged with nuisance for "creating" a dead mosquito every time they swatted one.

[1181] Piper also noted that if the man who first used fire had to file an environmental impact statement to assure numerous government agencies that it was perfectly safe before being put into use, we would be eating our food cold.

Mr. Piper then counterclaimed for his fee for eliminating the rats. The judge held Piper had not filed a timely notice of claim within 90 days, and his counterclaim was dismissed. He was distraught at first, but then left the courthouse, and was last seen playing his pipe in the streets with many curious children following him.

CAN THE COURTS PROSECUTE THE TOOTH FAIRY?

A strange turn of events took place recently in the courtroom of Judge Max Termm during what started out as a routine burglary prosecution. The female defendant was found masked and in dark clothing poking about with a flashlight in the bedroom of a residence at night without apparent authorization by the owner. She was in a child's bedroom at the time.

The police were alerted by a silent alarm system, and when they apprehended the defendant she refused to give her name and insisted that she was the tooth fairy. There was a tooth beneath the pillow of a young girl who slept in the room that night, and she said she put it there to exchange it with the tooth fairy for an unspecified amount of cash. Although the owner of the home testified that *he* had not invited the defendant onto the premises, the daughter testified that she fully expected a visit from the tooth fairy.

The District Attorney was unable to show that the "tooth fairy" defendant had taken any item of value, and, although the child did not own the home, Judge Termm acknowledged that children can and do permit people to come into their residences, and the invited individuals are not trespassing. It appeared that the burglary case would have to be dismissed.

However, the District Attorney was disturbed at the prospect of such a result. He noted on the record, "My office is alarmed that this case may become authority for fairies to bribe their way into children's bedrooms for purposes having to do with a minor's body parts. Certainly that must violate *some* provision of law!"

So, the District Attorney asked for a one day adjournment, and then moved to conform the indictment to the proof, by charging the tooth fairy with the misdemeanors of violating Public Health Law § 4302 and § 4307, and not being licensed to operate a tissue bank. The former section lists the persons and organizations who may be the donee of an anatomical gift.[1182] Accepting such a gift without being lawfully permitted to

---

[1182] § 4302. Persons who may become donees and purposes for which anatomical gifts may be made

do so is a misdemeanor. The tooth fairy was not a hospital, surgeon, school, society, educational institution, organ procurement organization or a donee for therapy or transplant purposes. The next night, when the case appeared on television, Judge Termm's young child asked him if he would really put the tooth fairy in jail. The Judge told her that he would have to do what the law required, and his daughter appeared visibly upset.

The following day, the attorney for the tooth fairy, Sy Bernatich,[1183] argued that a baby tooth is not the kind of "body part" contemplated by the statute. Baby teeth are meant to be shed, and thus are called deciduous teeth,[1184] he argued. They are thus no longer a "body part" after they have been severed from the body, any more than fingernails, hair or blood are. Blood can certainly be sold, as can human hair before or after separation from the donor.[1185]

Moreover, the tooth fairy was not a donee—she paid for the tooth.[1186] But the Judge pointed out that a different section defines what can

---

The following persons may become donees of gifts of bodies or parts thereof for the purposes stated:

1. any hospital, surgeon, or physician, for medical or dental education, research, advancement of medical or dental science, therapy, or transplantation; or
2. any accredited medical or dental school, college or university for education, research, advancement of medical or dental science, or therapy; or
3. any bank or storage facility, for medical or dental education, research, advancement of medical or dental science, therapy or transplantation; or
4. any specific donee, for therapy or transplantation needed by him.
5. an organ procurement organization meeting the requirements of article forty-three-B of this chapter.

[1183] Of the firm of Katz & Jammer.
[1184] See, *Whipple v. Goldsmith*, 202 App. Div. 2d 834 at 835, 609 NYS2d 377 (3rd Dept., 1994) in which they are called that.
[1185] Ours is a free market economy system, and we loathe the interference of the government in our commerce, it was argued to the judge.
[1186] There is no Uniform Gift *From* Minors Act, although there is a Uniform Gift *To* Minors Act (Estates, Powers and Trusts Law §7-4.1). The act concerns gifts

be given—Public Health Law § 4301,[1187] and that section only permits individuals over eighteen years of age to give body parts upon death.[1188] Here no one was charged with *selling* the tooth, only with buying it.[1189]

Further § 4307 makes it a crime both to buy and sell human organs,[1190] and prescinding from whether teeth are an organ or tissue, it only forbids buying and selling organs for transplant. There was no indication that the tooth was intended to be a transplant. The tooth fairy only indicated that it was for a secret fairy use, and declined to reveal that use, as a fairy "trade secret."[1191]

---

of all kinds (see Practice Commentary to §7-4.2) and is not limited to gifts of uniforms.

[1187] There is no Private Health Law.

[1188] He ruled it was not clear if the death referred to was of the person or the tooth donated.

[1189] Compounding the problem is whether the minor could sell the tooth without parental permission. However, her mother admitted that she did permit the child to place the tooth under the pillow and had told her that the tooth fairy would give her a dollar for it—the apparent going rate.

The District Attorney did not indicate that the rate was too low, but did remark that the tooth fairy, as the only known buyer for used baby teeth, could set the market rate arbitrarily. He did not, however, charge the tooth fairy with anti-trust violations under the Donnelley Act, General Business Law § 340 *et seq.*, as there appeared to be no "trade" that the Tooth Fairy was restraining.

[1190] A person can be the donor of an organ and carry a card identifiying him as such, which, it was patiently explained to the judge, did not involve giving a Wurlitzer to the church.

[1191] It was believed that the tooth fairy wanted them because they decay so fast they make excellent depreciable assets for tax purposes.

Others believed that the tooth fairy was engaged in some kind of a Ponzi scheme in which potential investors were convinced that the Tooth Fairy controlled valuable baby tooth futures, and they had an opportunity to get in on the ground floor of a new industry. The teeth were supposed to have some unspecified New Age alternative medicine purpose known to Druid fairy and pre-Christian culture.

However, the Commissioner of Health's regulations[1192] forbid any person to operate a nontransplant anatomic bank of body parts without being licensed. The tooth fairy had no license. The case went forward on that issue.

Certainly a tooth is a "body part," as Public Health Law § 1389-aa (1)(b) which defines "human pathological waste" as body parts except teeth, *et. al.* makes clear. But is it a body part, Bernatich asked, after it has ceased to be a *part* of a body, and the body has grown a new one? Or does it cease being a body part when it is no longer part of a body?

After all, a gift of a part of a mummy to a museum or a relic of a saint to a church does not come under the Uniform Anatomical Gifts Act because the "parts" have long ago ceased to be associated in the mind with the body from which they came. Reluctantly, the judge rejected this defense argument.

A controversy arose when the tooth fairy sought to testify. There are several reported cases in which a prosecutor was criticized for referring to a defendant's testimony as a "fairy tale," and sometimes a reversal of a criminal conviction resulted from that very comment.[1193] The District Attorney argued that those cases are an indication that the Appellate Divisions, in their wisdom, do not permit fairies to tell any tales under oath.

But, if the tooth fairy cannot be sworn, how could she defend herself against the allegations? The District Attorney argued that the tooth fairy could not testify because she was not "a person," and thus had no constitutional right to testify or be heard.[1194] Having no *"corpus"* as we know it, a fairy could not be *habeased*, and Mr. Bernatich could cite no case in which

---

[1192] at § 52.-2.1.

[1193] See, *People v. World* 157 App. Div 2d 567, pp. 568 - 569, 550 NYS2d 310; *People v. Jackson*, 143 App. Div. 2d 525, pp. 525 - 526, 515 NYS2d 105, *and People v. Simms* 105 App. Div. 2d 845, p. 846, 482 NYS2d 41.

[1194] Like a decedent's estate, which also has no constitutional rights, *East Harlem Pilot Block Building 1 v. Serrano* 153 Misc. 2d 862, 475 NYS2d 319 (1984).

a court acknowledged the rights[1195] or even the existence of fairies, the D.A. proclaimed.[1196]

However, Judge Termm replied, the District Attorney was required to prove each element of the offenses beyond a reasonable doubt. Fairies, being mythical, are not "persons" under § 4302, 4307 or the regulations, and hence, the prosecution had failed to prove one of the elements of the offense—namely that it was committed by "a person."

Therefore, the Judge ruled, no law prohibits tooth fairies from possessing all the teeth they need.

Small children everywhere whistled a sigh of relief through the gaps in their deciduous and permanent teeth.

[1195] "Fair trial" and "fairy trial" apparently do not come from the same etymological root.

[1196] But see *Stambovsky v. Ackley* 169 App. Div. 2d 254, 572 NYS2d 672 (1992) in which the First Department ruled that, for the purposes of that case, a house was haunted as a matter of law.

CHAPTER TEN

FROM THE DESK OF THE CHIEF SHOP STEWARD, UNION OF UNCONCERNED NUCLEAR SCIENTISTS

A PROPOSAL FOR AN INVESTIGATION OF THE MATING HABITS AND MORALS OF *HOSARIA MIDCALFUS*

We report on the interim results of our current investigation in which we have attempted to determine why socks no longer appear to mate for life. Stockings are believed to have mated for life since they were first domesticated by prehistoric man.[1197]

We conducted our investigation on one species of stockings (*hosaria midcalfus*) because of their availability and frequent use by mankind. We have concluded that socks used to mate for life when they were hand washed. However, since the middle of the twentieth century, when machine washing and mechanical drying threw socks together indiscriminately, dynamic new forces of attraction have led socks to stray from their mates.

The breakdown in sock marriage parallels the breakdown of society.[1198] The effects of global warming on the moral climate of sock drawers[1199] has yet to be proved. It was Prof. D.O.S. Formatt

---

[1197] See, R. Lee Kee, "Homo Erectus Tames the Rift Valley Argyle," National Geographic Television Special, 1991.

[1198] The breakdown of modern society can be quantitatively demonstrated by the dramatic increase in the number of repairmen of all kinds in the twentieth century.

See, N. Tropee, *Numbers of Repairmen per Capita in the Western World Since the Beginning of the Industrial Revolution* (Calcutta, 1979).

[1199] P. Ester, "Moral Fiber Content of Socks," 13 *Journal of Investigative Accouterment Dehydration* 1649 (1989), an article which concludes that socks of man made fibers or socks that have bold patterns are more likely to be promiscuous. The study was based upon 5000 pair of stockings and the results were rounded off to five digits per foot.

who posited in Formatt's Last Theorem "Global warming affects the moral climate is a true statement."[1200] Although it appears difficult to measure moral climate in degrees centigrade per decade, we have an elegant solution to the problem[1201] which also answers the question whether infinity is an odd or an even number.[1202]

Our study will also determine where the socks go when they migrate lemming-like from the hamper, washer, or dryer,[1203] and whether socks that cling to underwear in the dryer are compelled to do so by some predisposition, some genetic reason, an injury,[1204] or whether such deviant behavior is of their own choosing.[1205] The treatment of this deviation by the introduction of chemical agents (e.g., anti-static agents such as Bounce) is being explored, as well as the long term effect of those chemicals on the morbidity and mortality of the socks.[1206]

Polly Ester was also able to determine such difficult questions as which sock was the left one and which the right.

[1200] Prof. Formatt first formulated his last theorem when his students demanded a final examination that had only true or false questions.

[1201] And what existed before the Big Bang where there was no time and no space. We'd record it here in the margin, but for the moment we have no time and no space.

[1202] The answer is no.

[1203] Our colleagues working on black holes have some suggestions.

[1204] When socks were hand washed they were dried gently on lines in the open air. The buffeting they take in a modern dryer may cause some to suffer from post traumatic stress syndrome in which they deviate from prior imprinted behavior according to the Le Boyer Hypothesis.

[1205] See, O. Winfrey, *Socks Who Crave Underwear, and the Panties that Love Them,* La Salle Home Study Institute Press, 1993).

[1206] Sock predators include household pets such as dogs and cats, and long toenails. Holes in the toe or heel are the usual cause of mortality in socks, followed statistically by unraveling, or runs. Traditional healers (so called because of their use of darning with natural fibers on traditional heels) claim they can prevent runs by washing hosiery in a weak solution of kaopectate. Many others say this is just a folk yarn.

We realize this is an exciting and unique proposal, but we modestly confess that it is nothing that an infinite number of monkeys sitting at an infinite number of typewriters couldn't write.

A Finite Number of Gentlemen from Verona
    Committee on Crunching Imaginary Numbers
    Subcommittee on Sub Totals
    Ivory Tower
    Elephant Hall
    Donald Trump Junior College
    Roadkill, N.Y.

JAMES M. ROSE

RESULTS OF AN INTERDISCIPLINARY SURVEY AT A LARGE UNIVERSITY REVEAL THIRTEEN OF THE TOP TEN REASONS WHY

by James M. Rose[1207]

The main function of scientists is to answer the question "Why?" Because scientists are often frustrated in their search for the answer to the question "Why" by things such as stubborn or unruly data or recalcitrant experiments, Prof. David L'Etremann[1208] has come up with a handy list of thirteen of the top ten reasons why.

"Interdisciplinary" is a modern buzzword meaning that more than one person was asked the same question and each approached it from his own narrow and parochial perspective. Prof. L'Etremann consulted many students and University Departments, and the answer depended on the responder's narrow field of endeavor. Here is the fruit of his research, which did not fall far from the tree, but may have been bruised in accord with Newton's Fourth Law.[1209]

[1207] Who didn't check the math in this article.
[1208] Professor of Gratuitous Advice at the M.L.E. PostModern University, Entropee, Mass, where he is an Assistant Maven. He used to be a Cosmetologist, but now refers to himself as a Cosmologist after his dentist advised him to eliminate "teas" from his life because they stain teeth.
[1209] Sometimes attributed to Sir Isaac Newton and sometimes attributed to his cousin, Fig I. Newton, because of a fragment of a research paper in the hand of Sir Isaac containing the Fourth Law and the phrase "see Fig I." The Fourth Law was an embryonic concept at the time of Newton's death. Newton's death is considered to be his most successful experiment in inertia. The Fourth Law is stated "Any body that falls due to gravitational force is likely to be bruised, broken or battered in a ratio proportional to its worth."

THE REASONS WHY

1. Because. (This answer was derived from the Philosophy Department, and is considered to be the traditional answer.)
2. Why not? (This is the more modern, laid back answer of graduate students in the Philosophy Department who are Logical Positivists, Logical Negativists and Tautologists.)
3. It has always been that way. (Survey shows this is the number one answer given by Historians, who have the 3 X 5 cards with *facts* on them to prove it.)
4. It is the will of (fill in name of appropriate deity). (So saith the Divinity School Faculty).
5. Y= ab^2 + c (This is the answer of the Math Department.)
6. Complex interaction of many forces the decimal places of which, the chaos theory postulates, cannot be rounded off without changing Life as We Know It. (This is the answer of the Physics Department, and they'll throw in a Unified Theory for a Grand, but it may just be stringing you along.)
7. Subconsciously you willed the results to be so. (The white mice of the Psychology Department passed along this answer).
8. Why= (who+where)/ when divided by what (reports the School of Journalism.)
9. Y = Yttrium (The Chemists with periodic tables demonstrated. It has an atomic number of 39, and an atomic weight of 88.905, although experiments to prove that give off a foul smelling by-product.)
10. It was not my fault. (This is the answer favored by most undergraduates, especially those on the thirteenth step of a 12 step recovery program. It is also the answer given by the University's Office of Risk Management (which purchases No Fault insurance), and pledges of fraternities and sororities.)
11. "Y" is the sex chromosome associated with male characteristics. (Geneticists say, who often find it at mixers with X chromosomes on weekends all over campus.)
12. The penultimate letter of the alphabet. (according to the English Department who use vocabulary like "penultimate,"

and who often advise students to be politically and grammatically correct by changing "Y" to "i" and adding "e s" in a pluralistic society such as ours.)
13. Y is the letter invented by Phoenicians 1000 B.C. (Ye olde etymologists write.)
14. *Ours* is not to reason why (This answer was favored by most persons on athletic scholarships.)
15. There is no particular reason. (This answer was not favored by any group in particular.)
16. Why ask why? This dry, Wiser reply was the answer given by most fraternities and persons named "Bud".
17. The Law of Unintended Consequences compelled it. (It is unclear how this answer came to appear on the list).
18. "Define 'Why,'" (demanded the Linguists.)
19. 110110101000101010110 (is the answer of the Computer Science Department. When they were asked to translate it from the binary code, they replied, "Abort, Retry, Ignore?")
20. None of the above. (This answer was favored by most graduate assistants teaching large sections of introductory classes who are responsible for grading examinations, because this answer can be placed on a multiple choice grading key, whereas essay answers cannot.)

Next Question: Why *what*?

CONFIRMATION OF THE EXISTENCE OF THE SUB ATOMIC PARTICLE THE WISHON BY EXPERIMENTAL DATA[1210]

Experiments have recently been concluded that confirmed the existence of yet another sub-atomic particle—the wishon. The wishon was initially thought to emanate only from the first star seen at night. The wishon may actually come from a white hole in space[1211] located near each first star seen at night. It is hypothesized that the wishon either has or gives a positive charge, and has an atomic height of one. It has an atomic weight of minus ten. That is, it reduces the atomic weight of any particle with which it collides by ten. This is considered good news for dieters who will want to consume wishons in order to become light.[1212] Dieters reacted by saying that the wishon was too good to be true. Since something that is thought to be too good to be true usually is, that was considered a confirmation that a wishon "is."[1213]

To further confirm the existence of the wishon, the cloud chamber was employed (as with other sub atomic particles). However, no wishons were spotted because of inclement weather in the chamber.[1214]

[1210] By Prof. Jiminez Crickett, Undistinguished Fellow, Post Impressionist School of Art, and Shop Steward, Union of Unconcerned Scientists, and James M. Rose, J.D., The Moe Stappi Fellow, Nappa Valley Institute of Heretical Physics, and I. R. Hubris, Visiting Professor of Physiques, Close Cover Before Striking Institute of Home Studies.

[1211] White "holes" are invisible "rents" in the fabric of space, and are not composed of matter. White holes emit all sorts of particles that did not first enter them.

[1212] It is thought of as a counterbalance to dark matter, which has an atomic weight of ten, and so the wishon is also described as "lite matter."

[1213] By "is" we mean exists, as in the third person singular conjugation of the verb "to be." See ex-president Bill Clinton for a further and more complex discussion of what the meaning of "is" is.

[1214] It was too cloudy.

The wishon was posited to be the means by which wishes were transmitted both to and from the first star seen at night.[1215] Experiments to confirm the particle were then devised. A hundred volunteers of various ages, sexes, heights and weights were selected randomly[1216] by the head of the Campus Computer Science Department Professor Wi Gee. They were separated into groups by dividing their weight by the number of letters in their names. Slips containing their names were placed in weight/name ratio order in a 10 liter beaker which had first been sterilized in an autoclave. The names were then drawn out of the beaker by the winner of the Miss Behavioral Sciences contest.

The first group was told to wish upon the first star seen at night each evening for a period of a year. This was done to adjust for seasonal variations of the sky, the possibility of cloudy weather, and the orbit of the earth around the sun. No participants were placed in the southern hemisphere, since the saying being tested is thought to be of Northern Hemisphere origin,[1217] and the grant money did not permit it.

The participants were instructed to make a wish silently. The subjects were told that "no demand is too extreme" if their heart "was in their dream."[1218] Participants were permitted to wish for something not even scientifically thought possible—like the wishon itself.[1219]

[1215] The exact mechanism by which the wishon accomplishes its task of wish granting was not the subject of the experiment devised. It was thought that the scientific method required proceeding in logical steps, and that confirming the existence of the wishon is the first step in the process, since knowledge of the mechanism by which it worked would be of little value if, in fact, the wishon did not exist.

[1216] Specifically, the criterion was "If you wish upon a star, makes no difference who you are."

[1217] That is the Northern hemisphere of the Earth. No one has shown in which hemisphere of the brain it originated.

[1218] Participants who reported that they did not dream were eliminated.

[1219] However participants were told not to wish for wishons, as that might result in a an experiment for which no adequate control had been established.

A conundrum was presented because of the belief that if the participant revealed his wish it would not be granted. As a control, the participants were requested to memorize their wish in order to preserve it.

Preliminary training was necessary so that the participants would not inadvertently wish upon a planet such as Venus, or an orbiting satellite, airliner, or UFO.

A second control group was instructed not to wish for anything after dark during an entire year. They were able to do so, but it greatly inhibited the social life of certain participants who had difficulty not wishing for certain results at weekend social gatherings with the opposite sex.[1220]

A third control group was asked to wish upon a heavenly body other than a star. A fourth group was given a placebo upon which to wish. It was a standard laboratory placebo manufactured for its placebo effect to the standard purity for placebos established by the National Bureau of Standards.

A fifth group was asked to wish on a traditional wishing well by throwing a penny [1221] in it when making a wish.[1222]

One problem presented was the duration of the experiment, as the first star seen at night could be no closer than 8.8 light years away. Thus, for a wishon to travel to the wisher, back to the star and back to the wisher would require many years. A scheme was devised to select the outermost chronological limits of the experiment, and the computer surprisingly selected six months prior to the retirement date of the scientist who devised the experiment.

[1220] They assured the experimenters that nothing they would have wished for on those occasions came true.

[1221] + or - 5000% adjusted for inflation.

[1222] A grant from the National Aeronautical and Space Administration was used to help fund this control group until an artist lost his grant from the National Council on the Arts for giving away money to recent emigrants. It was then thought more prudent to build the pennies into the administrative portion of the grant.

Data from the experiment was then run on a computer using CHEAT software[1223]. A statistically significant amount of the first star wishers had wished to be thin again, to have cranial hair again, to see old friends, or have their baseball card collection back.[1224]

A statistically significant number of the control group wished for things unconnected with the past such as to win the lottery, to be famous, or be elected president, or to perform certain physical intimacies with Madonna or Richard Gere.[1225]

It was then concluded that because the first star wishers asked for things or conditions that **had** existed in the past, the wishon, like a positron,[1226] must actually travel backwards in time and grant the present wish sometime in the past. Evidence that people had seen their friends, had baseball cards, been thin or been hirsute when younger confirmed the hypothesis that present wishes are/were granted in the past, and hence confirmed the existence of the wishon.

CONCLUSION

Every scientific paper needs a conclusion, and this one is no exception.

For the reason stated herein, our currently pending application for a grant to study wishons should be granted, i.e., while you're up, get me a grant.

[1223] See, *Journal of Irreproducible Results*, 37:5)

[1224] Participants did not "tell" the researchers what their wish was, but the researchers were able to guess it by playing charades with the participants.

[1225] The sample was further corrected for statistical deviants.

[1226] which is an electron traveling backwards in time.

AN INQUIRY INTO THE PROXIMITY OF MOBILE HOMES AND TORNADOES: A STUDY TO DETERMINE IF MOBILE HOMES ATTRACT OR CREATE TORNADOES

by Prof. J. M. Rose[1227]

Laymen who read newspapers and watch television have themselves noted that when news of a tornado is reported, often photographs of demolished mobile homes accompany coverage. This anecdotal evidence has convinced bureaucrats that there is a mathematical correlation between the appearance of tornadoes and the location of mobile homes. It therefore presented a natural subject for an inquiry by Dr. Ipsi Dixit and Dr. Ray Ipsalocquitur whether the mobile homes created the tornadoes,[1228] attracted them,[1229] or had a symbiotic relationship with them.

Research had previously shown that there is a positive correlation between the type of building material and the safety of a residence in high winds. One such study is that seminal work by L. Pig, L. Pig, L. Pig and B. B. Wolf, *Anecdotal Evidence of Structural Integrity As it Relates to Building Materials: Results of Studies in Sticks, Hay and Bricks.*

The obverse of the possibility that mobile homes attract tornadoes is that tornadoes attract mobile homes, or that there is a

---

[1227] Prof. J. M. Rose is the occupant of the Folding Chair of Meteorillogical Studies at the Inquiring Minds Institute in Entropee, Mass. where he holds the title of Assistant Maven. He has done post graduate research at the M. L. E. PostModern School of Equittology.

[1228] The creator of chaos theory, Edward N. Lorenz, gave an address to the annual meeting of the American Association for the Advancement of Science on 29 December 1979 entitled "Predictability: Does the Flap of a Butterfly's Wings in Brazil Set off a Tornado in Texas?"

[1229] See, B. Franklin, "An Empirical Attempt to Attract Storms by the Use of Metallic Objects," rejected Doctoral Thesis, U. of Pennsylvania, 1752.

mutual attraction. There is no proof to establish those propositions.[1230]

Similarly, the proposition that mobile homes create tornadoes suggests the inquiry whether tornadoes create mobile homes, but photographic evidence establishes that tornadoes destroy rather than create structures. One researcher who believed he had proof of a tornado creating a mobile home has now been shown to have been rewinding his video recorder with the picture on at the time.[1231]

Recently Drs. Dixit and Ipsaloquitur[1232] received a large Federal grant pursuant to 42 U.S.C. § 5407 (b), which provides funds to study manufactured home safety.[1233] They proposed to build a trailer park in "tornado alley"[1234] to attract or create a tornado.

Tornadoes form when cool dry air from the west or northwest moves over warm moist surface air. They frequently occur in the Gulf States in February and March and in Iowa and Kansas in May and June. They are marked by a sudden reduction in barometric pressure. Some attempts to turn them into mere thunderstorms have been assayed by seeding clouds with dry ice.[1235]

By use of a computer model in conjunction with the mathematics department, Dixit and Ipsaloquitur were able to ascertain the exact location in an Iowa cornfield where it was predicted that the next

---

[1230] Critics have attacked Dixit and Ipsalocquitur for having flawed premises, but they have responded that their mobile home is "as good as the next guy's."

[1231] Since positrons are electrons traveling backwards in time, he was rewinding the tape in an attempt to create positrons to study.

[1232] who had done a pioneering study that proved that white mice attracted psychology majors.

[1233] The National Housing Act Section 308(c)(1) (Pub. L. 97-35) provided that all references to "mobile homes" in the statutes of the United States should be changed to "manufactured homes," and thus in one pen stroke wiped out more mobile homes than any tornado.

[1234] as a section of the Midwest of the country is called.

[1235] Dr. Dixit theorizes that the sudden depression in pressure should be treated

tornadoes would strike. Specifically, the computer predicted "If you build it they will come."

The methodology proposed was to man the mobile homes with expendable graduate assistants. When the tornado approached, the homes would be driven in a direction away from the storm's path, and video cameras would record if the tornadoes would consistently follow the vehicles. Multiple tests would be run in each compass direction. As a control, three identical mobile homes would be driven in different directions at the same time at the same rate to see if the tornado would remain equidistant from each. In addition, a non-mobile home would be placed on a flat bed truck and driven away from the tornado to see if it would also be followed.

The research sought to vindicate Newton's Fourth Law of Motion (sometimes attributed to Sir Isaac Newton),[1236] an embryonic concept at the time of Newton's death.[1237] The law is stated "Any body built to be put into motion will be put into motion when it attracts an outside force." Tornadoes by their very nature are outside forces, as no incident of a natural tornado forming inside has ever been reported.[1238] An attempt to lure them with mobile homes could be made it was theorized, using the chaos theory's "strange attractor" model.

Construction on the trailer park was commenced, however, before the instrument packages constructed to test the theory could be installed, the trailer park was destroyed by an earthquake.[1239]

---

by Prozac[R] and other anti-depressants, but is concerned by possible unknown side effects. On the other hand, some tornadoes rotate to the left and others to the right, so counter indications may be just what is needed.

[1236] and sometimes attributed to his cousin, Fig I. Newton, because of a fragment of a research paper in the hand of Sir Isaac containing the fourth law and the phrase "see Fig I."

[1237] Newton's death is considered to be his most successful experiment in inertia.

[1238] but Dr. Fujita has created a tornado machine that can simulate a tornado in the laboratory.

[1239] see, S. I. Velikowsky, *Earthquakes: Tectonic Blue Plate Specials of the Gods*, Olive Press.

WHERE PAPER PROFITS GO WHEN YOU LOSE THEM IN THE STOCK MARKET

A startling theory and prediction were advanced recently by Prof. Albert Zweistein over two steins of beer in his office at the PostModern Institute for Deconstruction of Physics. We met after I followed his directions to turn north outside Chickopee, Mass., pass through Entropee, and arrived in the hamlet of Critical, Mass.

At the Institute Prof. Zweistein occupies the Edwin Folding Chair[1240] and teaches the Physics of Economics, as well as heads the Claire Booth Luce Project to Study Economic Change—the Luce Change Project.

What he studies is where money goes when you "lose" it. Not the kind of pocket change you cannot find—exhaustive studies have proved that it goes into the interstices of the couch.[1241] Not that twenty dollar bill you left in your pants pocket that went into the wash and left you vulnerable to Federal charges of money laundering. Those items, he explained, are real and tangible. When they are lost, like a lost glove, they occupy some place in the space-time continuum, or are converted to energy according to the Laws of Conservation of Matter.[1242]

[1240] Edwin Folding not only established the Folding Chair years ago, he also endowed many studies in the physics of economics with Folding money. He made his money by shrewdly buying up tons of government surplus monosodium glutamate (MSG) cheaply from the government strategic stockpiles when it fell out of favor in this country in the early seventies. When Nixon opened China, he was able to sell it to millions of Chinese restaurants.

His story was fictionalized by Pearl S. Buck, who changed the commodity to polysaturated cooking oil in the novel *Oil for the Woks of China*. She made so much money that she and her publisher Dennis O'Day created a program to subsidize rental cars for deserving graduate students—the Buck—O'Day Car Rental subsidy.

[1241] A. Seely, B. Castro, et. al. "Unearthing Drachma in the Divan," 15 *Annals of Couch Archeology* 421 (1990).

[1242] To the extent that the Laws of Conservation of Matter can be considered environmental laws, the current Congress has either repealed them or transferred

He explains, for example that it is not the spring solstice that causes spring and summer to be warmer than winter, since that only makes the days longer. The days could be short and hot or long and cold, he explained. However, when enough gloves and scarves are lost, they are converted to energy, and the energy gives off heat—hence the heat of spring and summer.[1243]

What Zweistein studies is lost paper profits. Not real money you invest in some project[1244] but lose, but paper profits that disappear when some trader for Daiwa Bank or Barings Bank PLC bets them on the nutmeg futures market or arbitrage.[1245] Applying the laws of Conservation of Matter, do paper profits go anywhere, since paper profits are not really matter nor energy?

They are, he theorizes, virtual matter, and are converted into virtual energy. *Where* they are converted is in virtual space. But since we cannot see virtual space, how do we know that it is there? Zweistein explains that what exists in virtual space is the Internet—something we cannot see or touch and that "disappears" when we turn off our computers. Yet the Information Superhighway exists in cyberspace. The Internet has been growing so swiftly that it is important we understand why and how it expands.

He studies whether it is governed by the familiar formula $E=MC^2$ when the equation is solved for matter. His conclusion is a

---

the obligations for their enforcement to the states of matter—solid, liquid, gas, plasma, and North and South Dakota.

[1243] Not to be confused with "the greenhouse effect," a rare phenomenon in which all the plants in your garden suddenly develop price tags and growing instructions.

[1244] like Kevin Costner's film Waterworld. That's real money you earned, and it goes to pay real salaries, caterers, and necessary suppliers—such as drug dealers, etc. It is then converted to energy by them—so much energy that in that case that the film was not only a bomb, it was in the multi-megaton range.

[1245] "Arbitrage" is a complicated medico-legal procedure for surgically separating a sucker from his money via the Barnum-Leeson Maneuver. There are only three rules for succeeding at arbitrage—unfortunately no one knows what they are.

definite "Maybe, but I doubt it." He suggests that by multiplying both sides of the equation by 1, the result is M= E/C$^{.2}$

Thus, the more energy that disappears the more matter there should be. However, he points out, on the Internet the opposite is true. There has been a disappearance of matter (i.e., virtual money), and a corresponding increase of energy expended on the Net.

He concludes that (1) either he made a math mistake somewhere in the multiplication, or (2) the formula $E=MC^2$ does not hold for virtual matter/energy on the internet. Since the internet was created just moments ago (when its age is compared to the age of the Real Universe), it is his conclusion that a virtual Big Bang took place when lost money was converted to enough energy that it created matter in a virtual Big Bang like the universe. It has been said the universe is the Ultimate Free Lunch—an example of something[1246] for (or from) nothing.[1247] Since you are not charged to use the internet,[1248] you get it for nothing if you can afford to get on.

Moreover, the recent billions of dollars lost by Barings and Daiwa[1249] represent the potential for yet another big bang in cyberspace[1250] and the creation of either a second or alternative Internet.

Prof. Zweistein is now looking for a learned journal to publish his results in,[1251] and is the odds on favorite to win a Virtual Nobel Prize in Economics, Physics or Literature (in the "Fiction" or "Comedy" categories).

[1246] Indeed, everything!

[1247] Perhaps, then, the rule is *not* that we cannot make something out of nothing, but that we cannot make something out of nothing *twice*. The rule of physics may just be "One Something Out of Nothing per Customer."

[1248] or the real universe.

[1249] This article was written before the Enron collapse.

[1250] What existed in cyberspace before the first Big Bang is beyond the scope of this article, but we'll take a shot at it anyway. Prof. Zweistein theorizes that nothing, including cyberspace, existed in cyberspace before the first big bang since there was no money.

[1251] He is considering an offer from *Physics N' Things*.

THE EFFECTS OF GRAVITY UPON THE LAW AND VICE VERSA[1252]

What the Constitution of the State of New York has to do with bathroom odors is uncertain, Mr. Justice Heisenberg ruled in State Supreme Court recently.

The issue came to the fore in a case in which Mr. Strawman, an owner of an apartment building, was accused by his tenant, Mr. Javert, of violating Multiple Residence Law §171.[1253]

That section, as every schoolchild knows, provides that in Multiple Residences bathrooms containing water closets must have a window or skylight, or, if they do not, they must be ventilated by mechanical or gravity ventilation. A gravity ventilation system must be capable of four changes of the volume of air in the room per hour.

Mr. Javert, a former sewer inspector turned author, tested the air in his multiple residence bathroom by intentionally introducing a foul smelling gas of some sort into it. He did not reveal the source of the foul smell nor the method of propulsion he used in disseminating the gas. He then measured the rate at which the smell dissipated by coming into the room after an hour and claimed he could still smell the gas. This he claimed to do on three separate days, and when he detected the odor filed he filed the complaint.

Strawman's attorney, S. Crowe Czashijec[1254] first argued that the air in the room had in fact changed, but the smell (as opposed to the air) had not. The specific gravity of the smell could have

---

[1252] by James M. Rose, White Plains New York, the man who put the "fun" in fungible.

[1253] Not to be confused with the Multiple Dwelling Law, although it is not clear why not, nor is it clear why there is a need for both a Multiple Dwelling and Multiple Residence Law. It is possible that "Multiple" is intended to modify "Law" as well as "dwelling" and "residence."

[1254] Of the firm of Czashijec and Splitt.

been heavier than that of the air and lingered near the floor or on the towels, while the air that had been in the room with the smell turned over at the specified rate. The law did not say four *total* changes of air, he argued. However, the judge inquired what the purpose of the law was if not to rid the bathroom of the smell.

The answer was then amended to state that four total changes of air *had* occurred on the dates in question. In the first the bathroom air was removed to the adjoining bedroom and the air from that room imported into the bathroom. In the second the process was reversed, that is the air that had been obtained from the bedroom was then replaced by the air that had originally been in the bathroom. In the third change of air the first exchange was repeated. Unfortunately, when the last change occurred, all the air that initially resided in the adjoining bedroom was one again replaced in the bathroom by the foul smelling air that had been removed from the bathroom in the initial exchange.

Justice Heisenberg remarked that this explanation reminded him of the sergeant who told his platoon "The army says you men must change your socks every day. We have no fresh socks, so Jones change with Smith, Williams change with Johnson."

The plaintiff then argued that gravity ventilation works by the weight of air.[1255] On most occasions the air in the room was in fact replaced more than four times per hour, but when the wind was blowing strongly at right angles to the soffit vent opening (like a person blowing over the mouth of a glass beer bottle) it acted like a lid that prevented outside air from entering the opening, and thus was an exception to the law of gravity.[1256]

[1255] For a description of gravity ventilation see, Carl and Barbara Giles, *Ventilation: Your secret key to an Energy Efficient Room* (Tab Books, 1984) at 43.

[1256] He also referred to Newton's Laws in the motion papers. The reference is to Sir Isaac Newton and not his cousin Figuaro Ishmael Newton, also known as "Fig" Newton. While Isaac was sitting underneath apple trees, "Fig" conducted

It was argued that on average this occurred one tenth of the time, and thus by the law of averages nine tenths of the time all the air in the water closet room was replenished more than four times an hour.

Judge Heisenberg admitted that indeed there *were* laws of physics, but he was uncertain of their principles. He was concerned that he might have to learn those laws[1257] in order to deal with the case. He opined that an apartment owner attempting to comply with this law would have to retain a physics expert—perhaps by looking one up in the yellow pages under "Mechanic, Quantum."

Javert's lawyer, Peck Sniff[1258] argued that the volume of air in the room must always be capable of replacement four times an hour rather than *on average* four times an hour. Strawman asked the judge to apply to Law of Averages.[1259] Concepts from his high school math course such as median, mode, mean, average and percentile swirled uncomfortably in his head.[1260]

---

    many experiments blowing across the mouths of beer bottles, and even formed a jug band known as the Newton Ramblers. It is believed that Fig assisted Sir Isaac in his experiments concerning inertia because of a fragment of a research paper in the hand of Sir Isaac containing the notation "See Fig I."

    Fig's death is considered to be his most successful proof of Newton's First Law—that a body at rest tends to remain at rest unless acted upon by some outside force.

[1257] Something he was unable to accomplish in high school before turning to the law.

[1258] of the firm of Skratch & Sniff.

[1259] The judge admitted he knew nothing of the Law of Averages and believe it to have been an elective course he had not taken in at Law School. He only knew that it was infamous for catching up with you—like a mugger in a dark alley.

[1260] He was a schoolboy in the days before the "new math" and now he wondered if he would have to learn it. "What was wrong with the old math?" he wondered. "Wasn't it hard enough to understand?"

Sniff argued that "average" numbers were inapplicable because they were *imaginary*, whereas the law deals with the real world. If the average person has two point five children he does not have a Nancy, Fred and a Bi__. He remarked, "On this jury of six men and six women, the average juror has one breast and one testicle, but if any juror were so configured I could not address them as 'ladies and gentlemen of the jury!'"

The judge then inquired how Javert selected the days on which he ran the experiment, and was told they were selected randomly to comply with the law of averages. "You mean arbitrarily and capriciously?" Justice Heisenberg inquired. When the answer came back in the affirmative, the judge remarked that, if the law of averages demanded that something be done in an arbitrary and capricious manner it denied due process of law[1261]—so he declared that the law of averages was unconstitutional. Nevertheless he ruled that the bathroom would have to pass the test at *any* time.

In response, Czashijec argued that no case or statute defined "Gravity ventilation."[1262] Multiple Residence Law § 171 incorporated concepts of the weight of air and the operation of Newton's Laws of Motion.[1263] Having to know the weight of air and the operations and exceptions to the laws of gravity bothered the judge.[1264] Strawman's attorney urged him to invoke New York State Constitution Article III which prohibits the legislature from passing acts that incorporate by reference any existing law.

Judge Heisenberg's opinion quoted from a Court of Appeals explanation of the provision:

[1261] c.f., *American Ins. Assn. v. Lewis* 50 NY2d 617, 431 NYS2d 350 (1980).

[1262] One attorney was arguing for the application of the Law of Averages and the other for the Law of Gravity. The judge was concerned that he would have to apply the choice of laws doctrine. Since the demise of the *lex loci* test, New York has applied the center of gravity test. But that brought him back to gravity again! Like death and taxes, "gravity" too seems inescapable, he remarked.

[1263] He was barely able to understand the CPLR's laws for motions let alone Newton's, the judge thought.

The purpose of the constitutional prohibition against incorporation by reference is to prevent the Legislature from incorporating into its acts the provisions of other statutes or regulations which affect public or private interests in ways not disclosed upon the fact of the act, and which would not have received the sanction of the Legislature if fully understood by it, *People ex. rel. Board of Commrs. v. Banks*, 67 NY 568, 576; see *People ex. rel. Everson v. Lorillard*, 135 NY 2."[1265]

Judge Heisenberg doubted that the members of the Legislature fully understood the effects of the laws of gravity (from their high school days) when they incorporated Newton's Laws[1266] into the Multiple Residence Law § 171 without fully setting forth all those laws in the section.

He ruled that § 171 was unconstitutional. In this one case he had rules both the law of averages and the laws of gravity unconstitutional. As Javert was leaving the courtroom, he was arrested for violating Environmental Conservation Law § 71-2105 and 6 NYCRR § 21.2 [b] because he was alleged to have operated an air contamination source without a license. The famous novelist Javert left, muttering that the "whole thing stinks." The next day the tabloid New York *Voyeur* ran the story of his arrest under the headline "Author Voids Where Prohibited by Law."

[1264] The press, which dubbed this the "odor in the court" case, noted of the once athletic but now portly judge that gravity had not been kind to him—and this was his chance for revenge.

[1265] *Matter of Medical Society v. Doh*, 83 NY2d 447 at 453-3, 611 NYS2d 114 (1994).

[1266] "The Laws of Newton are not the laws of New York," Judge Heisenberg proclaimed, perhaps confusing Sir Isaac with the Town in Massachusetts.

James M. Rose

A PROPOSAL TO INVESTIGATE WHAT AN INFINITE NUMBER OF MONKEYS WOULD WRITE

edited by James M. Rose[1267]

We propose another project upon the completion of our current investigation in which we have concluded that stockings (*hosaria midcalfus*) used to mate for life when they were hand washed;[1268] however, since the middle of the twentieth century when machine washing and mechanical drying threw socks together indiscriminately, dynamic new forces of attraction have led socks to stray from their mates.[1269] The effects of this on the moral climate of sock[1270] drawers (i.e., posited global warming) has yet to be determined, as well as where the socks go when they migrate lemming-like from the hamper, washer, or dryer,[1271] and whether socks that cling to underwear are compelled to do so by some predisposition, some genetic reason, an injury,[1272] or

---

[1267] Editor, *Unpopular Science Magazine*, Unpleasantville, New York.

[1268] Stockings are believed to have mated for life since they were first domesticated by prehistoric man. See, R. Lee Kee, "Homo Erectus Tames the Rift Valley Argyle," National Geographic Television Special, 1991.

[1269] The breakdown in sock marriage parallels the breakdown of society (which can be quantitatively demonstrated by the dramatic increase in the number of repairmen in the twentieth century.)

[1270] P. Ester, "Moral Fiber Content of Socks," 13 *Journal of Investigative Accouterment Dehydration* 1649 (1989) which concludes that socks of man made fibers and that have bold patterns are more likely to be promiscuous. The study was based upon 5000 pair of stockings and the results were rounded off to five digits per foot.

[1271] Our colleagues working on black holes have some suggestions. Sock predators include household pets such as dogs and cats, and long toenails.

[1272] When socks were hand washed they were dried gently on lines in the open air. The buffeting they take in a modern dryer may cause some to suffer from post traumatic stress syndrome in which they deviate from prior imprinted behavior according to the Le Boyer Hypothesis.

whether such deviant behavior is of their own choosing.[1273] The treatment of this deviation by the introduction of chemical agents (e.g., Bounce) is being explored, as well as the long term effect of those chemicals on the morbidity and mortality of the socks.[1274]

Our new proposal is to test the heretofore untestable mathematical theorem first enunciated by Prof. D.O.S. Format (Format's Last Theorem) that an infinite number of monkeys sitting at an infinite number of typewriters would produce the entire works of Shakespeare[1275] is a true statement.[1276] What are the chances?[1277]

[1273] See, O. Winfrey, *Socks Who Crave Underwear, and the Panties that Love Them*, La Salle Home Study Institute Press, 1993).

[1274] Holes in the toe or heel are the usual cause of mortality in socks, followed statistically by unraveling or runs. Traditional healers (so called because of their use of darning on traditional heels) have begun to wash hosiery in a weak solution of kaopectate to prevent runs.

[1275] Not to be confused with Sir Arthur S. Eddington's statement in his 1927 Gifford Lecture (later in *The Nature of the Physical World*, Macmillan & Co. 1948, p. 72) "If an army of monkeys were strumming on typewriters they might write all the books in the British Museum. [Emphasis in the original]. He concluded "The chances of their doing so is decidedly more favorable that the chance of [all] the molecules [that were once in one half of a vessel] returning to one half of the vessel."

Although the odds of that happening are 1/2 to the quadillionth power, the odds of the monkeys typing the entire book collection of the British Museum may in fact be higher. (See footnote 11 *infra*.)

Eddington is also incorrect unless he establishes a time limit. If the monkeys are given an infinite amount of time then the chances of them reproducing the library are excellent. Bertrand Russell discussed the Tristram Shandy paradox. Shandy took two years to write up the events of the first two days of his life. He lamented that he could never complete his autobiography at that rate. Russell remarked that an immortal Shandy with all eternity at his disposal would eventually catch up. (Constance Reid, *From Zero to Infinity* Thomas Crowell Co., NY, 1964 at 142.)

[1276] Prof. Format first formulated his last theorem when his students demanded a final examination that had only true or false questions.

[1277] Assume that there are 54 keys on the typewriter that could make a mark on

The first problem inherent in testing the theorem is that an infinite number of animal rights groups may complain that monkeys are being used in the lab. Our proposed solution is to build a public relations component into the grant.

The next foreseeable problem is that we may develop an infinite amount of monkey excrement. Some of us believe that this is not a problem at all, since all research generates excremental results at times, and we have the possibility of selling it (spinning it off doesn't project the correct image) as fertilizer like some zoos are now doing.

Another problem we anticipate might occur if the monkeys type the complete works of Danielle Steele before they develop the Shakespearian masterpieces. They may well then hire an infinite number of agents and sell the stuff to the movies, especially the novels of Danielle Steele that have not yet been written.[1278] Once

---

the paper or affect the spacing of the outcome. There are six letters in the name of "Hamlet." It has been calculated that the odds of winning they 54 number lotto are one in 25 million. But in the Lotto once numbers are drawn they are not returned to the barrel, unlike the typewriter in which all 54 keys remain to be struck and can repeat, and in the Lotto the numbers do not have to be drawn in the correct order. Thus even if the monkeys strike the six letters in HAMLET they could type MELTAH or THEMAL, and if they repeat a letter and drop another they could type LATEHA and have the last laugh. The odds of randomly typing just the name "Hamlet" are 1 in 24,794,911,296. The odds of typing the actual name of the play, "Hamlet Prince of Denmark" with the correct blank spaces are 1 in 54^{24} or 3.78×10^{41}. Is Eddington correct that the odds of the monkeys randomly typing the British Museum's collection are better than 1/2 to the quadrillionth power?,

[1278] What will happen when Danielle Steele then writes the works of the monkeys and finds out they have the copyright is a question we have not yet explored. If the monkeys write it first, can one say that they wrote "the works of Danielle Steele" or that she subsequently (or even previously) wrote the works of monkeys?

they are independently wealthy, the monkeys may chose to go in their own creative directions and even run their own studios as some do now.

It is not clear whether Format's theorem hypothesized that the infinite number of monkeys would sit at an infinite number of typewriters for an infinite amount of time. If this is true, the experiment would be impractical to conduct because not even the National Science Foundation will fund a project of an infinite duration.

Paper will be a problem too. Each monkey will be given only one sheet of paper. This is a mathematical constraint on the project because if you have an infinite number of monkeys and they each have a sheet of paper you have (by definition) an infinite number of paper sheets, and if you gave each monkey two sheets you would have infinity times 2 sheets of paper—a mathematical impossibility.[1279]

This also limits the time frame of the project, because monkeys when typing become infinitely bored, and will soon long for an infinite number of bananas.

Another potential hurdle consists of identifying who will sit and review the infinite number of pages produced to check to see if the Theorem has been vindicated. Even though a notoriously cheap source of labor is available in graduate students, the number needed to review an infinite amount of paperwork could be a considerable expense.

Our colleagues in the English Department also inform us of another problem. They cannot agree what the complete works of Shakespeare are, as the authorship of various plays, sonnets and the like is disputed, and we do not know if some of the work of Shakespeare has been lost. What edition of Shakespeare would be standard? Would any spelling be acceptable to you, or only as you like it? Perhaps we ought to shoot for the complete works of Bacon instead—but should we include Shakespeare's, too?

[1279] Although a minority among us believe each monkey should be given an infinite amount of paper, creating infinity.

However, we have an elegant solution to the Last Theorem[1280] which also answers the question whether infinity is an odd or an even number.[1281]

We realize this is an exciting and unique proposal, but we modestly confess that it is nothing that an infinite number of monkeys at an infinite number of typewriters couldn't write.

Respectfully and hopefully submitted,

A Finite Number of Gentlemen from Verona
Committee on Crunching Imaginary Numbers
Subcommittee on Sub Totals
Ivory Tower
Elephant Hall
Donald Trump Junior College
Roadkill, N.Y.

[1280] And what existed before the Big Bang where there was no time and no space. We'd record it here in the margin, but for the moment we have no time and no space.

[1281] The answer is no.

INTERDISCIPLINARY RUMINATIONS ON THE ORIGINS OF LAW AND JUSTICE

By Professor Parker J. Schaeffer[1282]

Law, like many other fields, is now being looked at interdisciplinarily[1283]. Cosmologists from the Physics side of the campus have applied their expertise (and jargon) to determine the Big Questions in the law—such as where did law and justice originate? Not surprisingly, the conclusions depend on the discipline of the thinker.

Cosmologists believe that in the beginning there was no law. People sat around with unresolved controversies. All of a sudden, out of nowhere, there was a huge explosion (the "Big Bang") and since then the law has been expanding rapidly, some believe at the speed of light. Statutes and case law have expanded exponentially, and are receding from us rapidly.[1284]

Before there was law, there were no doctrines such as *res ipsa loquitur*. There is, therefore, no explanation of the Big Bang, and hence there have been no settlements of any lawsuits about the

---

[1282] Professor of English as A First Language for Academics, and Occupant of the Lounge Chair of Forensic Tautology At Hamburger University, San Diego, California.

[1283] For example, Kabalists from the Divinity have done well explaining the intricacies of the laws of taxation.

[1284] Some believe that they are receding as a speed that is so fast that even WESTLAW and LEXIS cannot keep up with them. These same professors also debate the ultimate question, i.e., what will the fate of the ultimate universe and law be? Will the universal (and law, by analogy) continue to expand forever, and flee beyond our reach, or will it all reach one point where it starts to contract? Will it shrink until there is nothing left but a few commandments and a leash law? It all depends on whether the weight of the law ("Gravitas") has reached critical mass or not. Those who believe that it has done so and gone beyond are denominated the School of Hypocritical Legal Studies.

explosion. However, if the matter were even fully and finally litigated, many people will have been held to have waived their rights to recover because of language normally found in form general releases.[1285]

Other physics professors who specialize in quantum mechanics have a different explanation of the law. To oversimplify, they believe that everything does not occur in the same way every time according to immutable laws, but within a range of probabilities. Therefore, laws will vary within a range of probabilities.[1286] Laws vary from state to state, and what would be forbidden in some countries is mandatory in others. Cases are decided not according to *stare decisis*, but within mathematical ranges, they reason. This adds a mathematical twist to the classic view of Oliver Wendell Holmes in *The Common Law* that "the Prophecies of what the courts will do, in fact, and nothing more pretentious are what we mean by the law."[1287] Quantum mechanics is used to predict where an electron might be in a cloud of electrons. You might be able to predict the general geographic location of the electron, but you cannot pin it down to any one location. Similarly,

---

[1285] "the . . . releasor . . . releases and discharges the releasee . . . from all actions, causes of action . . . claims and demands whatsoever . . . from the beginning of the world to the date of this release." (Blumberg Form B110—General Release, Julius Blumberg Law Blank Publishers.).

[1286] The Chaoticists, a new school of thought was a name that resembles a heavy metal band, believe that when formulas are extremely complex and there are many variables, we cannot predict the results at all (New York Times, October 15, 1987, p. C 28 col 3, "Books: Third Scientific Revolution of the Century," a review of J. Gleick, *Chaos: Making a New Science*, (Viking)). When scientists put the same figures into a very complex formula twice in a row but rounding them off slightly many digits out, the results are different, even with the use of a computer. Chaoticists apply this same principle to the law, and conclude that there must be a very complex pattern to it, because the same facts will not always result in the same verdict. They still struggle with the statement that there *is* a simple pattern to anti-trust law: The government always wins.

[1287] O.W. Holmes, *The Common Law*, quoted at page 75 of *The Mind and Faith of Justice Holmes*, (Max Lerner Ed. N.Y., 1943).

law is everywhere and nowhere specific place at the same time.[1288] Albert Einstein reacted with horror to the theory of quantum mechanics because he said that he could not believe that God plays at dice. Yet, if he would have looked at judges decisions, he would have seen some of the same random qualities physicists believe are evidence of quantum mechanics at work.[1289]

Social Darwinists have another theory about the organic development of the law.[1290] So do the Anti-Social Darwinists, but they refuse to express their views to other people. Darwinists theorize that the law is ever evolving and mutating like an organic entity, adapting to the conditions and environment on which we find ourselves. Their imagery is derived from biology, and is often unsuitable for dinnertime conversation with young children. They are presently caught up in the controversy that is preoccupying the evolutionists, i.e., whether there can be a quantum leap in adaptation, or whether changes must evolve slowly. If they are correct, successful mutations are the key to evolution, and the most successful practitioners of law today would be mutants. Only time will tell.

The Darwinists are opposed by the Creationists, who believe that God is the source of all laws.[1291] Most Legal Creationists have withered gone the way of the doctrine of Sovereign Immunity, a doctrine with similar origins (that is, if a Supreme Being makes laws on Earth through the reigning sovereign you can't very well

---

[1288] "Law must be stable and yet cannot stand still," Roscoe Pound said in *Interpretations of Legal History*.

[1289] A professor from the Mathematics Department on loan to the law school has developed the art/science of forensic topology. It uses arcane mathematical formulae to stretch legal precedents into completely new shapes without breaking them.

[1290] Arguments that the law grows organically should not be confused with Natural Law (*jus naturale*), although no one can say why. Organic Law theories are said to have originated at the Ag school.

[1291] They say that studying law and praying are therefore the same thing. They favor school prayer—at least in Divinity Schools.

sue him, can you?) The Creationists argue that Darwin was wrong, because our founding fathers were the intellectual giants Jefferson, Franklin, Adams, Hamilton and Marshall. Our two most recent presidents were an ex-peanut farmer and an ex-actor. Congress is peopled with intellects such as ex-baseball players and football players, and Sonny Bono. Is this where two hundred tears of evolution have brought us? The Anti-Creationists argue that law cannot be the manifestation of God's will on earth, or else his representatives would be the current Congress. That statement is its best refutation.

Perhaps there is still no better theory of justice for the Post-Modern Era[1292] that the one which the founding fathers derived from the Enlightenment to illuminate our Constitution. It is the Social Compact theory, which states that we have banded together for the common good to decide the greatest good for the greatest number, and that we express how we should behave in the contract that is our laws.

Close analogies to the contract theory suffer. Law is not a contract that must be in plain language, and one must carefully parse the small print. The legal system does not come with a warranty of fitness for a particular purpose, either.

In conclusion, there are many different theories of the origin of law when looked at in the narrow prospective of an academic who must publish in order to obtain tenure.

[1292] "Post Modern" is a current buzz word with little or no meaning.

SACHAROMYCES CARLSBERGENIS : THE BEER MAKING MICROBE THAT PUT THE FUN IN FUNGUS

by James M. Rose, J.D.[1293]

"A jug of wine, a loaf of bread—and Thou," wrote the famous scientist Omar Khayaam.[1294] What do they all have in common? If Omar's girlfriend "Thou" was suffering from a yeast infection (*candida albicans*), they are all intimately involved with members of the yeast family.

Yeast infection (*candida albicans*), baker's yeast (*sacharomyes cervistae*) and brewer's yeast (sacharomyces carlsbergenis) are all one celled plants without chlorophyll or roots that are known as yeast—the plants that put the "fun" in fungus.

Yeast has done much for mankind in supplying an essential catalyst to create both bread and beer[1295]—staples of our existence. Without the yeast microbe's metabolism, I would not have the beer that I am drinking now as I write this article. Alcoholic beverages inspire creativity of the kind that made the *Journal of Irreproducible Results* the type of publication that it is today. Moreover, yeast is now employed in several experiments that are changing the composition of fermented products that consumers find in retail establishments today.

Following the lead of pioneer scientists who grazed cows on Astroturf[c] in order to produce non-dairy creamer,[1296] several similar

---

[1293] The author *of YEAST—The Answer to the Question: What Makes it America's Fastest Beer?* Vanity Press, 1977.

[1294] *Rubaiyat of Omar Khayyam* Fitzgerald translation (NY, 1947) at 55. Extensive research shows that the next line of the poem is not "And soon I'll be drunk, fat and in trouble."

Khayyam once went to a wine tasting, and he liked the wine so much he bought the company.

[1295] Beer is not a microbe, although it has a head and "body." It has no feet, and does not even have a pseudopod.

[1296] These techniques were discovered accidentally after farmers in poorer countries

experiments were conducted in the fermentation process[1297] to combine natural and artificial constituents to produce innovative and novel products.

The first experiment involved endeavors to replace the glucose oxidase molecule in the fermentation process that provides the energy source to the yeast cell. A compound that chemically resembles it—1 aspartyl—1—phenyl—alanine methyl ester (APM)—known as aspartame, was substituted for it. When Martin and others are given the sugar substitute and are taken on long aerobic fermentation runs, they produce a less caloric beer that is known as "Lite Beer." It is lighter[1298] and less filling,[1299] but it possesses most of the properties of "heavy" beer.[1300] The only side effect that lite beer has manifest on those persons who consume it is the inability to spell correctly words with silent "gh" in them.[1301]

---

fed their cows marine animals of the phylum *perifera* (commonly known as sponges) which resulted in dry milk. (see, Symposium, 19 *Comparitive Studies in Experimental Bovinology* (1974), Speil & Berg, "Close Encounters of Third World Kine," and further experiments to completely dehydrate the compound, Anne Hydrous, "White Powdery Substances Fabricated in the Laboratory Prior to A DEA Raid," as well as Mo Tilliti, "The Mating Habits of Coffee Mate™" reprinted in the *Voyeur's Home Journal*).

[1297] In an allied experiment, non-dairy creamer was mixed with a slurry to form non-dairy curds, and was fed to cheese generating microorganisms in an attempt to produce non-dairy cheese for people with lactose intolerance.

The microorganisms digested the mixture, and then excreted a semi-liquid. The laboratory technicians named this excretion process cheese whiz.

[1298] That is, it has an atomic weight lower than that of ordinary beer.

[1299] That is, it has shorter strings of organic compounds.

[1300] Heavy beer is not to be confused with beer brewed with deuterium oxide, also known as heavy water.

[1301] See, D.O.S. Spelchzek, and Sherry Hite, "Disappearance of Silent GH in Light and Night," 16 *The Journal of Post Modern Spelling* 987 (1991).

Recent experiments were designed to produce alcohol by the non-aqueous method.[1302] This process involves introducing another microorganism—the sponge,[1303] at a critical point in the fermentation process to absorb superfluous H_2O, and produce anhydrous beer known commercially as "dry beer." Dry beer tastes like wet or non-dry beer according to recent double blind tests,[1304] but it is more easily transported to picnics, where water can be added later to taste.

Currently *sacharomyces carlsbergenises* have been fed aspartame in an aerobic fermentation environment while utilizing the anhydrous technique, but in total darkness from the commencement of the procedure to the termination.[1305] This method is currently being employed to produce the first "Dark Lite Dry" Beer. Among its physical properties are that it lacks color, taste, and alcohol. While this initially appeared to be an undesirable outcome because the liquid's physical attributes so closely resembled water, marketers[1306] report that this will not be an impediment to selling it. Dark Lite Dry Beer will compete in a market niche with colorless, caffeine free, sugar free, salt free soft drinks, and will be sold under the name Crystal Beer.[1307]

Excessive consumption of lite beer results in the inability to spell many other words, as well as the increased presence of alcohol by weight in blood fluids of motorists, according to arresting police officers and their laboratory technicians, who consistently refuse to grade blood alcohol tests on a curve.

1302 Water is a constituent of the manufacturing process of beer. "Spring" water is utilized, after it is run through a magnet to remove iron and rust that comes from old springs.

Springs are used to help keep the "head" of the beer up.

1303 See footnote 4, *supra*.

1304 "Double blind" tests were run by volunteers who got extremely intoxicated twice.

1305 Even the technicians involved in the process have been kept in the dark when necessary and where consistent with OSHA regulations.

1306 Specifically the firm of Spinmeister & Spinmeister, product representatives.

1307 It will be marketed by the R. Nixon Breweries, whose motto will be "Let us make one thing perfectly clear."

CHAPTER ELEVEN

SHORT RIBS

or

WHEN YOU FINISH CHAPTER ELEVEN, YOU'RE DISCHARGED

WHEN LIFE HANGS A U TURN

When I was young my step-father used to tell me "The first half of your life you spend your health trying to get wealth, and the second half of your life you spend your wealth trying to get your health back." (That was before HMOs. Now you can spend your wealth just trying to keep medical coverage.)

This opinion made me realize that the same is true for a lot of other things that do a one hundred eighty degree turn after midlife. I mean more than the obvious observation that you looked forward to your next birthday when you were young because you couldn't wait to be older.

I recall a villain in a movie about a runaway train who uttered what was then either a cliche or a cliche-to-be: "What doesn't kill me makes me stronger." Maybe that's correct if you are in the first half of your life (like most movie protagonists), but if you're in the second half you could just as well exclaim "What doesn't make me stronger kills me." The side effects of those prescriptions you're taking is a good example. However, Kinky Friedman has been quoted as saying that his motto is: "Find what you like [in life] and let it kill you."[1308]

Some of the turnabouts are obvious. The first half of your existence the media and your parents sternly caution you not to do drugs or pills. Later in life health professionals tell you not to forget to take pills. The evening news **encourages** you to inquire of your physician about a cornucopia of pharmacopoeia you could be taking. When you were a flower child your tie dye clothing was rainbow hued, now the contents of your pill box is.

[1308] (New York *Law Journal,* October 4, 2002 p.16 col. 5M.)

When you're a kid they tell you stop running all over the neighborhood and come in and do your homework. But in your advanced adulthood your doctor tells you stop working so much and run (or at least jog) around the neighborhood.

On weekends your parents would yell at you not to spend all day in front of a TV screen, but to go out and socialize with the neighborhood kids by playing games. Now, in the era of on-line and CD-ROM legal research, word processors, and E-mail you're encouraged to spend all day in front of that screen and not to go out and play golf with your friends instead.

Mom always told me to eat everything that was put on my plate when I was growing up. That counsel went along with admonition that "Children are starving in China," to which the nascent humorist in me would reply "Name three." Now, however, when we're growing in a different direction than up, nutritionists are telling us to eat less and leave a little of that big restaurant portion on the plate.

Now that I think of it, when I was young my mother admonished me not to be such a wise guy too, but now that I'm a geezer my editors encourage it.

When you were young you had to get new clothes because you were growing too tall for your old ones. As you shrink in your dotage you need to get new clothes because the old ones are too big.

When you're a pre-schooler they try hard to get you to go to sleep early at night and to take naps, but you resisted. In the nursing home they tell you to try not to nap so much and you look forward to going to sleep early.

When you were a kid they used to tell you that children should be "seen and not heard." Now your children don't come to visit you, but they call you with some frequency on the telephone. This is evidently because senior citizens should be heard, but not seen!

In the beginning of your married life you spend a lot of time changing your **children's** diapers, but in your declining years they'll spend time changing **yours**.

ST. PATRICK AND THE SNAKES

In March we celebrate the holiday on which Saint Patrick drove the snakes out of Ireland. Contrary to popular opinion, he did not do this because they had missed their train, and he was being a good Samaritan and offered them a lift.

Few know, and fewer cite the obscure case about the occurrence, *Matter of 1,947,364 Snakes v. Saint Patrick*, 11 AllIreland Reports 989. St. Patrick was distantly related to The Pied Piper of Hamlin. The relation was through a very ancient ancestor on his grandmother Eve's side. Legend has it that she had once personally conversed with a serpent who was later named a co-respondent in a messy suit involving the rights to fresh produce, (In which the court declared the well known rule *"Fructus pendentes pars fundi videntur"* . . . 2 Bouv. Inst. No. 1578);[1309] and in which her husband, Adam, alleged that she had been led astray by express and implied warranties of fitness (or at least ripeness of fruit).[1310]

Adam claimed that he knew nothing about it, so he entered a general denial.

When Saint Patrick read about how the Pied Piper had rid Hamlin of vermin, he paid little attention to the deleterious side effects of the pesticide used, which also had a dramatic effect on the village's children. No environmental impact studies had been conducted concerning the safety of the method employed, or the environmental effect of removing rats from the Village.

Saint Patrick likewise filed no environmental impact statement before removing the snakes from Ireland. He did not consider the effect on the rat population upon which the snakes had preyed.[1311]

[1309] "Hanging fruits make a part of the land," *Black's Law Dictionary*).

[1310] The fruits of the poisonous tree is an altogether different doctrine with a much different story.

[1311] He saw no irony in the fact that snakes "preyed" while he "prayed," a situation he did not raise (or raize).

He paid no attention to the rights of the snakes[1312] who were on the land for generations and ran with (or at least slithered on) the land. He ignored their arguments that they had evolved before humans and thus had rights superior to humans because they had been in possession longer.[1313]

St. Patrick argued that if an environmental impact statement has to be filed each time someone killed a predator the world as we know it will grind to a halt. He noted that if the caveman who discovered the beneficial uses of fire had been required to file an environmental impact statement and consider all the harm that fire could cause before re-using it we would all be eating our food cold.

The case was resolved when Saint Patrick agreed to a voluntary protective order prohibiting him from approaching within four rods (sixty-six feet) of a snake.

[1312] Vigorously asserted by the Hibernian Interspecies Society for the Suppression of Scandalous Slanderous Statements about Snakes or HISSSSSS.

[1313] This argument did not avail the Native Americans either, did it?

NAFTA'S WHY SANTA CLAUS IS NOT COMIN' TO TOWN[1314]

by James M. Rose[1315]

On the Mexican border, Texas safety inspectors have applied rigorous safety standards in an effort to turn back the tide of Mexican trucks seeking to do business in the United States under the North American Free Trade Agreement ("NAFTA").[1316] NAFTA[1317] provides that regulations of the Secretary of Transportation concerning the safety of vehicles entering this country apply to those who seek to bring goods into this country.[1318]

> On the night before Christmas[1319].
> When all was in order,
> Kris Kringle's sleigh was stopped at the border.
> Agents in kerchiefs and ear flapped fur caps
> stopped his sleigh full of toys at a spot on the map
> where customs inspectors make travelers pause
> to check they're complying with all of our laws.

[1314] This case referred to in this article is fictitious, although the references to the U.S. Code are correct (we hope). NAFTA, GATT, and the FAA are figments of an overactive regulator's imagination.

[1315] White Plains, New York. Mr. Rose is the lawyer with a dog known as "Royal Child." It was formerly known as Prince, but he had it neutered.

[1316] "Truckers Face Safety Crackdown on Day Border Was to Open," New York *Times*, December 19, 1995 p. B 10.

[1317] 19 U.S.C. §§ 3301 *et. seq.* NAFTA applies to United States trade with Mexico and Canada. It defines "Mexico" in § 3301 (1) as "the United Mexican States" *if* the agreement is in force there. It does not say what Mexico would be called in this country (or in what language) if the agreement were not in force there, no doubt because those kind of terms are not normally found in a family-rated code of laws.

[1318] 18 U.S.C. § 3411.

[1319] December 24, 1995.

James M. Rose

Sue S. Grinch, an Inspector, said something's the matter
with Kris Kringle's sleigh and his toys, as the latter
failed some of the tests that exist under NAFTA
while in prior years he knew he "didn't haveta."
And, Sue Grinch said, "You can't enter this nation
'cause your sleigh's not equipped for air navigation."

The sleigh was just lit with a single red light
on the nose of a reindeer, and can't fly at night
unless its equipped with required transponders,
and the right colored lights placed on Blitzen and Donder.
The arraignment occurred in its proper progression,
and Judge Hawley Smoot ruled at that evening's session:

"The vehicle Kris Kringle drove was a sleigh,
It wasn't an aircraft, this court holds today.
"Foreign aircraft" is a term defined in forty nine U.S.C.,
at section forty thousand one hundred three (C).
In that definition we are given directions
To where "aircraft" is defined in the previous section.
A "contrivance invented, used," (the law recites there)
"or designed to navigate or fly in the air."[1320]
A Sleigh is not "aircraft" the trial court opined,
because it won't "fly" as *that* term is defined.
If a sleigh hits a bump and just leaves the ground
to judge that it's aircraft's not legally sound.
"Must Olympic ski jumpers," her Honor then queried,
"Wear lights on their skis if I follow your theory?"
Judge Smoot told Ms. Grinch, the chagrined prosecutrix,
"The government's certainly up to some new tricks!
Toys may be carried by carrier pigeons,
but they don't become aircraft, not even a smidgen."
"The means of propulsion for Kris Kringle's sleigh

[1320] in 49 U.S.C. § 40102 (a) (6).

was actually reindeer,[1321] large mammals that weigh
quite a bit, and do not achieve aviation
in Mexico, Canada or in this nation.
"Reindeer" are defined in an unhelpful way
in Twenty five U.S. Code Five hundred (j)
as "reindeer and caribou."[1322] But it doesn't say
In section forty thousand one hundred two a,[1323]
In the Forty ninth title ("aircraft engines" defined)
that Congress had caribou herds on its mind.
And the magistrate simply could not fathom why
the government argued that reindeer could fly.[1324]

"There *is* one section of federal law
that defines "off road vehicles." Congress foresaw
the need for some guidelines for when snowmobilers
drive off road vehicles or use three wheelers.
But in snow or on sand or on land used by voters,
Defined "off road vehicles" all employ motors.[1325]
A reindeer drawn sleigh, it takes no erudition
to find, is not motorized by definition.

If a sleigh hits a bump it may vault in the air,
But nobody makes one to *navigate* there.[1326]

[1321] *Rangifer tarandus.*

[1322] Which is only logical, if not tautological. 19 U.S.C. § 500 (a) permits the Secretary of Commerce to take reindeer by eminent domain and give them to "native Alaskans." However, that term includes descendants of those who inhabited Alaska in 1867, and it was unclear if Mr. Kringle qualified to hold reindeer under that definition.

[1323] 49 U.S.C. § 40102(a)(7).

[1324] As a youth she found that even believing strongly in Tinkerbelle and fairy dust did not allow her siblings to fly to Neverland.

[1325] 16 U.S.C. § 670 (k).

[1326] She attributed too much Christmas spirits (of whatever kind or definition) to

A sled's not an aircraft that's *meant* for the sky,
Your argument—just like a reindeer—can't fly."

Kringle however, remained at the bar.
He had no passport. He said he lived far
away in a workshop he built near a shoal
Assembling toys at the globe's Northern Pole.
"I don't long for Florida as I grow older,
I want to live in a place that is colder.
A stateless world citizen." (What could be dumber!)
He said that he lived at the *South* Pole in summer.
A doctor who testified to the reporter,
Said Kringle must have a bi-polar disorder.[1327]

Kris Kringle had written detailed information
required by customs in his declaration.
His purpose for coming here he wrote was "pleasure",
and not to sell toys—he was not seeking treasure.
All the toys that sat piled so high in his sleigh
Kringle said he had planned to just give away.
But Santa's not recognized (as he should be)
pursuant to 501 sub (c) sub (3)
as a charity safe from the Revenue Code.
Gift taxes were levied on all of the load.

Kringle was sworn in, and said on the stand
That the toys were all made on Canadian land.
Assembled by elves[1328] in a workshop at night.
At the North Pole that's lit by the cold northern lights.

---

the story that a heavy sled filled with toys and a corpulent man pulled only by reindeer could navigate in the air.

[1327] Since he called himself both Kris Kringle and Santa Claus, and because he was stopped at the Canadian border, he was a classic borderline schizophrenic.

[1328] NAFTA requires that labor standards in the exporting countries be similar to those in the United States, and inspectors could be sent to Santa's Workshop

THE SUPREME COURT JESTER

Kris Kringle's *one* license must be poetic,
(The North Pole he spoke of must be the Magnetic,
Because at the true Pole—at ninety degrees
North latitude—one will find nothing but seas.)
The magnetic pole is to what he referred,
Because that's in Canada—Kringle demurred.
"No NAFTA duty is owed *you* because,
My goods are Canadian under the laws."

Kringle's luck had run out—for the Federal sage has
read all of NAFTA—all 2000 pages.[1329]
"The *parts* in your toys were made, my good man,
in Pacific rim countries—Hong Kong and Japan."
It seems under NAFTA and its terms of art
the whole's less important than some of its parts.
One thousand pages in total defined
The formula three country's bureaucrats signed.
It takes all those pages to figure what's meant
by NAFTA's term "regional value content,"
and "transaction value" and other mind numbers
"Bewildering reading" and all truly bummers.
"Unworkable ultimately" say trade reporters.[1330]
Still Kringle was pinched by Ms. Grinch on the border.
He summed up in rambling phrases disjointed.
He pleaded our children would be disappointed.
"NAFTA," he said, "needs one *more* page because,
the drafters forgot to include Santa's clause."

Ltd. where the toys were assembled to see if fair labor standards were employed there. Canadian officials had received complaints under their discrimination laws that Kringle (d/b/a/ Santa's workshop) would not hire tall people, or even those of average height, for example.

[1329] C. Siegle "Report Card: World Trade," *World Trade* June 1994, Vol. 7 No. 4 P. 123-124.

[1330] *Ibid.* See also, C. Russell, "Tariff shifts and NAFTA," *Global Trade and Transportation* Vol. 11 No. 2 February, 1994 p. 21-2.

447

James M. Rose

Kris had no passport and no bills of lading
for his toys or components. As the evening was fading
he was warned with *Miranda* just as the judge ordered,
and then was turned back across Canada's border;
And we heard him exclaim as he drove out of sight,
"You all have a right to sing "Silent Night."[1331]

[1331] If you cannot afford to carry a tune and a mortgage at the same time, a caroler will be assigned to you free of charge.

IF YOU CAN'T SUE YOURSELF, WHO CAN YOU SUE?

The headline "Client Sues Herself; Lawyer Criticized" appeared in the New York *Law Journal* for May 20, 2002 in the third column below the fold.

The facts were these: A grandmother backing her car out of the driveway hit and injured her nine year old granddaughter. The grandmother was the sole custodian of the child. The mother had previously had the custody of the child taken from her, and the child had no other living relative.

A lawyer attempted to sue on the mother's behalf, but ultimately the Supreme Court, Ulster County declared that the mother had no standing. The attorney to whom the headline referred had obtained a retainer from the grandmother, to defend her against the mother's claim and to assert a claim on behalf of the granddaughter as her legal guardian. The Supreme Court opined that the grandmother's lawyer "wore too many hats." But the grandmother, not the lawyer, was the one with dual (or dueling) chapeaux—being both the guardian of the child and the tortfeasor. A woman can't be too thin or too rich according to conventional wisdom,[1332] but apparently she *can* have too many hats!

Actually, the lawyer had too many *ties*—his tie to the grandmother and his tie to the granddaughter. The lawyer understood that he had a conflict, so he asked to have a guardian *ad litem* appointed for the granddaughter, which the judge ultimately did. However, the lawyer asked, when he was stung by criticism for his tactics "How *do* you bring this lawsuit?" Only the legal guardian of the child can bring the action, but she is the only defendant, too.

The lawyer was perplexed because if you can't sue *yourself* who *can* you sue? Recently, Al Goldstein, publisher of the pulp philosophical journal *Screw*, was convicted of harassing his longtime secretary, prompting the parallel inquiry "If you can't harass your own secretary, who *can* you harass?"

[1332] Or in the case of Imelda Marcos, never have too many shoes.

The case of the grandmother with *dos sombreros* raises some perplexing questions. How do you get into court if not with the grandmother as the moving party? Where the ultimate bearer of the loss will be some insurance company, is the suit against public policy because of the likelihood of collusion between the grandmother and her ward? If you represent the plaintiff and defendant in the same action, how do you structure your fees? If clients can waive jurisdictional defenses, can they waive conflicts of interest as well?

Perhaps the grandmother said to the attorney she wanted to cross claim, and he replied "Suit yourself," and she just misheard him. How would *you* bring this action on behalf of the granddaughter? Reader's replies are invited.

ERRATA, CORRECTIONS, APOLOGIES AND *MEA CULPAS*

In an article in the last newsletter we implied that J. Radley Herold is both omnipotent and omniscient. We and Mr. Herold regret that the statement is not correct.

A piece contained in the December issue referred to the new court rules requiring written retainer agreements and a pamphlet about them from OCA entitled "Retainer Agreements for Dummies" by Mortimer Snerd and Joe Krazchtesdtdummi, Esqs. To the extent that the article indicated that dummies were required to retain attorneys we were in error. That is merely the Inevitable Result.

In the October newsletter we repeated the quotation, "These are the times that try mens' souls." To be excruciatingly accurate, mens' souls are not *actually* being tried now. They are only being marked "Ready for trial." When mens' souls will be reached for trial God only knows.

December's newsletter contained no scathing editorial about The Lack of Progress. We are sorry about the omission. To the extend that we indicated that the antonym of *Pro*gress was *Con*gress we regret that we are correct.

Recent issues contained articles by Anthony Anea about growing old and infirm (hereinafter "Senior Moments"). Letters to the editor have complained that this is a depressing topic. The Westchester County Bar Association and its newsletter regret that people become aged. We meant to stop mentioning it, but it slipped our minds. We also pledge to stop referring to the author of the column as "Señor Moments."

A recent article contained a quotation from T. S. Eliot's *The Wasteland*: "April is the cruelest month." We apologize to April. Some other months are just as bad, the fifteenth of April not withstanding.

In the Christmas Poem in the December edition there were eight typographical errors on the second page. Since James M. Rose was given the task of proofreading the poem he sincerely apologizes to himself for those mistakes.

A letter to the editor by Anonymous slated for the November edition described the plan to search all attorneys entering courthouses as "a nonsensical, time wasting piece of failed public relations" due to a typographical error. It should have read "ill advised." The error appeared in an early draft of the Newsletter and never made it to print. Perhaps it's just as well.